Global Africa

GL●BAL SQU■RE

Edited by
Matthew Gutmann, Brown University
Jeffrey Lesser, Emory University

The Global Square series features edited volumes focused on how regions and countries interact with the rest of the contemporary world. Each volume analyzes the tensions, inequalities, challenges, and achievements inherent in global relationships. Drawing on work by journalists, artists, and academics from a range of disciplines—from the humanities to the sciences, from public health to literature—The Global Square showcases essays on the histories, cultures, and societies of countries and regions as they develop in conjunction with and in contradiction to other geographic centers.

Each volume in The Global Square series aims to escape simplistic truisms about global villages and to provide examples and analysis of the magnitude, messiness, and complexity of connections. Anchoring each book in a particular region or country, contributors provoke readers to examine the global and local implications of economic and political transformations.

1. *Global Latin America: Into the Twenty-First Century,* edited by Matthew Gutmann and Jeffrey Lesser

2. *Global Africa: Into the Twenty-First Century,* edited by Dorothy L. Hodgson and Judith A. Byfield

Global Africa

INTO THE TWENTY-FIRST CENTURY

EDITED BY

Dorothy L. Hodgson and
Judith A. Byfield

UNIVERSITY OF CALIFORNIA PRESS

University of California Press, one of the most distinguished university presses in the United States, enriches lives around the world by advancing scholarship in the humanities, social sciences, and natural sciences. Its activities are supported by the UC Press Foundation and by philanthropic contributions from individuals and institutions. For more information, visit www.ucpress.edu.

University of California Press
Oakland, California

Library of Congress Cataloging-in-Publication Data

Names: Hodgson, Dorothy Louise, editor. | Byfield, Judith Ann-Marie, editor.
Title: Global Africa : into the twenty-first century / Edited by Dorothy L. Hodgson and Judith A. Byfield.
Other titles: Global square ; 2.
Description: Oakland, California : University of California Press, [2017] | Series: Global square ; 2 | Includes bibliographical references and index.
Identifiers: LCCN 2016059240| ISBN 9780520287358 (cloth : alk. paper) | ISBN 9780520287365 (pbk. : alk. paper) | ISBN 9780520962514 (e-edition)
Subjects: LCSH: Globalization—Africa—21st century. | Africa—Economic conditions—21st century. | Africa—Social conditions—21st century. | Africa—Politics and government—21st century. | Africa—Foreign relations—21st century. | National characteristics, African.
Classification: LCC HC800 .G54735 2017 | DDC 303.48/26—dc23
LC record available at https://lccn.loc.gov/2016059240

25 24 23 22 21 20 19 18 17 16
10 9 8 7 6 5 4 3 2 1

CONTENTS

ILLUSTRATIONS

MAPS

FIGURES

ACKNOWLEDGMENTS

We are grateful, first and foremost, to our many contributors for their commitment to the mission of the book, willingness to revise their pieces numerous times, and patience with us as editors. Several authors were already friends and colleagues; others were complete strangers willing to take a chance on our project. All are very busy scholars, activists, policy makers, journalists, artists, and/or public intellectuals who found time to write (and rewrite) their articles under tight deadlines. Thank you.

The idea for the volume began with a conversation between Dorothy and Matthew Gutmann, coeditor, with Jeffrey Lester, of the series The Global Square. We thank them for their encouragement, good humor, and innovative vision. Naomi Schneider, executive editor at the University of California Press, has been a stalwart supporter from the beginning. Will Vincent and Renee Donovan, her editorial assistants, responded calmly and quickly to our many questions.

Many of these pieces were presented in draft form at a two-day workshop on Global Africa held at Rutgers University in September 2015. The workshop provided a vibrant space for debate, discussion, and learning among presenters and with our engaged audience. We all left excited about the intellectual and political possibilities of the volume. But the logistics of organizing travel, accommodations, food, and more for almost twenty participants from around the world were formidable. Thankfully, Renée DeLancey, the business manager for the Center of African Studies at the time, coordinated everything with her usual grace, goodwill, and extraordinary management skills. Many Rutgers units cosponsored the event: School of Arts and Sciences, Centers for Global Advancement and International Affairs, Institute for Research on Women, Department of Anthropology, Center for

African Studies, Department of History, Department of Africana Studies, and Department of African, Middle Eastern, and South Asian Languages and Literatures. We also received support from the History Department and the Africana Studies and Research Center of Cornell University.

Several authors also presented drafts of their papers at a double session on Global Africa that we organized for the annual meeting of the African Studies Association in November 2015 in San Diego. Provocative questions and comments from several audience members helped authors focus their arguments and assisted us in sharpening our introduction.

The volume also benefitted tremendously from two sets of readers' reports: the first on the prospectus, and the second on the draft volume. Thank you to Jonathan Reynolds, reviewer extraordinaire, for helpful (and pointed) comments in both rounds of review; Mary Osirim and an anonymous reviewer for thoughtful comments on the prospectus; and Laura Mitchell and an anonymous reviewer for detailed suggestions on the full manuscript.

Finally, Dorothy would like to thank the School of Arts and Sciences and Graduate School–New Brunswick at Rutgers University for the generous research account that supported the workshop, permission fees, and other costs.

MAP 1. The African continent. Rutgers Cartography, 2016.

Why Global Africa?

Dorothy L. Hodgson and Judith A. Byfield

THE CONTINENT THAT WE CALL AFRICA is as much a space as an idea. Africa is huge (a surface area of almost twelve million square miles), and diverse in every possible way—socially, ecologically, culturally, politically, linguistically, and economically. Over a billion people, living in vibrant urban centers like Nairobi and Dakar or rural homesteads in the Rift Valley, speak more than two thousand languages. Ecologically, the country of Tanzania alone contains coastal beaches, highland savannas, mountain forests, and one of the largest lakes (Lake Victoria) and mountains (Mount Kilimanjaro) in the world. Because of their extraordinary diversity and dynamism, Africa and Africans have been central to transformations throughout the world: from the food we eat, to the music we listen to, to our philosophies, technologies, scientific innovations, and political innovations, to name a few.

Africa, in other words, is global. Africa has a long history of global interactions that have shaped the rest of the world in significant ways—from the early migrations of our evolutionary forbearers, to the precious metals that supported international economies, to the forced displacements of enslaved adults and children, to contemporary circulations of people, music, ideas, and resources. Many of the world's significant concepts, art forms, diasporas, and material goods have their origins in the African continent. The deep history, vast geography, and complex local, regional, and global entanglements of people, ideas, and goods within and beyond the continent place Africa at the center of global historical processes rather than on its periphery.

In this volume, we seek to disrupt narratives that frame the ways many people imagine Africa as both an idea and a place. We begin that task by dispelling the geographical and political division of Africa into North Africa and sub-Saharan Africa. These all-too-common distinctions ignore historical and contemporary connections and perpetuate troubling racialized divisions between "Arabs" and "black Africans." We also challenge those narratives that contain African history and cultures within the continent. In the past, the migration of Africans across the Atlantic Ocean, the Indian Ocean, and the Mediterranean Sea helped transform societies in these new locales and on the continent. The cathedral-inspired mosques of the Republic of Benin, for example, exemplify the dynamic relationship between West Africa and Brazil born during the transatlantic slave trade. New African diasporas are emerging as technological developments and shifting global economic powers inspire movement. Nigerians, among other African peoples, belong to far-flung diasporas that move freely and frequently—in their case, between Nigeria, England, the United States, and South Africa.

Together, the pieces also complicate conventional narratives of Africa as a place of violence, despair, and victimhood—a place and space that other people, states, and organizations act on and steal from. Instead, our contributors document some of the significant global connections, circulations, and contributions that African people, ideas, and goods have made in the world—not just in the United States, but in Asia, Latin America, Europe, and elsewhere. Although the collection foregrounds new framings of Africa, none of the authors romanticize the conditions and circumstances in which too many people on the continent currently live. Instead, they amplify those voices that offer complex and insightful explanations, strategies for solutions, and inspiration for the future.

Global Africa includes almost forty short essays, profiles, interviews, photo essays, and reflections. Our contributors represent diverse perspectives, politics, and positions—journalists, activists, scholars, policy makers, photographers, artists, curators, and writers. Many are African or of African descent; others have spent years working with Africans on the continent and beyond. We have asked them to write short, engaging, journalistic pieces that are accessible to smart readers and do not rely on (or hide behind) the usual scholarly apparatus of citations, footnotes, and bibliographies. Our purpose is to educate, surprise, excite, and challenge you—and, we hope, spark you to seek more information from the additional readings, documentaries, and other resources included at the end of every piece.

We have divided the volume into five thematic sections that showcase different aspects of Global Africa. Part 1, "Entangled Histories," highlights the long history of the movement of African peoples, ideas, and goods in the world. Authors challenge and complicate narratives of "globalization" that seem to begin and end with slavery, colonialism, and conquest; or that presume that enslaved or colonized Africans were merely passive victims. Ibn Khaldun, for example, was born in Tunis in the fourteenth century and became for some the father of the social sciences. Long before he wrote his famous book, the *Muqaddimah,* many other traders and travelers from Europe, Asia, and Africa itself roamed throughout the continent during the "Golden Age" (AD 700–1500). And not all these travelers were men, as revealed by the journeys of Fatma, Odette, and Sophie across the Sahara in the twentieth century. Africans, of course, traveled elsewhere, often as enslaved captives but sometimes as part of the colonizing force. But whether in early Spain, colonial Mexico, or India, their lives were far more mobile and meaningful than many presume. These oceanic voyages were not one-directional. African Americans like Charles Morris traveled to South Africa and returned to the United States with new ideas for advancing the American civil rights struggle. These entangled histories link the past and present, demonstrating that Africa and Africans remain deeply implicated in the histories of other global regions.

In part 2, "Power and Its Challenges," contributors explore the sites and sources of intellectual, economic, and political power and conflict that have shaped global policies and practices. Imperialism and the racial discrimination that defined the lives of blacks in the diaspora gave rise to Pan-Africanism—a political movement that advocated for the unity of all people of African descent and helped lay the ideological foundation for decolonization. Julius Nyerere, the first president of Tanzania and a strong proponent of Pan-Africanism, also argued for interregional cooperation within the "Global South." He sought to restructure the inequality of the world economy in order to improve the social and material conditions of Tanzanians. However, structural-adjustment programs, authoritarian rule, and civil strife in many parts of the continent led some pundits to anoint Africa "the hopeless continent." Roundly condemned at the time, this characterization is especially untrue today. Conflicts have declined, in part because organizations such as the African Union have instituted practices and policies to manage power and mediate conflict. One such practice was the Truth and Reconciliation Commission (TRC) in South Africa, which has been praised as a model for healing long-standing conflicts. But the experiences and legacies of the TRC have been much more ambivalent, at least within South Africa. Individuals have made a difference as well. Leymah Gbowee, the Liberian peace activist and Nobel Peace Prize winner, helped coordinate Liberian women activists to force the country's leaders to sign a peace accord. African activists and leaders are challenging the international community, and especially corporations, to be good global citizens as they call attention to corrupt corporate practices that facilitate the illicit flow of money out of the continent; to environmental damage; and to the conditions of work in foreign-owned enterprises. Across the continent individuals, associations, and governments offer new ways of thinking about power, resources, and the human condition.

Part 3, "Circulations of Communities and Cultures," examines the complicated circulations, connections, and conjunctures of African peoples, arts, and ideas that demonstrate their global importance and challenge easy understandings of "Africa" and "Africans." Marcus Samuelsson's delectable cuisine at Red Rooster, in Harlem, New York, fuses his Ethiopian heritage with his Swedish upbringing and love of African-American soul food. Like food, the production of textiles also easily combines diverse aesthetic and material flows, both mapping and creating networks of exchange. Africans, at least some Africans, also move as well—in this case, to Guangzhou, China, as Christian missionaries, traders, and businesspeople. Language and literature are also mobile, malleable forms—but ones that, like food and cloth, reflect and reproduce politics. Mukoma Wa Ngugi's interview with his father, the renowned Kenyan novelist Ngũgĩ wa Thiong'o, explores the intertwined politics of African language and literature, global commerce, and local knowledge. And the story of African soccer (football) is also a global tale of leisure, but also of colonialism, competition, cooptation, and contestation. Africans—as the lives and work of Senzeni Marasela (from South Africa) and Lalla Essaydi (from Morocco) attest—have become increasingly visible and influential in the global art world. Similarly, the emergence of raï music and hip-hop/rap in northern Africa challenges the predominance of Europe and North America as sites for the production and circulation of global soundtracks.

Part 4, "Science, Technology, and Health," explores some key African innovations and issues in these fields. Dr. Sarah Eyangoh, a leading microbiologist from Cameroon, discusses the opportunities and challenges of biomedical research in Africa, especially for female scientists. What lessons, if any, have been learned from efforts to eradicate the long-standing HIV pandemic in Africa, especially given the more recent outbreaks of Ebola? In contrast to enduring assumptions, Africans have contributed numerous technological innovations—from geometric, architectural, and aesthetic forms that provide the basis for bottom-up technosocial innovations like open-source software, to advanced digital technologies for the transfer of and access to money through mobile phones. But Africa is also the site of ongoing resource extractions, including the mining of coltan in the Democratic Republic of Congo and the relentless search for indigenous "miracle" drugs like hoodia in South Africa. What are the social and political consequences of these global invasions and investments for the lives and livelihoods of local peoples? In the case of Tunisia, the drive for economic growth by certain African governments, in alliance with international corporations, can literally leave behind piles of stinking garbage—a visceral legacy of corporate greed, social inequality, and environmental negligence.

Finally, the pieces in part 5, "Africa in the World Today," provide examples of some of the unique contemporary contributions of African peoples and ideas to global conversations. Entrepreneur Mo Ibrahim, from Sudan, created Celtel, one of the largest cellular-network companies in Africa, and, eventually, the Mo Ibrahim Foundation to support good governance and peaceful democratic transitions on the continent. Keiso Matashane-Marite, currently the Social Affairs officer for the UN Economic Commission for Africa, describes her journey for gender justice from her rural home in Lesotho to the corridors of the United Nations. The acclaimed artist Meschac Gaba, from Benin, created *Museum of Contemporary Art,* a provocative twelve-room installation that critiqued and challenged the lack of spaces for contemporary African art in galleries and museums in the Global North. Similarly, Nollywood, the name given to popular Nigerian cinema, has forged new creative forms and spaces in Africa and beyond. In the 1970s and 1980s, two Senegalese Sufi masters moved to the United States to proselytize. By adapting Sufi teachings to accommodate Western perceptions and concerns, they built vibrant religious followings. Many younger, wealthy Africans in the United States and elsewhere have come to be referred to (and refer to themselves) as "Afropolitans," to signal and celebrate their identities as cosmopolitan Africans. How is this identity understood and experienced by Afropolitans and their critics? Ethiopian filmmaker Salem Mekuria's photo essay of a model "utopian" community in Ethiopia suggests that Africa and Africans continue to innovate and inspire the rest of the world.

CONCLUSION

Given the immense size, diversity, and long history of the continent, the contributions in *Global Africa* could never be exhaustive. But we do hope they are tantalizing, intriguing, and, at times, surprising. We hope that as you read the profiles, articles, and photo essays, you will develop new frames for conceptualizing Africa's past, present, and future. We also hope that Africa will cease to be that exotic space where "tribes" live locked in tradition and outside of history. Instead, these pieces will help you appreciate that the continent is populated by dynamic communities whose material, intellectual, and cultural resources have shaped—and been shaped by—other world regions. But African communities also exist within a matrix of uneven relations of power that contribute significantly to the unequal distribution of resources between men and women, social classes, and nations. Therefore, efforts to improve the material, economic, and social conditions of people on the continent require much more than empathy; they require an understanding of how power is exercised and practiced in a globalized world. *Global Africa* provides the tools.

PART I

Entangled Histories

INTRODUCTION

How many times have you exclaimed, "What a small world!"? The speed at which we travel, send goods, and communicate with people in other parts of the world seems to erase the tremendous distances that separate us. Historically, distance and lack of comfort in travel did not compel Africans to remain bound to one location or dissuade others from visiting the continent. Ibn Khaldun, the fourteenth-century scholar considered the inventor of the social sciences by some, was born in Tunis to a prominent family that ventured from Yemen to Spain before settling in Tunis. Oludamini Ogunnaike's biographical profile of Khaldun reveals the breadth of the intellectual universe in which Khaldun operated as he received visitors from Andalusia (Islamic Spain) and northern Africa and as he lived and worked in important centers such as Fez and Cairo.

Luxury goods also traveled along the pathways traversed by Khaldun. François-Xavier Fauvelle introduces us to works by Arabic geographers and travelers that document the extensive international trade in which West African kingdoms such as ancient Ghana participated. Gold lubricated this trade between the eighth and fifteenth centuries that linked elites as well as Christians and Muslims and crossed the Sahara, Mediterranean, Red Sea, and Indian Ocean. Thus, Africa has long belonged to shifting multiregional networks through which products, ideas, and people flowed. In the process, different African societies have been entangled in the development and histories of other parts of the world and vice versa.

"Entangled Histories" offers rich examples of these networks at different historical periods and illuminates how people lived and experienced them.

The Sahara is a desert, but it is not a lifeless place, as some dictionaries inform us. To help us understand the experiences of those whose lives crosscut the Sahara, E. Ann McDougall introduces us to three women whose trans-Saharan crossings were profoundly shaped by the big "isms" of our time—colonialism, capitalism, and nationalism. The linkages that connected the lives of these women to global processes were pioneered in an earlier period when glory seekers ventured across the Atlantic. The transatlantic trade opened a new geopolitical era sustained by the wealth of the slave trade and slave labor. People of African descent were on multiple sides of this process. Some were among the colonizers from the Iberian Peninsula who laid claim to the "new" world. Leo J. Garofalo explores the life of one such itinerant, Diego Suárez, an actor who journeyed to Mexico and Peru as a member of the conquering forces. Others were among the millions of bonded laborers whose toil inscribed the landscape with their presence. Only traces are left of the places where enslaved Africans worked and lived in seventeenth-century Mexico City. Nonetheless, by mining wedding records, Frank Trey Proctor III reveals how enslaved Africans simultaneously held on to aspects of home while they created new families and new lives in this cosmopolitan city. The experiences of Pedro Sánchez and Mariana, who appeared at the Metropolitan Cathedral in 1640 to apply for a marriage license, also remind us that the institution of slavery varied considerably.

The formal end of slavery did not create equal citizens in former slave societies. The promises of reconstruction after the American Civil War were largely overturned by the end of the nineteenth century. The rise of the Ku Klux Klan and legalized racial segregation generated many parallels in the histories of the United States and South Africa. Their shared histories supported transnational politics as African Americans and Black South Africans traveled across the Atlantic engaging in spiritual and political fellowship. Benedict Carton and Robert Trent Vinson introduce us to the transatlantic Pan-African crusade of Charles Morris, a black Baptist missionary and protégé of Frederick Douglass. The alliances Morris helped to forge during the nineteenth century would become even more urgent in the twentieth century as African communities both continental and diasporic struggled to purge democracy of white supremacy.

Africa did not only populate slave societies across the Atlantic. Enslaved Africans were taken to the Arabian Peninsula and to the Indian subcontinent. Renu Modi reminds us of the long-standing relations between India and the African continent. Slavery was one small facet of a relationship that is being reinvigorated as the Siddis, the descendants of enslaved Africans in India, establish ties to African countries and to African diasporic communities in other regions, and as the Indian government expands political, social, and economic ties with African governments. Collectively the chapters in part 1 reveal the dynamic and enduring entanglements that put Africa at the center of world history.

PROFILE

IBN KHALDUN: THE FATHER OF
THE SOCIAL SCIENCES

Oludamini Ogunnaike

Abstract: Ibn Khaldun has been called the father of economics and sociology, and his ideas and methods anticipate developments in European thought five centuries after his death. He applied his extensive political experience and learning to understand how societies rise and fall, and is still studied and cited today by economists, politicians, and sociologists.

Keywords: Islam, economics, sociology, political philosophy, North Africa, Arabic

> In the Prolegomena (Muqaddimat) to his Universal History he
> [Ibn Khaldun] has conceived and formulated a philosophy of
> history which is undoubtedly the greatest work of its kind that
> has ever yet been created by any mind in any time or place.
>
> —BRITISH HISTORIAN A. J. TOYNBEE

ABŪ ZAYD ʿABD AL-RAḤMĀN IBN Muḥammad Ibn Khaldūn al-Ḥaḍramī (1332–1406 CE), better known as Ibn Khaldun, has been called the father of economics, the father of sociology, the inventor of the social sciences, and the forerunner of Western intellectual giants such as Machiavelli, Vico, Weber, Durkheim, Keynes, and Marx. But Ibn Khaldun and his ideas are far more than a foreshadowing of developments in European thought centuries later; he was a shrewd statesman, a gifted writer, an adventurer, a political theorist, a philosopher, a theologian, and a remarkably creative and original thinker and student of the human condition. In his work, he sought to synthesize and describe the numerous branches of knowledge that had been developed in Western lands of the Islamic world, and bring them all to bear on the questions, How do human societies work? What makes them rise and fall?

Ibn Khaldun was born in Tunis to a prominent family of scholars and court officials who had migrated from Yemen in the eight century to settle in Seville and then migrated to Tunis shortly before Seville fell to Christian forces in 1284. At the time, families like Ibn Khaldun's maintained their status, and lucrative administrative and judicial posts in the courts of Andalusia and northern Africa, through their erudition. As such, Ibn Khaldun received a first-rate education, memorizing and studying the Qur'an, the Arabic language, Arabic rhetoric and poetry, Islamic jurisprudence, logic, mathematics, and Islamic theology, political theory, and philosophy. However, when he was only seventeen, Ibn Khaldun lost his parents and many of his teachers to a widespread outbreak of the plague.

After a brief, boring stint in Tunis as a calligrapher of royal decrees, he left to join his philosophy teacher and mentor in Fez, which was the political and intellectual center of the Maghreb. In his autobiography, Ibn Khaldun recounts his delight at meeting the many scholars from Andalusia and North Africa who passed through the city. However, he felt that the new positions open to him in Fez were still "beneath those to which his ancestors had aspired," and so he leapt into the turbulent political intrigues of court politics in the hopes of winning a high position for himself and reforming society according to his philosophical ideals.

These political maneuvers cost Ibn Khaldun his job several times and landed him in jail for two years. He even had to flee for his life a few times as he moved from court to court in northern Africa and Andalusia. He often carried out diplomatic missions among the Arab and Berber tribes of North Africa on behalf of his patrons. After alienating nearly every major dynasty in the region, he took advantage of these relationships to take something of a sabbatical from the intrigues of political life, retiring to a remote fortress under the protection of the Banu Arif tribe for four years (1375–79). During this time, he wrote his groundbreaking *Muqaddimah,* or introduction to his ambitious larger work of the history of Arabs and Berbers in northern Africa, the *Kitāb al-'ibar,* or "The Book of Lessons." He also reflected upon his repeated failures to cultivate and create the ideal philosopher-king and state as described by Islamic philosophy and political theory. And so, following the example of earlier Islamic philosophers, he redirected his ambitions away from reforming society through political means and toward investigating, discovering, and formulating the true governing principles of society through scholarly means.

After completing the *Muqaddimah,* in which he outlined his new philosophy and approach to history, Ibn Khaldun briefly returned to Tunis before leaving for Cairo in 1382. In Cairo, he found work as a judge and attracted a number of students eager to learn his new science of society (*'ilm al-'umrān*). He also completed his massive world history (*Kitāb al-'ibar*) (which he expanded to include the history of the Middle East) and his autobiography. When the Mongol conqueror Timur (Tamerlane) besieged the city of Damascus in 1401, Ibn Khaldun brashly went out to meet and study the conqueror who seemed to prove so many of the scholar's theories about power and social organization. In his autobiography, Ibn Khaldun records that the Mongol leader was very impressed with him and his ideas, which Timur saw as explaining and legitimating his own military and political successes. According to Ibn Khaldun, both men learned a great deal from each other during the month they spent together. Timur even tried to recruit Ibn Khaldun to his own court, but Ibn Khaldun made his excuses and returned to Cairo, where he died just a few years later, in 1406.

By the time of his death, Ibn Khaldun had completed a few works on logic, arithmetic, philosophy, and Sufism, but he is most famous for his autobiography and his magnum opus, the *Kitāb al-'ibar*—especially its introduction, or *Muqaddimah.* This large work (seven volumes in most modern printings) is divided into three books: the celebrated *Muqaddimah,* which outlines Ibn Khaldun's new theory and approach to historiography and the science of human social organization (*'ilm al-'umrān*); a history of the Arabs from pre-Islamic days to the present and of neighboring peoples and dynasties (such as the Persians, Turks, Greeks, etc.); and a history of the Berbers of North Africa.

THE IDEAS

What distinguished Ibn Khaldun from earlier historians was his development of a critical approach to history that combined philosophical reasoning and analysis with empirical observations. In the beginning of the *Muqaddimah,* Ibn Khaldun explains that one must have an understanding of the "laws of history"—why and how historical events occur—in order to critically evaluate historical accounts and data. But one must also have recourse to historical data in order to discover these "laws of history," just as one needs data from the natural world in order to formulate the "laws of nature." He writes, "The inner meaning of history, on the other hand, involves speculation and an attempt to get at the truth, subtle explanation of the causes and origins of existing things, and deep knowledge of the how and why of events. [History,] therefore, is firmly rooted in philosophy. It deserves to be accounted a branch of [philosophy]."

Ibn Khaldun criticized the shortcomings of earlier historians. He argued that they had failed to take into account the biases of sources, relied on implausible accounts, and, most important, failed to rationally and systematically determine why and how historical events occurred. In contrast, his new approach to history included a new science of human social organization that could explain how and why historical events occurred. On the basis of this science, he argued, one could logically and rigorously distinguish the necessary, possible, and impossible in the course of human social organization, and thus judge the plausibility of historical data about human societies.

According to Ibn Khaldun, man is by nature a social creature, and differences between peoples and their social organizations can be explained by different physical environments and related ways of making a living: "It should be known that differences of condition among people are the result of the different ways in which they make their living. Social organization enables them to cooperate toward that end and to start with the simple necessities of life, before they get to conveniences and luxuries."

He then develops a dialectic between Bedouin societies—those tribal societies that live in the wilderness and desert and maintain a subsistence-level existence with few luxuries—and settled or urban, sophisticated societies in which luxuries, social hierarchies, and specialized labor and fields of knowledge proliferate. Bedouin societies are characterized by strong 'aṣabiyah—a key term in Ibn Khaldun's thought that can be roughly translated as "group solidarity"—because it is necessary for their survival in such difficult conditions. On the basis of his own experience, Ibn Khaldun also notes that the conditions of Bedouin life tend to make its members more brave, tough, vigilant, hardworking, and pious than their urban counterparts. Thus, Bedouin societies give rise to strong tribal dynasties and militaries. Out of desire for security, tranquillity, and luxury, once they become strong enough, these dynasties either found their own cities or, more commonly, invade and take over already existing cities.

In perhaps the most famous discussion of the *Muqaddimah,* Ibn Khaldun explains how and why these dynasties usually decline within three or four generations. The founder of the dynasty is a stereotypical tough man of the desert who maintains the Bedouin virtues that led to his success, while his generation maintains the strong *'aṣabiyah* (group solidarity) that brought them into power. The second generation learns these qualities and virtues from their parents, and maintains them to a certain extent. They are also the first to master and excel in the urban arts of administration and bureaucracy. But, raised in a more luxurious environment, they are one step removed from the Bedouin qualities that brought their parents to power. The third generation is even further removed from these qualities, and maintains them as "tradition," not as practical necessities, as in the first generation, or lessons learned, as in the second generation. Under the rule of law and relative ease of urban life, the self-sufficiency, courage, group solidarity, and general toughness of the third generation are much weaker than their predecessors'. They begin to focus more on the pleasures and luxuries of urban life than on pursuing glory and greatness. As a result of their decreased group solidarity and toughness, the rulers of the second and third generation must increasingly rely on mercenaries from outside their dynasty to maintain their rule and fend off rivals within their own dynasty. This further diminishes group solidarity and increases the resentment of the ruler among the other members of the dynasty.

By the fourth generation, the members of the dynasty have become accustomed to easy living and luxuries, which they take for granted, having lost the memory and the qualities of their ancestors' struggle that led to their acquisition. The group solidarity and strength of the earlier generations have all but vanished as this fourth generation abandons itself to the pursuit of pleasures, and the dynasty "progresses toward weakness and senility." As the rulers become more inept and pay more attention to their own hedonistic pursuits than to the supervision of their kingdom, they appoint more sycophantic and inept administrators, and in the absence of oversight, corruption and mismanagement set in. The result is the eventual collapse of the dynasty, usually at the hands of a new Bedouin dynasty that sweeps in from the desert to take over and reinvigorate the state.

In summary, Ibn Khaldun argues that Bedouin life precedes and leads to settled, urban life, which will, in turn, decay and collapse under the weight of its own sophistication, returning to the simplicity of wilderness life—unless it is revived by an influx of fresh Bedouin spirit from the wilderness.

Ibn Khaldun developed and "proved" his theory not only through logical demonstration and philosophical reasoning, but also by citing numerous examples from North African and broader Islamic history, demonstrating how his theory models and explains the mechanisms of state formation, expansion, and decline. After establishing these and other general theories of human social development and decline, Ibn Khaldun applies them to judge the plausibility of various historical accounts and to suggest causal links between, and general principles that can be adduced from, the various events he records in his history of the Arabs, the Berbers, and neighboring peoples (books 2 and 3 of his *Kitāb al-'ibar*).

Although the *Muqaddimah* contains many other original discussions of topics—such as government (which he famously defined as "an institution that prevents injustice other than such as it commits itself"), various modes of labor, profit and taxation, religion and religious propaganda, different intellectual disciplines and their pedagogical methods and roles in societies—it is the dialectic outlined above for which the work and its author became most famous.

THE CONTEMPORARY LEGACY

Although Ibn Khaldun first became known to the Western world in the seventeenth century, his work was not widely read in Europe until the nineteenth century, when it was translated into German and French. (Ibn Khaldun's history of North Africa and its peoples may have been of particular interest to the French at this time, as they were in the process of colonizing northern Africa.) Scholars throughout Europe soon took note, characterizing him as a "genius ahead of his time," whose ideas and methods anticipated developments in the Western social sciences by several centuries.

These positive appraisals of Ibn Khaldun led to a revival of interest in his work in the Arab and broader Muslim world, which in turn led to an appreciation of Ibn Khaldun not only as a source of historical data and a forerunner of Western social theorists, but as a thinker whose ideas have contemporary relevance. His theories have been used to explain contemporary politics and conflict in the Middle East (such as the rise and decline of contemporary monarchies and regimes), patterns of immigration, and street gangs and cartels. Former president Ronald Reagan even invoked him to defend his supply-side economics (much to the chagrin of scholars), and a recent article in the *Atlantic* employs Ibn Khaldun's theory of dynastic decline to explain the slide of retail giant Walmart's share prices.

Ibn Khaldun's impressive legacy demonstrates that Africa is rich not only in natural resources, but in intellectual ones as well. His writings are a rich mine of theories and ideas, many of which have yet to be explored. Scholar, statesman, and theorist, Ibn Khaldun and the work he did in fourteenth-century northern Africa continues to shape and influence our world and the ways we understand it. This is exactly as he hoped, as he wrote in the conclusion of his *Muqaddimah:* "We have dealt—as we think, adequately—with the problems connected with [the nature of civilization]. Perhaps some later [scholar], aided by the divine gifts of a sound mind and of solid scholarship, will penetrate into these problems in greater detail than we did here."

ADDITIONAL RESOURCES

Alatas, Syed Farid. *Ibn Khaldun.* New Delhi: Oxford University Press, 2013.

Baali, Fuad. *The Science of Human Social Organization: Conflicting Views on Ibn Khaldun's (1332–1406) Ilm al-umran.* Mellen Studies in Sociology. Lewiston, NY: Edwin Mellen Press, 2005.

Fromherz, Allen James. *Ibn Khaldun: Life and Times.* Edinburgh: Edinburgh University Press, 2010.

Heck, Paul. "Theo-Humanism, Lecture 3: Ibn Khaldun; The Introduction to History." Georgetown University, n.d. www.youtube.com/watch?v=i_oJNkoTbQE.

Ibn Khaldûn. *The Muqaddimah: An Introduction to History.* Abridged ed. Edited by N. J. Dawood. Translated by Franz Rosenthal. Princeton, NJ: Princeton University Press, 1969.

"Ibn Khaldun (1332–1406), Muslim Philosopher." N.d. https://www.youtube.com/watch?v=2D13izXNZAc.

Mahdi, Muhsin. *Ibn Khaldun's Philosophy of History: A Study in the Philosophic Foundation of the Science of Culture.* Chicago: University of Chicago Press, 1971.

. . .

Currently an Assistant Professor of Religious Studies at the College of William and Mary, Oludamini Ogunnaike is a scholar of Islamic, African, and Religious Studies, with a focus on the intellectual and artistic dimensions of West African Sufism and Ifa, an indigenous Yoruba religious tradition. He is a graduate of Harvard College, earned his PhD from Harvard University's Department of African and African American Studies, and completed a postdoctoral fellowship at Stanford University. His research examines the Islamic and indigenous religious traditions of West Africa, seeking to understand their philosophical dimensions by approaching them and their proponents not merely as sources of ethnographic or historical data, but also as distinct intellectual traditions and thinkers.

Trade and Travel in Africa's Global Golden Age (AD 700–1500)

François-Xavier Fauvelle

Abstract: Between the eighth and the fifteenth centuries, vast regions of the African continent were in direct contact with the Islamic world and, through it, the rest of the world, from Mediterranean Europe to the Far East. From the Atlantic Sahel to the coastal areas on the Indian Ocean, these regions formed a long interface stretching between the African interior and the external world. The African elites of these regions exported and imported luxury and prestige goods, adopted and adapted ideas that were originally foreign, especially religious ideas, and developed political formations that, through the prism of the narratives of travelers and traders, acquired an echo tinged with legend and mystery. The golden age of Africa was thus an age during which African powers were able to act as indispensable partners in a global commercial system.

Keywords: Africa, Middle Ages, Islam, gold, travels

ARABIC GEOGRAPHER ABÛ ABAYD ABD Allâh al-Bakrî probably never left his native Andalusia (then Islamic Spain), but his *Book of Routes and Realms* (written in 1068) is one of the most valuable descriptions of the Maghreb and West Africa, and one of our very few pieces of written evidence about the kingdom of Ghâna, which was probably located in today's southern Mauritania (and has nothing to do with today's Ghana). It is not always easy to figure out whether al-Bakrî borrowed his information from archives then available in Cordova or if he obtained them from contemporary Muslim travelers who had crossed the Sahara. But whatever the case, what he writes about the apparatus surrounding the king of Ghâna is probably as mesmerizing today as it was a millennium ago: "The king ... puts a high cap decorated with gold and wrapped in a turban of fine cotton. He sits in audience ... in a domed pavilion around which stand horses covered with gold-embroidered materials. Behind the king stand ten pages holding shields and swords decorated with gold, and on his right are the sons of the [vassal] kings of his country wearing splendid garments and their hair plaited with gold. At the door of the pavilion are dogs of excellent pedigree.... Round their necks they wear collars of gold and silver studded with a number of balls of the same metals" (Levtzion and Hopkins 2000, p. 80). In a diametrically opposed region of Africa, Mapungubwe Hill in South Africa, has yielded several tombs from which a small but famous gold-foil rhinoceros and other animals of the same metal, a possible "scepter" and a gold-leaf headrest, thousands of beads, and several solid-gold items of jewelry were found. These objects date to the thirteenth century.

These are only two examples—one from written sources, the other from archaeology—that demonstrate the role of gold for African elites during the medieval period as signs of power to their own population, but perhaps especially as signs of prestige and wealth to outside visitors. We do not know if there were visitors to Mapungubwe; if they came, none left written evidence or gave an account to an author such as al-Bakrî. But in Ghâna, if we are well informed on the uses of gold in the royal court, this is precisely because such a profusion of the yellow metal was destined to make the eyes of foreign merchants in the capital sparkle and, through their accounts (transmitted by al-Bakrî), to strike the imagination of the outside world—in other terms, to find outlets on the foreign markets for their gold.

In this, one could say that the African powers entirely succeeded. And if the period between the eighth and fifteenth centuries (what is called the Middle Ages in Europe) can be called the golden age in Africa, this is due as much to the tons of gold exported each year from Africa as to the agency of African political and economic elites who, controlling gold fluctuations, succeeded in imposing themselves in foreign markets as powerful and reliable economic partners. Gold here played the role that luxury brands play today by contributing to the creation and maintenance of a commercial reputation, allowing the sale at the highest price of other export products such as slaves, ivory (elephant, rhinoceros, warthog), cattle hides and feline skins, ambergris (a secretion of the sperm whale that served as the basis for perfumes and unguents), and so forth. A good example of this political and commercial success is provided by the famous Catalan Atlas, a map of the Mediterranean world drawn by Jewish cartographers from Mallorca, in the Balearic Islands, in 1375: at the bottom of the map, a black figure called Musse Melly holds all the signs of royalty (crown, scepter, etc.) and is described (in Catalan) as "the richest and most noble lord of all this region by the abundance of gold that can be obtained from his lands." This "Musse Melly" is Mûsâ, king of Mâli, who a half century earlier had made a strong impression when he visited Cairo. Egyptian chroniclers describe the ostentation surrounding Mûsâ during his visit en route for the pilgrimage to Mecca in 1324; he spent so much gold, it was said, that the value of the dinar (Arab money) was significantly affected.

Merchants are often more careful and scrupulous with the products they buy than with those they sell. As a result, the written documentation is more prolific for products purchased by foreign merchants with African partners in African warehouses and capitals and then exported toward the outside world than it is for products imported in Africa. For the latter, the written documentation is typically terse, and one needs archaeological documentation to have a more detailed idea of them. Unlike the Muslim and Christian tombs, which generally do not have grave goods, the "pagan" tombs often yield, when they have not been looted, funerary goods that reflect the social status of the deceased. Such is the case at Mapungubwe as well as in many rich burials of the "Shay culture" in Ethiopia from the ninth to fourteenth century and the tombs at the end of the first millennium AD in the Lake Chad region. In most of these, grave goods include stone beads from Pakistan and Gujarat in India, glass beads from Egypt or the Near East and other, tiny ones, from a vast Indo-Pacific area, cowry shells from the Maldives, and sometimes even plates or fragments of plates of Islamic or Chinese ceramics. Despite the fact that these objects are found in "pagan"—that is, pre- or early Islamic—contexts, such an archaeological "assemblage" reflects very well the diversity of the economic catchment area of the Islamic world of the time. Further, that some objects from sometimes distant provenances had acquired prestige status in line with Islam is seen in the Chinese porcelain plates (only the Chinese possessed this technique during this period) found from Tanzania to Mozambique and Madagascar, sometimes embedded in the prayer niches (*mirhab*) of the old mosques.

The African golden age is thus also a global age, which took shape within the new global geography established with the rapid spread of Islam and Muslim powers in the seventh century. From the seventh century, vast regions of Africa came progressively in direct contact with regions subject to Muslim powers and Qur'anic law (but which were not necessarily Muslim in their majority and whose populations sometimes did not speak Arabic)— what we call the Islamic world.

The Africa connected to, and that traded with, the Islamic world and through it the rest of the world was not the same as during antiquity. It was a new frontier now reached by the crossing of the Sahara or the Indian Ocean— in both cases, at a cost of two months' travel—by merchants, diplomats, and travelers. From the Atlantic Sahel to the Lake Chad Basin and the Middle Nile Valley, from the Horn of Africa to the coastal areas on the Indian Ocean and the confines north of Madagascar, these regions formed a long crescent stretching between the Islamic world (to which the Maghreb and Egypt now belonged) and the African interior. These regions formed not only a geographic but also a political, religious, and cultural interface. This is, for example, evident in Ethiopia, where "pagan," Christian, and Muslim powers were closely interacting for several centuries, and in the famous kingdom of Mâli, where in the fourteenth century the king had a dual legitimacy, both as sultan (an Islamic noble title) for foreign visitors and major dignitaries of the kingdom, and as *mansa* (a Malinke royal title), intercessor of his people, with the local deities and ancestors.

That these were foreign traders, ambassadors, and travelers who came to the commercial cities and capitals of the African kingdoms does not mean that people from these African kingdoms did not travel the other way. Beyond the case of Mûsâ, king of Mâli, we know of a number of African kings who together with their large parties of followers made pilgrimages to holy places in Arabia. But the fact is that the production of information on medieval African civilization is very largely dependent on the asymmetry in the conditions of encounters between Africans and foreigners. One may regret that medieval African societies (with the exception of the manuscript tradition in Ethiopia and the epigraphic traditions in Mali, for example) did not produce their own written sources until after the sixteenth century. But this unequal relationship in the production of information should be remembered if only because the narratives available show the observation biases of their authors: as men, orthodox Muslims, city dwellers, and traders, these authors were rarely interested in subjects other than cities and trade, leaving rural areas and most ordinary aspects of daily life unexamined. Their writings also reflect the strong prejudices regarding women, African forms of Islam, and non-Muslim beliefs.

The inequality in the conditions of encounters between Africans and foreigners did not prevent the African powers from reaping economic and political benefits from this relationship. By monopolizing some of the benefits of long-distance trade, and by converting to Islam, as they often did, the reigning elites gained both in power (with regard to their population) and in moral authority (with regard to foreign merchants). This led to the emergence of hierarchical forms of power that merit the name of empire. Such is the case of Mâli, which was established in the thirteenth century by its hero-founder, Sunjata Keita. His actions, largely surrounded by an aura of folklore and mythology, are known to us via a great epic poem orally transmitted for centuries by bards attached to the aristocratic families. In the fourteenth century, Mâli was indisputably the principal polity south of the Sahara. Its strength came from the fact that the kings were able to ensure a monopoly on the gold and slave supply from populations in the backcountry and on selling to Arab, Berber, and Egyptian traders from North Africa.

One characteristic of the global world of the Middle Ages was that people and goods did not travel directly from one extreme point to another, but rather through a number of commercial segments that were operated by different specialized groups or guilds with strong ethnic or religious ties. Another characteristic was that luxury goods on demand in another part of the world would usually be trans-shipped from one segment of the trade route to another and thus handed over from one specialized group or guild to another. This meant that the long-distance transport of merchandise did not require merchants to travel along with it. In other words, the medieval period was a global age of a different kind than our modern world, in the sense that there was no need, and only little possibility, to travel from one end of the world to another. Weren't there exceptions? We all know, at least by name, famous travelers who journeyed from one corner of the then known world to the other. Consider, for example, Benjamin of Tudela, a Jewish rabbi from the Christian Kingdom of Navarre, in today's Spain, who traveled extensively in the twelfth century; Ibn Battûta, the Arab traveler born in Morocco who left a travel account of the entire known world of the fourteenth century; and Zheng He, the famous admiral of the Chinese fleet at the time of the Ming dynasty in the fifteenth century. Interestingly, not only can we justifiably see these three figures—a Jew, an Arab, and a Chinese—as emblems of the global world of the medieval period; their very experience and travel agenda would not even be conceivable without the setting of the specific interconnectedness of the world permitted by the Islamic civilization.

Interestingly, these travelers lied, as scholars have shown, or rather allowed themselves uncertainties that left room to conflicting interpretations of the extent of their travels, especially when it involved the part of their journeys that touched Africa. The tacit agenda of Benjamin's account was to encompass, in the form of an itinerary, the entire Jewish diaspora of the time, from its western to eastern ends—that is, from Spain to China. However, the very objective of comprehensiveness of Benjamin's first-person account is precisely why doubts can be raised about the reality of some legs of his supposed travels: it was too tempting for him to complement the narrative with fictitious or secondhand details, thus creating for his readers (presumably Jewish coreligionists) the reassuring narrative of a cohesive global Jewish community. For this reason, Benjamin included in his account the mention of a powerful Jewish kingdom supposedly grounded in the mountains of Ethiopia—a Jewish kingdom that probably never existed, and that he certainly never visited. But whatever the reasons for Benjamin's lie or error, it is meaningful in the sense that it betrays his intention: this otherwise unattested Jewish kingdom of Ethiopia was included in his account only because Benjamin felt he could not take the risk of leaving a Jewish community outside the perimeter of his all-encompassing description.

In this regard, Benjamin can be compared with the famous fourteenth-century Muslim traveler Muhammad ibn Abdullah ibn Battûta. He was born in 1304 in the Marinid kingdom of present-day Morocco, and he departed at the age of twenty-one for a pilgrimage to the holy places of Islam in Arabia. This was to be the beginning of almost three decades spent traveling all over the known world of the time, only stopping for a few years at some places (such as Delhi, the Maldives, and Mecca) to set up as a Qur'anic judge or an office holder in some ruler's court. After he returned home, the account of this exceptional life was written down and embellished by an official scribe of the Marinids, Ibn Djuzayy. This book in Arabic is commonly known as the *Rihla,* or "Journey." Its documentary value for the fourteenth-century Muslim world is by and large outstanding. Of unique interest is Ibn Battûta's idiosyncratic preference for inventorying and describing in detail Muslim sanctuaries and princes' etiquette. For again, the aim of the account was to depict the entire Muslim community, if not the world, in both its unity and its diversity.

Yet for this same very reason, Ibn Battûta felt the need to "fill the gap" between the global world as it was recorded to exist and the mundane limits posed to an individual's experience. Modern scholarship has shown or suggested the unlikelihood of the most remote parts of the journey—for instance, to the north (in Russia) and east (the travel beyond the Malacca Straits and especially in China is demonstrably a piecemeal of information and legends from various origins). Already in the fourteenth century, some doubts were also cast by the great Arab historian Ibn Khaldun on the authenticity of Ibn Battûta's journey to the south, across the Sahara. Staying in the court of the king of Mâli—the *mansa* Suleyman, brother of Mûsâ—Ibn Battûta gives a very detailed description of his audiences and ceremonies. Yet, although for other regions of the world his inventory of sultanic powers is complemented by vivid details about daily life, the account of his stay in the capital of Mâli is limited to a narrative outline, thus presenting the shortcoming of describing in detail only aspects that any foreign residents could have described in similar terms, and giving no supplementary information that would support the veracity of his own visit. But it is particularly regarding the voyage from Mogadishu (today Somalia) to Mombasa (today Kenya) and Kilwa (today Tanzania) that the most serious doubts are raised: for each of these city-states on the east coast of Africa, the descriptions of Ibn Battûta deviate more or less significantly from the other available historical and archaeological data. Even more so, the pace of the journey that is related in the *Rihla* is in complete contradiction with the practical conditions of a voyage on the Indian Ocean during this period, as if the secondhand narration was satisfied here with espousing the fictive form of a travel account.

If there exists today a tendency to overestimate the scale of travels such as those of Benjamin and Ibn Battûta, this is probably because we compare their achievements by using the standards of our time, when our world has become comparatively so small as to make it possible for one person to travel around it several times over the course of a lifetime. Overestimations of these ancient travels are anachronistic and lead to an underestimation of their exceptional nature. Zheng He, the famous admiral of the Chinese fleet in the early decades of the fifteenth century, is possibly such a case where there is a discrepancy between the scale of his real travels and the romantic view promoted by some scholars and on the Internet about the Chinese fleet discovering America, or even passing the southern tip of Africa. Between 1405 and 1433, Zheng He, a Muslim Chinese, led seven naval expeditions toward the Indochina Peninsula, Indonesia, and, more distantly, the shores of the North Indian Ocean. The goal of these travels was to buy exotic goods such as perfumes, feathers, horn, and precious woods, no doubt also to record information on the sources and routes of supply of these luxury items, and occasionally to obtain the submission of local rulers to the emperor—if necessary, by soliciting them for hostages and gifts. Twice, in 1417–19 (during the fifth trip) and 1421–22 (during the sixth trip), Zheng He reached Africa. The primary reports of these expeditions are lost, but scanty information is preserved in a map by Huan Ma, the translator of the expeditions, in the annals of the Ming dynasty, and in a stone inscription engraved by Zheng He himself in a temple near the mouth of the Yangtze River. These documents contain some information on Mogadishu, Brava, and Juba—three places in today's Somalia. We learn that the country exports wild cat skins, "camelbird" (ostrich) feathers, "dragon saliva" (ambergris), and incense, and that local people are potentially interested in merchandise such as silks and satins, porcelains, rice, and cereals. And that's all: descriptions of these places are both fascinating and deceiving. Fascinating because such an episode fans our interest in remote medieval encounters. Deceiving because we cannot help imagining what might have been the encounter between China and Africa if both had attached to this event the same significance that we do today.

CONCLUSION

It is of note that the three travelers did not come from the center of the Islamic world (for instance, Cairo or Baghdad) but rather its distant peripheries. It is remarkable that it is these men coming from one end of the world who traveled to the opposite end, or at least claimed to have done so. It is difficult to find an explanation for this, except that these travelers from their respective peripheries possibly found it easier to experience the finiteness and completeness of the world because they themselves were proof that the world really had limits that were reachable and describable. It is also of interest that, despite their coming from the periphery, all three travelers were in some way typical products of the Islamic world. Certainly Ibn Battûta was, as an Arab Muslim from Morocco under a Muslim power. Benjamin, a Jew from bordering Christian Spain, could circulate across the Islamic lands thanks only to Jewish solidarity networks and the protective status provided to Jews by Islamic law. Zheng He's personal trajectory as a converted Chinese also made him the product of an Islamic network extending to the gateway of South China, probably providing him with a universalist Muslim viewpoint, and certainly creating opportunities for him to make connections with Muslim authorities and coreligionists while exploring the northern waters of the Indian Ocean. And it is also of interest that for them Africa was the ultimate truth test. In that, minor forgeries and shortfalls in their descriptions are not just meaningless flaws. They reveal that the meaning and ideal of the travel to Africa was to probe the completeness of the world, and that even if the world remained too big for a traveler, it was no longer too big for a writer.

From the fifteenth century, a new global geographic structure developed: the Portuguese caravels that circumnavigated Africa by the Atlantic competed with and replaced the trans-Saharan caravans and the sambuks of the Indian Ocean. With Portugal leading (the first voyage of Vasco da Gama dating to 1497–98), European powers began to regularly circumnavigate Africa via the south. Bypassed, the medieval global system of circulation and trade collapsed and a new political geography took shape. Some famous and brilliant African powers still had a role, but nearly everywhere the medieval African powers were replaced by new regional hegemonies; the glorious commercial cities and capitals of the golden age declined, when they did not disappear entirely under the sands of the Sahara or in the mangroves of the East African coast.

ADDITIONAL RESOURCES

Duyvendak, J. J. L. *China's Discovery of Africa.* London: Arthur Probsthain, 1949.
Fauvelle, F.-X. "Desperately seeking the Jewish Kingdom of Ethiopia: Benjamin of Tudela and the Horn of Africa (Twelfth Century)." *Speculum: A Journal of Medieval Studies* 88, no. 2 (April 2013): 383–404.
———. *Le rhinocéros d'or: Histoires du Moyen Âge africain.* Paris: Alma, 2013.
Gibb, H. A. R., and C. F. Beckingham. *The Travels of Ibn Baṭṭūṭa, A.D. 1325–1354.* 4 vols. London: Hakluyt Society, 1956–1994.
Levtzion, N., and J. F. P. Hopkins. *Corpus of Early Arabic Sources for West African History.* Princeton, NJ: Markus Wiener, 2000.

. . .

FRANÇOIS-XAVIER FAUVELLE is an Africanist historian and archaeologist. He is a senior researcher at the CNRS, University of Toulouse, France. He was the head of the French Center for Ethiopian Studies in Addis Ababa, Ethiopia, and is now the director of TRACES in Toulouse, one of the leading international laboratories in archaeology. His research focuses on the history and archeology of ancient and medieval Africa. His geographical focus is on southern Africa, the Horn of Africa, Morocco (where he leads a French-Moroccan program of excavations at Sijilmâsa), and West Africa. He is the author or editor of fifteen books and the author of around a hundred academic articles. His book *Le rhinocéros d'or: Histoires du Moyen Âge africain* [The golden rhinoceros: History of the African Middle Ages] (Paris, 2013) received the Grand Prix du Livre d'Histoire (the main French award for academic history books) in 2013.

Three Women of the Sahara

FATMA, ODETTE, AND SOPHIE

E. Ann McDougall

Abstract: This chapter explores the Sahara through the lives of three women. Snapshots from their experiences bring to life the rich patterns of trade, communications, and political movements that shaped communities in the desert. Collectively they challenge the image of the Sahara Desert as an empty space that divides communities on its northern and southern shores.

Keywords: French colonialism, trans-Saharan commerce, decolonization, Timbuktu

This is for John, who always loved Fatma's story.

FATMA, ODETTE, AND SOPHIE. They never met, yet their lives intersected with the lived history of the Sahara for much of the twentieth century. Their life trajectories crossed paths even if their lives did not.

They did so in what is often thought of as an "ocean of sand," an "empty space" that people crossed between a "civilized" North Africa and a "noncivilized" black Africa rich in gold and slaves. A place where (somewhat contradictorily) ferocious blue-veiled nomads lived and waged war on all who dared to enter. Or most recently, a "menacing void" in which al-Qaeda terrorists disappear and reappear, as if by magic. This is the "Great Desert," the Sahara, which stretches across Africa from the Atlantic to the Red Sea and whose very existence shapes perceptions of the continent itself: today, we speak mostly not of Africa but of "sub-Saharan Africa."

The lives of Fatma, Odette, and Sophie belie these stereotypes in just about every way. Each, albeit differently, actually lived in or on the margins of the Sahara, experienced "trans-Saharan" travel as a part of life, and defined themselves in terms of their relation to Saharan culture and economy. Fatma and Sophie have been (to date) invisible to history; and while Odette's writings are

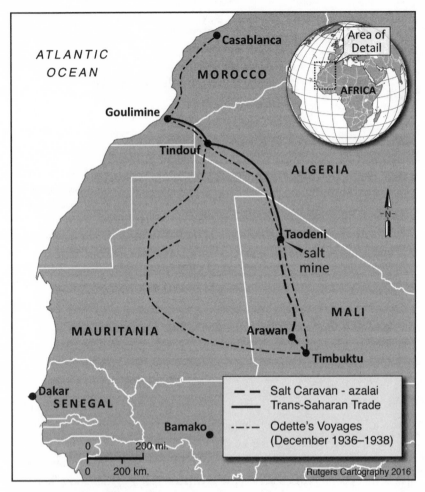

MAP 2. Northwest Africa. Rutgers Cartography, 2016.

prolific, she has rarely been taken seriously as either a witness to or a participant in Saharan history. Yet, their lives shed new light on major themes of academic research—slavery, commerce, and colonialism. Moreover, they were women. Their desert experiences were embedded in relationships with men—Fatma with her master, Sophie with her husband, Odette with the (entirely) masculine local colonial administration. But apart from Odette's somewhat "orientalist" view of Saharan nomads (the "true" Saharan man was proud, defiant, and nomadic), and Fatma's experience of one memorable warrior *razzia* (raid) during her only desert crossing, their real lives did not reflect the largely "male," uninhabitable Sahara with which we are most familiar.

Fatma was born (or taken) into slavery near Timbuktu in the early years of the twentieth century as part of a wealthy Moroccan merchant's household. She traveled across the Sahara by caravan as a young girl with her master, Mohamed Barka, when he returned to Goulimine (southern Morocco) in 1914. She lived most of her life as a domestic slave to that family but also as a concubine to Barka. She knew many years as a "freed-slave," with a husband, child, and property of her own, yet her intimate ties with the Barka family continued to shape her life. She died in Goulimine in 1995.

Odette du Puigaudeau was born to impoverished French aristocracy in 1894. She challenged norms of her class and gender in both professional and personal choices, being attracted to Marion, her life-long female companion, and to adventure in the Sahara. She also wanted acceptance in the male world of French academics as a scientific ethnographer. She and Marion traveled extensively in the Sahara in the 1930s and 1940s, invested in helping Saharans make the most of colonialism and eventually, postcolonialism. To this end, the couple moved to Rabat, Morocco, in 1961, where Marion died in 1977 and Odette in 1991.

Sophie mint Ali ould Ali Wali was born in Timbuktu (possibly c. 1920) to a commercial family from Tindouf that had longstanding connections to what was then "the Sudan" (black Africa). She married a merchant from an equally prominent trading family who worked the desert-salt trade out of Timbuktu. With him, she lived eight years (1954–62) in the middle of the Sahara, in Taodeni, at the salt mine itself, then spent the next almost thirty years in Timbuktu. She experienced the transition from colonial French West Africa to independence in Mali, Algeria, and Morocco—all of which affected her life. In the early1990s, her husband, M'Rabih, was wounded in a rebellion by local Saharan Tuareg "nationalists." Although not politically involved himself, as a Saharan merchant he was assumed by the Malian army to be sympathetic to the Tuareg. He was seriously wounded and was evacuated to Goulimine, where Sophie cared for him until his death. She remained in Goulimine—a widow of desert politics.

COLONIAL MEANINGS

Fatma, Odette, and Sophie: three women of the Sahara whose lives teach us so much—not in spite of their differences but because of them. Fatma was a young girl who became a slave in the household of a typical Timbuktu merchant probably around 1910. Sophie's grandfather's business was well established, also in Timbuktu, at the same time; the families had business connections. This was a Sahara of slave trading between "black Africa" and "North Africa," one that integrated Goulimine (southern Morocco), Tindouf (an Algerian frontier town contested by Morocco), and Timbuktu (Mali). Fatma's trip across the Sahara was made as a slave, but unlike other slaves who made that trip over the centuries, she was not for sale. She proudly told the tale of that desert crossing and gloried in the telling of being "feted" upon arrival in Goulimine. It was here, in Barka's new household that she became a trusted "family" member—the one who "carried the keys to the pantry." When freed years later, she drew upon relations with women the family had known in Timbuktu and Tindouf to support a brief "adventure" (as she put it) as a baker and bread seller in Tindouf.

Sophie's mother might well have been among those women because her father, although born in Tindouf and involved in his own father's Goulimine-based trans-Saharan business, had relocated to Timbuktu following the French occupation of the Niger Bend. Sophie was born in Timbuktu, probably not long after Fatma's memorable desert crossing. But unlike those for whom Timbuktu was the southern terminus of their family network, Sophie's father represented a new generation. He took advantage of colonial commercial opportunities in Senegal, where he also took a second wife and gave Sophie a Senegalese half-brother who later facilitated her husband's business.

The imposition of French colonial rule over the Sahara and its neighbors underlies each woman's personal history. First Sophie's father, then her husband, M'Rabih, saw his commercial career reshaped by the growing French West African colonial market. Grandson of one of Timbuktu's famous slave traders, M'Rabih made his initial fortune in desert salt mined at Taodeni (seven hundred kilometers north of Timbuktu) between 1935 and 1950. He bought camels in Timbuktu, sent salt to Goulimine, purchased Moroccan and French imported goods, then sent them to Tindouf, partly on trucks, partly on camels. He kept camels at Tindouf for use in this trade. The success of this business prompted him to take up residence at Taodeni, where he could more closely control his affairs. While M'Rabih managed the macro side of business, Sophie dealt with local purchases (such as tobacco from Timbuktu) and the food supplies brought by the annual caravans (*azalai*), with which she regularly fed her husband's salt miners. And she carried out her own petty commerce, making an onion-and-hot-pepper paste that she sold alongside the tobacco. She described herself as "well looked after," with a large household at her command.

Sophie would still have been living in Timbuktu when one of the 1938 annual *azalai* arriving at Taodeni brought with it not only supplies but two French women, Odette du Puigaudeau and Marion Senones. Sophie had likely heard about them in any event, Timbuktu being a small community. Odette and Marion had waited there for over two frustrating weeks because no one wanted to rent them the camels they needed to make the trip to Taodeni (where they were to meet a French escort for the rest of their desert crossing). This was their second Saharan voyage. Previously, in 1933–34, they had traveled through Mauritania's desert, visiting nomadic camps and date-palm oases.

The desolate and dangerous desert that lay north of Timbuktu, however, was another story. This voyage of more than seven hundred kilometers was particularly unwelcoming—and unforgiving. After the town of Arawan, with the one hundred wells for which it was famous and where *azalai* rested to graze and water camels, there was neither pasture nor water until Taodeni—some five hundred kilometers and eight days later. When supply caravans did not reach Taodeni because of these natural dangers or political disturbances, the mine workers were left to die. Several times in the past, conflict generated by local Saharans' opposition to the French presence had obstructed commercial traffic—and neither the Timbuktu administration nor its military had intervened.

Odette gathered information from the leader of the *azalai* about how work at Taodeni was organized. Traditionally, it had depended on the slave labor now abolished under French law—a policy about which Odette had mixed feelings, as it happens. How, she asked, had abolition affected the mine? Taodeni proved to be home to an industry in which "the past" coexisted easily with a rapidly changing present—as true in the 1950s, when Sophie lived there, as it was during Odette's four-day stay. There were those who were still slaves (the law notwithstanding) but more who had been legally freed (*haratine*); yet their lives were still dependent. Without "masters" to provide for them, they were now indebted to merchants in Timbuktu and labored in Taodeni to work off their debts. Some were working on their own behalf; they had the better chance of realizing profit. But everyone depended on people with access to camels for transport to and from Timbuktu. Transport costs were high; those who could afford both "workers" (slaves or otherwise) and camels were the real winners in this lucrative business. As Odette pointed out, Taodeni kept a whole sector of the

Timbuktu regional economy going: those who wholesaled the salt, those who retailed it, those who "tailored" it, those who made cords for it, those who made/repaired the leather straps used to load the salt, those who in turn transported it by boat, donkey, and head loads into the Sahel and forest zones; also, those who grew the millet and tobacco that Sophie in turn "retailed," who filled leather sacks with liquid butter and dried cheese. All depended on the annual *azalai* for their livelihood.

What Odette described seeing in Taodeni in 1937–38 was the life Sophie lived in the 1950s. According to Sophie's account, little had changed, including the range of "freedoms" present among those who lived and worked at Taodeni. Sophie had her own *hartaniyya* (female freed slave), and her "well-off" household included others of servile status. She noted that the government-appointed mayor in charge of the mine (with the right to one-tenth of the salt it exported) had married a *hartaniyya* from her own family. And at least one of the few "black families" at the mine was also descended from one of her family's (former?) slaves. Taodeni provided a window on significant economic and social change as it related to French policies regarding slavery and the slave trade: both Odette, who bore witness to this moment, and Sophie, who lived it a few years later, were each in their own way elements of the change itself.

THE GREATER SAHARA

Resistance to colonial rule in Morocco in the 1950s also became a reality for these women. For Sophie, the actual "liberation movement" that emerged in the southern regions in 1954 was far from her Taodeni household; the 1956 declaration of independence in Rabat, farther still. But the negative impact on her family's all-important trade into southern Morocco was felt during the disturbances. That said, she explained in a seemingly approving way that the army was fighting "for the freedom of the Sahara and Mauritania," implicitly understanding "the Sahara" as a unity. Fatma's son joined that army. She worried that his absence prevented him from marrying and providing her with the daughter-in-law she needed in her old age. With the help of a woman who housed Liberation Army officers in Goulimine, she arranged for her son to get leave for a wedding. A former Barka slave, Messoud, with whom Fatma had worked years earlier, helped her; "the family" provided the requisite (but expensive) bride's horse. Fatma was "honored by army men eating at the house for a week."

Odette's experience was not with the local liberation army per se. Rather, it was with issues around the meaning of colonialism by the 1950s and the ultimate goals of that army. If for Fatma the issue was her son's marriage and her own prestige, and for Sophie her family's commercial interests, for Odette the situation was more complicated. The Liberation Army opposed the 1953 forced exile (by the French) of the Moroccan king; they were fighting the French military. Her many Saharan trips had been assisted by that military. Officers had shared their local knowledge, provided appropriate accommodation and company, and in one instance (reportedly), romance. Mauritania's Sahara was not France, but its principle of "social respect" between clearly delineated, hierarchical classes resonated with Odette. She believed that colonialism meshed with the true Saharan "soul" vis-à-vis humanity. When she returned to Mauritania between 1949 and 1951, she was bitterly disappointed in what that relationship had brought to the postwar world. Modernization was not, in her opinion, a good thing for Saharans, who now wanted to move into towns, take up wage labor, embrace materialism, and essentially abandon the desert and its values. Even as Fatma's son was joining the Liberation Army and Sophie was hoping it would be successful, Odette was despondent about what had happened to "her" Sahara and the declining role of the honorable French military.

Less than a decade later, that Sahara had become Morocco, Algeria, Mauritania, and Mali. The French military was gone. The impact was again enormous, but different for each woman.

The independence of Morocco for Fatma equated with her son's army experience; it simply did not figure in her own sense of self. She continued to define herself in terms of her desert crossing with the Barka family half a century earlier. This in itself is intriguing. How many others of slave and freed-slave origin saw themselves as so tied to family and community, because this was where their identity was rooted, that the politics of anticolonialism and independence in Morocco simply did not register?

For Sophie, not just Moroccan but "African" independence was a crisis. Because of her family's longstanding trans-Saharan commercial relations, they, along with others, fought against the new boundaries that attached Goulimine to Morocco and Tindouf to Algeria. Members of Sophie's family were imprisoned. M'Rabih's camel trade with Goulimine ended. While it could not have been an easy period in her life, Sophie calmly recounted that "as a consequence of this," her husband, her brother, and their partner adjusted their commerce once again: they worked between Timbuktu and

Dakar (via rail for the most part) and Casablanca, Morocco (by ship). Her husband frequently flew back and forth to handle business, which now depended heavily on importing a highly valued Sudanese incense to Morocco.

Independence had a second impact. The new Malian government had little interest in Taodeni. Another Saharan clan claimed control of the mine, and in the subsequent conflict the community was left to starve—revealing once again the vulnerability it had known under early French rule. For Sophie, this situation reflected the widespread fear that the government was "anti-Arab." She and M'Rabih left Taodeni in 1962 as a consequence, and by 1964 had quit the salt business; but they remained in Timbuktu, developing the Dakar–Casablanca commercial network described above.

Odette was French. In terms of nationality she was part of the problems Sophie and Fatma experienced. But she did not see herself that way. She thought colonialism could unite the Sahara. With the information she could provide as an academic and writer about Saharans' traditional values and social hierarchy, she could help protect them. This explained her ambivalence about the abolition of slavery—an institution that she saw as embodying both "values" and "hierarchy." As the tsunami of independence swept North and West Africa in the late 1950s, Odette advocated a political position that had strong support in Mauritania and Morocco: the creation of a Greater Morocco that embraced the Malian and Mauritanian Sahara. Pointedly, Odette preferred the term "Greater Sahara." In spite of other significant differences, she and Sophie would have (literally) shared some common ground on this question. In 1961, Odette was enticed to settle in Rabat (the Moroccan capital) by a job offer with the national radio station to promote the cultural basis for Morocco's Saharan claims. By leaving France, Odette felt she was helping to create a "new Sahara," one in which the traditional past would be respected even as the future beckoned.

DESERT CROSSINGS

To the best of my knowledge, if Sophie ever crossed the Sahara, it was in an airplane to take M'Rabih to Goulimine. Her Sahara was the one between Taodeni and Timbuktu, her "crossing" the one she undoubtedly made annually with the *azalai*. But when interviewed in Goulimine, she suggested that there was little difference between life in Mali and the one she now lived. Poignantly, given her husband's critical condition at the time, she chose to show us one of the few precious things she had brought with her—a *melhafa* (veil worn by Saharan women) of an exquisite, handmade indigo cloth. It was produced only in the Sudan, worn only for special celebrations. It seemed that in the unwrapping this treasure, Sophie also "unwrapped" the memories of Saharan living it embodied.

Odette's Sahara, in contrast, was defined precisely by her multiple desert crossings. With Marion, she had spent (in total) more than three years traveling down the ancient Triq-Lamtuna (the route from Morocco through Mauritania, named for the famous eleventh-century [Lamtuna] Almoravids), across the desert edge populated with rich date-palm groves, east to Timbuktu, then north through Taodeni and Tindouf to Goulimine ("the salt route"). This is the Sahara she defended. In the 1940s, she was an ardent spokesperson for the French colonial state, having been commissioned to write a book about its highly politicized Trans-Saharan Railway Project. Neither the book nor the railroad materialized. But Odette's intimacy with the desert was seen as something that could work for French goals in West Africa. That Morocco recognized a similar potential in Odette's Sahara obsession in the early years of its own imperial ambitions (1960s) is not surprising. While Odette was clearly a foreigner, a colonialist, and an aristocrat who experienced the Sahara in a particularly privileged and protected manner, she felt herself defined by it. While visiting a southern Mauritanian school during her 1949–51 trip, she recounted, to a rapt audience of young chiefs' sons, her memories of the traditional Mauritania she remembered from her earlier voyages. She referred to "her Moors," as one convinced she knew Saharans better than anyone else. "I would be proud to call any of these young men my son," she later wrote in her journal—articulating her own "maternalist" colonialism.

Then there was Fatma, in whose "desert-crossing footsteps" Odette traveled. Although Odette referred to her travels as adventures, Fatma's trip from Timbuktu to Goulimine truly *was* an adventure: not only did their caravan face the desert's natural challenges; it was robbed by *grands nomades* who regularly traveled thousands of kilometers across the Sahara, and then left their victims to perish. The caravan was rescued by Tindouf residents, who came out to meet it with camels and water. On the surface, the story reflects the stereotypical Sahara—an empty space through which camel caravans travel, vulnerable to attacks by fanatical warriors. But Fatma's telling of it was so much more revealing. She spoke repeatedly of her master's bravery, his wisdom in burying their wealth (in gold) before the pillagers arrived, and the assistance of her master's friends from Tindouf. This is a Sahara in which information moved with lightning speed through various family/merchant networks—in this instance, the source of both their attack and rescue. It was also one in which legendary "heroes" and "villains" were made. Their arrivals first in Tindouf and finally in Goulimine were celebrated because of her master's famous wealth and generosity, and the bravery of his slave Messoud, who was soon freed in recognition of his Saharan service. Fatma also emphasized how important it was that the people of Goulimine knew she was arriving "not as a daughter" but as a slave.

There was a reason for her insistence on this point: she later became Barka's concubine. In this Muslim community, only slaves could legitimately be concubines, give birth to free children, and ultimately, as *umm al-walad* ("mother of the child"), become free themselves. On his deathbed, according to Fatma, Barka told his children that she "was their mother and not a slave." While not literally true (Fatma later gave birth, but not to Barka's children), by obliquely referencing her status, he was asking that she be given her freedom *as if* she were *umm al-walad*. While Barka's children chose to ignore his request, freeing her only years later, they acknowledged her special status in the ongoing family relationship of which she was so rightfully proud.

Fatma's repeated telling of "the desert crossing" over the years established the social and religious credentials of her master and, by extension, herself. The performance literally defined her identity. When she said, "I am the mother of a very large tent," echoing Barka's last words, she was also not unlike Odette in finding a "self" outside her class and her culture. And making it her own.

ON "BEING SAHARAN"

I do not know if Sophie is still living, but I believe that she would say she was more Saharan than Moroccan, having family from what became Algeria and living most of her life in what became Mali before burying her husband in Goulimine, which had never been her home. Odette wanted to be Saharan—although, in contrast to Sophie, that meant being a nomad. Her self-positioning vis-à-vis imperialist visions of France and, latterly, Morocco was entirely about that sense of self. The fact that she spent the last third of her life in Rabat devoted to all things Saharan but was never rewarded with Moroccan citizenship must have been devastating.

Fatma declared her "Saharaness" when she applied for her national identity card shortly after we interviewed her. Her famed "crossing" and Malian slave status notwithstanding, she claimed to have been born in Goulimine in 1900 to Aisha, probably a reference to Barka's daughter, and Uthman, apparently her real father's name. As for herself: she became Faytma Barka. "Faytma" is the intimate form of "Fatma"; it was Barka's name for her. In this act, she officially imprinted her relationship with Barka onto her own national identity. As recently as the late twentieth century, this is what being Saharan meant to one woman in Goulimine named "Faytma."

These women were neither typical nor untypical. Fatma, Odette, and Sophie were real women whose lives reveal something to us today that historians looking for "big events" and "great men" miss: the ways in which people—non-important people, both men and women—brought the Sahara to life. Because these three people were even more "nonimportant" than most—they were women in a patriarchal world—their lived experiences provide an even more precious glimpse of past realities.

Slavery was still a way of desert life. Fatma's story suggests that for some, it could be a path to social mobility. Odette's observations of slavery were ambivalent, in part reflecting her colonial position. But still she addressed a crucial moment of labor transition as seen in the Taodeni salt industry. Sophie lived that moment and testified to its impact on social relations. Trans-Saharan commerce did not "die" under attack—not the traditional attacks of *razzia,* nor the colonial attack on slave trading, nor the "attack" indirectly created by the imposition of national boundaries at Independence. Instead, Sophie's story highlights the resilience and flexibility of the trajectories and merchants of trans-Saharan commerce over three generations.

Colonialism had many faces. Odette's life from the mid-1930s through to her death was one of them. Her romanticism, combined with her knowledge of Saharan life and dedication to "Greater Morocco" as a way to protect what she thought she understood so well, makes her invaluable as a window onto contemporary colonial/postcolonial politics. She was right. The Sahara she saw and recorded (her words, Marion's drawings) could not, would not, stand still in time.

NOTE

Information on Fatma and Sophie: interviews by author and Mohamed Nouhi in Goulimine (July 1994). Information on Odette: her own numerous publications and biography (Monique Verité, *Odette du Puigaudeau: Une Bretonne au désert*

[Paris: Editions Jean Picollec, 1992; reprint, 2002]). Sheila (Donnelly) Dobbs began PhD work on Odette with the generous assistance of Monique Verité; their research confirms Odette's right to historical recognition in Saharan history.

ADDITIONAL RESOURCES

du Puigaudeau, Odette. *Barefoot through Mauretania*. Translated by Geoffrey Sainsbury, with a new Introduction by Caroline Stone. London: Hardinge Simpole, 2009.

Lydon, Ghislaine. *On Trans-Saharan Trails: Islamic Law, Trade Networks, and Cross-Cultural Exchange in Nineteenth-Century Western Africa*. Cambridge: Cambridge University Press: 2009.

"Mali: The Last Salt Caravan." Journeyman Pictures, 1999. www.journeyman.tv/8948/documentaries/the-last-salt-caravan.html.

McDougall, E. Ann. "A Sense of Self: The Life of Fatma Barka." *Canadian Journal of African Studies* 32, no. 2 (1998): 281–315.

McDougall, James, and Judith Scheele, eds. *Saharan Frontiers: Space and Mobility in Northwest Africa*. Bloomington: Indiana University Press, 2012.

Savage, Elizabeth, ed. *The Human Commodity: Perspectives on the Trans-Saharan Slave Trade*. London: Frank Cass, 1992.

. . .

E. Ann McDougall is Professor of History at the University of Alberta. Her research interests include the economic, social, and political history of the Sahara and slavery in French and Northwest Africa. Her publications include *Engaging with a Legacy: Nehemia Levtzion (1935–2003),* London: Routledge, 2012); "'To Marry One's Slave Is as Easy as Eating a Meal': The Dynamics of Carnal Relations in Saharan Slavery," in *Sex, Power and Slavery,* ed. Gwyn Campbell and Elizabeth Elbourne (Athens: Ohio University Press, 2015); and "On Being Saharan," in *Saharan Frontiers: Space and Mobility in Northwest Africa,* ed. James McDougall and Judith Scheele (Bloomington: Indiana University Press, 2012).

Afro-Iberians in the Early Spanish Empire, ca. 1550–1600

Leo J. Garofalo

Abstract: From the 1470s forward, Afro-Iberians constituted a European chapter in the African diaspora. Both free and enslaved, Afro-Iberians labored in homes, artisans' workshops, markets, and in shipping and soldiering. With a heritage reaching south of the Sahara, these black Europeans participated in the Catholic Church and the conquest and colonization of the Americas.

Keywords: Black Europeans, Catholic Church, diaspora, Spanish empire, sailor, soldiers

AN ACTOR AND A SOLDIER, and considered a mulatto by all who knew him in Spain and the Americas, Diego Suárez was born in 1548 and grew up in the mid-sixteenth-century metropolis of Seville, in southern Iberia. Even before taking up soldiering in Spanish America, Suárez had bolstered his status around town by dressing as a soldier. In fact, his extensive acting wardrobe proved an important asset when he decided to sail to the Americas as a soldier to help protect Spanish shipping against the British, Dutch, and French pirates and privateers infesting the Atlantic and Caribbean. By all accounts, he simply dressed as a soldier, strapped on a sword, and appeared at the Board of Trade—the customs house that controlled travel and commerce to the Americas. He easily gained permission for passage to the Indies. In theory, legal restrictions limited Afro-Iberians' access to both weapons and travel to the Americas. However, Suárez saw himself as a loyal Crown subject and a pious Catholic with both a right to travel to the Americas and Africa and an obligation to defend Spain's interests and faith, with his sword if necessary. The officials of the Board of Trade agreed, and they gave him and many other Afro-Iberians permission to travel and serve the Crown.

In sixteenth-century Seville, Suárez lived with his mother, Barbola Hernandez. They occupied a house near the Straw Market in the Iglesia

Mayor neighborhood, surrounded by hat makers, shopkeepers, and wine sellers who worked in that area. The people in the neighborhood knew his mother well because she sold them traditional Spanish sweets. As an adult in Seville, Suárez made a name for himself first as a man with a profession and second as an active Christian: he acted in plays, and he raised money for the church institutions in Seville. After multiple voyages to Mexico and Peru, Suárez died in 1589, far from that European home, without access even to a scribe or priest at the moment of his death. He died in a farming valley in Spain's Peruvian viceroyalty, with his trunk still containing scripts for plays, a sword, and a half-full alms-collection box for a Seville brotherhood.

THE AFRO-IBERIAN DIASPORA

By the time Suarez was acting on the stage in southern Spain in the 1570s and 1580s, the sales in Iberia of people taken from western and central Africa had been going on for a hundred years. Lisbon was Europe's largest slave market, and people were brought by land from Lisbon and Lagos in Portugal for resale in southern Spain. This enslavement of people from western and central Africa and their dispersal throughout the Atlantic world constitutes one of the earliest and longest-lasting European interactions with Africa. This early chapter in the diaspora illuminates the complexities of global Africa. Diplomatic, religious, commercial, and military exchanges long linked Portugal and the Kingdom of Kongo and other polities. In short, interactions between Iberians and people from south of the Sahara have a long and complex history stretching back to at least the 1400s.

Scholars tend to recognize the presence and importance of enslaved and free people from western and central Africa in forming Europe's American colonies from the 1500s forward. However, the collective and individual acts of incorporation, resistance, and movement of Africans in Europe also shaped southern Iberian society. And these Afro-Iberians influenced Portugal's and Spain's imperial projects in Africa, the Americas, and Asia. Despite their importance, black Europeans and their claims to community and belonging often remain unrecognized in descriptions of global Africa. Afro-Iberians offer another of the many stories of diaspora. Often their stories involved multiple displacements.

One way to visualize more of global Africa is to examine these Afro-Iberians and their experiences at the local level, where opportunities to negotiate status, privileges, and obligations frequently appeared. In the 1400s-1600s, a population of people with origins from south of the Sahara became integral parts of southern Iberia's urban society. Many Afro-Iberians came directly from Africa. Other Afro-Iberians were born in Portugal or Spain, or on the Atlantic island colonies of Spain and Portugal (the Canaries, São Tomé, and Cape Verde). In some cases, Afro-Iberians' origins were unclear or purposefully hidden. In most cases, early modern Afro-Iberians identified as much with Iberian places of origin (and Iberian or Afro-Iberian practices and institutions) as with African ethnic identities or slave-trade labels—or even more. The display or negotiation of these origins or identities occurred through both everyday and exceptional acts throughout the Atlantic world of the 1500s and 1600s.

Within the movement of people and ideas that linked Afro-Iberians to Africa, Europe, and the Americas, certain institutions and practices stand out as potential sites for identity affirmation or formation. They provided opportunities for people to define their relationship to the state, religion, and even notions of nation. Particularly revealing are Afro-Iberian membership in religious confraternities or brotherhoods and other claims to Christian status or royal service. Laypeople organized confraternities to express devotion through saints' feast-day celebrations, care for the bodies and souls of the deceased, and carrying out charitable acts. In acts of self-definition, Afro-Iberians used religious confraternities, service to the Crown, and legal arguments to prove their freedom from the "taint of Muslim or Jewish practice." These acts of affirmation before religious and secular authorities brought opportunities to travel within the Spanish empire and the benefits of Crown service to Afro-Iberians.

NAVIGATING RACE AND RELIGION IN THE IBERO-ATLANTIC WORLD

Diego Suárez offers an illustrative case of Afro-Iberian movement through the early Ibero-Atlantic world. He shows the possibilities of mobility—in particular, how participation in the church helped both travel and social status. Born in 1548 in Seville, Suárez lived with his mother in a neighborhood of artisans and people engaged in petty commerce. Everyone knew Barbola Hernandez because they bought her *turrones* (a sweet made from honey and almonds). In particular, they noted her death and her burial in the Church of San Francisco accompanied by the brothers of the San Buenaventura Brotherhood. The family association with San Buenaventura proved strong. When Suárez's detractors tried to establish that his mother's burial by the brotherhood was a charitable act performed for a destitute woman, others testified to the contrary. Evidence entered the court record of a long history of monetary contributions to the church. The Suárez family members identified closely and successfully with an image of themselves as faithful and active Christians, and unabashedly claimed the privileges that came with that religious participation.

Suárez's stage acting gained him recognition and admiration that far exceeded his mother's renown in the neighborhood. Among the men and women in Seville who testified in support of honoring the will he dictated on his deathbed in Peru, most had attended plays in which he acted. Despite the standard prohibitions against Afro-Iberians' possession of offensive weapons and a ban on licenses for them to travel abroad, Suárez's actions demonstrate that Afro-Iberian community members considered themselves Crown subjects. As such, they demanded the right to travel and embraced the obligation to defend Spain. Local royal officials shared this view of Afro-Iberians. Furthermore, the need to complete crews and defend the slaving and trading ventures setting forth from Seville, Cádiz, and Sanlúcar de Barrameda—not to mention many Portuguese ports—meant exceptions were frequently made to the rules limiting Afro-Iberians' movement to the Americas.

A brief chronology of Diego Suárez's Life

1548—Born in Seville

1570s-80s—Worked as a stage actor in Seville and elsewhere

1584 [?]—Began sailing between Spain and the Americas

1586—Last embarked with the fleet in Seville headed to the Americas

1587—Mention of Suárez's absence and replacement in ship's log

1588?—Death of Suarez's mother, Barbola Hernandez, in Seville

1589—Suárez's death in Vitor Valley, Peru

1590–1601—Legal battle over Suárez's property and legal status

A significant seafaring and soldiering population developed among Andalusia's male Afro-Iberians. From the fifteenth century forward, they moved back and forth between the Americas and Spain, and western Africa and Spain. They worked as soldiers, gunners, mariners, common sailors, and cabin boys. At least one reached the level of a highly skilled pilot. Both enslaved and free Afro-Iberian men can be found working in these capacities. As with all sailors and soldiers sent to defend the ships and slaving expeditions, but particularly in the case of Afro-Iberians, Crown law insisted that these people be returned to Spain and not remain in the Americas without a specific license for immigration. In practice, many like Diego Suárez remained or partially settled in American ports and their hinterlands. These black European sailors and soldiers became traders and engaged in petty commerce or even agricultural work in order to survive until the fleet returned to Spain.

Although Suárez added sailing to the Indies as his second profession and made multiple voyages to the Americas as a soldier, he also continued to work as an actor in Mexico and Peru. In fact, he was still carrying scripts of plays with him when he died. Acting and soldiering supported Suárez economically, and his local social standing depended on these professions and his religious activities.

Participation in a confraternity reinforced Suárez's identification with an artisan sector that placed him well above his father's manual-laborer status (a marketplace porter) and his mother's position selling sweets. Suárez and the artisans who counted themselves among his friends and neighbors favored two confraternities under Franciscan tutelage in Seville: San Buenaventura, and Souls of Purgatory. Confraternity activities became another link that bound them together as men who practiced diverse professions in Seville. The intensity of the struggle over his legacy opens an unusual window into his religious attachments and bequests, the way he constructed his status and identity, and how these identifiers traveled with him to the Americas. Suárez's religious acts represented an important part of his formal relationship with the church. In Seville, Suárez enjoyed a close connection to the brotherhoods of San Buenaventura and Souls of Purgatory. When he embarked on his final trip to the Americas in 1586, Suárez packed all of his possessions, including an alms-collection box for Seville's San Buenaventura Brotherhood. In 1589, the collection box contained 34 pesos raised in Peru. Each brotherhood that he named received approximately 398 pesos from his estate. Even when he was displaced to the Americas, Suárez's strongest attachments were to confraternities associated with artisans and his home neighborhood in Seville.

In Peru, those who witnessed his death knew him as an actor, a mulatto, and a pious man. Suárez had also established links with the local church, although perhaps not as strong as those in Seville. Perhaps he had resettled in Arequipa. He designated money for specific Masses in Arequipa's Mercedarian, Franciscan, and Dominican monasteries and in the Convent of Santa Catalina de Siena. He requested that money be donated for the construction of Arequipa's cathedral. He asked to be dressed in a Franciscan habit and buried in the city's Franciscan monastery. In short, confraternity membership and participation and donations to prominent church institutions where he lived or worked proved to be an important part of Suárez's identity on both sides of the Atlantic.

Despite the strong presence of confraternities organized for and in some cases by Afro-Iberians and Africans in Seville and Peru, Suárez chose not to identify with them. Founded to help sustain the slaves and other blacks receiving treatment in Seville's hospital for blacks, the Brotherhood de Los Angeles (later de la Presentación or, popularly, de los Negros) won considerable prestige as the city's oldest confraternity (and enjoyed the right to certain privileged positions in processions). However, it was just one of several brotherhoods specifically serving Seville's black population, with the goals of instructing newly arrived and converted slaves in Christian practice, providing charity for the destitute among the slave and free black community, and providing a place of supervised congregation and identification with the established social order in the city. In the Andes, and especially in places with large black populations like Lima and certain agricultural valleys with black plantation laborers, specifically black confraternities were organized. Lima, in fact, boasted fifteen, and the archbishop in 1619 praised the mixed-race and black Brotherhood of Nuestra Señora de los Reyes. It was a "confraternity with much luster and ornaments and it is one of the best and best financed in this city thanks to the care of the *morenos* [blacks]." The size and importance of Lima's African-descent population also allowed for the formation of confraternities linked directly to African ethnic groups or slave-trade groupings, or to the higher social status of the American-born creoles or the mixed-race status of mulattos. The official ecclesiastical inspections carried out in Peru during this time period also noted black religious brotherhoods in the rural agricultural areas using black slaves and wage laborers. Specific African origin (or distance from that origin) and level of Christian practice thus became important markers of individual and group identity in both Seville and Lima. Although Diego Suárez chose not to identify directly with black confraternities on either side of the Atlantic, the Christian status and geographical origin of his family did become an important topic of debate when it came time to distribute his bequests.

The complex origins and identities of Seville's Afro-Iberians, even after death, appear in competing claims over inheritances. The effort to determine if Suárez's mother was still alive, or at least alive when he dictated his will, generated two new claims to his money. As was typical in such cases over the property of the deceased, the town crier circulated in Seville, announcing both Suárez's death and the court's search for any heirs. Because his mother had apparently died, the Franciscan monastery in Seville claimed the right to distribute the money according to the terms of Suárez's will. In addition, after hearing of the case, the owner of Suárez's enslaved nephew and a bailiff of the Board of Trade each submitted petitions that challenged the Franciscan confraternities' rights to the dead man's money. Both new petitioners based their arguments on genealogical descent and the special religious and legal standing of people of African origins. The slave owner's petitions first appeared to attempt to hide the heir's status as a slave, although it openly embraced parentage with the deceased mulatto Suárez and his mother. The petition is written in the first person, in the name of the nephew, Geronimo Castro, identifying him as a householder of Seville. The petition argued that Castro was the only surviving heir of this family of Seville mulattos. Only when pressed by the opposing sides to appear in court and submit witnesses did Castro's bondage come out, forcing the owner to make clear his intention to take Suárez's possessions as his own. (After all, he reasoned, he owned the heir, Castro.) However, the slave owner's attempt foundered on two counts: the argument that bondsmen lacked legal right to property or inheritance, and the owner's failure to produce witnesses to bolster his case.

The bailiff's suit proved more serious. If it had prevailed, not only would Suárez's bequests have been ignored, but his family would also have been legally barred from travel and office, and they would have been marked as religiously suspect. Apparently a status worse than *negro* [black] or mulatto existed in the eyes of the judges and local opinion: being of Jewish or Muslim heritage. The bailiff alleged that Barbola Hernandez was a *Berberisca*—a Muslim woman captured and enslaved in North Africa. Consequently, Suárez, regardless of his current Christian status, was of Muslim origin and thus barred from travel to the Americas. According to the 1560 Royal Decree, his property could be confiscated and donated to the Mercedarians to use to buy the freedom of Christian captives. Of course, a quarter of the property seized would go to the bailiff as the denouncer of this infraction! The witnesses the bailiff called forth gave different accounts of the family's origin: the mother was a *Berberisca* because she spoke Spanish with an accent, as people who speak "Arabiago" do; her face was branded; she was a Moorish woman either from Granada in Spain or North Africa; she was an Iberian convert from Islam; her son had marks on his face such as North Africans have; they were simply mulattos. Obviously there was some confusion as to where the family came from and what ethnic markers might help determine its origin. Slaves and their descendants populated Seville, and they hailed not only from sub-Saharan Africa, but also from Granada and North Africa. This alleged connection to Muslim or former Muslim populations posed a threat to the mulatto family even after death. For Spaniards, a status more damning than *negro* or mulatto and even more indelible than "slave" could mark a family.

To counter such charges, Afro-Iberians and their advocates successfully asserted "Old Christian" status. Again the Suárez case proves instructive. The lawyer Diego Vazquez vigorously denied the claim that Suárez was a Moor or an Iberian convert from Islam. He defended the Franciscan monastery's interests in obliging the Board of Trade to honor Suárez's will and donate his money to the family's confraternities and a Franciscan charity for prisoners of the city's public jail. The lawyer argued that Suárez was known as an "Old Christian and an honorable man." He further stated that accusations to the contrary were malicious. In fact, Afro-Iberian claims of "Old Christian" status proved quite common in the effort to secure the religious and genea-logical standing needed to travel legally to the Americas. Often petitioners for passengers' licenses presented documents in which they openly acknowl-edged parents or grandparents born in Senegambia or Angola and brought as slaves to Spain or Portugal. Nevertheless, the petitioners in many other cases go on to emphatically state that they themselves are not from the prohibited categories of foreigners, heretics, "New Christians," or "those newly con-verted to the faith." Their petitions use the label "Old Christian" just as in Suárez's case. Therefore, Afro-Iberians pushed successfully, at least before Andalusia's Crown courts, to establish new claims to full membership in the Catholic Church. They strove to appropriate the rights, privileges, and pro-tection of an "Old Christian" identity at the same time that they suffered the marginalization and stigma of slavery and African origin.

This brings us back to the mulatto soldier and actor Diego Suárez, who successfully invested time and money in building a strong Christian identity that included confraternity membership, donations to the church and charities, and the collecting of alms. Diego Suárez's identity spanned the Atlantic and even earned his family "Old Christian" legal status before Seville's royal court. The dynamism evident in the Afro-Iberian cases suggests that Afro-Iberians played key roles in shaping their local identities and the transfer of these identities to the Americas and back.

CONCLUSION

Diego Suárez represents the reality that faced many of the Afro-Iberians both in southern Iberia and traveling as free individuals to and from the Americas. Participation in confraternities was an important part of life for many. Membership could help them associate with ethnic kin or people of similar occupational status or both. Of course, not all Afro-Iberians or Afro-Peruvians participating in confraternities chose to emphasize links to African descent. These confraternity associations could take on real significance in confraternity members' lives, leading them to retain and renew those obligations even after they had moved to other continents and lost touch with family members and friends. As in Suárez's case, effective claims to Christian identity and the emerging ideas of popular and legal ethno-racial categories developed within the ample and diverse Afro-Iberian population and spread throughout the early Spanish Atlantic world. It is clear from these cases that in some contexts Afro-Iberians *were* "Old Christians" and that confraternity membership and donations to the church played an important role in establishing and renewing Afro-Iberians' familial and individual status and ethnic and social identities. It is also clear that the diverse black African presence in Spain today is not solely a recent phenomenon. Debates about belonging, rights, and obligations have deep roots in southern Iberia.

ADDITIONAL RESOURCES

Bryant, Sherwin, Ben Vinson III, and Rachel Sarah O'Toole, eds. *Africans to Colonial Spanish America: Expanding the Diaspora.* Champaign: University of Illinois Press, 2012.

Earle, T. F., and K. J. P. Lowe, eds. *Black Africans in Renaissance Europe.* Cambridge: Cambridge University Press, 2005.

Garofalo, Leo J. "Afro-Iberian Sailors, Soldiers, Traders, and Thieves on the Spanish Main." In *Documenting Latin America,* edited by Erin O'Connor and Leo J.

Garofalo. Vol. 1, *Gender, Race, and Empire*, 25–34. New York: Pearson/Prentice Hall, 2010.

McKnight, Kathryn Joy, and Leo J. Garofalo, eds. *Afro-Latino Voices: Narratives from the Early Modern Ibero-Atlantic World, 1550–1812*. Cambridge: Hackett, 2009.

Northrup, David. *Africa's Discovery of Europe: 1450–1850*. New York: Oxford University Press, 2009.

Pike, Ruth. "Sevillian Society in the Sixteenth Century: Slaves and Freedmen." *Hispanic American Historical Review* 47 (1967): 344–59.

. . .

LEO GAROFALO is an Associate Professor of History at Connecticut College. His research draws attention to the central roles of Native Andeans and Afro-Peruvians in colonial cities. Currently he is exploring the Afro-Iberian roots of Andean witchcraft and the Atlantic and European routes of the West African diaspora in the sixteenth- and seventeenth-century Andes. Professor Garofalo coedited, with Kathryn Joy McKnight, *Afro-Latino Voices: Narratives from the Early-Modern Ibero-Atlantic World, 1550–1812* (Hackett, 2009); with Paulo Drinot, *Más allá de la dominación y la resistencia: Ensayos de historia peruana* (Instituto de Estudios Peruanos, 2005); and, with Erin O'Connor, *Documenting Latin America*, 2 vols. (Pearson/Prentice Hall, 2010).

"From the Land of Angola"

SLAVERY, MARRIAGE, AND AFRICAN DIASPORIC IDENTITIES IN MEXICO CITY BEFORE 1650

Frank Trey Proctor III

Abstract: Tens of thousands of enslaved Africans lived and labored in the colony of New Spain (colonial Mexico), particularly in urban centers like Mexico City, in the mid–seventeenth century. This article employs marriage records for such Africans to introduce the contours of their experiences in this early urban form of slavery and to explore how the enslaved began to construct new identities and communities within slavery based on their regionally specific African origins.

Keywords: Mexico City, slavery, marriage, African diaspora, West Central Africa

PRIOR TO 1650, Mexico was home to the second-largest population of enslaved Africans in the Americas, exceeded only by Brazil. Nearly 175,000 Africans had been imported into colonial Mexico. Tens of thousands of enslaved Africans and their descendants toiled in such colonial industries as sugar and woolen textiles as well as in urban contexts like Mexico City. Well before the "sugar revolution" in Barbados in the 1640s, the transition to African slavery in the Chesapeake in the 1670s, and the explosion of sugar production in the Caribbean, the slave trade into Mexico dwarfed the approximately one hundred slaves imported into Virginia by 1650.

As a result, Mexico City was home to one of the largest populations of displaced Africans in the Americas before 1650. Urban slavery, in particular, was a very important manifestation of early Atlantic African slavery. Population figures for Mexico City, and particularly for slaves, are exceedingly scarce. An estimate from 1572 indicates that as many as 8,000 Afro-descended slaves lived in Mexico City alongside 8,000 Spanish heads of household. An observer from 1612 suggests that as many as 50,000 Afro-descended peoples, predominantly African slaves, lived in Mexico City alongside 15,000 Spaniards and 80,000 Indians. Importantly, following on the heels of a significant (purported) slave rebellion that rocked Mexico City in 1611, culminating in the execution of 35 accused black and mulatto rebels, these numbers may well be exaggerated to highlight the perceived threat posed by Africans and their descendants. Conversely, a modern scholar suggests that as many as 19,000 Africans and 43,000 Afro-descended peoples resided in the archbishopric of Mexico, which included Mexico City, in 1646, compared with just over 102,000 persons of European descent. In either case, Africans and their descendants made up a sizable portion of the population of Mexico City before 1650.

Whatever images "American slavery" conjures in our minds, the world that many enslaved Africans inhabited in Mexico is likely not it. The term "slavery" generally evokes images of the nineteenth-century rural slavery like the cotton kingdom institution in the US South so vividly portrayed in the motion picture *Twelve Years as Slave* or sugar-plantation slavery throughout the Caribbean and Brazil. Those visions focus on the height of African slavery in the Americas, but the institution had a nearly four-hundred-year history before abolition. The expansion of African slavery in Mexico took place much earlier, and the urban form of slavery that many enslaved Africans experienced in early colonial Latin America differed in myriad ways from rural plantation slavery.

SLAVERY, PLACE, AND CULTURE

Enslaved Africans in Spanish America operated within a very different judicial and religious framework than seen in the nineteenth-century rural contexts of the US South. As Catholics, for example, enslaved people in Spanish America (all had been forcibly converted) could officially marry in the Church, whereas they were expressly forbidden to do so in the US South. The Spanish state even provided limited protections for those unions.

Different, however, should not be confused with *kinder, gentler,* or *more humane*. This was racialized slavery with all the physical, emotional, psychological, and cultural violence that nineteenth-century plantation slavery entailed. Enslaved Africans had been kidnapped, ripped from their families and communities, forced across the Atlantic Ocean in the hold of a slave ship, only to find themselves defined as property and sold to the highest bidder.

We rightly see this as a profoundly isolating, desperate, heart-wrenching reality. Every step in the process served to further remove the enslaved from his or her family, community, home, and, some would say, very sense of self. But in the wake of all this destruction and desolation, the enslaved began to create new connections, new relationships, and new communities—and that is the story that interests us here.

In January 1640, two enslaved Africans named Pedro Sánchez and Mariana (who, like many enslaved people, had no official listed surname) appeared at the Metropolitan Cathedral in the heart of Mexico City to apply for a wedding license. They brought Juan de la Cruz and Ana María, also enslaved Africans, to witness their union. All four claimed to hail from the "land of Angola," meaning that they had been born in Africa and brought forcefully to Mexico via the infamous Middle Passage. In a similar example from August 1648, Manuel, an enslaved Malemba, and Juana, an enslaved Angola, sought to marry, with two enslaved Congos, Manuel de Santiago and Domingo, as their witnesses (the terms "Malemba," "Angola," and "Congo" are explained below). These eight individuals were among the thousands of enslaved Africans living, laboring, and seeking to create new families and communities in Mexico City.

Clues left by Africans in their wedding applications provide traces of the social worlds they inhabited. For example, there are hints that suggest that the foundation of the communities that individual Africans created in Mexico sometimes began in Africa or during the Middle Passage. In the 1630s, pairs of siblings, enslaved in Africa and transported to New Spain together, appear in the sources. For example, Pedro, a Congo, testified that he and his brother Manuel had been captured in Africa and sent to Mexico in 1626, where they were promptly separated when purchased by different owners. Manuel remained in Veracruz, while Pedro's owner took him to Mexico City. These brothers, who had likely relied quite heavily on each other to survive the horrors of their capture, forced march to the African coast, and the Middle Passage, probably had no idea what happened to each other after their separation, fearing the worst. After four years, however, the brothers were reunited in Mexico City when Manuel's master moved him there. We can only imagine just how significant this reunion was, and how other Africans would have sought out such connections in the absence of real kinship ties.

Tantalizing, but scarce, evidence indicates that the foundations of the nascent communities created by Africans in slavery were actually formed by strangers during the Middle Passage. For example, Pedro and Christina de la Cruz became acquainted with Francisco, a witness to their wedding, in 1646, when they left Africa onboard the same slave ship. Francisco's testimony suggests that they became acquainted after their capture in Africa. We can only image just how significant those connections made during the Middle Passage were. Amazingly, despite the fact that the three shipmates had different masters, they were able to maintain those bonds of comradeship forged onboard a slave ship in the streets of Mexico City. Similarly, the couple Antonio and María de la Cruz, and their wedding witnesses, had all four made the Middle Passage together. The importance of such "shipmates" as pillars of nascent slave communities in the Americas cannot be overstated.

Many enslaved peoples were likely not so fortunate as to be able to rely on family from Africa or even shipmates in their search for camaraderie and support in colonial Mexico. For those Africans, however, wedding applications allow us to begin to envision the relationships they formed and the communities they created. For example, the bride, groom, and their witnesses rarely had the same owner, and thus they were making these connections with other Africans *outside* the confines of their masters' households. This reality highlights that these unions were likely initiated by the enslaved themselves, and not forced upon them by their owners, and that the enslaved enjoyed a modicum of physical mobility throughout the urban landscape of Mexico City, allowing them to interact with each other.

These relationships were also deep and long lasting. Pedro and Mariana's witnesses testified that they had been friends with either the bride or groom for at least twelve years in Mexico City before they married. Similarly, the average age of wedding witnesses was approximately forty years, indicating that they had likely been in Mexico for some time because most had been enslaved in Africa as adolescents and young adults. Numerous African-born enslaved people appeared as witnesses for multiple couples, suggesting a developing slave community. At the extreme, Pedro García, a forty-year-old enslaved Angola, officially witnessed at least twelve marriages between 1631 and 1634, highlighting his connections with at least thirty other enslaved Africans. Within the developing networks created by Africans in Mexico City, men like Pedro García may well have been recognized as community leaders or "elders."

Many were domestic servants, day laborers, and marketers who likely interacted in the major markets and storefronts throughout the cityscape. A major site of these interactions may have been the large open-air market that operated in the plaza of the very cathedral where our protagonists married. The plaza, memorialized by the painter Cristóbal del Villalpando in his 1695 painting *View of the Plaza Mayor* (*Vista del Zócalo*), still exists, as does the Metropolitan Cathedral.

Now that we have established that these marriages seem to have been emanating out of an established and dynamic slave community, we can turn our attention to the contours of identity within it. To do so we can focus on the racial or ethnic labels that slaves self-applied to describe themselves. Among enslaved people who married in the 1640s, nearly three in four described themselves as originating from Africa. Conversely, just over one in four were creole (*criollo*) or American born. These two groups exhibited very different marriage patterns, with very little intermarriage between the two. Africans married Africans, and creoles tended to marry other creoles. Based on this information, we may not be able to speak of a single "slave" community in Mexico City grounded in shared blackness or Africanity.

Reality, it turns out, was even more complicated than saying "Africans married Africans" might suggest. The enslaved members of these wedding parties did not define themselves as Africans as such. No such identity existed then. Rather, they self-identified as Angola, Biafara, Terranova, Mozambique, and so forth—some of the many monikers used by slaves and slavers to mark important differences among enslaved sub-Saharan Africans in the Americas. For masters and slavers, these terms referred to general regions along the African coast where they purchased captives. The question under consideration here, however, is whether such terms could be more than just an indicator of point of origin when self-applied by Africans themselves.

THE SIGNIFICANCE OF A NAME

Terms like "Congo" and "Angola" did not refer to shared identities as recognized in Africa. Rather, they were created in the diaspora, and the slaves who claimed them in the diaspora imbued them with specific meanings. Historian James Sweet demonstrates this reality in his study of a single African slave, Domingos Álvares, in the Portuguese Atlantic. Álvares described himself as originating from the town of Naogon (in present-day Benin), but other enslaved peoples from that region described him as a Cobû—a larger ethnic group that encompassed the residents of Naogon and neighboring villages. In Portuguese America, however, Álvares came to be identified (and self-identified) as a *Mina,* which referred to the West African slaving region that consists of modern Ghana, Togo, and Benin. Once he was ripped from his local African context and thrust into the diaspora, the term "Mina," which had no meaning for him in Africa, came to describe the important connections that he made with other people with common regional origins from within Africa (and distinguished him from those enslaved peoples from other regions of Africa). Most colonial Spanish-American records do not include such detailed information on enslaved Africans. But examining whom Africans married and who served as their wedding witnesses suggests that these self-applied ethnonyms had particular meanings for enslaved Africans in the diaspora.

The question becomes, on some level, With whom did Africans interact intimately, and why? We can imagine a newly arrived African slave on the streets of Mexico City. Having just survived the harrowing Middle Passage, the horror of the slave market in Veracruz, and being torn away from whatever relationships he/she formed with other slaves during the Atlantic crossing, knowing little or no Spanish (or even Portuguese), these slaves likely gravitated toward other Africans with whom they could communicate minimally. The linguistic and cultural complexity of Atlantic Africa made this no small feat. These linguistic ties would have been derived from being drawn from neighboring regions in Africa, or more specifically from within the major language groupings that seem to overlay the general slaving regions there. Within the cacophony of European, indigenous, and African languages spoken in Mexico City, the recognition of individuals with whom a newly arrived slave could communicate must have been a balm of sorts. That initial pull toward people who our imagined slave could understand would likely result in his or her continued integration into a larger group of Africans whose linguistic and cultural heritages were similar enough to his or her own to be mutually intelligible.

As a result, multiple and often overlapping and intersecting communities were under constant (re)creation by enslaved Africans in Mexico City. And thus, ethnonyms like "Angola," "Congo," "Terranova," and the like potentially marked African diasporic identities. The foundations of these identities were not fully intact African ethnicities (articulated at the village or lineage level). Nor were they Pan-African (i.e., shared by all Africans) or race-based (i.e., shared by everyone of African descent) identities. Rather, they were spontaneously articulated in the diaspora by the enslaved, who would not have identified as having common origins *in* Africa, but who were creating new identities and communities based upon shared regionally specific cultural beliefs and practices *from* Africa. Those identities became identified by terms such as "Angola" and "Congo" because such terms marked distinctions between "us" and "them" that had resonance for the enslaved in this particular historical and geographic context.

The "Angola" group represented a sizable majority of slaves who married in Mexico City (nearly eight in ten Africans in marriage applications) before 1650. Angolas chose to marry other Angolas in a great majority of cases. While the term "Angola" clearly obscures the village-level and regional identities of people in Africa (like Naogon and Cobû for Domingos Álvares), it seems to have reflected some sense of potential connection among those slaves who claimed it.

It is actually among the smaller African groups that we can more clearly see how these ethnonyms may have reflected a sense of commonality among slaves who claimed them. Among self-identified Terranovas (Yoruba speakers from modern Nigeria), a majority selected spouses with the same ethnonym. The significance of this pattern is clear when we consider that Angolas outnumbered Terranovas nearly fifteen to one in Mexico City before 1650. Additionally, those Terranovas who did not marry another Terranova often had at least one Terranova witness in their wedding party. For example, when Maria sought to marry Cristóbal, an enslaved Angola, she presented another Terranova also named Maria as her witness. These two women had known each other for over ten years in Mexico at this point. Even as the bride Maria chose to marry someone who claimed a different ethnonym, she still demonstrated a strong, long-lasting connection to at least one other person with whom she shared common African origins. This same general pattern is true for most West African groups in Mexico City, who tended to marry other slaves and/or present wedding witnesses who claimed the same ethnonym.

The preceding discussion has operated on the assumption that if these ethnonyms had significance in the Atlantic World, they were mutually exclusive. However, there are patterns within marriages wherein the enslaved participants claimed *different* ethnonyms that *also* suggest the construction of regionally specific African diasporic identities. Let's reconsider the marriage of Manuel, a Malemba, and Juana, an Angola, and their two Congo witnesses introduced above. How does this example of four slaves claiming three different ethnonyms fit within the African diasporic identity argument?

The ethnonyms "Angola," "Congo," and "Malemba" from this example all referred to West Central African origins. If we turn our attention to that region in the first half of the seventeenth century, we can see that these terms should not necessarily be treated as mutually exclusive. Historian Jan Vansina, in his seminal *Paths in the Rainforests,* charts how West Central Africa came to be populated by a single linguistic family—the Western Bantu—over the last two millennia BC. Subsequently, these peoples with a common ancestry developed distinct local traditions and dialects over time. Thus, in Africa the peoples who inhabited these regions would *not* have identified themselves as having a common ethnicity. Yet within the areas most involved in the slave trade, West Central Africans spoke two languages—Kikongo and Kimbundu—that were as linguistically similar as Spanish and Portuguese. Similarly, scholars argue that precolonial West Central Africans shared a single overarching cultural and political tradition *before* they arrived in the Americas. In other words, the languages, cultures, and societies of the area constituted a single unit when compared with the outside even if Western Bantu speakers failed to recognize it as such in Africa.

Furthermore, the region from which captives were taken in Central Africa before 1650 focused on a fairly small geographic area between the Zaire and Kwanza Rivers, extending perhaps two hundred kilometers inland and falling under the political control of the Kingdom of Kongo; on the expanding Portuguese colony of Angola; and on those regions' interior borderlands. From the perspective of slaver traders and masters, terms like "Angola," "Congo," and "Malemba" referred to general areas. The majority of slaves shipped from the port of Luanda were called "Angola" by Portuguese slave traders even if they originated in the territories once controlled by the Mbundu peoples (Kimbundu speakers) around Luanda, or were Ovimbundu, Imbangala, or Congo (subdivisions within the Western Bantu language group). "Congo" slaves originated in or near the areas controlled by the Kingdom of Kongo, a powerful African principality between the Kwanza River and the Zaire River to the north. Many, but not all, of these slaves were likely Kikongo speakers and/or subjects of Kongo, but again it would be a mistake to assume heterogeneity. "Malemba," the third ethnonym in our example, referred to a principality formed along the eastern edge of the Portuguese colony of Angola that was populated, in part, by refugees from Kongo and Angola. Other West Central African ethnonyms used in Mexico City included "Anchico," "Matamba," and "Banguela." The peoples who inhabited the relatively small region encompassed by these six ethnonyms had a long history of political, economic, and cultural interaction *before* the initiation of the Atlantic slave trade. Thus, the great majority of slaves drawn from West Central Africa shared common cultural and linguistic heritages and had long-lasting connections in Africa that could have facilitated the generation of new ethnicities within the diaspora—identities that might not have been contained to a single ethnonym.

Such descriptions of the cultural unity of West Central Africa before 1650 suggest that unions between slaves originating from that region, regardless of ethnic appellation, *could* be treated as ethnically endogamous and reflecting the construction of a broader African diasporic identity in Mexico City grounded in common West Central African origins. For example, the minority Congo slaves (outnumbered ten to one by Angolas) tended to marry other Congos and Angolas at approximately the same rate. Based on the discussion above, it seems plausible that those unions could be treated as endogamous—that the differences between Angola and Congo were important enough to name, but not so great as to make them mutually exclusive in the specific context of seventeenth-century Mexico City.

The distinctions between "Angolas" and "Congos" in the minds of slaves is impossible to know. They might have been geographic, or linguistic (Kikongo versus Kimbundu), or they might have been cultural, in that Congo identity might have recognized the deeper associations with Christianity in the regions dominated by the Kingdom of Kongo. The rulers of Kongo converted to Christianity in 1491, initiating the spread of an Africanized Christianity among their subjects. We should never assume mutual exclusivity or inclusivity, but based on the cases like Manuel and Juana's particular marriage, it seems reasonable to conclude that in particular times and places the union of two slaves with *different* ethnonyms might suggest a collective diasporic identity uncontainable with a single ethnonym but still not so broad as to be understood as based in shared blackness or Africanity.

If we return to the marriages of Pedro Sánchez and Mariana and of Manuel and Juana described above, these mundane acts invite us to contemplate the significance of Mexico in the broader history of early Atlantic slavery; the lives and experiences of enslaved Africans in Mexico; and their ability to construct communities and identities under unspeakably harsh conditions. Ripped from their homes in Africa, these enslaved peoples would find potential spouses, and long-lasting friendships, in the streets of Mexico City and begin the process of (re)constructing their social worlds. That they claimed provenance from Angola, Congo, or Malemba tells us that while they originated from the same slaving region in Africa, it wasn't until they were in the diaspora that they could think of each other as being connected in any meaningful way. These slaves were a small portion of the thousands of enslaved Africans in Mexico City at this time, all of whom, I would like to believe, were seeking out similar sorts of connections.

ADDITIONAL RESOURCES

Bennett, Herman. *Africans in Colonial Mexico: Absolutism, Christianity, and Afro-Creole Consciousness, 1570–1640*. Bloomington: Indiana University Press, 2003.
O'Toole, Rachel. *Bound Lives: Africans, Indians, and the Making of Race in Colonial Peru*. Pittsburg: University of Pittsburg Press, 2012.
Proctor, Frank T., III. *"Damned Notions of Liberty": Slavery, Culture, and Power in Colonial Mexico, 1640–1769*. Albuquerque: University of New Mexico Press, 2010.
Sweet, James H. *Domingos Álvares, African Healing, and the Intellectual History of the Atlantic World*. Chapel Hill: University of North Carolina Press, 2011.
Vinson, Ben, III, and Matthew Restall, eds. *Black Mexico: Race and Society from Colonial to Modern Times*. Albuquerque: University of New Mexico Press, 2009.

. . .

FRANK TREY PROCTOR, III, an Associate Professor in the Department of History at Denison University, writes on the lived experience of slaves of African descent and master–slave relations in Spanish America. His first book, *"Damned Notions of Liberty": Slavery, Culture, and Power in Colonial Mexico, 1640–1769* (University of New Mexico Press, 2010), explores master–slave relations in Mexico. He has published articles in the *Hispanic American Historical Review* and the *Americas* and a chapter in the edited volume *Black Mexico: Race and Society from Colonial to Modern Times* (University of New Mexico Press, 2009).

"Ethiopia Shall Stretch" from America to Africa

THE PAN-AFRICAN CRUSADE OF CHARLES MORRIS

Benedict Carton and Robert Trent Vinson

Abstract: In 1899 a sacred song, "Let My People Go," embodied the suffering and striving of black peoples in the United States and South Africa. This hymn had become the clarion call of Charles Morris, a black Baptist missionary, and his Xhosa converts in the Cape Colony, seeking deliverance from white supremacy through Pan-African faith, education, and politics. Their crusade would shape the course of twentieth-century democracy.

Keywords: South Africa, transnational, imperialism, white supremacy, uplift, Ethiopianism, Pan-African, Wilmington, Jim Crow

PRELUDE

In 1899 a black Baptist missionary named Charles Morris traveled from the United States to South Africa. His sojourn through the British Cape Colony illuminates the shared suffering and striving of black people in South Africa and the United States, and their transnational contributions to democracy in both countries. Morris sailed an old route to Cape Town taken by black New England whalers and the Confederate warship *Alabama* carrying "human cargo" to Africa. When he docked in Cape Town, the Virginia Jubilee Singers, black American performers, had just finished their acclaimed tour of South Africa. The troupe regaled spectators with Booker T. Washington's parable about moving "up from slavery" to Christian education—a tale captivating black congregations of the National Baptist Convention (NBC) and the African Methodist Episcopal (AME) Church throughout the United States. Graduates of Virginia's Hampton Institute, the Jubilee Singers and their maestro, Orpheus McAdoo, performed the anthem of Emancipation,

"Go Down Moses." They soulfully conjured "When Israel was in Egypt's land," a metaphor for plantation bondage. Defiant verses ensued: "Let my people go, / Oppress'd so hard they could not stand, / Let my people go." This Negro spiritual not only resonated across the Atlantic but also deeply affected black audiences enduring racial discrimination under British colonialism.

The Jubilee Singers, the AME Church, and the NBC paved the way for black Americans, "sing[ing] praises unto the Lord," to evangelize in South Africa. A trailblazer in this effort, the Reverend Charles Morris envisioned Christianity "stretching forth" to the "continent where the Kingdom of Heaven and its righteousness must first be sought." He would gladly depart the segregated United States for segregated Cape Town as a self-styled "Twentieth Century Ethiopian," adopting the biblical persona of Psalms 68:31: "Princes shall come out of Egypt; Ethiopia shall soon stretch out her hands unto God. Sing unto God, ye kingdoms of the earth; O sing praises unto the Lord." Such scripture vindicated the sacred claim of black people to worldly freedom. For men like Morris facing violent racism at home, the missionary fields of South Africa offered solace and opportunity. Morris would leave behind a country celebrating Theodore Roosevelt's "Anglo-Saxon" exploits, if one believed this future president's account of his Rough Rider conquests in Cuba. Morris was among those who did not. Before embarking for South Africa, he praised the unsung "manhood" of "colored troops" supporting the Rough Riders in combat. Upon arrival in South Africa, he felt the "degrading" weight of "imperial" America lift from his body. Morris had come home to the place he had dreamed of as a youth, intending to develop "Negro manhood" through his understanding of Old Testament prophecy: "'Ethiopia shall arise . . . and suddenly stretch forth her hand unto God.' If this taxes credulity, quarrel with God."

BEGINNING

Morris's religious destiny took shape in his childhood. Born during the final year of the Civil War, he grew up in Kentucky. As a teenager Morris studied at Wilberforce University, the historically black school in Ohio that would offer a professorship to Pan-African pioneer W. E. B. Du Bois and open its doors to Xhosa and Zulu converts of South African missionaries. Morris's education included stories of the "splendid continent of his forefathers" and headlines of an 1881 circus featuring "heroic" South Africans. Barnstorming through Kentucky and Ohio, this "ethnological showcase" spotlighted Princess Amadaga, the reputed niece of the Zulu king Cetshwayo, deposed by British military conquest in 1879. A brochure described her retinue and their "life and adventures in Zululand; how they fought their foes in defense of their homes; . . . how their King Cetewayo [sic] was captured; how they and Princess AmaZulu were induced to come to this country." Ringmasters lauded the royals: "[N]o true Zulu will ever break his word or insult a woman." Other "virtues" were highlighted, among them the ritual praises of an American missionary bowing to King Cetshwayo, who in turn saluted her with the phrase "'*Utali witu mina niam!*' (My white sister!)." This Zulu phrase and scene appeared centrally in the brochure. Morris was also inspired by an encounter in Ohio one decade later with members of a "Kaffir choir" from South Africa. Then a music promoter, he heard the vocalists explain that the slavery lamented in Negro spirituals was anathema to their people. Members of the choir went on to attend Wilberforce in defiance of colonial bans back home prohibiting their entrance in premier schools.

Around this time Morris's own talents were destined for the stage. In 1888 he was a magnetic speaker for the Republican Party, stumping for candidates as Frederick Douglass's protégé. At campaign rallies Morris flanked the eminent abolitionist, whose eloquent plea for a more perfect union was legendary. (See figure 1.6.1.) Douglass counseled his apprentice: "It will be said . . . that you are putting on airs . . . but . . . I know your ability and worth, and rejoice in every blow you strike at wrong." From the dais Douglass introduced his "thunder and lightning," the young Morris, who urged black voters to vindicate their rights to a democratic Promised Land. "Voting always," Morris intoned, and "when the Ku-Klux" stand "armed about the polls," come "up to the danger line.'" If "the negro" be "bitterly denounce[ed]," he assured his audience, the Bible divined "centuries ago" that black liberation was imminent. Psalms 68:31 foretold that the "Ethiopian shall stretch forth his hands to God." While he revered Douglass, Morris did not share his mentor's views of African "barbarism."

The semantic differences between *Ethiopian* and *barbarism* reveal the "ambivalent place Africa [held] in the imaginations of its 'New World' descendants," write historians Sidney Lemelle and Robin Kelley—an ambivalence expressed in rhetoric "conservative and atavistic," but invariably oppositional to racism. Indeed, by the early 1890s Morris's political homilies were assailing the Jim Crow system, which entrenched white supremacy and "savage" lynching in many states. If America would not accept its emancipated

FIG. 1.6.1. Charles Morris and Frederick Douglass, ca. 1888. HU Mooreland Library.

millions, another continent would. "A quarter of a century after slavery," Morris reminded black Republicans, their "million and a half children in the public schools, twenty thousand in academies and colleges, . . . [and] as many ministers" should assist the "missionary effort" in Africa.

Such ideals of transnational "racial uplift" entailed solidarity with the anti-lynching movement of Ida Wells, Morris's one-time romantic interest. During the 1880s Wells had corresponded with her "Challie boy," as she teased Morris before he wed Annie Sprague, the granddaughter of Frederick Douglass. By the early 1890s, Wells was urging African Americans to question the "doctored reports of lynchings" in the mainstream press. She published *Southern Horrors,* a best-selling pamphlet attributing "lynch law in all its phases" to the "lie that Negro men rape white women." Morris remained in touch with Wells while he was the personal secretary of Douglass, who applauded *Southern Horrors* as having "no equal to it in convincing power."

Douglass introduced Wells to his enthusiasts on the other side of the Atlantic, principally the English Quaker Catherine Impey, editor of *Anti-Caste,* a journal devoted to fighting racial discrimination. In 1892 Impey sailed from London to meet Douglass in the United States, staying briefly with Annie Sprague. British readers of *Anti-Caste* helped Wells navigate complex humanitarian networks during her anti-lynching tours of Europe in 1893 and 1894. She convinced stewards of "human rights in Empire," including associates of Cecil Rhodes in South Africa professing to be "friends of the native," to condemn American lynching. Her overseas accomplishments laid a foundation for Morris's plan to unite black Americans, British allies, and African subjects in a global quest for "racial uplift."

PREPARATION

By the mid-1890s, however, Morris was no longer pursuing politics. Grieving for loved ones, he pivoted from Republican favor to God's grace. Frederick Douglass had passed away in 1895—a blow Morris felt more acutely after the tragic death of his wife, Annie Sprague, two years prior. She succumbed to illness while carrying the couple's first child. He, too, began to mourn the loss of his party, gravely infected by "martial" Republicans urging intervention in a Cuban war of independence waged by former slaves. Late in 1895 Morris entered Newton Theological Seminary as Roosevelt demanded America annex Cuba (while drafting his treatise on the "perfectly stupid" Negro). Affording a sanctuary of anti-imperialism and civility, Newton Theological instructed "men to preach the gospel" like "foreign missionaries of distinguished usefulness." Graduates were groomed for careers in the "American Baptist Missionary Union and ... American Board of Commissioners for Foreign Missions," which furnished "opportunities to meet ... those who" preached the gospel of peace in South Africa and elsewhere.

Morris's years at Newton (1895–98) coincided with a wave of "anti-Negro jingoism" driven by currents of social Darwinism and its imperialist exemplars such as Roosevelt, then considered a racial liberal, whose Republican cause Morris once served. The upsurge in racial oppression brought lynch mobs from the South to the Midwest, US Supreme Court legalization of "separate-but-equal" (*Plessy v. Ferguson, 1896*), and violent raids on state authority. The most notorious invasion occurred in Wilmington, North Carolina, where white supremacists murdered African Americans. In November 1898, a coup d'état overthrew this city's ruling coalition of black Republicans and white populists. Wilmington was initially overrun by a paramilitary unit known as the Red Shirts. Unlike Klansmen, Red Shirts wore no disguise. Yet this was a minor deviation in brotherhoods of terror goaded into action by neo-Confederates, like the South Carolina senator "Pitchfork Ben" Tillman, who aimed to destroy black churches, businesses, and governments. The ex-congressman Alfred Waddell reinforced the Red Shirts with the First North Carolina, a regiment of white army veterans wielding weapons from the Cuba theater. Waddell incited his vigilantes: "You are Anglo-Saxons. . . . [I]f you find the negro outvoting [*sic*], tell him to leave the polls, and if he refuses, . . . [s]hoot him down in his tracks." This command turned to duty. Thomas Dixon, one of Roosevelt's political donors and favorite novelists, whose book *The Clansman* would script D.W. Griffith's *Birth of a Nation,* hailed the white "Wilmington revolutionists . . . [for] important work in the preservation of our civilization." By contrast, an African-American woman begged the White House to provide her safe passage from Wilmington to Africa.

As a newly remarried pastor of Myrtle Baptist Church outside Boston, Morris spoke publicly of witnessing the Wilmington massacre. Fearing for the future of his own family—including his wife, the former Sadie Waterman—he recounted how households escaped their torched homes only to be hunted down, with one "Negro shot twenty times in the back . . . thousands of women and children fleeing in terror . . . [all] in the name of civilization . . . [and] the reformation of . . . Wilmington." Was this "Russia"? No, he retorted; the pogrom occurred "within three hundred miles of the White House . . . thanking God for having enabled it to break the Spanish yoke from the neck of Cuba." Morris likened US imperialism to a brutal "crusade" that installed the "white pulpit of Wilmington." He concluded with a story of the "Good Samaritan" traveling from Jerusalem to Jericho to get help for his son wounded by criminals. Morris compared the fate of this descendant, "bleeding at his own threshold," with that of African Americans awaiting rescue. Shortly after the birth of his first child with Sadie Morris, christened Charles Jr., the new father cast his eyes to South Africa, where he would proselytize for the Baptists.

Morris set sail in June 1899 for his "Jericho," Cape Town, conveying the spirit of activism enjoined by Ida Wells and his hero, Booker T. Washington. Like Wells, in leaving the nascent American empire (and its "anti-Negro jingoism"), Morris would pivot to an older English empire, his symbol of opportunity in South Africa. Morris knew that Cecil Rhodes was the embodiment of British power in Cape Town. If Rhodes, from a certain distance and in a certain light, could be seen as a moral champion of black rights, he had another appeal. Morris carried seed money from the NBC and the endorsements of Booker T. Washington and the AME clergy, who had gone to South Africa three years before. These sponsors and the NBC contingent in Cape Town led by the Reverend R. A. Jackson could not fund very much. Thus Morris looked to Rhodes, the mining magnate, for a grant to build vocational schools.

When Morris reached South Africa in August 1899, he was awed by the rich resources and serenading echoes of his youth. Morris's impressions were published by a Xhosa Christian newspaper in the Cape, *Imvo Zabantsundu*. "The soil in many places is exceedingly ... fertile," he reported, producing "everything from wheat, oats and corn, back from the coast, to oranges, bananas, sugar, cotton, tobacco." He listened "day and night" to "Kaffir ... jubilee hymns." Morris's rapturous amazement provoked distressing memories as well: "After one gets here he wonders why our people have such an everlasting dread of coming to Africa. Why we will be shot down," lynched, and "burned to a handful of human cinders or 'Jim Crowed' ... when here is a vast continent." Not yet attuned to his South African milieu, Morris contrasted the slayings of African Americans in North Carolina with Xhosa Christian dedication to the British Crown: "So much for my treatment in the Queen's dominions. ... God bless her, I don't wonder that her African subjects are loyal to her. They certainly have infinitely more reason to sing 'God save the Queen' than we have to sing [the] hypocrite 'My Country Tis of Thee, Sweet Land of Liberty.'" He contemplated "a black man singing that" with "Negroes slowly bleeding to death in the red gutters of Wilmington." Morris was drawn to the notion of British "equality under the law" but did not mention how Cape "liberalism" limited the franchise to a small group of African Christian men.

Through NBC channels Morris secured an appointment with Rhodes, confident the patron would finance schools that would hire "young men and women ... [from] America as leaders of this work." The Boston *Colored American Magazine* described their meeting in grand terms, comparing its scope to Rhodes's dream of "cast[ing] up a highway" from Cape to Cairo. How much the American Baptist learned of his prospective benefactor's opinions is difficult to know. Prolific and observant, Morris was silent on Rhodes's notorious boast that he "preferred land to niggers."

Departing empty-handed, Morris reflected, "Poor as I am, I would not have changed places with the empire builder of South Africa." The Baptist missionary quickly moved to develop partnerships with African ministers who shared in a "providential design" famously articulated by the AME minister Absalom Jones: "Who knows but that a Joseph may rise up among them who shall be the instrument of feeding the African nations the bread of life?" Such prophesy animated Morris as he visited NBC missions in Port Elizabeth, East London, Middledrift, Queenstown, and Qumbu. During these travels through the Eastern Cape, he noted prejudice against "the native ... in many of the English churches [which] ... were not willing to allow a Kaffir to come within the doors and worship God." Unlike colonial clergy, Morris relished the chance to pray with Africans. Fatefully, he met a progenitor of the "Ethiopian Movement, who ... was driven out of the Church of England because ... as the Europeans and the Kaffirs bowed around the altar, the rector whispered to this man, 'Tell your people there is not enough bread to go around.'" Morris marveled at the results—more and more black preachers singing a familiar spiritual with their local congregation: "Oh! go down, Moses, / Away down to Egypt's land, / And tell King Pharaoh / To let my people go." Such full-throated pride in African Christianity, historian Robert Edgar argues, challenged white churchmen who refused "to allow their black counterparts in leadership posts."

Morris stayed in hotbeds of independent African Christianity like Lovedale—a mission guided by the Reverend Walter Rubusana—exulted in revivals, and baptized hundreds of Ethiopian followers. These experiences deeply touched Morris. "If anyone had told me I should find such intelligent, bright faced, thoughtful people," he gushed, "I would have said that it is absurd to expect to find men of such breadth, such culture, such ability in Africa." In September he wrote from Lovedale to Booker T. Washington, rejoicing in the industriousness of "strong and vigorous" neophytes who were "breaking away from the churches which evangelized them," establishing independent congregations, and arranging "to ... contact ... American negro religious teachers."

FIG. 1.6.2. Founding members of the SANNC (forerunner of the ANC), with the Reverend
Walter Rubusana standing on the left. HU Mooreland Library.

The Cape preachers with close ties to Morris, such as Rev. Rubusana of
Lovedale and the Reverend Jonas Goduka of the African Native Church,
used their Sunday schools to train activists. Several of their teachers started
Nelson Mandela's political party. In fact, Rubusana was a founder in 1912 of
the South African Native National Congress, or SANNC, forerunner of the
African National Congress (ANC). (See figure 1.6.2.) For his part, Rev.
Goduka welcomed "Dear Brother" Morris: "Loyalty to the Scriptures ...
Baptist views ... [and] independency of churches." Their spiritual commitment to Ethiopianism hinged on revolutionary action, with Africans at the
vanguard, according to the *Voice of the Negro*, W. E. B. Du Bois's medium.

Not long after Morris landed back home, the *Voice of the Negro* publicized
Ethiopian "doctrines which have inspired the natives with a spirit of independence" and filled the Cape government with fear. The official alarm was
not narrow-minded but global facing, for "English colonial" authority realized that "the American Negro is most active in stirring up the cause. He
knows by experience of the haughty white man and is advising the natives to
seize time by the forelock and be at least master of his own country." At a
large ecumenical conference in 1900 Morris proclaimed this cause: "[T]he

American Negro had been marvelously preserved and Christianized for a purpose ... destined to play a star part in the great drama of the world's development." The returned Baptist had acolytes to prove it. While in South Africa, Morris converted African chiefs, including one who sent sons with the returning missionary to study at Lincoln University and Virginia Theological Seminary. Morris helped build an educational pipeline that gave four hundred black South Africans opportunities to attend US colleges and universities by the early twentieth century. Two graduates, John Dube and Pixley Seme, became the first president and treasurer, respectively, of the ANC—future stars in one great drama of world development: the birth of democracy in South Africa.

HORIZON

Morris's experience in South Africa imbued him with an appreciation of the twentieth-century "color line," a concept coined by Du Bois to describe how racism scarred the hemispheres. By 1905 Ethiopian fervor had shifted Morris's politics from civilizing-mission gradualism to assertive self-determination. The next year Morris participated in the Niagara Movement, which would lay the foundation for the National Association for the Advancement of Colored People (NAACP), the preeminent civil rights organization in the United States. Meanwhile, he straddled his pulpit in the (now-famous Manhattan) Abyssinian church, where he repudiated President Roosevelt for disparaging black freedom fighters at home and abroad. The *New York Times* quoted the Baptist firebrand: "'Theodore Roosevelt, once enshrined in our love as our Moses, now enshrouded in our scorn as our Judas.'" Morris amplified black nationalists who, in the words of Du Bois, linked the mentality of "colonial exploitation" in Africa with Roosevelt's mind-set at home, slamming the door of equality "in the black man's face."

While Morris recognized Du Bois's definition of white supremacy as the "possession ... of the dark millions," they both rejected this fate, electing instead to foster African alliances in advance of a gathering struggle to erase the color line. In this regard Morris's Cape sojourn was a gateway act of the unfolding twentieth-century play called Pan-Africanism. This long-running drama, codirected by Du Bois and his rival Marcus Garvey, thrilled and chilled the United States and South Africa during the interwar years. Their diasporic disciples encouraged new leaders educated by American Christians, including ANC presidents Dr. Alfred Xuma and Albert Luthuli, to look beyond the nation-state for social justice. Indeed, as Morris had before, the Reverend Martin Luther King Jr. would ally himself with kindred South Africans like Luthuli, and together they would stretch out their hands singing an Ethiopian jubilee spiritual, "Let My People Go," still today the global chorus of civil rights.

NOTE

The authors wish to thank Robert Edgar, Michael O'Malley, Jennifer Ritterhouse, and Greg Robinson for their scholarly contributions.

ADDITIONAL RESOURCES

Bay, Mia. *To Tell the Truth Freely: The Life of Ida B. Wells.* New York: Hill & Wang, 2010.

Campbell, James. *Songs of Zion: The African American Methodist Episcopal Church in the United States and South Africa.* Durham: University of North Carolina Press, 1998.

Edgar, Robert. "New Religious Movements." In *Missions and Empire,* edited by Norman Etherington. Oxford: Oxford University Press, 2005.

Gaines, Kevin. *Uplifting the Race: Black Leadership, Politics and Culture during the Twentieth Century.* Durham: University of North Carolina Press, 1996.

Magubane, Zine. *Bringing the Empire Home: Race, Class, and Gender in Britain and Colonial South Africa.* Chicago: University of Chicago Press, 2003.

Vinson, Robert Trent. *The Americans Are Coming! Dreams of African American Liberation in Segregationist South Africa.* Athens: Ohio University Press, 2012.

Williams, Walter. *Black Americans and the Evangelization of Africa, 1877–1900.* Madison: University of Wisconsin Press, 1982.

· · ·

BENEDICT CARTON is Robert T. Hawkes Professor of History and Africa Coordinator of African and African American Studies at George Mason University in Fairfax, Virginia. He studies the transnational dimensions of southern African history. His publications include *Blood from Your Children: The Colonial Origins of Generational Conflict in South Africa* (University of Virginia Press, 2000) and *Zulu Identities: Being Zulu Past and Present* (Columbia University Press, 2009; coeditor and coauthor). His next book, with Robert Trent Vinson, is called *Shaka's Progeny,*

a Transnational History: Americans, Zulus and the Making of Diasporic Worlds,
1820–2000.

. . .

ROBERT TRENT VINSON is the Frances L. and Edwin L. Cummings Associate
Professor of History and Africana Studies at the College of William and Mary. He
teaches and writes on ancient and modern Africa, Latin America, the Caribbean,
and the United States. He is interested in cultural and intellectual histories, impe-
rialism, and colonialism. His publications include *The Americans Are Coming!*
Dreams of African American Liberation in Segregationist South Africa (Ohio
University Press, 2012), and *Before Mandela, like a King: The Prophetic Politics of*
Chief Albert Luthuli (Ohio University Press, forthcoming).

Africans in India, Past and Present

Renu Modi

Abstract: We can trace relations between India and Africa through three
defining historical periods: the precolonial era; the postcolonial, Nehruvian
era; and the globalized multipolar age of today. In examining these periods,
we can attempt to capture the myriad lived experiences of African sojourn-
ers who came to India as seafarers, merchants, and slaves in the precolonial
as well as the postcolonial era, and as students, medical tourists, expatriate
professionals, and traders in the contemporary context.

Keywords: Africans, India–Africa, Siddis, racism, South–South cooperation,
globalization

ON SUNDAYS IN MUMBAI, over a hundred people from various African
countries congregate at a local Methodist church near a railway station.
Africans are also visible in and around major hospitals, clutching large paper
packets containing their X-rays. Although the number of African immigrants is small, many have been in India for decades. The shores of Asia,
Africa, and Arabia were linked many years before colonialism drove them
together into the category of the Third World. These oceanic connections
have been alive all along and in the postcolonial period evolved further
within the framework of South–South cooperation. Since the dissolution of
the Iron Curtain, India–Africa engagements have intensified, becoming new
poles of growth in the twenty-first century. This chapter provides a brief over-
view of India's and Africa's historical relations as well as a portrayal of life in
Mumbai for current African residents. This picture is drawn from interviews
with a cross-section of Mumbai's African residents.

SIDDIS: HISTORICAL LINKAGES

Seafarers and traders have been plying the western Indian Ocean between the
west coast of India and the hinterlands of the Swahili coast since antiquity.

Later, soldiers and slaves, mainly from East Africa, traversed the maritime highway of this ocean until the abolition of slavery in the 1830s by the British colonialists. The slaves came to serve Hindu and Muslim royalty in India, and their descendants have become known as Siddis. The origins and early history of the Siddis (whom some people refer to as the "lost Africans") is difficult to reconstruct. In Sachin, a former principality near Surat, these former slaves rose to power, and some of them became royalty, such as the late Siddi nawab Ibrahim Mohammad Yakut Khan II of the princely state of *Sachin* (1833–73). There were others, too—like Siddi Wazir Malik Ambar, who was the regent of Ahmadnagar, Aurangabad, and Janjira, in the state of Maharashtra. The nizam of Hyderabad (a state in southern India) retained his Siddi cavalry guards until they were disbanded in 1948—a year after India's independence. The royal Siddis of Jafarabad, Hyderabad, and Aurangabad liaised with upper-class Muslim Indians. Other Siddis worked as domestic servants, in dock-yards, or in the agricultural sector as farm laborers.

Despite a lack of documented history, Siddis have a rich oral tradition, including dance and stories, through which they craft a collective identity premised on their historical linkages with Africa. *Goma-dhammal,* for example, is a high-energy rhythmic African dance form accompanied by Sufi songs. Some performances include peacock-feather costumes to venerate the black Sufi saint Siddi Mubarak Nobi, also referred to as Gori Pir or Bava Gor. According to oral traditions, Gori Pir was a trader in agate beads who came from Abyssinia via Mecca in the thirteenth century, along with his sister Mai Mishra and brothers. Siddis also maintained a corpus of *jikkars* (sacred songs), healing rituals, and mytho-poetic renditions to honor Siddi ancestral saints. Together these cultural expressions retained the link to Africa and probably helped overcome the rupture of slavery and forced migration. Today, some Siddis have gained access to education and professional occupations such as health care and banking, but the majority of Afro-Indians live on the margins within Indian society.

A general awareness about the African origins of the Siddis was ignited over the past two decades when ethnomusicologists and a UNESCO project on slave routes, called the African Diaspora in Asia (TADIA), tried to delve into the African connections of the Siddis. The project introduced members of the Siddi community to other African diasporic communities and gave them a greater appreciation of their own community in India. A Siddi *goma* (dance) performer was amazed to see similar musical instruments in Brazil. He noted that the *malunga,* a one-stringed percussion instrument that is a remnant of the Siddis' African ancestry was "akin to the *berimbau* that I saw at a museum in Bahia." Material culture was obviously transported by the transatlantic as well as the Indian Ocean slave and trade routes. Reminiscing about a TADIA conference, Abbas Siddis, one of its participants, told me, "I did not know there were so many of us scattered across Gujarat, Karnataka, Goa, and Hyderabad." He spoke proudly of his African heritage, although that identity had been somewhat latent all these years.

The Siddis who have been in India for multiple centuries have blended into the multicultural fold of the country through the adoption of local customs and languages. They follow the customs and traditions of the states in which they reside while at the same time retaining their distinct cultural heritage, music, dance forms, and veneration of Bava Gor. Though they are Indian citizens, their distinctive physiognomic features—in particular, the texture of their hair—lead some Indians to assume they are recent African migrants. When Usmaben Siddi started her new job at a bank in Gujarat, for example, the staff thought she was an African tourist and guided her to the foreign-exchange counter. Other Siddis have been asked to pay a higher entry fee in US dollars during their visits to monuments of national importance such as the Taj Mahal. The reverse has happened outside of India. When Ahmad Siddi, from Ratanpur, in Gujarat, went to perform with the Siddi *goma* dance troupe at the Zanzibar International Film Festival (ZIFF) in Tanzania, "[t]he immigration officials mistook me for a local and were surprised to see me with an Indian passport!" he told me. "Likewise, on return to India, the immigration officials were puzzled to see me with an Indian passport."

NEHRU'S VISION OF SOUTH–SOUTH COOPERATION

After independence in 1947, Prime Minster Jawaharlal Nehru's foreign policy was anchored firmly on principles of antiracism and the decolonization of countries under the colonial yoke. He accorded great priority to India–Africa relations. South–South cooperation grew into a philosophy of development in the 1960s and 1970s, at a time when the Third World countries of Africa and India looked for collective self-reliance on dealing with common issues such as poverty and underdevelopment, both individually and through common platforms such as the United Nations. Nehru's vision of prioritizing India–Africa relations shaped India's long tradition of hosting international students. "India has always been special for the Africans because of our common struggle against colonialism," explained Tony, a student from Malawi. Tony followed in the footsteps of Bingu wa Mutharika, the late president of Malawi, who graduated in economics from the Shri Ram College of Commerce in New Delhi. Salim Ahmad Ali, the former secretary of the Organization for African Unity (OAU), also studied in India. The trend continued into the 1960s, when East Africa's tertiary-education institutions were aimed at producing only civil servants and staff for corporations in the three East African states. Africans from Francophone and Lusophone countries have also studied in India. India was the preferred destination in the days of the nonaligned movement.

The subsequent decades were challenging times for India and Africa. The countries of the Global South were besieged by structural adjustment programs (SAPs) and mired in a debt trap and negative growth rates—hardly a condition for collective action. The situation was further aggravated by proxy wars through self-aggrandizing dictators and the militarization of the continent during the Cold War period. By the 1990s other countries, particularly China, emerged as alternative destinations for studies. In spite of these challenges, India's commitment to training African students continued. The three India–Africa Forum Summits (IAFS) of 2008, 2011, and 2015 enhanced the scholarship programs and strengthened relations between India and the continent. Bilateral trade between the two regions has increased, and political relations between India and Africa have always been positive. The cost-effective nature of Indian higher educational institutions and the lack of adequate opportunities in most African nations are some of the prime factors behind the surge of Africans into India for further studies. "It is a way of extending our soft power and generating goodwill in Africa," says a government official from the Africa desk.

Between 2008 and 2015 about twenty-five thousand students from across Africa received government of India (GoI) scholarships. Students from Mauritius, Ethiopia, Kenya, Rwanda, and other African nations have sought admissions across 150 universities in India. Of the over six thousand successful applicants for the GoI scholarships in 2014, about one-sixth are enrolled at Osmania University in Hyderabad, South India. Pune University in Maharashtra, technological universities in Gujarat in western India, Ananthpur in the state of Andhra Pradesh, and universities in Bangalore and Mysore in southern India draw a bulk of the students. Students opt for science, humanities, Indian music and dance, Ayurvedic medicine, yoga, and Hindi as well, says Arop, a postgraduate student from Nairobi. "How do you like your stay in India?" I ask. "Ah, well! I have had a good experience. I love my school and my friends here. They invited me home for Diwali this year. Maybe I am at home in India because we have so many Asians in Nairobi. I am used to seeing Asians in Kenya, even if the interactions are limited to public spaces. Most of the shopkeepers in Westlands [an upmarket Nairobi neighborhood] and in other parts are Gujaratis. I know how to greet them. "Namaste," he says, folding his hands as he bends his head forward in a reverential manner.

BEING AFRICAN IN INDIA

Despite the continuing support of the Indian government, Africans living in India, especially Nigerians, are subject to unwarranted racial profiling. Bless, a Rwandan student, says that, unfortunately, Nigerians are stereotyped as drug peddlers and criminals. "Well, there are good Nigerians and bad Nigerians, just as there are good Indians and bad Indians," he explains. "Besides, the added problem is that all blacks are called Nigerians." At the church in Mira Road, Vincent, a young Nigerian student, introduces me to his fellow African worshippers. They are in the city for higher education or business. I meet an elderly-looking gentleman who has been traveling between India and Nigeria for the past two decades. Vincent also introduces me to Nigerian families who have come to attend the church service. They seem to be just like any other family who love to spend Sunday morning singing hymns at church. After the service I ask one of Vincent's friends about the issue with Nigerians in Mumbai. I can sense the frustration. "Reciprocity, reciprocity," he says, repeating himself. "Indians in Nigeria live such a comfortable life. Most of them are rich. We do not harass them." He continues, "In Africa, Indians are allowed to live and run their business, whereas here in India it is the opposite. Most of us want to operate our small shops under a legal license, but that is not possible. Should we not be treated on the basis of reciprocity?" Instead, Nigerians, like other Africans, are not encouraged to engage in business activities in India or even market their products locally. "Nigerians" he says, "are unable to open even a bank account, leave alone start a business." According to another young student at the church, "some Africans, a very small number, are caught dealing with drugs and violating the law, but that is not a justification for stereotyping all the Africans."

Stories in the leading news dailies confirm Vincent's narrative. Students and traders at the church described being harassed by the police when they approach them to extend their visas, and are asked to return to their country of origin. "It is easy to get fresh visas from Indian embassies in African countries, but the travel means a lot of money," says Wandoh, a Nigerian national. The reluctance of landlords to rent out apartments and the stereotyping of Africans as drug dealers have periodically strained relations between the Indian Ministry of External Affairs and African embassies and consulates in India.

Matters reached a low point in the wake of the murder of Nigerian national Obado Uzoma Simeon in Goa in October 2013. His death led to clashes between the small community of Nigerians in Goa and the local population. The media reported a drive by the government in Goa to identify and deport Nigerians allegedly in the country without valid visas as well as a move by landlords to evict Nigerian tenants. The Goa police explained the tense relations as a law-and-order problem that did not involve every African immigrant. The police blamed the killing on a rivalry between local and Nigerian drug traffickers, and the state government asked the police to track down Nigerians living illegally in the state, to deport them and thus settle the matter amicably. Early the following year, a midnight raid was conducted on Ugandan nationals in New Delhi, alleging their involvement in illegal activities such as prostitution and drugs. The coordinator for the Association of African Students in India, Mbaya Guy Davis, regrets such events and attributes discrimination against Africans to "misperceptions" about them. He adds that it was only the "uneducated and illiterate" who ill-treated Africans. Patrick, from Johannesburg in South Africa, a doctoral scholar at Jawaharlal Nehru University in New Delhi, clarifies: "Certain Africans may be involved [in illegal activities], but this doesn't make every African the same." But there is yet another constituency who live as illegal immigrants in India. Either they have lost their passports or their visas have expired. So they, when caught, can be either deported as per law or imprisoned. Ikeorah Junior, from Lagos, who runs a café for Africans in a crowded Mumbai market on Mohammed Ali Road, does not agree with the detainment of fellow Africans. They should be deported, he affirms. But a government official in the state who is in charge of maintaining law and order says it is not that simple: "In most cases they have no passports. So, unless their nationalities are determined, they cannot be deported."

Two other Africans, Puku and Omo Okhuoya, have overcome these barriers and added to the city's multicuisine landscape by establishing modest restaurants. They sell *moi* bean cakes and chicken *onugbo* (African bitter leaf) soup along with *garri* (cassava) *fufu*. Omo is affectionately called Mama Maharashtra. Her menu card also has spicy mutton *ogbono* soup made from small dried mango seeds, and food cooked in red palm oil imported from Nigeria.

THE NEW FACES OF SOUTH–SOUTH COOPERATION

Despite the discrimination and harassment some Africans have faced, cooperation between both regions is expanding and evolving in new directions, including sports, health services, and outreach. Soccer is a popular sport in India, and there are about four hundred or so African (mainly Nigerian) footballers in the country, including "star" Africans like the high-profile Ranti Martins. Local clubs are allocated a quota of two or three spaces for foreigners, which are regularly filled by Nigerian match winners. Martins, a coveted soccer player, now plays for the United Sports Club in Kolkata, though initially he played for the Dempo Sports Club in Goa after moving to India in 2004. His children were born in Goa. Martins expressed his views about racism in India thus: "It's something that was different when I came to India. . . . I'm enjoying it, I'm enjoying my football, but it's not an easy situation as a Nigerian. Goans don't really appreciate other cultures. . . . They don't like the change to their culture. But Indians are going outside India— they are in Nigeria and the US and UK. It's something that Indians have to reflect on, because we are living in one world, we are the same. It's up to the government to make sure it educates Indians not to discriminate." Martins continues to thrive in his profession. "With my personality they [Indians] see me as a role model for their kids in Indian community. . . . India loves stars. I'm happy to be a star here." But he laments the racist incidents against his fellow compatriots. He is "hopeful [that] kids who are born and raised in India will have fewer problems when they grow up. Hopefully when Indian and African children grow up going to school together they will have a better understanding of each other."

Africans also come to India to take advantage of the high-quality, low-cost medical services. As Peter, from Kenya, exclaimed, "First World facilities at Third World costs! Be it education or accessing health services, for us it is very cheap here compared to the US or European countries. The Indian-made generic drugs are so cheap and lifesavers as well." He tells me about his uncle who was flown in from Nairobi for a knee replacement in a Mumbai hospital. "There is no pain, and he can walk now. Once you are away from home, a few things happen," he adds stoically.

The Indian government is also supporting new kinds of South–South collaborations. As part of the government's Indian Technical and Economic Cooperation grants, women from countries in Africa who have little or no formal education are invited to receive training at the Barefoot College in Rajasthan, a state in western India. These women are trained to harness the sun's energy through solar electrification and learn to light up their homes and villages using this technology. "Where is it written that if you can't read or write, you can't become an engineer or a designer?" asks Bunker Roy, the founder of Barefoot College. "It has to be bottom-up, it has to be indigenous, it has to develop solutions from the ground up, and it has to be both community based and community managed," he argues.

CONCLUSION

Amid several challenges, India–Africa South–South linkages are on the ascendance like never before. People-to-people interactions have become more intense, partly facilitated by increased connectivity by air and the Internet. Several Africans are in India for business as usual. They come to India in pursuit of higher education, for medical treatment, as highly paid expatriates, or as traders. The latter source merchandise for day-to-day consumption back home in Africa. Shoes, apparel, leather bags, kitchenware, bling jewelry, braided hair, colored beads, and decorative items all can be purchased at reasonable rates from wholesale markets in Mumbai. Kanga and wax prints in dark shades are sold at the wholesale textile market or the old colonial-style Crawford Market, located near the city center.

Those Africans who have settled in India have had mixed, but generally positive, experiences. Most of the African expatriates I interviewed enjoy their postings in India despite some of the racial stereotypes and incidents. Like the students, expatriates, and patients who come to India for, respectively, higher education, work, or access to affordable health care, they have become goodwill ambassadors for India. They invoke Nehru's vision of strong India–Africa relations based on a shared colonial history and common developmental challenges, and they reinvigorate South–South cooperation in the twenty-first century.

ADDITIONAL RESOURCES

Basu, Helena. *Journeys and Dwellings: Indian Ocean Themes in South Asia*. Hyderabad: Orient Longman, 2008.

Hawley, John, ed. *India in Africa, Africa in India: Indian Ocean Cosmopolitanisms*. Bloomington, Indiana University Press, 2008.

Modi, Renu, ed. *South–South Cooperation: Africa on the Centre Stage*. Basingstoke, UK: Palgrave Macmillan, 2011.

The Siddi, an African Community in India. Video. https://www.youtube.com /watch?v=UD7sp-L9lUk.

• • •

RENU MODI is a faculty member in the Centre for African Studies at the University of Mumbai. Her research areas include international migration, the political economy of international development, diasporas, and India–Africa relations. Her recent publications include, with Rhea D'Silva, "Liminal Spaces: Racism against Africans in India," *Economic & Political Weekly* 51, no. 41 (8 October 2016); and "The Indian 'Birds of Passage' in South Africa: Renegotiating Identities in the Local and Global Context," *World Focus* 409 (January 2014).

PART II

Power and Its Challenges

INTRODUCTION

In his satirical film *History of the World: Part I,* Mel Brooks, as King Louis XVI, declares, "It's good to be the king!" However, having power can be a precarious responsibility. Imperial rulers, coup leaders, and beneficiaries of electoral manipulations often assume that control of the reins of political and economic institutions, armies, and judiciaries gives them absolute power and control. However, history has demonstrated that control is never as all-powerful as imagined; it can be challenged and sometimes dismantled. The chapters in this section explore the dynamic relationship between those who exercise power and those often deemed "powerless."

European colonial powers imagined that they would retain their African colonies well into the twenty-first century. However, as Hakim Adi illustrates, they did not anticipate the powerful intellectual and social movements that would launch the process of decolonization by the mid–twentieth century. These movements were indebted to Pan-Africanist thinkers such as W. E. B. DuBois, Marcus Garvey, and Jane and Paulette Nardal, who challenged colonialism and the racism that framed the lives of black peoples in Africa, the Caribbean, the United States, and Europe. Students of Pan-Africanism, such as Julius Nyerere, were among the first generation of Africa's postcolonial leaders. As Tanzania's first president, Nyerere challenged the structural and moral efficacy of World Bank and International Monetary Fund programs. Equally important, Chambi Chachage illustrates Nyerere's efforts to make the end of exploitation and inequality the cornerstones of his government's policy. While Nyerere tried to transform Tanzania, war and destruction raged in other parts of the continent. Leymah Gbowee, a formidable Liberian woman, mobilized other women to challenge Charles Taylor and the warlords destroying their country with their violence and greed. As Pamela Scully's thoughtful profile makes clear, Gbowee has forever changed the way we theorize building peace by making women's concerns for personal security and healing central to peace-building agendas.

As Liberian women spoke truth to power, their deliberations confirmed that the inequalities that shape the continent's present are not the product of Africans alone; they are, in part, products of Africa's engagement with other regions of the world. Masimba Tafirenyika exposes the looting, theft, and other mechanisms through which multinational corporations and organized crime syndicates divert approximately US$50 billion annually from Africa. Solutions to address this outflow of money require political action by African leaders as well as the international community. African states are gradually improving their capacity to address issues like the illicit outflow of money. Stephen Mogaka and Stephen Ndegwa reveal hopeful political signs on the continent. Conflict has declined, in part because the African Union and regional organizations have developed early warning systems to help prevent or minimize civil strife.

The increasing capacity of African states to manage power and conflict is critical as they try to correct the ills of the past. In South Africa, the end of apartheid, the subsequent election of Nelson Mandela as president, and the implementation of the innovative Truth and Reconciliation Commission (TRC) inspired many people around the world. South African activists and scholars Sarah Malotane Henkeman and Undine Whande helped usher in this new era in South Africa, but their reflections question whether justice has been served. Their somber assessment, however, is not a call to disillusionment. Instead, it reminds us that there is much work to be done to fulfill the promises of the antiapartheid movement and overturn inequalities in South Africa, as elsewhere in the world. Indeed, a new generation of activists are pursuing justice through environmental action. Jacklyn Cock introduces us to activists who are fighting to stem toxic pollution in the heartland of South Africa. They have linked environmental activism and social justice in new and exciting ways that will further the movement for justice in postapartheid South Africa. They are also forging new types of relationships and alliances across South Africa and internationally.

New economic relationships are also unfolding across the continent as China's economic engagement with African countries intensifies. Jamie Monson, Tang Xiaoyang, and Liu Shaonan explore the rich and diverse interactions as Chinese and Africans work in multiple settings and locations, from the "China shop" in a Ghanaian marketplace to Chinese-owned leather factories in Ethiopia. Together these articles strip away notions of a static Africa and reveal the dynamic ways in which Africa is reinventing itself in the twenty-first century and providing lessons and examples for us all.

2 . 1

Profile

LEYMAH GBOWEE: SPEAKING
TRUTH TO POWER

Pamela Scully

Abstract: Leymah Gbowee received the Nobel Peace Prize for her contributions as a leader of the Liberian women's movement for peace. Through her courage and example, she helped to reframe the meaning of peace building in Africa and elsewhere to include women's grassroots organizing and notions of personal security and social healing.

Keywords: Liberia, postconflict, women, peace building, gender, Nobel Prize

IN 2003, LIBERIAN WARLORDS (including then-president Charles Taylor) met in Accra, Ghana, to engage in peace talks. But these dragged on for weeks, with observers beginning to think that leaders liked the relative comfort of the hotel rooms so much they would just keep talking without reaching conclusions. Had it not been for Leymah Gbowee, this situation might have continued. Gbowee had had enough. She staged a sit-in with other Liberian women, effectively barricading the men in the hall. When men tried to force the women to leave, Gbowee made a ruckus and refused to move until the warlords promised to discuss peace in good faith. She promised to return if they did not. Thanks to Gbowee and the efforts of many other Liberian women and men, peace finally came to Liberia. Ellen Johnson Sirleaf, the first elected female president on the African continent, was inaugurated as president in 2006. Her ascendancy owed much to the grassroots organizing of Liberian women who took on warlords, forged a path for peace, and were not scared to speak truth to power.

In Leymah Gbowee's life we see exemplified the old feminist adage that the personal is political. Gbowee turned the challenges of being born female and coming to adulthood in a time of great violence into the fuel for a powerful transformation of what it meant to be a peace builder in Liberia and beyond.

In a world of men at war, Gbowee matched that fierceness with a different kind of ferocity: by taking on warlords, calling out sexism, and demanding respect, she unified Liberian women in the call to end the war. Liberia has a long history of division: areas of what is now known as Liberia were settled by African Americans under the auspices of American missionary societies and Africans taken off slave ships by the British. The area became independent as Liberia in 1847. Until 1980, descendants of the American settlers, known as Americo-Liberians, governed the broader country with little regard for the rights of indigenous Liberians, causing tensions that ultimately fueled the civil wars of the 1990s and early 2000s. Gbowee came to fame through her efforts to end the Liberian civil war, and, eventually, through her starring role in the 2008 documentary *Pray the Devil Back to Hell.* Her work and her international exposure garnered Gbowee the Nobel Peace Prize in 2011, along with her more famous compatriot, Ellen Johnson Sirleaf, and Tawakkol Karman of Yemen.

Before she was famous, Leymah Gbowee was a social worker, a founder of women's peace groups; and also a mother, a survivor of domestic abuse, and, for a time, a broken woman whose family, particularly her mother, helped her find the internal resources to build a life amid war. She was born in Monrovia, Liberia's capital, in 1972 to a poor couple, with connections to the Liberian countryside, and thus to indigenous Liberian societies. Her mother and father worked hard to provide for Leymah and her four sisters, all of whom went to private school and became part of Liberia's urban elite. As Gbowee recounts in her memoir, *Mighty Be Our Powers,* when she graduated from high school in 1989, she thought she was set for glory, preparing to go to university to become a doctor.

War, however, intervened. Liberia was wracked by civil war from 1989 to 1996 (the First Civil War) and again from 1998 to 2003 (the Second Civil war). These wars resulted in the virtual destruction of Liberia, and the displacement of some five hundred thousand people between 1989 and 2003. Warlords such as Charles Taylor used child soldiers and sexual violence as a means of spreading terror in Liberia. In the years between 1993 and 1998, Gbowee lived in many places in Monrovia and its environs, and in Ghana, as she sought to stay one step ahead of hell. As she explained in her Nobel lecture: "Women had become the 'toy of war' for over-drugged young militias. Sexual abuse and exploitation spared no woman; we were raped and abused regardless of our age, religious or social status. A common scene daily was a mother watching her young one being forcibly recruited or her daughter being taken away as the wife of another drug emboldened fighter."

In the midst of the disintegration of Liberia, Leymah Gbowee's world started to fall apart. A bad relationship, which resulted in four children in quick succession in the mid-1990s, trapped her in dependence. With no work, and an abusive partner, Gbowee fell into depression. Education saved her, as did the support of her mother and sisters, and perhaps the derision of her father, who worried aloud that she was becoming a "baby machine." In the late 1990s, as part of a program of social work at Mother Patern College, Gbowee started an internship at St. Peter's Church, in the Trauma Healing and Reconciliation Program. In this work, Gbowee met Sam Doe, the founder of the West Africa Network for Peacebuilding (WANEP). She also began to travel the countryside and become familiar with women's concerns. She was motivated by her involvement with women from Sierra Leone and their "zest for life." Inspired also by a song from her church, "Count your blessings, name them one by one," Gbowee began to focus on peace building, to think about how to practice nonviolence in the midst of war. As she says in her autobiography, "We would always look up to Gandhi. We would always look up to Nelson Mandela, the Dalai Lama, Rosa Parks. Those were the kind of leaders Liberia needed now. . . . We needed to help ourselves."

The Second Civil War started in 1999, with the infiltration of a new army, LURD (Liberians United for Reconciliation and Democracy), which unleashed a new round of terror. People also realized that being in power had intensified rather than blunted Taylor's evil. Existing organizations such as WANEP and the Liberian Women's Initiative had tried to bring about reconciliation for many years. Gbowee admired their efforts, but she felt the need for more direct action. In 2000, she helped form the Women in Peacebuilding Network (WIPNET), which united women from different faiths and backgrounds across the region to advocate for peace. Gbowee became head of the Liberian Women's Initiative of WIPNET.

By 2002, Gbowee believed that ordinary women might hold the key to opening the door to peace. Gbowee began to organize a coalition of women willing to challenge Taylor. The female-centered grassroots organization that she built drew on strong networks of religious women's groups, existing practices of women's leadership in the Sande secret society, and forms of female chieftainship in different indigenous societies. The Liberian women's peace movement was thus not only a revolutionary movement but also one that drew on older histories of female spiritual and social power.

Gbowee's major contribution to peace building was to recognize the power of solidarity and grassroots organizing by women. Eschewing the formal political realm, Gbowee built Women's Mass Action for Peace, a coalition of groups that began to create patterns of solidarity and staged ongoing protests to shame Taylor into peace negotiations. In her Nobel Prize lecture she recalled the hard work of women: "We worked daily confronting warlords, meeting with dictators and refusing to be silenced in the face of AK 47 and RPGs. We walked when we had no transportation, we fasted when water was unaffordable, we held hands in the face of danger, we spoke truth to power when everyone else was being diplomatic, we stood under the rain and the sun with our children to tell the world the stories of the other side of the conflict. Our educational backgrounds, travel experiences, faiths, and social classes did not matter. We had a common agenda: 'Peace for Liberia Now.'" With their white (for peace) T-shirts, women started becoming part of the public land-scape, most notably through their daily outdoor protests on a soccer field on the president's daily route to work. In June 2003, Taylor granted the women an audience at the presidential mansion. Gbowee was chosen to speak for the women. Quietly but powerfully, she told Taylor: "We are tired of war. We are tired of running. . . . We are tired of our children being raped. We are now taking this stand, to secure the future of our children."

In 2003, after many years of fighting, warlords came to peace talks in Accra, Ghana, under pressure from the international community. Seven leaders of WIPNET traveled to Ghana to mobilize the thousands of Liberian women living there as refugees. When the talks still yielded no progress after six weeks, Gbowee was fed up. She organized a sit-in of the women who had been protesting for peace outside the hotel. Lining up in the corridors, they barricaded the delegates in the hall for two hours. As Gbowee explained in a note to General Abubakar, the head of the peace talks: "We are holding these delegations, especially the Liberians, hostage. They will feel the pain of what our people are feeling at home." As a result of this pressure, peace talks pro-ceeded. The Comprehensive Peace Agreement was signed two weeks later.

But Gbowee and other women did not stop their organizing after the peace accord. They helped create dialogue between Liberian women and the United Nations Mission in Liberia (UNMIL). For example, WIPNET and the Liberian Women's Initiative organized a two-day symposium with some eighty women from around the country to discuss the terms of the peace agreement and to encourage the women's peace-building efforts. In addition, they assisted the disarmament, demobilization, and reintegration processes. WIPNET and women from Bong County made public the fact that ex-combatants had not been paid after handing in their guns as agreed upon.

Gbowee and her colleagues in many ways transformed the way that people understood the very concept of building peace. She helped put women's concerns for personal security and social healing on the peace-building agenda. In a way one could say that she helped contribute to the field of gender and security studies. No longer is security seen only as a matter of police and armies. Instead, scholars working on security studies now talk about the need for freedom from domestic violence, and for women to feel secure while walking down the street. Gbowee also reanimated grassroots organizing, including civil-society and religious organizations. She practiced a contentious politics that called on society and on the state to realize peace.

In the mid-2000s, Gbowee decided to bring theory together with practice and completed a one-year master's degree in conflict resolution and peace building at Eastern Mennonite University in the United States. The philanthropist Abigail Disney approached Gbowee in 2006 about making a film about the women's peace movement that Gbowee had done so much to shape. The film was released as *Pray the Devil Back to Hell,* with Gbowee as the main narrator: a new kind of star was born.

When the Nobel committee awarded Gbowee the peace prize in 2011, they recognized her incredible energy and ability to bring women from different walks of life together in solidarity for peace. In a country as historically divided as Liberia between urban (Monrovia) and rural, between Christian and Muslim, between Americo-Liberian and indigenous, and by ethnicity, Gbowee's accomplishment was truly remarkable. As the committee stated: "Leymah Gbowee mobilized and organized women across ethnic and religious dividing lines to bring an end to the long war in Liberia, and to ensure women's participation in elections. She has since worked to enhance the influence of women in West Africa during and after war." Leymah Gbowee closed her lecture by saying: "And, finally, Liberian women: thank you for making our country proud. Thank you for sitting in the rain and under the sun. This is your prize. This is our prize. The world used to remember Liberia for child soldiers but they now remember our country for the white t-shirt women. Who would have ever thought that Liberian women would have been among faces of women's global victory, but you did it. So thank you!"

Leymah Gbowee and Liberian women helped show that social mobilization and women's participation are key to the ending of war. Gbowee created a space for grassroots organizing and thus widened the scope of politics. She showed that ordinary women could change the future. The landscape of twenty-first-century peace building looks different because of the efforts of Gbowee.

ADDITIONAL RESOURCES

Berger, Iris. "African Women's Movements in the Twentieth Century: A Hidden History." *African Studies Review* 57, no. 3 (2014): 1–19.

Gbowee, Leymah, with Carol Mithers. *Mighty Be Our Powers: How Sisterhood, Prayer, and Sex Changed a Nation at War*. New York: Beast Books, 2011.

Pray the Devil Back to Hell. Directed by Gini Reticker. Produced by Abigail Disney. Fork Films, 2008.

Scully, Pamela. *Ellen Johnson Sirleaf*. Athens: Ohio University Press, 2016.

Tripp, Aili Mari, Isabel Casimiro, Joy Kwesiga, and Alice Mungwa. *African Women's Movements: Transforming Political Landscapes*. Cambridge: Cambridge University Press, 2009.

· · ·

PAMELA SCULLY is Professor of Women's, Gender, and Sexuality Studies and Professor of African Studies at Emory University. She is also Assistant Vice Provost for Academic Innovation. She has her PhD in history from the University of Michigan. Her publications have focused on comparative women's and gender history, and most recently on sexual violence in conflict and postconflict. Her most recent book is *Ellen Johnson Sirleaf* (Ohio University Press, 2016). She works closely with the Institute for Developing Nations, a partnership between Emory University and The Carter Center, which focuses on collaborative research regarding issues of poverty and development.

2.2

Pan-Africanism

AN IDEOLOGY AND A MOVEMENT

Hakim Adi

Abstract: Pan-Africanism emerged at the end of the nineteenth century as a political current advocating the unity of all those of African heritage in order to advance the common interests of Africa and all Africans. Emerging first in the diaspora, it has become of major significance for the African continent.

Keywords: Pan-African, Pan-Africanism, diaspora, Négritude, intellectuals

IN MAY 2013 THE AFRICAN UNION (AU), an organization of African states, held its twentieth summit—fifty years after the founding of its predecessor, the Organisation of African Unity. The AU, barely ten years old, adopted the theme "Pan-Africanism and African Renaissance" for its anniversary summit. A special anniversary publication explained that "Pan-Africanism is an ideology and movement that encouraged the solidarity of Africans worldwide. It is based on the belief that unity is vital to economic, social and political progress and aims to 'unify and uplift' people of African descent. The ideology asserts that the fates of all African peoples and countries are intertwined. At its core Pan-Africanism is 'a belief that African peoples both on the continent and in the Diaspora, share not merely a common history, but a common destiny.'" Nothing could exemplify this belief better than the AU itself, an organization with a membership that includes not only fifty-three out of the fifty-four African states but also the entire African diaspora. The diaspora, or people of African origin living outside the continent, is designated the "sixth region" of the AU. As if to give added emphasis to the unity of Africa and its diaspora, Haiti, birthed by the revolutionary action of Africans in the Caribbean from 1791 to 1804, has been granted AU observer status and is seeking to become an associate member. Haiti continues to maintain and affirm its close ties with Africa—yet another contemporary manifestation of Pan-Africanism.

Pan-Africanist thought and action were provoked by the modern dispersal of Africans resulting from the trafficking of captives across the Atlantic to the Americas and elsewhere from the end of the fifteenth century. Pan-Africanism evolved as a variety of ideas, activities, organizations, and movements that, sometimes in concert, resisted the exploitation and oppression of all those of African heritage, opposed the ideologies of racism, and celebrated African achievement and being African.

THE FORERUNNERS

Before the concepts of Pan-African and Pan-Africanism emerged at the end of the nineteenth century, there were various organized efforts by Africans in the diaspora to join together in order to combat racism, to campaign for an end to enslavement, or to organize to repatriate to the African continent. It was enslavement, accompanied by anti-African racism, that made Africans in the diaspora aware of their common African heritage and the importance of coming together to ameliorate the oppression they faced outside the continent.

In eighteenth-century Britain, for example, the African abolitionists Olaudah Equiano and Ottobah Cugoano formed the Sons of Africa, one of the earliest Pan-African organizations, to collectively campaign to end Britain's participation in the transatlantic trafficking of enslaved Africans. The best-selling writing of Equiano and Cugoano also established the "slave narrative" as a new form of African political literature. This writing, sometimes a collective endeavor, also established a central role for the African intellectual as one who places intellect in the service of the Pan-African cause—that is, for the advancement and liberation of Africa and all Africans.

In the nineteenth century those in Africa and the diaspora who were Western-educated, many of whom were personally connected with the struggle against enslavement, contributed to the development of emancipatory ideas with a broad Pan-African rather than just local character. Such figures as James Africanus Horton from Sierra Leone, Martin Delany from the United States, and Edward Blyden from the Caribbean were concerned not only with combating the virulent anti-African racism of the period but also with encouraging those who suffered from racist oppression in the diaspora to return to and develop their ancestral African homeland.

Delany, an abolitionist, writer, and medical practitioner, clearly stated his policy: "Africa for the African race and black men to rule them." Blyden, a politician, writer, educator, and diplomat, has been seen as one of the key thinkers in the development of Pan-Africanism. He returned to his ancestral home in West Africa and established a newspaper, *Negro*, specifically aimed at audiences in Africa, the Caribbean, and the United States. Blyden believed that Africans had their own unique contribution to make to the world and an equally unique "African personality." His ideas, although often contradictory, influenced later Pan-Africanists such as Marcus Garvey and Kwame Nkrumah.

THE FIRST PAN-AFRICAN CONFERENCE

The first Pan-African Conference was held in London, the heart of the British Empire, in July 1900, convened by the African Association led by Henry Sylvester Williams, a Trinidadian lawyer. The association was formed in 1897 in London by African and Caribbean intellectuals, including one woman—Anne Victoria Kinloch, from South Africa—and was concerned with combating various injustices in Britain's African and Caribbean colonies, in the period following the European "scramble for Africa." After Williams met with Benito Sylvain, a Haitian journalist, lawyer, diplomat, and anticolonial activist based in Paris, the scope of the conference was broadened to include "the treatment of native races under European and American rule." One important aim was to demonstrate that those of African descent could unite and speak for themselves against the injustices they faced throughout the world.

Among the distinguished participants of this international gathering were Benito Sylvain, representing Emperor Menelik of Ethiopia; the African-American educator and activist Anna J. Cooper; and W. E. B. Du Bois. The conference's "Address to the Nations of the World" was drafted under the chairmanship of Du Bois and included the famous phrase "[T]he problem of the 20th century is the problem of the color-line." The organizers intended to establish branches of a new group, the Pan-African Association, in Africa, the Caribbean, and North America, and Williams was able to launch the first few issues of a magazine, the *Pan-African*. However, both the Pan-African Association and its publication were short-lived.

Following the London conference, several years passed before such a major event was again organized. Yet the problems facing Africans and those of African descent grew more acute. In the United States, for example, between 1900 and 1914 over eleven hundred African American men, women, and children were murdered by racist mobs. In Africa the violent European conquest of the continent was almost complete by 1914. In just one colony, Belgium's ironically named Congo Free State, conquest and colonial exploitation led to an estimated ten million deaths. Anti-African racism was ubiquitous, suffered equally by those in Africa and in the diaspora.

Du Bois had emerged as one of the key figures in London and three years earlier had elaborated his views on what he referred to as "Pan-Negroism," and on the "uplifting of the Negro people" by their own united efforts. Du Bois, a prominent African-American intellectual, believed that African Americans had a special responsibility to organize and speak for all those of African descent. He therefore sought to continue the tradition of major international gatherings when he organized the first Pan-African Congress in Paris in 1919, with fifty-seven participants from Africa, the Caribbean, and the United States.

Du Bois convened the congress at the conclusion of World War I as the victorious powers were meeting to discuss the postwar world in France. He proposed the creation of new states in Africa, supervised by the major colonial powers, from the confiscation of some of Germany's former colonies. He considered that they should take account of the views of the "civilized Negro world," by which he mainly had in mind intellectuals such as himself. He also called for a permanent Pan-African secretariat based in Paris and hoped that the congress would enable the voice of the "children of Africa" to be heard at the postwar peace conferences held in the city. However, the first Pan-African Congress had little lasting influence, and its demand that the rights of Africans and those of African descent be protected by the League of Nations was ignored.

Du Bois then took the initiative to organize a second congress, held in 1921 in London, Paris, and Brussels, then a third in London and Lisbon in 1923, and a fourth, originally scheduled to take place in the Caribbean but finally held in New York in 1927. In 1929 he also made plans to hold a fifth congress in Tunis but was denied permission by the French colonial government. The four congresses established the idea of Pan-Africanism, consolidated Pan-African networks, and drew activists from the United States, Liberia, Ethiopia, and Haiti, as well as from Africa, and also from the Caribbean residing in Europe. They took a stand against racism and began to raise the demand for self-determination in the colonies. However, few representatives from organizations on the African continent participated, there was little support from African-American organizations, and no permanent organization, organizing center, or publication was established. The congresses were also criticized for the moderate political views expressed and for the exclusion of Marcus Garvey, perhaps the leading Pan-Africanist of the time.

The Jamaican writer and activist Marcus Garvey first established the Universal Negro Improvement Association and African Communities League (UNIA) in Jamaica in 1914 jointly with Amy Ashwood, who later became his first wife. It included among its aims "a universal confederacy amongst the race," as well as promoting "racial pride," education, commercial enterprises, and "conscientious Christian worship" and assisting in "the civilizing of backward tribes in Africa." Garvey was also concerned with "upliftment" and stated that he wherever he traveled he "saw the injustice done to my race because it was black."

He reestablished the UNIA in New York in 1917, where it soon attracted thousands of adherents, first throughout the United States and soon afterward internationally. At its height the UNIA's membership has been estimated at over four million, but no precise figures exist. Undoubtedly it was the largest political movement of Africans during the twentieth century, embracing not just a few intellectuals but the masses both on the African continent and throughout the diaspora. The organization's newspaper, *Negro World,* preached an anticolonial message, "Africa for the Africans at home and abroad," challenged notions of white supremacy, and extolled the greatness of Africans and Africa's history. It circulated throughout the diaspora, often illegally in colonial Africa and the Caribbean.

The UNIA's Declaration of Rights of the Negro Peoples of the World, launched by Garvey in 1920, demanded self-determination, condemned anti-African racism, and defended "the inherent right of the Negro to possess himself of Africa," as well as the "necessity of Negro nationalism, political power and control." It also envisaged a "Negro independent nation on the continent of Africa" to which those in the diaspora could return. In the meantime Garvey attempted to forge links with the government of Liberia and declared himself provisional president of a future independent African republic. Garvey's politics, overtures to the Ku Klux Klan, and links with the masses put him at odds with Du Bois and other leading African-American intellectuals, while his movement was feared by the major colonial powers and the US government. He was deported from the United States in 1927 but remained active until his death in 1940. Garvey exerted a considerable impact on Africa and its diaspora during the interwar years, as has been acknowledged by other Pan-Africanists, most notably by Kwame Nkrumah.

RADICAL PAN-AFRICANISM AND NÉGRITUDE

Some of the most significant critics of Garveyism were those connected with the international communist movement, who developed a different Pan-African vision. Although acknowledging that Africans globally faced similar problems of racism and various forms of colonial oppression and exploitation, the "Black Bolsheviks" advocated the need for an African political struggle in unity with working and oppressed people of all countries. They disseminated their views in Africa, the Americas, and Europe and in 1930 held their own Pan-African conference, in Hamburg, Germany, drawing participants from Africa, the Caribbean, the United States, and Europe. The politics of the communists did not attract as many adherents as the UNIA, but the conference was significant for its critique of colonialism and imperialism, and its insistence on the need for an organized struggle around specific demands that would lead to a socialist future in which all Africans would be empowered. One of the most notable of these communists was the Trinidadian journalist and writer George Padmore, a former student at Howard University, who acted as the editor of the *Negro Worker,* the publication of the Comintern's International Trade Union Committee of Negro Workers. After he parted company with the communist movement, Padmore became a leading Pan-Africanist.

Yet another strand of Pan-Africanism developed among African and Caribbean intellectuals living in France between the two wars. The Négritude movement was principally developed by three male students, Aimé Césaire from Martinique, the Senegalese Léopold Senghor, and Léon Damas from Guyana, as well as two female intellectuals, Jane and Paulette Nardal from Martinique. The founders came under a variety of influences including Marxism, Surrealism, Garveyism, and the Harlem Renaissance. Négritude propounded a reconciliation between Africans from the continent and the diaspora through a rejection of assimilation, colonialism, and Eurocentrism and encouraged a common struggle to embrace and celebrate African culture and the uniqueness of being African, at times almost a harking back to the notion of "African personality" espoused by Edward Blyden. Its impact was greatest in the Francophone world and was exemplified in Jane Nardal's essay "Internationalisme noir," published in 1928, and Césaire's poem "Cahier d'un retour au pays natal," first published in 1939.

In the mid-1930s Pan-Africanism became radicalized by the influence of Marxism, especially in Britain and France and the colonies of these two imperialist powers. It was the Comintern that first promoted the idea of a United States of Socialist Africa and provided an uncompromising critique of colonialism. A more radical approach to colonial rule was also the consequence of the dire economic situation during the years of the Great Depression, which led to major strikes and rebellions throughout the Caribbean as well as to fascist Italy's invasion of Ethiopia in 1935. The latter led to a major international campaign to support Ethiopia that was particularly strong in many parts of Africa and throughout the diaspora. The outbreak of World War II only strengthened Pan-African demands for an end to colonial rule, while in Britain, Padmore and his Pan-African Federation made preparations for a new Pan-African congress.

THE MANCHESTER PAN-AFRICAN CONGRESS

The Fifth Pan-African Congress, held in Manchester, England, in 1945, has been seen as the most significant of all the Pan-African congresses. It was dominated by the thinking of Padmore and other British-based intellectuals, including Kwame Nkrumah and Amy Ashwood Garvey. It grew out of the radicalism of the 1930s and the war years, as well as Padmore's experience as an organizer of the communist-led Hamburg conference in 1930. One of its main features was that participation was restricted to representatives of workers' and farmers' organizations—"the masses," who were considered to be the main force that would end colonial rule, by force if necessary. It therefore broke with previous gatherings comprising only intellectuals, which merely aimed at lobbying the imperialist powers. The congress expressed its opposition to the "rule of capital" and the imposition of Eurocentric political institutions in the colonies, as well as condemning the colonial borders that had been imposed on African states. The participants were mainly from

Britain's colonies in Africa and the Caribbean, and there was both an increasing emphasis on African liberation and an internationalist spirit, reflected in the slogan "Oppressed People of All Countries Unite."

PAN-AFRICANISM IN AFRICA

After Manchester the center of the Pan-African world shifted away from the diaspora to Africa, where Kwame Nkrumah played a major role as an anticolonial leader in the Gold Coast. In 1957, as the newly named Ghana celebrated its independence from British colonial rule, Nkrumah declared that the change was "meaningless unless it is linked up with the total liberation of Africa," and he began to organize to achieve that liberation and his vision of a United States of Africa. In 1958 he hosted the Conference of Independent African States and, later the same year, the All-African Peoples Conference, which brought together over three hundred representatives from twenty-eight African countries, including those still under colonial rule. Both conferences aimed to encourage a spirit of Pan-African unity among the participants and to discuss the removal of colonial rule throughout Africa. Even at this early stage Nkrumah urged the African states to consider measures to enhance economic cooperation and to develop a common foreign policy, and both conferences looked forward to a commonwealth of independent African states. Similar initiatives were organized in other parts of the continent. There were, however, differing approaches to the question of African unity and whether this merely meant increasing economic cooperation or implied a more immediate political union. But these did not prevent the founding in 1963 of the Organisation of African Unity (OAU) by thirty-two African states.

The main aims of the OAU were to increase cooperation and unity between African states and to rid the continent of colonial rule. Although it was handicapped by the impact of neocolonialism, its formation was clearly a major victory for Pan-Africanism on the African continent, although it also had a significant influence among those in the diaspora. This was particularly evident in the work of the African-American activist Malcolm X, who in 1964 established his Organization of Afro-American Unity in order to address the many problems still faced by those not just in the United States but also throughout the diaspora. At the end of his life Malcolm X spoke for a whole generation when he called for the diaspora to identify and learn from

Africa but also demanded that the OAU take up for solution the problems confronting the diaspora. The militant approach of Malcolm X and others ushered in a new era and a demand for what was referred to as Black Power. This new Pan-Africanist trend exerted its influence not only among those in the diaspora but even among those in parts of the African continent—most notably in South Africa, in the Black Consciousness Movement led by Steve Biko, a South African student leader, who was also influenced by Négritude.

After the founding of the OAU there were continuing attempts to strengthen links between the diaspora and Africa and between governments and NGOs in an era when Pan-Africanism appeared to be mainly concerned with the liberation and unity of Africa and dominated by African governments. At the Sixth Pan-African Congress, in Tanzania in 1974, critics complained about the hijacking of Pan-Africanism by the unrepresentative member governments of the OAU. A key figure at the congress was the well-known Guyanese historian and activist Walter Rodney, who spoke for many when he asserted that "the OAU does far more to frustrate rather than to realize the concept of African unity." In his remarks before the congress Rodney had urged that the Pan-African movement should again reestablish the orientation it manifested at the time of the Manchester congress.

The years that followed did nothing to minimize the differences that existed among all those claiming adherence to Pan-Africanism. In addition there were diverse cultural manifestations of Pan-Africanism, the music of the Jamaican Bob Marley, the South African Miriam Makeba, and the Nigerian Fela Kuti, for example, serving as unifying factors. Such cultural manifestations had long existed and included the two Conferences of Negro Writers and Artists, held in Paris and Rome in 1956 and 1959, respectively, and the World Festivals of African Arts and Culture held in Senegal and Nigeria in 1966 and 1976. New intellectual currents, such as Afrocentrism, that emerged at the end of the twentieth century only contributed to the diversity of opinions but did not prevent the convening of a seventh Pan-African congress, in Uganda in 1994, and an eighth, in Ghana in 2015.

In addition to external criticisms of the OAU there was also a recognition from member states that the organization was no longer appropriate for the challenges of the twenty-first century. It was the initiative of the Libyan leader Muammar Gaddafi to convene an extraordinary summit of the OAU in 1999, and from this emerged the Sirte Declaration and a new organization of African states, the African Union (AU). The AU was an attempt at revitalization, since the OAU had become discredited as a "club of dictators," but also to establish a more robust organization in the era of globalization. Gaddafi was the most enthusiastic proponent of Nkrumah's dream of a United States of Africa and of a strong and united continent able to stand up for itself. Although other leaders were more cautious, there was an agreement to expedite the founding of continental institutions such as the Pan-African Parliament. The aims of the AU are much wider than those of the OAU and specifically include accelerating "the political and socio-economic integration of the continent." The AU was officially founded in May 2001, and although it also has many critics, one of its most important acts was to recognize the importance of involving the African diaspora in its activities and deliberations. The problems and challenges confronting Africa and its diaspora remain, and so, too, does a sense of common purpose and aspiration—the basis for Pan-Africanism of the twenty-first century.

ADDITIONAL RESOURCES

Adi, Hakim. *Pan-Africanism and Communism: The Communist International, Africa and the Diaspora, 1919–1939*. Trenton, NJ: Africa World Press, 2013.
African Union. "History of the OAU and the AU." www.au.int/en/history /oau-and-au.
Ewing, Adam. *The Age of Garvey: How a Jamaican Activist Created a Mass Movement and Changed Global Black Politics*. Princeton, NJ: Princeton University Press, 2014.
Festival panafricain d'Alger. Directed by William Klein. ONCIC, 1969.
Sherwood, Marika. *Origins of Pan-Africanism: Henry Sylvester Williams, Africa and the African Diaspora*. New York: Routledge, 2010.

. . .

HAKIM ADI is Professor of the History of Africa and the African Diaspora at the University of Chichester, UK. Hakim has written widely on the history of Pan-Africanism and the African diaspora, including three history books for children. He is the author of *Pan-Africanism and Communism: The Communist International, Africa and the Diaspora, 1919–1939* (Africa World Press, 2013); *West Africans in Britain, 1900–1960: Nationalism, Pan-Africanism and Communism* (with M. Sherwood; Lawrence and Wishart, 1998); *The 1945 Manchester Pan-African Congress Revisited* (New Beacon, 1995); and *Pan-African History: Political Figures from Africa and the Diaspora since 1787* (Routledge, 2003).

Mwalimu Nyerere as a Global Conscience

Chambi Chachage

Abstract: As the first president of Tanzania, Mwalimu Julius Kambarage Nyerere was instrumental in the liberation of the continent of Africa from colonialism. But he also connected that liberation to similar struggles in the African diaspora and between the Global South and Global North. To do so, he championed the formation of a "new economic order" that could reduce the gap between and within rich and poor countries. Thus the socialist policy of *ujamaa*—"familyhood"—that he pursued in his home country was a building block toward the creation and consolidation of a worldwide brotherhood/sisterhood based on equality and dignity.

Keywords: liberation, equality, *uhuru* ("freedom"), unity, *ujamaa* ("familyhood")

> If the blessed Lord had wanted a planet for myself, He would have done it. He could have made a planet for every single individual but He never did it. He put us in community, and we jolly well have to live as part of it. Of course, I'm an individual and a member of a community. And the community has conditions. All the commandments—Thou Shalt Not—are about community ... individuals, yes—but individuals in the community. Individuals, yes—because I myself am an extremely assertive individual. Nobody can doubt my own commitment to my own individualism, but I am still an individual within the community.
>
> —JULIUS NYERERE

INTRODUCTION

When Julius Kambarage Nyerere died on October 14, 1999, the British Broadcasting Corporation (BBC) called him "the conscience of Africa." Fondly called Mwalimu—"the teacher"—in his Swahili-speaking country, where he started as a schoolteacher before deciding to enter politics, Nyerere led the struggle for the independence of Tanganyika from Britain in 1961 and spearheaded its union with Zanzibar in 1964 to form the United Republic of Tanzania. Mwalimu was also one of the leaders of what he referred to as the "crusade for liberation" of southern African frontline states, such as Mozambique and Angola, that were still under colonial rule (until 1975). This mission was accomplished with the ending of white minority rule in Zimbabwe (in 1980), of the occupation in Namibia (in 1990), and of apartheid in South Africa (in 1994). Mwalimu's leadership, however, was not confined just to his country and region. He was a key player in Africa and on the global stage. As such he became a leading thinker and—as a man of action, or "actionist," to borrow Erna Brodber's terminology—an advocate of the Global South vis-à-vis the Global North.

MWALIMU AND GLOBAL AFRICA

As the first president of Tanzania, Nyerere is well remembered for introducing and implementing *ujamaa* ("familyhood") as a philosophy and policy of African socialism and collective self-reliance. Born in the small village of Butiama in 1922, he observed how his extended family cooperated in their daily activities and later on imagined how such an attitude could be extended to the whole nation. However, he also observed that rudimentary technology and visible gender inequality hindered the progress of his peasant community. As early as 1944, when he was a student at Makerere University College in Uganda, Nyerere penned an essay titled "The Freedom of Women." Here was a young man attempting to come up with a way of uplifting his society from the shackles of poverty that primarily stemmed from human inequality.

Ujamaa thus started as an idea that Nyerere outlined during the struggle for independence against the British. However, it was not until 1967 that he managed to translate his ideas into policy through the Arusha Declaration on Socialism and Self-Reliance. Aiming to do away with exploitation and inequality, *ujamaa* attempted to create a society that would work together to create wealth and share it equitably, based on common values such as mutual respect and human dignity. According to Nyerere, to realize such an egalitarian community, the state had to control, on behalf of the people, all common resources.

In his own words, the public, through the government, had to own and manage "such things as: land, forests, minerals; water; oil and electricity, news media; communications; banks; insurance, import and export trade, wholesale trade; iron and steel, machine-tool, arms, motor-car, cement, fertilizer, and textiles industries; and any big factory on which a large section of the people depend for their living, or which provides essential components of other industries; large plantations, and especially those which provide raw materials essential to important industries." For him, letting only a few individuals, especially the wealthy, own these public goods as private properties would continue to ensure that the majority of the people remain in poverty.

Not surprisingly, the enduring legacy of *ujamaa* remains a contentious issue. On the one hand, advocates of the private sector argue that *ujamaa* undermined the very sector they felt was the engine of development. On the other side, critics of capitalism claimed that *ujamaa* helped to reduce the gap between the rich and the poor. Others believed that although *ujamaa* did not bring prosperity to the whole country, it consolidated national unity and identity at a time when many countries were—and continue to be—in turmoil. To them, Tanzania's political stability and social harmony are the primary legacy of Nyerere and *ujamaa*.

For Nyerere, the values of *ujamaa* were inextricably linked to the freedom and unity of Africa and Africans. As such, even though *ujamaa* was developed for, and in the context of, a particular locality, Nyerere envisioned its ideals of equality and solidarity beyond his country. It is instructive to recall that in 1960, two years before he published *Ujamaa: The Basis of African Socialism*, Nyerere was invited to give a talk, titled "Africa's Place in the World," at a symposium on Africa at Wellesley College. After observing the apparent conflict between the rights of the individual and the rights of the state, he asserted that, in this sense, Africa was fortunate in that it still had a form of social organization that could also fundamentally solve that conflict globally.

It is this form—in which the rights of the individual are balanced with the rights and welfare of the society as embodied in the rights and welfare of his/her fellow members of the community—that he saw as the building block of a global Africa that was rising from the clutches of colonialism. The Africa of "our own dreams" that "we must create" and "bequeath to posterity," he thus stressed, "must be an Africa that the outside world will look at and say: 'Here is a continent which has truly free human beings.'" And so exiles from other countries arrived in droves. As the famed song "Tanzania Tanzania" puts it, "the castaways" were always welcome.

Nyerere's conception of what Africa is and what Africans are was broad enough to transcend the color line. Although he agreed with the motto Africa for Africans, Nyerere believed in unity in diversity. "A united Africa," he wrote in 1961 to a magazine published by a whites-only secondary school in the then-apartheid South Africa, "does not mean uniformity." As he explained: "Because whether or not Africa even becomes united, whether or not we manage to overcome the present poverty in our continent—both of which I believe will happen—there is one thing which is quite certain. Africa will belong to Africans. I believe that this word 'Africans' can include all those who have made their home in the continent, black, brown, or white. I think this is what the majority of the people now want. Yet it can only happen if people stand as individual citizens, asking only for rights which can be accorded to all other individuals. This means forgetting colour, or race, and remembering humanity." Thus for him, men and women are, first and foremost, humans.

An early witness of this postracial state of affairs was Nelson Mandela. When Mandela arrived in Tanzania soon after its independence in 1961 to seek Nyerere's support for the armed struggle in South Africa, he remarked: "For the first time in my life I was a free man. Though I was a fugitive and wanted in my own land, I felt the burden of oppression lifting from my shoulders. Everywhere I went in Tanganyika, my skin colour was automatically accepted rather than instantly reviled. I was being judged for the first time not by the colour of my skin but by the measure of my mind and character. Although I was often homesick during my travels, I nevertheless felt as though I were home for the first time." Later, in the wake of civil wars and genocides, refugees from Rwanda, Burundi, and Somalia must have had the same feelings when Tanzania sheltered them and, in some cases, granted them citizenship.

Nyerere put his ideas on race into practice. One only has to take a glance at the composition of his first ministerial cabinet in 1961. It included, among others, Amir Jamal, a Tanzanian of Asian/Indian origin; and Derek Bryceson, a Tanzanian of European/British origin. Given that Tanzania no longer has ministers of European or Asian origin, one could easily assume that Nyerere did this in the wake of independence only to contain the then-simmering racial tensions. But he continued this practice into the 1970s, as evidenced by the appointment of Leader Stirling (a British citizen) and Al Noor Kassum (of Asian descent) as ministers. Moreover, he signed an inclusive bill that ensured that race was not a criterion for citizenship.

Some have claimed that Nyerere's policy of *ujamaa* led to a large exodus of people of Asian descent, especially after his government passed the Acquisition of Buildings Act in 1971. But the law also affected relatively wealthy Tanzanians of African descent. Its main aim was simply to reduce the gap between the rich and the poor that was exacerbated by rent and speculation in the housing sector. Many Tanzanians of Asian origin thus stayed. In contrast, Idi Amin, the then president of Uganda, expelled them. In line with his ethos, Nyerere denounced that approach: "Physically what do you do to such people? If you can give them thirty days to get out—or any other period—what do you do when it is expired? Where are they supposed to go—to the moon?" In some ways, Nyerere was already anticipating a postracial—and indeed postnational—world in his own worldview. For him, lives—whether African or not, black or not—mattered.

MWALIMU AND THE GLOBAL SOUTH

By the dawn of the so-called lost decade in 1980 it was clear that Nyerere's country—Tanzania—and his version of African socialism—*ujamaa*—were in a crisis. So were other African countries, whether they were pursuing socialist or capitalist policies. The problems, it seemed, were not simply internal. They were also external.

These problems also faced most of the countries in what is known as the Global South. Simply put, politically, this is a symbolic area that encompasses the majority of former colonized countries in Africa, Asia, and South America. It is defined in relation to the Global North, which is mostly composed of former colonizing countries in Europe and North America. Since colonial relations continued in different exploitative forms after independence, the Global North continued to benefit from human and natural resources from—and at the expense of—the Global South.

In the 1970s Nyerere intensified his engagement in global affairs in an attempt to restructure the unequal international economic order. For him, the solution to inequality had to involve both South/North halves or divides. So he crisscrossed the globe, attempting to redress global capitalist relations.

Thus in 1974, a year after his country started to face severe economic crises due to external forces such as the rise in oil, capital-imports, and food prices as well as internal forces such as droughts and involuntary relocations to *ujamaa* "development villages," he visited a number of countries in the Caribbean. His message was "A New World Economic Order." On September 13, in Georgetown, Guyana, he inaugurated the Non-Alignment International Program of Cooperation, with a "Trade, Industry and Transport" theme.

Among other things, he argued that the so-called Third World nations must act together, "like a trade union of the poor, in negotiations with the rest of the world." He believed that the existing world economy worked in favor of "developed countries: hence they preferred it to continue unchanged." Yet the optimist—and indeed the strategist—in him believed, almost naively, that those "First World nations" could "absorb and adapt to changes on the margin, and they will do so if they believe that this will safeguard their long-term interest." In this regard, he supported a coalition of developing countries known as the Group of 77 that was working out a joint strategy before each United Nations Conference on Trade and Development (UNCTAD) with the hope that, in their unity, "Third World countries" would reform the unequal structure.

He then headed to Kingston, Jamaica, where he commended the "united stand" that had been taken by the forty-four "countries of the Caribbean, the Pacific, and Africa, in the negotiations with the European Economic Community." For "the first time," Nyerere affirmed, our "nations have not been pygmies, begging concession from giants," and concluded that "we have been real negotiators." He reiterated this optimism a few days later in Cuba by asserting that those nations were, then, recognizing such "correct answers" on economic freedom. His "idealism," however, was to soon fade.

As the economic crisis intensified, Nyerere became more and more vocal. One gets a glimpse of this in his animated speech at the Royal Commonwealth Society in London on November 21, 1975. In the speech, aptly entitled "The Economic Challenge—Dialogue or Confrontation," he claimed that the situation in Tanzania was so bad that Tanzania now belonged in the Fourth World, not the Third World. Asserting that he was not there to plead for aid for his country, Nyerere strongly critiqued the whole concept of aid, demanding change. "As far as we are concerned," he continued, the "only question at issue is whether the change is made by dialogue or through confrontation." A year later, in India, he called for a "new economic order" when receiving the Nehru Award for International Understanding. He stated, long before the popularization of globalization, that "[n]ever in history has the human race been so aware of its one-ness." The world is so interconnected, he argued, that a rise in the price of oil affects a person in India as well as Tanzania, just as a failure of the wheat crop in the United States impacts all countries. Thus, no country could afford to ignore any other country in the worldwide web of interdependency. "Even when a small country like Tanzania begins to process its own agricultural products," Nyerere explained, "nations as far apart as

India, Britain and Jamaica . . . find that some of their citizens lose their normal jobs." It is thus ironic that in 2013, when Nyerere was no longer in the picture, Tanzania banned the export of tanzanite, a gem that is found only within its borders, and India had to request the lifting of the ban because it affected those of its citizens who depend on processing it.

Nyerere's relationship with the financial face of the global economic order reached its nadir in 1980. When did the International Monetary Fund (IMF) "become the International Ministry of Finance?" he asked. Tanzania was experiencing high inflation and a shortage of commodities. Its balance of payments was in a dire deficit, not least because of—though it predated—the war to oust Idi Amin, support for the liberation struggles in southern Africa, and yet another hike in the global price of oil. Shrewdly, the IMF laid down conditions for using its fund facilities. Furiously, Nyerere initially refused: "Tanzania is not prepared to devalue its currency, just because this is a traditional 'Free Market' solution to everything, regardless of the merits of our position. It is not prepared to surrender its right to restrict imports, by measures designed to ensure that we import quinine rather than cosmetics, or buses rather than private cars for the elite. My government is not prepared to give up on our national endeavour to provide primary education for every child, basic medicine and some clean water for all our people." After stepping down voluntarily from the presidency in 1985, he stood by, reluctantly and critically, as the IMF and the World Bank spearheaded structural adjustment programs (SAPs), especially in the first years of the tenure of his successor, Ali Hassan Mwinyi. In undoing *ujamaa,* SAPs made Tanzania, in the words of a Tanzanian report, "Liberalize, Marketize, and Privatize (LIMP)."

Reminiscing about that showdown, Nyerere recalled an ironic encounter in Washington, D.C., with one of the Bretton Woods institutions in 1997: "At the World Bank the first question they asked me was 'how did you fail?' I responded that we took over a country with 85 per cent of its adult population illiterate. The British ruled us for 43 years. When they left, there were 2 trained engineers and 12 doctors. This is the country we inherited. When I stepped down there was 91 percent literacy and nearly every child was in school. We trained thousands of engineers and doctors and teachers." He then settled the scores with them: "In 1988 Tanzania's per-capita income was $280. Now, in 1998, it is $140. So I asked the World Bank people what went wrong. Because for the last ten years Tanzania has been signing on the dotted line and doing everything the IMF and the World Bank wanted. Enrolment in school has plummeted to 63 per cent and conditions in health and other social services have deteriorated. I asked them again: 'what went wrong?' These people just sat there looking at me. Then they asked what could they do? I told them have some humility. Humility—they are so arrogant!" Finally, Nyerere and *ujamaa* seemed vindicated.

Mwalimu had retired from the presidency of Tanzania but was not tired of furthering his principles in what he referred to as the Economic South. At the Non-Alignment Movement (NAM) meeting in 1986, he was nominated to chair the South Commission, which he chaired from 1987 to 1990, when it became the South Centre. "The Commission's search for a successful programme for the South-South cooperation and solidarity," he reiterated, "is thus essential for any possibility for a restructuring of North-South nations." Hence he crisscrossed and transcended the South/North divide, attempting to influence the leaders of the world to bridge it, as the following titles of his speeches highlight: "One Humanity on One Planet," "The World Is One; But Not One," "The Challenge to the South—and the North," "The South and the North Together." When submitting his report on the outcome of the commission's search, a 287-page document, he accordingly stressed that nothing in it was "'anti-North'"—that it was "simply 'pro-South.'" What remains to be seen is a full implementation to undo global inequality.

CONCLUSION

As I watched the South African Broadcasting Corporation (SABC) air the procession of Mwalimu Nyerere's funeral in 1999, I wondered how much he meant to Africans. The then president of the Republic of South Africa, Thabo Mbeki, referred to him as "one of the wise sons of Africa who guided our journey towards placing Africa in her rightful place in the world." Fittingly, he ordered their flag to fly at half-mast. Why, some seemed to query sarcastically, honor a leader from a faraway country whose policy of *ujamaa* is said to have disastrously failed to uplift his people from poverty?

It is precisely such questions that I have tried to address from Nyerere's vantage point. Here was a leader who genuinely cared, not only for people in his home country, but also for those in other countries who were under the yoke of an unequal global economic system. For him, the national or global economy ought to be, first and foremost, for—and about—our humanity rather than the other way around.

When one looks at the current crises that have led to Occupy movements in the United States against the 1 percent who are apparently controlling the global wealth, to Fees Must Fall protests in South African universities, and to the refugee crisis in Europe, it is tempting to conclude that Nyerere was far ahead of his time. Who could have thought, for instance, that in 2015 the people of Greece would attempt, through referenda, to stand up against the kind of austerity measures that Nyerere defied—in defense of social provision—to the ridicule of the international financial institutions in 1985? One can only wonder who was actually listening when Mwalimu uttered these words in 1975 in London, one of the global financial capitals: "At the present, the world is moving towards a confrontation between the rich and the poor which will do damage to both. I want there to be a dialogue. But dialogue depends upon mutual understanding, and upon action beginning now." That is the voice of—indeed the need for—a "global conscience."

ADDITIONAL RESOURCES

Chachage, Chambi, and Annar Cassam, eds. *Africa's Liberation: The Legacy of Nyerere*. Nairobi: Pambazuka Press, 2010.

Legum, Colin, and G. R. V. Mmari, eds. *Mwalimu: The Influence of Nyerere*. London: James Currey, 1995.

Mazrui, Ali. A., and Lindah L. Mhando. *Julius Nyerere, Africa's Titan on a Global Stage: Perspectives from Arusha to Obama*. Durham, NC: Carolina Academic Press, 2013.

Mwalimu Nyerere Foundation. *Freedom, Non Alignment and South-South Cooperation: A Selection from Speeches, 1974–1999*. Dar es Salaam: Oxford University Press, 2011.

. . .

CHAMBI CHACHAGE is a PhD candidate in African Studies/History at Harvard University. He is also the coeditor of *Africa's Liberation: The Legacy of Nyerere* (Pambazuka Press, 2010), a blogger at *Udadisi: Rethinking in Action,* and a political commentator in print and electronic media such as *Pambazuka News, African Arguments,* and the *Citizen.*

Power, Conflict, and Justice in Africa

AN UNCERTAIN MARCH

Stephen Mogaka and Stephen Ndegwa

Abstract: The African continent has come a long way. In the 1990s, following the end of the Cold War, the continent experienced an outbreak of conflicts and other crises. Developments at the time served as validation of the 'Afro-pessimism' discourse on the continent's prospects. However, the continent has turned a corner in the last decade, marked by significant progress in political inclusion, conflict management and mitigation, and the rule of law. The outcome of these processes has been a reduction in conflicts and related fatalities, as well as economic growth. Challenges remain, but the overall momentum is one of progress primarily driven by indigenous efforts and processes, emphasizing Africans' own agency in this transformation. Africans themselves have seized upon the opportunity to transform the continent for the better.

Keywords: Africa, conflict, ICC (International Criminal Court), justice, African Union

THE 1990S WERE THE AGE of Afro-pessimism. Several commentators and media outlets lined up to portray the African continent as the epicenter of human suffering, facing a range of challenges such as state collapse, poor governance, disease outbreaks, and conflicts. The consensus among most of these commentators was that Africa faced a bleak future and lacked the agency to resolve most of the challenges it faced, thus necessitating international intervention. We believe, however, that the African continent has largely confounded such gloomy predictions. Though challenges remain, remarkable progress has been made in the last decade particularly in the areas of political inclusion, conflict management, and the promotion of the rule of law. Africans themselves have been at the forefront of transforming the continent for the better. In the process, indigenous initiatives and processes have been appropriated to address modern challenges.

The pessimism about Africa was epitomized at the time by the influential *Economist* magazine. The issue of May 13, 2000, was headlined "The Hopeless Continent," accompanied by a map of the African continent that contained a photograph of a young African man, presumably a rebel fighter, holding a rocket-propelled grenade. The magazine described the continent's various problems: "Floods in Mozambique; threats of famine in Ethiopia (again); mass murder in Uganda; the implosion of Sierra Leone; and a string of wars across the continent. The new millennium has brought more disaster than hope to Africa. Worse, the few candles of hope are flickering weakly." The manner in which the magazine framed the African continent provoked outrage, controversy, and debate within and outside the continent. Fast-forward to December 3–9, 2011: the magazine's cover read "Africa Rising." Below those words was a picture of a child holding a string attached to a fluttering multicolored kite in the shape of the African continent. The issue detailed the impressive economic growth achieved across most of the continent. In particular, the magazine noted that "[s]ince *The Economist* regrettably labelled Africa 'the hopeless continent' a decade ago, a profound change has taken hold."

In the last five years a significant amount of scholarly writing on Africa has pointed to the general decline of wars and conflicts. Besides the decline in conflict, Africa has turned around many aspects of its political and economic life, and several of the trends simultaneously reflect and influence trends elsewhere. Africa is both incredibly integrated into the global dynamics and integral to them. This is true in the contemporary dynamics of conflicts, conflict prevention, the management of contentious politics, and justice between citizens and states.

THE ESTABLISHMENT OF CONFLICT EARLY WARNING SYSTEMS

Since 2000 there has been an overall decline in conflicts in Africa despite a spike in conflict after 2010. The decline in conventional conflicts has been attributed to factors such as the end of the Cold War, war fatigue, and the improvement in Africa's conflict-prevention and conflict -resolution mechanisms. A keen examination of the data from sources such as the Armed Conflict Location and Event Data Project (ACLED) reveals that the situation is a bit more complex. While interstate and civil wars have declined, other forms of political violence remain a source of concern. A key trend is the decline in the role played by conventional rebel groups. The most important conflict actors in Africa today are political militias. According to ACLED, "political militias" are entities that are allied with the political elite and are established with the aim of serving a political objective through the use of violence. The difference between a conventional rebel group and a political militia is the objectives of each. The rebel group seeks to overthrow the government, while the political militia seeks only to further a political goal that does not include the overthrow of the government.

The decline of conflict in Africa has not been entirely accidental, nor has it been largely exogenously driven. Regional and continental bodies have especially invested in mechanisms to predict and respond to early signals of conflict. The first basic structures for early warning were established under the now-defunct Organisation of African Unity (OAU) in 1998. But the structures that emerged were undeveloped and underfunded. In 2002 the OAU's successor organization, the African Union (AU), announced plans for its Continental Early Warning System (CEWS). Despite initial delays in setting up the system, significant progress has been made in recent years in the realization of key parts of the system.

Meanwhile, various regional organizations such as the Economic Community of West African States (ECOWAS), the Southern African Development Community (SADC), and the Intergovernmental Authority on Development (IGAD) have also established their own early warning mechanisms. These organizations, in turn, provide information to the African Union's CEWS.

One of the most elaborate systems in place is the ECOWAS Early Warning and Response Network (ECOWARN). ECOWARN has received praise for the manner in which it has incorporated civil-society organizations into the system. Civil-society monitors from the West Africa Network for Peacebuilding (WANEP) play an important role in providing on-the-ground information on the latest conflict dynamics.

Conflict early warning systems have also been adopted at the national level, where they have been used to prevent and minimize conflict. In Kenya important lessons were learned during and after the 2007–8 postelection violence. A group of bloggers came together to establish the Ushahidi (Swahili for "testimony") platform, which mapped the violence in different parts of the country from crowd-sourced information. Ushahidi, an open platform, has subsequently been used across the world to map the dynamics of various threats, including pandemics and natural disasters. In 2010 the Uwiano (Swahili for "cohesion") platform was launched and used during a referendum for a new constitution in Kenya. The Uwiano platform was set up jointly by the government, UNDP (United Nations Development Programme), and civil-society actors to collect information about potential flashpoints. Trained peace monitors were then dispatched to areas where conflict was seen as likely to emerge based on the information. One estimate suggests that 122 incidents of potential violence were prevented by the Uwiano platform.

Despite progress in the establishment of regional and continental early warning systems, challenges remain. A key challenge for some of the systems is funding, which in turn is linked to limitations in human-resources capability. In particular, the African Union's CEWS has grappled with challenges related to the recruitment of experts with relevant country knowledge as well as thematic expertise on some of the key issues related to conflicts. A second challenge has been the lack of coordination between regional systems and the continental system.

THE STRENGTHENING OF AFRICA'S MEDIATION CAPACITIES

In a continent where effective mediation in conflict has historically been lacking, wars have continued for decades (forty years for the civil war in Sudan) or sputtered in repeated cycles of violence (as in the conflicts in the Congo/Zaire, Somalia, and the western Sahara). A major challenge in resolving conflicts has been the limited capacity of mediators to effectively and skillfully mediate and sponsor credible commitments between warring parties. In a surprising admission, a Tanzanian diplomat who facilitated the Arusha talks before the 1994 Rwandan genocide observed that his team of mediators had lacked the understanding and knowhow to conduct the talks. The failure of mediation initiatives often resulted in inconclusive peace agreements that over time resulted in renewed conflicts in such countries as the Democratic Republic of the Congo (DRC) and Burundi.

The failure in mediation initiatives in the past was attributed to a number of factors. A key factor was the lack of the institutionalization of conflict mediation. Mediation was typically undertaken by heads of state, many of whom had a limited grasp of mediation and were not considered entirely neutral. The situation has changed over the years. First, the African Union and several regional organizations institutionalized conflict mediation not only by establishing standing mechanisms staffed by professionals but also by utilizing respected statesmen such as former presidents Olusegun Obasanjo, Jerry Rawlings, and Thabo Mbeki as well as prominent personalities such as Nobel laureate Desmond Tutu. The AU established the Panel of the Wise as a key pillar of the African peace and security architecture. ECOWAS established the Council of the Wise, a group of renowned individuals (mostly of national or regional repute or local jurists) who can be called upon to assist in the mediation of a conflict. Similar efforts to institutionalize mediation have been embraced elsewhere in Africa. The lessons and experiences from the past can better inform future initiatives. Furthermore, the institutionalization of conflict mediation through regional and continental bodies has arguably reduced conflict by bringing coordinated pressure to bear on conflict actors.

Second, there is greater recognition that mediation is a skill and an art, and that training for mediators can make them more effective. At the level of both the AU and regional organizations, a number of initiatives have been launched that provide training and exchange of knowledge about mediation. Third, the AU and the various regional organizations have shown a new willingness to experiment with the choice of mediators. This flexibility reflects a welcome tendency to look at each conflict carefully before choosing the right mediator. Depending on the conflict, incumbent or former heads of state and prominent individuals have been chosen as mediators. Fourth, institutions established to carry out mediation, such as the Panel of the Wise, have become important actors for fostering discussion and knowledge creation on various issues having to do with conflict in Africa. In 2008, the Panel of the Wise organized an international workshop on election-related violence that proposed recommendations on what the panel could do before and after elections.

COALITION GOVERNMENTS

An emergent mechanism for establishing credible commitment in managing power and conflict in Africa is the creation of governments of national unity to manage the exclusionary politics that often fuel violence. Unlike the traditional unity government that arises in parliamentary systems when no party wins a majority to form a government on its own, the coalition governments in the last decade in Africa have been formed explicitly as a transitory solution following conflict, often as a part of a peace agreement or as a mechanism to hold the country together following contentious electoral outcomes.

The South African government of national unity, following the fall of apartheid that transformed the country to a democracy, was an early and iconic example. While the South African experience was the most successful—measured by ushering in a new constitution and democratic government and avoiding a predicted conflict—it was also short-lived by design and limited despite its ambitious goals. Less impressive but still credible examples of coalition governments elsewhere on the continent include the Sudan and South Sudan national unity government as part of the Comprehensive Peace Agreement, and the Rwanda and Burundi governments following periods of conflict. These transitional arrangements hark back to several experiments to stitch together broad-based democratic governments following independence, often under the tutelage of the departing colonial power—in Zambia and Kenya in 1962–63 and, as late as 1980, in Zimbabwe. Mediated by departing colonial powers and foisted on an unengaged but ethnically aligned citizenry, these early efforts did not last long.

By contrast, the recent ones have been orchestrated by national elites mediated by international or African institutions and mandated to not only govern collaboratively for a term but also usher in new constitutional arrangements to provide for institutionalized management of the deep divisions. This represents the second variant of coalition government, one that is intended to govern fully in a shared manner. Success is not guaranteed; but neither is failure preordained. Both Kenya and Zimbabwe returned to a unity-government formula to avoid elections-related collapse with better success (if measured by the survival of the coalition for at least one full electoral term). There is debate on how successful these kinds of governments have been in assuring good governance or good economic management, but data indicates that in terms of peace, these power-sharing formulas have been successful. In both the Kenyan and Zimbabwean cases, it is clear that the coalition-government model was an essential implement for stopping the violent political crises that had arisen following flawed presidential elections. In Sudan, the coalition government between the northern elites and the southern rebel movements provided a safe space to navigate the intricate steps to a peaceful secession of the south, including the final negotiations of thorny boundary issues in the oil-rich borderlands. Indeed, a study of thirty-eight such cases, of which fifteen were African, found that such arrangements did contribute to peace—defined as avoidance of full-scale violence. Others have been less successful—for instance, the coalition government of postgenocide Rwanda, which became an instrument of consolidation; or the DRC, which was underlain by a coalition of regional fiefs that could and did easily break off, leaving the country in perpetual violence and with a weak central government.

This range of outcomes is reflective of the fate of these kinds of coalition governments in the global context, especially as a mechanism for managing conflict. For instance, in the case of Iraq and Afghanistan, the two countries reflect the experience of Kenya and Zimbabwe, in which a government of national unity is an outcome of a negotiated exit from a spiral into violence but remains deeply divided rather than conclusive. Yemen, on the other hand, parallels the collapse of a unity government very much along the lines of the governments of Burundi and Rwanda, with a similarly catastrophic collapse of the state. Beyond these examples, for several states riven by deep ethnic division, a coalition government is often proffered as an alternative to a predicted decline into political chaos (e.g., Afghanistan, Fiji, and Papua New Guinea). The rising literature on national unity governments, mostly drawn from African examples, offers lessons that would be universally useful. However, the judgment of the success or failure of these should not be based on the robustness of governance that ensues—and that often reenacts the original divisions—but rather on the peace holding.

JUSTICE AND THE ACCOUNTABILITY OF STATE ELITES

In addition to giving birth to new ways of managing conflict around how power is acquired, the last two decades in Africa have produced significant change in how state elites are held to account for excesses while in power. An enduring image of African politics since the independence era was the impunity of leaders who visited untold suffering on their people either through economic mismanagement or, more often, through the unleashing of blatant violence. Iconic outsize personalities such as Idi Amin of Uganda (1971–86), "Emperor" Jean-Claude Bokassa of the Central African Republic (1966–79), and rebel leaders such Jonas Savimbi of Angola went to their graves in the safety of exile or, less often, summarily executed without a public reckoning. Since the early 1990s an important departure from such impunity has been the notable rise of juridical justice.

Reflective of how integrated into the world African politics remains, this change has been driven by internal and external factors and has had measurable impact on global discourse on the accountability of political leaders for acts carried out in the name of sovereignty or the immunity of the sovereign. First, the democratic movements that have liberalized politics since 1990 insisted on accountability writ large and rejuvenated judiciaries to become conduits for pressing accountability of executives. Second, globally, the rise of the International Criminal Court (ICC)—though that institution remains contentious—has provided a sharp tool to deal with the violent excesses of incumbents and rebels. Regionally, local or regional tribunals, some drawing from UN mandates but others invoking "universal jurisdiction," have prosecuted dictators for the abuses that occurred while they were in office.

There are three significant trends that are redefining accountability in the exercise of political power in Africa. First is the ubiquitous ICC, which has indicted several prominent African individuals—most notably, Sudanese president Omar Bashir, who was the first sitting president indicted by the court. In 2011, the court summoned prominent Kenyan political leaders, including Uhuru Kenyatta, who in 2013 went on to become president. African countries freely supported and endorsed the ICC, even as several global powers such as the United States and Russia refused to ratify its writ over their citizens. Africa plays an important role in the ICC. The African continent provides the largest delegation of countries at the ICC, with thirty-four states. Africa also supplies four of the court's eighteen judges, and both the chief prosecutor and the vice president of the court are Africans. While the ICC has investigated different situations across the globe, it has to date issued indictments only to personalities from the African continent, thus raising accusations of political and racial bias. However, in each country where the indictments have been meted out, the citizenry is not uniformly opposed, and in fact some see the ICC as an important implement to force accountability where local institutions fail. In Kenya, for instance, the court summoned individuals to appear before it only after the local process to investigate the postelection violence of 2007–8 was stymied in parliament.

If one looks past the controversy of the evenhandedness of indictments (e.g., in spite of allegations of war crimes and crimes against humanity in

Syria and Sri Lanka, the court has yet to make investigations or indictments), the African experience has done more to legitimize the ICC than the experience of any other region. The voluntary attendance at trial by the sitting president and deputy president of Kenya and the handover of the former president of Côte d'Ivoire for trial have done much to solidify the reputation of the ICC as a recognized international body to address serious crimes and to signal the importance these political systems give to seeking internationally sanctioned justice even for incumbent leaders. This effect overshadows the media circus—ultimately insubstantial—around the perennial refusal of signatory countries to arrest the indicted President Bashir of Sudan or the Libyan authorities' refusal to hand over former Gadhafi officials for trial in favor of national prosecution. Both of these are important in the discourse of establishing credibility for the notion of an international interest for justice within other sovereign nations: both escapes are based not on counterclaims of freedom from accountability but rather on a preference (perhaps spurious at times) that national institutions carry out the trials.

A second effort to redefine accountability has been the international tribunals set up under UN mandates but locally or regionally executed, such as the Rwanda Tribunal following the Rwandan genocide and the Special Court for Sierra Leone, which focused on crimes committed during the Sierra Leonean civil war. Both of these have succeeded in bringing to trial dozens of actors, including key leaders, who as part of incumbent governments or antigovernment forces during civil wars committed indiscriminate violence against civilians—for example, the arrest and prosecution of former Liberian president Charles Taylor in Nigeria, and of several *génocidaires* from the Rwandan civil war. An important extension of these tribunals is the initiative by some African governments—in part as a way to avoid the ICC—to pursue the prosecution of former dictators under the claim of "universal standing." Exercised at the global level, this principle undergirds the ICC. Outside immediate war victories, the last decade has seen the most rigorous exercise of this principle, with Africa entering this fray for the first time in its history. The fact that the Chadian case is ineligible for ICC action (the ICC can act only against crimes occurring after 2002) did not deter the Senegalese state from pursuing the case. Whether successful or not, this has important implications for justice in Africa. First, it establishes an important principle: that the power of leaders is not unrestrained or unaccountable. Second, for deposed African leaders who rest in exile in comfort thanks to friendly leaders (e.g., Mengistu Haile Mariam in Zimbabwe), it indicates an unlimited exposure should the regime under which they shelter be succeeded by another.

Finally, a third strand is the local tribunals or court actions that variously assert the right of citizens and the sovereign, subsequent to the ancien régime, to prosecute the mistakes of the past. This includes prosecution for abuse of office, prosecution for violence, or claims against illegal actions. Thus, former Zambian presidents Frederick Chiluba and Rupiah Banda were both prosecuted (and acquitted) for stealing millions of dollars while in office. Other examples include the trials of former president Kamuzu Banda of Malawi for conspiracy of murder, and of Simone Gbabgo, the wife of the ex-Ivorian president, who was jailed for the role she played in the 2010–11 postelection violence for which her husband is to stand trial at the ICC. Interestingly, few presidents from the single-party eras—themselves perpetrators of vast corruption and sometimes violence—have been touched by these recent assertions of legal accountability, which seem to affect mostly the leaders who ascended to power under democratic elections.

Spotty in their application, often regarded as victor justice or a Western-backed conspiracy against African leaders, do these trends in justice in African politics amount to much? The answer must be yes. Each of these movements contributes to Africa's own attempts to reset expectations of the proper exercise of political power, especially with regard to the use of violence and, less emphatically, to the use of state resources for personal or narrow political gain. Internationally, they contribute to a necessary discourse of deterrence; nationally, they revise expectations of accountability to comport with the legal foundations of a democratic politics. But similar reckonings elsewhere (Central America, Cambodia) have shown that these are not straightforward and quickly concluded events but slow, often painful processes with fits and starts and a significant cost to the national psyche and political potency. While justice is not guaranteed, the process is an important step in the emerging institutionalization of just politics.

CONCLUSION

African countries have witnessed remarkable economic growth in the last decade. Underpinning such growth have been the positive developments across issues such as political inclusion; conflict management and prevention; and governance and rule of law. Notwithstanding the role of external actors in these developments, the role of indigenous processes has been very important. Africa has become a mover of its destiny on a whole range of issues. Increasingly, the role of the international community has become less one of launching initiatives on the continent than one of supporting programs launched by Africans themselves. Civil-society actors have played an important role in shaping the processes at both national and regional levels. As Africa responds to its various challenges, it has had to innovate. In a sign of the times, the March 2, 2013, issue of the *Economist* offered a special report on Africa entitled "A Hopeful Continent." Among the themes addressed in the report were the decline in conflict across the continent, the rise of institutional government, the increase in foreign investment, and expanding economies.

NOTE

The views expressed in this chapter are of the authors as independent scholars and do not reflect the views of the World Bank Group or its board of directors

ADDITIONAL RESOURCES

African Union. "Prevention Is Better Than Cure." Conflict Prevention and Early Warning Division, Peace and Security Department, 2015. https://www.youtube.com/watch?v=9t2PwDBMf1Q.
AU Panel of the Wise. "Peace, Justice, and Reconciliation in Africa: Opportunities and Challenges in the Fight against Impunity." International Peace Institute, 2013. www.ipinst.org/2013/01/peace-justice-and-reconciliation-in-africa.
Parler de Rose: Prisonnière de Hissène Habré / Talking about Rose: Prisoner of Hissène Habré. Directed by Isabel Coixet. Miss Wasabi Films, 2015. https://www.youtube.com/watch?v=7DqJiIN2VBs.
Strauss, Scott. "Wars Do End! Changing Patterns of Political Violence in Sub-Saharan Africa." *Africa Affairs* 111, no. 443 (2012): 179–201.

• • •

STEPHEN MOGAKA (MA, University of Nairobi, 2011) is a political scientist with the Fragility, Conflict and Violence Group at the World Bank, Nairobi. He is a coauthor of *The Challenge of Security and Stability in West Africa* (World Bank, 2015).

Stephen Ndegwa (PhD, Indiana University, 1993) is the Operations Manager for the World Bank in Afghanistan. He was a lead author of the *World Development Report on Conflict, Security and Development* (World Bank, 2011). Before joining the World Bank he was Associate Professor of Government at the College of William and Mary and the author or editor of several books and articles.

Where Truth, Lies, and Privilege Meet Poverty... What Is Hope?

REFLECTING ON THE GAINS AND PAINS OF SOUTH AFRICA'S TRC

A dialogue between Sarah Malotane Henkeman and Undine Whande

Abstract: Two peace builders in South Africa dialogue as a black woman and a white woman in 2015 to reflect on the efforts and effects of the Truth and Reconciliation Commission after twenty years. They contemplate the experiences—professional, political, and personal—that left them disillusioned with "peacebuilding interventions" while charting a heart-and-soulful way forward for their work.

Keywords: Truth commission, structural violence, transgenerational transmission, peacebuilding/justice, historical trauma

We all lied about the deaths of your sons. I have now come to the TRC to tell the truth. I have sinned on this earth. Will you please forgive me.

> —*paraphrased excerpt of testimony by a black policeman who infiltrated and led seven activists to their death at the hands of police in Gugulethu*

We forgive you, my son.

> —*mother of one of the seven men, during the TRC mediation process*

We have been devastated by the depths of depravity that the process has revealed, especially with regard to the diabolical projects in the Chemical and Biological Warfare Programme. But we have been amazed, indeed exhilarated by the magnanimity and nobility of spirit of those who, instead of being embittered and vengeful, have been willing to forgive those who treated them so horribly badly.

—ARCHBISHOP DESMOND TUTU, *TRC report, 1998*

IN 2014 SOUTH AFRICA CELEBRATED twenty-one years since the first "free" elections—a kind of coming-of-age of the young democracy. The year 2015 brought about a realism that certain realities the republic had been blind to could no longer be ignored in the face of a new generation maturing into new questions and new forms of political and social struggles for justice. This meant picking up some of the threads from where the South African Truth and Reconciliation Commission (TRC) had left off in 1998, when the main operations closed, and from 2005, when it finally ended its lengthy amnesty process.

This past year, 2016, forced us to reexamine the compromise and delicate balance between peace and justice needed in the post-apartheid scenario, and to shift our focus onto questions of justice not served. The question of justice appeared urgent as we surveyed the economic disparity around us. It was a root cause of the structural violence that had been veiled in the "rainbow nation" discourse. Efforts had been made to park questions of redistribution, reparation, and compensation for past harm in favor of a more centralized political reconciliation for decades. Critical tenets are posed now to ensure that the promise of freedom no longer remains just that—a promise—for future generations, especially around socioeconomic rights and needs.

The conversation about "truth" and "reconciliation" you read here started about nineteen years ago, in a back room at the Centre for Conflict Resolution (CCR) and at U Managing Conflict (UMAC), both in South Africa. This was a time when the two partners in this dialogue were mostly swimming along the tide of euphoria and enthusiasm that swept the country after the free and fair elections of 1994: two peace builders who had witnessed and engaged the TRC close up. Sarah was then a full-time employee and a part-time student, the descendant of a mix of colonized, enslaved, and oppressed people— oppressed during her own lifespan until 1994, when she was in her thirties, married, and had two young children. Undine was a twenty-three-year-old white youngster who had engaged in the German anti-apartheid movement and arrived bright-eyed and bushy-tailed from abroad to "see" and take part in the "miracle." Both felt privileged to be part of building a new era. The conversation invites the reader into the journey they traveled, within and alongside the TRC's process over nearly two decades, and shares some of today's concerns and potentials for truth, justice, and peace in South Africa.

Sarah: As a black woman who was raised during apartheid, I feel very strange sitting here now in 2015, discussing the impact of the Truth and Reconciliation

Commission with a white woman activist. It is an experience that is hard to describe, given that we were oppressed by white people. Maybe you and I connect because you were born in Germany, and your life is about working for peace, equality, and social justice, as is mine. How does it feel for you?

Undine: To me it feels like the questions the TRC raised have been my bread and butter as a "memory worker" for so many decades. Probably because of the German experience and having witnessed South Africa's pain from the lens of personal stories, as well as sharing my experiences being myself a child of parents who were war children and never spoke of their deeper experiences, it does not feel strange to speak with you as a black person. But, yes, we are on opposite sides of a spectrum racially and historically. I have been very aware of the contradictions in my own perceptions of such conversation. I feel it sits between wishing we could deconstruct race for real, so it would not have an impact any longer on our relations as humans, or on our children, and then seeing the very racialized environment we live in and the severe consequences of pigmentation levels inherited.

Sarah: Yes, I see the parallels, and then, the composite image that stands out for me about the TRC is one that merges the testimonies I witnessed with my own eyes and other oppressed people's experiences from colonial and apartheid times. These were of course not regarded as "gross violations of human rights," but they were human rights violations of the "routine" and "ordinary" kind. It is with deep sadness that I reflect on the hugs between victims and offenders and realize, with hindsight, that the offenders went back to privilege and the victims mainly back to poverty. This continues as global and national inequality has risen steadily over the years.

Undine: What I recall mostly are the testimonies of the "Gugulethu Seven" mothers at the human rights hearings vis-à-vis their later experiences of being face-to-face with the perpetrators [*referred to in the opening quote*]. The initial gesture of honoring each story and personal memory was striking. Yet later the experience was one of disregard and disillusionment when the amnesty hearings revealed not only the scope of brutality and systematic planning behind violations, but the unapologetic if not denialist stances of the perpetrators. In addition we had the absence of white beneficiaries reflecting publicly on their privilege. This awareness is only beginning to emerge now into the discourse around race relations.

Sarah: I agree with regard to the bigger theme of denial as the shadow side of the "miracle" nation. The documentary *Long Night's Journey into Day* is about the young American woman, Amy Biehl, who was killed in Gugulethu.

The story of the "Gugulethu Seven" is part of that documentary along with the stories of the "Cradock Four," who were killed by police, and the story of the ANC Umkhonto we Sizwe soldier who bombed the Magoos Bar in Durban. I used that documentary while teaching peace building in Norway, so I saw it several times, and many times had to debrief participants and myself afterward! I have often wondered about those perpetrators—specifically, Thapelo Johannes Mbelo, whose first name means "prayer" according to one of the mothers. And in that poignant moment she declared on behalf of all the other mothers, "We forgive you, my son." That still hooks me particularly because during 1996, I managed a project that sought to resolve conflicts between communities and police. This was a difficult process, as the police "force"—the former "strong arm" of the apartheid government and the "enemy" of the oppressed—were in the process of transforming into a "service" for all South Africans. This was hardly a decade after hit-squad units of the police murdered activists who opposed the system of apartheid. The most notorious of these units were the Vlakplaas police, headed by Eugene de Kock, and consisting of apartheid police and "*askaris*" [double agents] who initially fought on the side of the oppressed but later lured activists into police traps and many to their death, as revealed by the TRC. During early democracy the police were demilitarized. However, during 2010 the "service" was again changed to a "force" as crime rates soared. Mainly historically oppressed people are disproportionately overrepresented throughout the criminal-justice system at present. I believe that this is a direct result of society's denial about the uninterrupted role that symbolic, structural, and psychological violence plays in the production of physical forms of violence. It is our task as peace builders to lead the charge in rendering this invisible/ visible structure of violence visible so that violence can be reduced in its structure.

Undine: The Gugulethu Seven were a group of young activists that was infiltrated by so-called *askaris*—black policemen who pretended to be activists. They were supplied with weapons and some training, only to be set up and led into an ambush on March 3, 1986. Attacked by police from several sides, the seven young men were killed. During the TRC hearings—to the shock of the families and all present—it surfaced that the entire operation was devised in order to fund-raise for the police. They needed a police video that would show a successful "anti-terrorist" operation. On this justification the plot to take the lives of the activists was founded. When the police video was shown, one of the daughters of the deceased had a serious breakdown. I recall that an aunt threw a shoe at the video screen, which nearly hit one of the commissioners. The proceedings had to be paused. Emotions ran very high that day. I remember another moment at the hearings: after Thapelo Mbelo had been the one honest enough to divulge how he had worked as an *askari*. He divulged a lot of the actual truth about the case. When we walked out he wanted to enter the lift to go downstairs. As he tried to do so, the entire family of Christopher Piet walked out of the lift. He got in and proceeded to ride down alone. Downstairs, as we followed him in a second round of taking the same lift, I saw him picking up four! guns at the exit, tie them to his belt, and then leave the building. I remember wondering what his life was like at that moment, the levels of fear he must have been experiencing. Yet later he was the one the families felt able to forgive because he shared what happened and what he knew. But that moment of social ostracism stood out as probably a bigger punishment than being locked up.

Sarah: That information about the lift is quite telling: it speaks to a "performance" of forgiveness, but not yet felt then perhaps? I also thought that the one mother, after the "leader mother" chose to forgive him and spoke about God, simply nodded her head because of the social pressure. Thanks for telling what you witnessed; it confirms the "messiness" for me. The business of forgiveness is a process and not an event.

Undine: I recall the stories of people at the Healing of Memories workshops at the time. We came together as groups to tell ordinary personal stories about life under apartheid, as well as speak about now the real-lived consequences—black, white, coloured—all stories were welcome. As you said, the ordinary stories mattered: needing to get off the sidewalk for the "white *baas*" [Afrikaans for "boss"]. We also heard about the extraordinary pain of seeing torturers walk free. Not only did they walk free, they walked free with riches, leaving those they harmed in poverty. There was little restoration, and the sense of an ongoing process of violation.

Sarah: Thanks for mentioning that there was no sense of "restoration" for many whose experiences made up the bulk of the "ordinary," seemingly banal history of uninterrupted violations. I have no doubt that many of the instances of extreme violence we currently experience as "violent crime" have their roots in unresolved historical trauma in the context of ongoing inequality. This intersection is what I am in the process of researching more in depth in relation to other aspects and forms of violence. Many countries replicated South Africa's TRC model; it would be interesting to see which themes arise out of their experiences.

Undine: Forgiveness was experienced as a process of back-and-forth, with many gradations. There is no such thing as "I have forgiven." There seems only a gradual sense of being less severely affected. And there also is a choice to focus on one's own well-being that could be equated with first forgiving oneself by not focusing on the deed anymore, nor on revenge, nor allowing the perpetrator's energy to hook one's own energy.

Sarah: I think it is more useful for us to tell our stories as they are lived in relation to the TRC. That was one "event" that intervened to steer our society toward peace, instead of making the assumption that it was immediate nirvana for the majority of people. Unfortunately, the first beneficiaries of democracy are still mainly white; and the continued victims of inequality remain black. It is this image of the forgiving, openhearted ongoing victim that rips my heart apart. I do not suggest that "nothing was done" after apartheid. I state what I observe, and I am trying to make sense of it. But I struggle in the face of ongoing poverty and privilege. I am also troubled by what appears to be a form of deep denial by "the world" as they look to South Africa as the miracle and Archbishop Tutu's "rainbow nation," as if South Africa is delinked from global inequality and advances. Colonialism, which informed apartheid, was a global economic enterprise, and thus South Africa's problems and successes are also shared by others in the world—"the family of nations."

Undine: The paradox is that white society in SA is very psychologically damaged inside, and it is also not sure where to take that pain. White pain becomes personalized, and there is not really a place for it in the political discourse except owning it as an inherited legacy and stepping into historical responsibility. Having lived here for twenty-two years with German roots, I recognize this "hidden guilt" immediately. It is very familiar from my upbringing; just white society here is not in touch with its own sense of guilt, or seeks to suppress it. This is still a time of telling the story that one is not affected and was not part of it all. I feel there is a real chance here if sentiments of guilt are not silenced but spoken and lived in ways that lead to courageous action, confronting the facts and owning the legacy of the ancestors' deeds.

Sarah: That is an interesting theme, which only white people can take up among themselves. Similarly, there are themes that only we as black people can take up among ourselves. It could be parallel processes that weave in and out of a "third space" where we figure out how to "walk together," not only with hugs and kisses, but with a solid plan to deal with inequality—that is, at the societal *and* interpersonal levels. What would you say the effect of this waxing and waning of interest in the TRC was on yourself, your life's work, and globally?

Undine: I agree with the idea of a "third space" for healing. Early on after 1994 there was amazement that South Africa actually dared confront the horrors of apartheid so directly in the TRC. I felt some excitement that denial was no longer possible, and I was awed by the courage of people to remember and speak. Midway through the process was the start of disillusionment. There was a palpable exhaustion, and many were feeling that the amnesty hearings were overshadowing the process of honoring victims. The process of collecting testimonies was done, but, comparatively, only few people could make it into the hearings. There was the concern about the focus only on gross violations and not the more "ordinary" stories. Mahmood Mamdani pointed out that apartheid's beneficiaries did not need to confront anything because of the focus on gross violations.

In the end, I remember total exhaustion, a sense of having gone to the dark deep side of the human psyche. I concluded the TRC meeting at a place beyond judgment in myself: "Those perpetrators are also me." That could have been my grandparents or my parents. Would I have stepped out and up to oppose if I had been socialized here? What would I have risked?

There was empathy for the survivors and a sense of their lives continuing to be very difficult. This was the failure of the reparations process. Post the TRC process the South African government mostly ignored the report. It was debated in parliament and victims were told by the finance minister that "they performed so well at the TRC, they were aiming for Oscars." This was painful to those who had gone through the difficulty of digging up their pain once again. There was little follow-up with regard to the TRC recommendations. Reparations came late and were paid through an individual reparations process, which meant a lump sum was paid to few. Victims often had no support with creating something sustainable from 30,000 South African Rand (ZAR). Money dried up fast and had no real impact on poverty because of structural challenges manifesting through alcohol abuse, money being diverted away from children and women, and so forth.

What about you? What would you say the effect of this waxing and waning of interest in the TRC was on yourself, your life's work, and globally?

Sarah: At the moment, I feel I cannot allow myself to "die a disillusioned and defeated life." I have made a clear decision that the action research I do for the rest of my life will primarily be directed at imparting skills to oppressed people who work for social justice and the common good. This does not mean I will not work with progressive white practitioners, but I recognize that, initially, separate processes are needed for healing to take place in a third space. For all its flaws, the TRC did "start" the process for some of us to "see," and now we cannot "unsee," as Arundhati Roy states so eloquently. We are duty bound to pass on the skill of "seeing," "hearing," and breaking complicit silence, nationally as well as globally. I cannot see myself other than as part of a "category" (oppressed); so personal ambition as well as monetary gains are secondary and subsumed within a social-justice agenda, to which I am completely devoted.

Undine: After the TRC there was what some referred to as the "memory circus." Those who had been insiders to the TRC got invited and traveled all over the world to share the experience. This led to a kind of external romanticism with the TRC process internationally, while internally we faced avoidance, exhaustion, and disappointment with the process. While we were, to some extent, still advertising the rainbow nation outside at conferences and workshops, a new period of "forgettery" had also set in. No nation can deal with the past publicly 24/7 and attempt do this forever. Yet nothing goes away either; dealing with the past is more like a stream that goes underground for a while until the next generation surfaces it again, which is happening now. My work is with creative healing processes and emphasis on the intergenerational conversation. Through my research I realized how memory is lodged in the body at the cellular level and how it transfers to descendants. I feel no more need to engage in frontline confrontational activism; instead I engage in personal healing work that impacts at a bodily level. I am interested in the subtlety of experience and believe that inner transformations matter. My current work is offering leaders space to reflect on their innermost processes of transformation and affirm their quest for healing.

What South Africa is experiencing with regard to race, class, privilege, and exclusion is global, but it is not confronted in the same way elsewhere. I remain with a sense of a deeper connectedness among South Africans that becomes visible when abroad. Collectives are bound by suffering and historical debt to one another. There is no place to flee from that, even when emigrating to another country. The descendants may have to return and, metaphorically, "pay" ancestral debts, as has been observed in German-Jewish relations.

NOTE

The Gugulethu Seven were Mandla Simon Mxinwa, Zanisile Zenith Mjobo, Zola Alfred Swelani, Godfrey Jabulani Miya, Christopher Piet, Themba Mlifi, and Zabonke John Konile.

. . .

SARAH MALOTANE HENKEMAN is an independent conflict and social justice researcher/practitioner, and a senior staff associate of the Centre of Criminology in the Faculty of Law, University of Cape Town (UCT). Before, during, and after the end of apartheid she worked in the sectors of public interest, human rights, community safety, and conflict resolution. She conducted TRC research and provided facilitation, mediation, training, and research in conflict resolution, restorative justice, and community safety in South Africa. She also facilitated training processes in Ethiopia, Tanzania, and Norway and led evaluation processes in South Africa, Botswana, Kenya, Uganda, Mauritius, and Zimbabwe. For more information, see http://www.criminology.uct.ac.za/dr-sarah-henkeman.

UNDINE WHANDE, born in Germany, has lived and worked continuously in southern Africa since the mid-1990s. She holds a PhD in social anthropology from the University of Cape Town. In the political and social transition in South Africa she worked as a conflict mediator, coach, and facilitator in social-change processes with, among others, the South African Truth and Reconciliation Commission and the Healing of the Memories processes, the Centre for Conflict Resolution, U Managing Conflict, and the Centre for the Study of Violence and Reconciliation (CSVR). She currently works as a dialogue facilitator and systemic leadership coach.

2.6

Commerce, Crime, and Corruption

ILLICIT FINANCIAL FLOWS FROM AFRICA

Masimba Tafirenyika

Abstract: Africa currently loses about US$50 billion every year to illicit finan-
cial flows. A highly complex and deeply entrenched practice of underreporting
profits or diverting funds has thrived over decades, with devastating impact,
while barely making it into the news headlines. Experts have proposed practical measures to curb the practice.

Keywords: finances, crime, corruption, taxes, poverty

AFRICA IS POOR, ALWAYS POOR—or so we hear. Despite its fabulous
wealth in natural resources—agriculture, diamonds, copper and other
minerals—Africa remains barely able to provide sufficiently for its people.
Schools are few, hospitals are understaffed, women die in childbirth, and
education is denied to many girls. All the while, great sums of money are
changing hands and escaping to foreign banks in a fast-moving river of illicit
outflows.

Africa is losing money through exotic illicit outflows, of which 60 to 65
percent are business transactions by respectable multinational firms. Money
obtained through bribery and embezzlement accounts for only 3 percent of
these outflows. Dirty money from drug trafficking and smuggling make up
the rest (30 to 35 percent) of all illicit outflows, says a joint report by the
African Development Bank (AfDB) and Global Financial Integrity, a US
research and advocacy group.

The scale of these lost monies—over US$50 billion annually by some
estimates—tells only half the story. According to the joint report, a highly
complex and deeply entrenched practice of underreporting or diverting funds
has thrived over decades, with devastating impact, while barely making it
into the news headlines. "The illicit hemorrhage of resources from Africa is
about four times Africa's current external debt," says the joint report, *Illicit*

Financial Flows and the Problem of Net Resource Transfers from Africa: 1980–2009.

Another report, commissioned by African finance ministers, reckons that total losses are even higher because of the lack of searchable documents, or documents kept out of the reach of independent regulators or fiscal auditors. Illicit financial flows are monies acquired illegally and transferred elsewhere.

A NEW MODEL OF EXPLOITATION

The illegal movement of money out of Africa has its origins in the era of colonial rule by Europe in the nineteenth and twentieth centuries. During this period, the outright and brutal exploitation of Africa's rich natural resources flourished without restriction. Today, illicit outflows, often with a veneer of legality, have replaced the earlier expropriation of natural resources, usually obtained with military might. Hidden business transactions and the illegal transfer of wealth out of Africa are no longer the domain of colonial governments but are largely the work of multinational corporations. Yet the outcome is the same: illicit financial flows deprive Africa of the resources it desperately needs to finance its own development.

Not surprisingly, experts see a direct link between these outflows and Africa's turn inward in an effort to raise monies for needed development. The continent's annual economic growth has averaged 5 percent over the past decade, thanks to increased stability, a business-friendly environment, and the ease of repatriating profits. But low or negative growth in rich countries has dampened foreign investment, forcing Africa back on its heels, acquiring new debt from private and international sources, often with punishing interest rates.

The prospect of falling incomes and investment shortfalls linked to illegal transfers of money was so alarming that in 2011 African finance ministers urged the United Nations Economic Commission for Africa (UNECA) to establish a high-level panel on the subject. Former South African president Thabo Mbeki chaired the ten-member panel. Its tasks were: (1) to assess the scale and sources of illicit outflows; (2) to understand how these outflows occur in Africa using case studies of six countries—Algeria, Democratic Republic of Congo, Kenya, Liberia, Mozambique, and Nigeria; and (3) to come up with practical, realistic short- and medium-term measures that can be taken by Africa and the rest of the world to confront what is in fact a global challenge to ensure that sufficient resources remain within Africa for its development needs

TRACK IT! STOP IT! GET IT!

From the start, the Mbeki panel faced a daunting task. Data on illicit outflows flows was "scanty, clouded in a mixed mass of information and scattered in disparate locations," warned Charles Goredema, a senior researcher at the South Africa–based Institute for Security Studies, adding that most resistance to sharing data would come from tax-collection agencies and mining departments.

In early 2015 the panel released its long-awaited report, *Illicit Financial Flows: Track It! Stop It! Get It!* This document is a must-read for African government officials and policy makers. It confirms Africa's status as a net "creditor" to the world—that illicit outflows are immense and increasing and that ending them is a political issue. The report identifies large corporations as the major culprits of illicit outflows, followed by organized crime. It concludes that these outflows are to blame for reducing Africa's tax revenues, undermining trade and investment, and worsening poverty. While the report says corrupt practices in Africa and weak governance capacity facilitate illicit outflows, it argues that the problem "should be understood within the context of large corporations having the means to retain the best available professional legal, accountancy, banking, and other expertise to help them perpetuate their aggressive and illegal activities."

The panel's policy recommendations target both African governments and recipients of illicit financial flows. It concedes that although the sources of these outflows are within Africa, the means by which funds are moved involve global players who take advantage of policies adopted outside Africa. The panel calls for African governments to engage with these external actors to ensure that their practices do not facilitate the illicit outflows of funds from Africa.

Conclusions by the Mbeki report corroborate the findings by research and advocacy groups, including Transparency International, Global Financial Integrity, Action Aid Christian Aid, Oxfam, and the Tax Justice Network, which are all on the front lines of the war against illicit financial flows. The extent of such outflows is still under debate, but the figures on Africa range between US$50 billion and US$80 billion per year.

"The absence of unanimity on [the amount lost to illicit outflows] is probably attributable to the fact that the terrain concerned is quite broad, and each organization can only be exposed to a part of it at any given point in time," noted Mr. Goredema, who argues that it is less important to achieve consensus on the scale of illicit outflows than it is to achieve it on the measures to be taken to stem them.

THE THREE C'S OF ILLICIT MONEY: COMMERCE, CRIME, CORRUPTION

How is illicit money moved out of Africa? There are three broad categories: commerce, crime, and corruption. Commercial or trade-related activities—the largest category—consist of questionable financial operations such as tax evasion through international tax havens, secrecy jurisdictions (countries or cities whose laws enable people or entities to keep their financial information secret from other jurisdictions), shell companies, anonymous trust accounts, fake foundations, trade mispricing, and money-laundering practices. A common technique used by corporations to avoid paying taxes is through a practice known as transfer pricing or tax avoidance. Transfer pricing occurs when a multinational decides how much profit to allocate to its subsidiaries operating in different countries, and the tax to be paid to each government.

Under global trade rules, multinationals should pay for products from their subsidiaries at the same price they would expect to pay when buying on the open market. However, corporations circumvent this rule by moving profits to countries with low or no taxes and relocating expenses to high-tax countries, which is effectively tax avoidance (designed to comply with the law, although often ethically questionable), unlike tax evasion, which is illegal. A tax haven is a country or jurisdiction whose tax system is exploited by nonresidents to keep their money to avoid or evade taxes where the money is earned.

"Transfer pricing (really mispricing) is also used to load costs onto countries that offer generous subsidies, especially in extractive industries. It has become a key plank of multinational tax strategies," says the *Economist,* a UK-based weekly. The fact that about three-fifths of global trade is conducted by multinationals demonstrates the scope of the problem.

To illustrate how transfer pricing works and how profits are shifted into a tax haven, the Tax Justice Network, a coalition of groups against tax avoidance and tax havens, provides the following example on its website:

> World Inc., a multinational corporation, grows a crop in Africa, then harvests and processes it and transports and sells the finished product in the United States. It has three subsidiaries: Africa Inc. (in Africa), Haven Inc. (in a zero-tax haven) and USA Inc. (in the US). Africa Inc. sells the produce to Haven Inc. at an artificially low price. So Africa Inc. has artificially low profits—and therefore an artificially low tax bill in Africa. Then Haven Inc. sells the product to USA Inc. at a very high price—almost as high as the final retail price at which USA Inc. sells the processed product. So USA Inc. also has artificially low profits, and an artificially low tax bill in the U.S. But Haven Inc. is different: it has bought cheaply and sold at a very high price, creating very high artificial profits. Yet it is located in a tax haven—so it pays no taxes on those profits. And this is how the tax bill disappears.

The Mbeki report cites an example of aggressive tax avoidance. The case involves a multinational company (name not disclosed) in South Africa that avoided $2 billion in taxes by claiming that a large part of its business was conducted in the United Kingdom and Switzerland, which at that time had lower tax rates than South Africa. The company's headquarters was declared to be in the two European countries. After investigations, South African authorities found that the UK and Swiss subsidiaries/branches had only a handful of low-paid workers with relatively junior responsibilities, and that these offices did not handle any of the commodities in which the company dealt (nor were they legally able to take title to those commodities). The company's customers were often in South Africa, but for each transaction, a paper trail was created that would route the transaction through the Swiss or UK offices to give the impression that these offices were critical to the business. The South African authorities were able to reclaim the tax that was avoided because it was clear that the core of the company's activities were conducted in South Africa.

The Tax Justice Network has found that millions of companies and thousands of thinly capitalized banks, funds, and insurers in tax havens or secrecy jurisdictions are engaged in the same activities as the South African corporation. These institutions provide "facilities that enable people or entities to *escape* (and frequently undermine) the laws, rules, and regulations of jurisdictions *elsewhere,* using secrecy as a prime tool." However, in their public operations, tax havens try to assume a veneer of legitimacy, helped in part by international accounting firms. Reports say almost three-quarters of the five hundred biggest companies in the United States have tax havens in the shape of foreign subsidiaries in countries with low or no taxes. Analysts have accused many of these so-called tax havens of going to great lengths to cooperate with international efforts to stamp out gigantic tax avoidance, but only in ways that mean they can continue with the same practice but in disguise.

"UNCONSCIONABLE ACTS"

The Africa Progress Panel, chaired by former UN secretary-general Kofi Annan, is critical of the current rules on corporate transparency. In its *Africa Progress Report 2013*, Mr. Annan wrote: "It is unconscionable that some companies, often supported by dishonest officials, are using unethical tax avoidance, transfer pricing and anonymous company ownership to maximize their profits while millions of Africans go without adequate nutrition, health and education." The Mbeki report found that illicit outflows from commercial activities suggest unreported wealth and reveal the ways corporations evade or aggressively avoid taxes and dodge customs duties and domestic levies—in many cases with the acquiescence of supposedly reputable international accounting firms that help multinationals to structure complex tax-avoidance schemes.

Criminal activities make up the second-biggest channel for illicit outflows. These include activities that range from "trafficking of people, drugs and arms" to "smuggling, as well as fraud in the financial sector, such as unauthorized or unsecured loans, money laundering, stock market manipulation and outright forgery." In 2011, the UN Office on Drugs and Crime compiled a "study of studies" or meta-analysis on estimating illicit financial flows resulting from drug trafficking and related crimes. Results showed that in 2009, money from global criminal activities amounted to US$2.1 trillion of the world's gross domestic product. The study also revealed that higher profits were generated from crimes committed in poor countries, and the proceeds were laundered abroad. Less than 1 percent of these proceeds were seized or frozen by authorities.

Examples of Illicit Financial Flows
(Source: Global Financial Integrity)

- A drug cartel using trade-based money-laundering techniques to mix legal money from the sale of used cars with illegal money from drug sales;
- An importer using trade misinvoicing to evade customs duties, VAT, or income taxes;
- A corrupt public official using an anonymous shell company to transfer dirty money to a bank account in the United States;
- A human trafficker carrying a briefcase of cash across the border and depositing it in a foreign bank; or
- A terrorist wiring money from the Middle East to an operative in Europe.

Beneficiaries of illicit financial flows argue that because corruption—the third component of illicit outflows—is so common in Africa, its leaders should shoulder most of the blame. Even the Mbeki panelists agreed that corruption in Africa has "facilitated all other aspects of [illicit financial flows]." To be sure, most African countries rate poorly on global anticorruption indices. But the ground is gradually shifting as a handful of African leaders reject unorthodox or illegal past practices.

REPATRIATING STOLEN MONEY

Given the enormity of the problems created by illicit financial flows and their damaging effect on African economies, the question to be asked is, What can be done to track, stop, and get back the more than US$50 billion that Africa is losing every year? While the Mbeki report recognizes the need to arm African governments with the technical capacity to curb illicit outflows, it nevertheless concludes that ending these outflows is a political issue that requires the political will of all governments, particularly those of the recipient or destination countries. It wants recipient countries of illicit outflows to assist Africa in repatriating the stolen money and prosecute the perpetrators, and it asks that banks desist from using frozen funds while the law takes its course.

Several African countries are now fighting for the repatriation of stolen wealth. For example, Nigeria's new leader, President Muhammadu Buhari, has pressed US president Barack Obama to assist Nigeria "in locating and returning US$150 billion in funds stolen in the past decade and held in foreign bank accounts on behalf of former, corrupt [Nigerian] officials." Getting the money repatriated to Africa will be an arduous task complicated by host countries' laws that shield bank-account holders and the amounts deposited. In a sign of progress, the US Department of Justice announced in 2014 that it had frozen more than $458 million in corruption proceeds stashed in various accounts in the United States and around the world by the late Nigerian president Sani Abacha and his allies.

Despite evidence that the Paris-based Organization for Economic Cooperation and Development (OECD), a group of thirty-four rich countries, is taking a harder stance against corruption, about half of its members had yet to prosecute a single case by the end of 2014. The group admits that it lacks effective mechanisms, including stiff penalties, to unearth bribery and prosecute bribe payers. What is telling in the OECD research, though, is not the findings it unearthed or the remedies it proposed, but its use of moral suasion as a weapon to compel members to institute the changes necessary to curtail illicit outflows. Experts concur that effective legislation to deter bribery or plug loopholes in current antibribery laws is what is needed, not a slap on the wrist of wrongdoers.

GLOBAL SOLUTIONS TO GLOBAL PROBLEMS

Because illicit financial flows are facilitated by individuals as well as corporate and public institutions and involve both rich and poor countries, global efforts are needed to deal with the problem. Support for new rules to rein in offshore tax shelters and curtail related illicit outflows has come from the leaders of the world's biggest economies—the G8 and the G20 countries. The economic meltdown sparked by the 2008 global financial crisis was a wake-up call for rich countries, which have long resisted universal rules to fight tax evasion and bank secrecy.

In 2014, the US Foreign Account Tax Compliance Act (FATCA) came into effect; it requires foreign financial institutions worldwide to reveal to US tax authorities the assets and identities of US citizens working and living overseas for purposes of identifying tax evasion. Institutions that fail to comply are denied access to US financial markets. Analysts view the law as a crucial weapon in global efforts to curtail illicit money. In the same year that FATCA came into effect, all OECD members, along with more than a dozen other countries, signed on to a new system—the Automatic Exchange of Information

(AEOI). Under this system, countries and jurisdictions are called on to obtain information from their financial institutions and automatically exchange that information with other jurisdictions on an annual basis. This gives tax authorities access to the data they need to detect and prevent tax evasion.

While tax-reform advocates welcomed the new law, they were not satisfied with the absence of a mechanism that would compel all countries and tax havens to sign up. Further, they argued that under the new law, some countries could collect tons of information on corporate or individual assets and still keep this data secret instead of sharing it with poor countries who need it the most to stamp out tax evasion. To address this concern, experts have called for illicit financial flows to be discussed under the purview of the United Nations–supported Committee of Experts on International Cooperation in Tax Matters, a tax forum for both rich and poor countries. The Mbeki report, for example, has called for global best practices—including those crafted by the OECD, the G8 and G20, the European Parliament, and the African Tax Administration Forum—to be universally applied.

For their part, a number of African countries have legislation that penalizes economic and financial crimes, according to Ambassador Segun Apata of Nigeria, a member of the Mbeki panel. However, the reality is that they lack the capacity to track and prosecute such activities. Raymond Baker, another panel member and the director of Global Financial Integrity, says the fight against global money laundering should be guided by two principles: the goal should be to curtail illicit outflows rather than the impossible one of stopping them; and the campaign should include both rich and poor countries. To this end, Mr. Baker recommends five steps to curtail illicit outflows.

First, all financial institutions should be required to know the identity of the person who owns and manages any account of theirs. He dismisses the case against full disclosure, arguing that transparency is a strong weapon against corruption, crime, terrorism, and tax evasion. Second, the global system should adopt consistent anti-money-laundering policies because current efforts are more geared toward looking for the money after it has passed from one party to another instead of curtailing the flow before it begins. Third, a global automatic exchange of tax information should be implemented because the argument that African nations and other developing countries cannot deal with the volume of data that would be produced through automatic exchange does not stand up to scrutiny. Fourth, trade mispricing should be curtailed. And finally, he argues, the world should adopt country-by-country reporting to bring greater integrity to the global financial system. This would ensure that corporations do not claim to be losing money in places where they are in business and making money in places where they are not in business.

It's easy to appreciate the realism behind Mr. Baker's arguments, particularly his recognition that the immediate goal should be to curtail rather than attempt to put a complete end to illicit financial flows. The secrecy and lack of transparency surrounding financial transactions, combined with the loopholes that exist in global tax laws, make it virtually impossible to completely eliminate the practice. Civil society, for the most part, backs the effort to tighten global tax laws. Academics Stand Against Poverty, a global association of antipoverty researchers and teachers, has called for, among other things, reforms in the transfer pricing system and international accounting standards, greater access to public registers of the real beneficiaries of financial assets, speedy repatriation of stolen money, and a boost in foreign aid to poor countries to strengthen domestic capacity on tax matters.

African citizens, says Mr. Annan, must demand the highest standards of propriety and disclosure from their governments, and rich countries must demand the same standards from their companies. Multilateral solutions are needed to address global problems because "tax evasion, illicit transfers of wealth and unfair pricing practices are sustained through global trading and financial systems." The African Union's development blueprint, Agenda 2063, emphasizes the need to reverse, and eventually eliminate, the flow of illicit capital from the continent. Initiatives by African institutions, coupled with global support—particularly from rich countries—to curtail illicit financial flows from Africa, raise hopes for strict rules against the practice.

A good start has been made by both sides in taking practical steps to stamp out the practice, but comprehensive laws with teeth are needed. Mr. Annan has warned that although ending illicit outflows will be difficult, "squandering opportunities to do so would be unforgivable and indefensible." Meanwhile, the high-level panel report's slogan—"Track it. Stop it. Get it"—aptly captures the call to action that global citizens and all involved must heed in response to this grave fiscal crisis confronting Africa.

NOTE

The views expressed in this article are the author's and do not necessarily reflect the views of the United Nations.

Diesing, Lena. "Money Laundering, Bribery and Tax Evasion: How to Freeze Illicit Flows." *Guardian* (UK), March 25, 2014. www.theguardian.com/global-development-professionals-network/2014/mar/25/tackling-illicit-financial-flows-oecd.

Global Witness, Tax Justice Network, Christian Aid, and Global Financial Integrity. "The Links between Tax Evasion and Corruption: How the G20 Should Tackle Illicit Financial Flows." Global Witness, 2009. https://www.globalwitness.org/en/archive/how-g20-can-stop-money-pouring-out-worlds-poorest-countries/.

Reed, Quentin, and Alessandra Fontana. "Corruption and Illicit Financial Flows: The Limits and Possibilities of Current Approaches." *U4 Issue,* no. 2 (January 2011). www.u4.no/assets/publications/3935-corruption-and-illicit-financial-flows.pdf.

Reuter, Peter, ed. *Draining Development? Controlling Flows of Illicit Funds from Developing Countries.* Washington, DC: World Bank, 2012.

Tafirenyika, Masimba. "Illicit Financial Flows from Africa: Track It, Stop It, Get It." *Africa Renewal,* December 2013. www.un.org/africarenewal/magazine/december-2013/illicit-financial-flows-africa-track-it-stop-it-get-it.

. . .

MASIMBA TAFIRENYIKA is the editor-in-chief of the United Nations' *Africa Renewal* magazine. He has worked for the United Nations in several African countries including Liberia, Sierra Leone, and South Africa, and visited many others. Prior to joining the United Nations, he worked as a journalist in his native country of Zimbabwe, writing extensively on African economic and political issues for different publications in Africa and in Europe. He holds a bachelor honors degree in Economics from the University of Zimbabwe and a master's degree in International Affairs from Columbia University in New York.

Working History

CHINA, AFRICA, AND GLOBALIZATION

Jamie Monson, Tang Xiaoyang, and Liu Shaonan

Abstract: In the last two decades Chinese economic engagement with African countries has increased, and with it new working relationships. Work provides an ideal lens for understanding the China–Africa relationship over time, because it involves both large- and small-scale interactions, and both state and nonstate actors. The outcomes of this engagement are similarly diverse, shaped not only by contemporary circulations of global capitalism, but also by history. There are therefore multiple sites and spaces where Africans and Chinese have come together at work, over a long historical trajectory. Most important, Africans themselves have profoundly influenced the labor situation in Africa, from the very beginnings of Afro-Asian engagement up to the present.

Keywords: China, Africa, work, labor, history, globalization

ASK ANY CASUAL OBSERVER OF Chinese engagement in Africa over the last two decades—whether that observer is in Africa or abroad—and you are likely to hear something about Chinese labor practices. From media broadcasts to statements made by politicians, a global understanding has emerged that there is a "Chinese way of work" in Africa. This way of work can sometimes be phrased positively—for example, when work on Chinese development projects is viewed as uplifting for Africans, who learn new skills and gain needed experience. Frequently, however, the "Chinese way of work" is described negatively, either because Chinese managers are accused of importing their own workers and depriving Africans of job opportunities, or because working conditions in Chinese enterprises are viewed as harsh and exploitative. Some reports go further, accusing Chinese projects of benefitting from prison labor; one scholar found in 2008 that Namibians from all sectors of society believed a rumor that Chinese convicts had chosen to serve out their sentences by working on Chinese construction sites in that African country.

Is there a Chinese way of work in Africa—or are Chinese employers behaving in the same ways as other foreign investors in this era of neoliberal economic reform and globalization? Work provides an ideal lens for understanding the China–Africa relationship over time, because it involves both large- and small-scale interactions, and both state and nonstate actors. The outcomes of this engagement are similarly diverse, shaped not only by contemporary circulations of global capitalism, but also by history. For Chinese and African workers have labored side by side over a long historical arc, from the ports of the eastern Indian Ocean in the twelfth century to the sugar plantations of the Caribbean in the nineteenth to the construction of Africa's colonial railways in the twentieth. There are therefore multiple sites and spaces where Africans and Chinese have come together at work, over a long historical trajectory. Most important, Africans themselves have profoundly influenced the labor situation in Africa, from the very beginnings of Afro-Asian engagement up to the present.

Labor also forms the background for some of the most powerful stories we tell about the larger China–Africa relationship, and these, too, have historical antecedents. African and Chinese workers are frequently racialized in relationship to one another, in ways that reflect imperial, colonial, and postcolonial ideas about African and Asian working bodies. Images of the "industrious" and hard-working Chinese have been contrasted with the "laziness" of Africans—stereotypes that have stubbornly persisted over time. In more recent accounts, African workers have been described as having little agency in the face of new forms of Chinese economic expansion that seek profit at the expense of workers' rights and wages.

In what follows, we investigate China–Africa engagement using the prism of work at diverse scales and locations, from the "China shop" in a Ghanaian marketplace to Chinese-owned farms in rural Zambia to leather factories in Ethiopia. Our case studies show that there are diverse experiences throughout the continent and that African responses are similarly varied. Africans are not only employees but also supervisors, managers, and contractors. There are joint ventures and enduring connections with other parts of the world (Dubai is one example), making China–Africa labor engagement truly global. Chinese enterprises on many levels operate within the same global capitalist frameworks as other economic actors. Yet at the same time, there continue to be unique "Chinese characteristics" in the workplace that set the China–Africa labor experience apart. There is, in the end, a "Chinese way of work" in Africa. But what does it really look like?

The earliest workplace encounters between Africans and Chinese probably took place on the southern coast of China in today's Guangdong Province, when Africans arrived aboard merchant ships from across the Indian Ocean in the seventh to tenth century, and likely much earlier. People of African descent worked in ancient China as soldiers, government officials, traders, artists, and laborers. During the T'ang dynasty (618–906), port cities like Guangzhou became known and valued destinations for global trade. According to the sparse records that remain, there were many foreigners in Guangzhou at that time, including enslaved African maritime workers who arrived aboard Arab trading dhows. Chinese observers marveled at their remarkable ability to swim and dive deeply into the ocean waters—skills they may have honed as enslaved pearl divers in today's Dubai.

In later centuries African and Chinese workers came together on the colonized "sugar islands" of the Indian Ocean (Mauritius and Réunion) and in the Caribbean. Following slavery's abolition in the nineteenth century, the ensuing labor crisis led to the importation of large numbers of indentured Asian workers from China and from India. From Réunion to Cuba to Louisiana, workers of African and Chinese origins began to work the same sugar plantations. And they responded in similar ways to their working conditions: using petitions, rebellion, desertion, and other strategies to contest coercive labor practices.

In colonized Africa starting in the late nineteenth century, Chinese laborers were again recruited to travel to Africa on contract to participate in colonial projects that ranged from mining (South Africa) to railway building (Congo and German East Africa). Colonial ideas about race and hierarchy also spread widely at this time, so that Africans and Chinese found themselves not only in the same working sites but also in an emerging imperial narrative about work that racialized worker characteristics. Chinese and African laborers encountered one another not only in the gold mines but also in the imaginations of the European colonizers. British colonial officials testified in parliament about Chinese qualities of "industriousness"—a theme that is echoed today in the concept of an Asian "model minority." This purported proclivity for hard work was contrasted in imperial reports with African "laziness." Then as now, this racialized hierarchy of labor was appropriated, contested, and used strategically not only by Europeans but also by Chinese workers and African intellectuals.

Following the Second World War, China turned toward communism just as African countries were decolonizing and moving toward independence. During this period a new narrative of work developed as China supported revolutionary movements while promoting a new model of independent modernization through "self-reliance." China promoted its own example of overcoming historical backwardness through state-led projects and through everyday "hard work." In the mid–twentieth century, therefore, the narrative of Chinese industriousness shifted, as the qualities of "eating bitterness"— perseverance and endurance for collective prosperity—were held up as a model for African people to adopt. Practices of hard work, discipline, and self-reliance were key components of labor models in Chinese assistance programs to Africa through the 1970s. These ideals meshed well with those of many African leaders as they fashioned independent states, economies, and new citizens.

The decade of the 1980s brought shifts once again into the China–Africa relationship that transformed the experience of work. Following the death of Mao in 1976, China began the era of "opening up and reform" under the leadership of Deng Xiaoping. During this same time period, African economies were under pressure to undergo similar economic reforms as international monetary bodies required market liberalization and structural adjustment policies. Currencies were devalued, markets were deregulated, and government bureaucracies were scaled back across Africa in response to externally imposed conditions. China's widening engagement with Africa starting in the 1980s took place within this larger global context of economic restructuring. By the 1990s, Chinese enterprises were actively investing in Africa, first by taking over many of the older socialist-era Chinese donor projects, and later by initiating new projects in sectors that met China's own development needs.

A CHINESE WAY OF WORK IN AFRICA?

Has a new "Chinese way of work" in Africa developed over the last two decades as a result of these economic reforms and China's adoption of "going out" policies? In what ways is this way of work similar to, or different from, that of other foreign investors? Some scholars, like C.K. Lee, provide evidence that it is the economic logic behind a firm that matters most for African workers, rather than the firm's national or cultural identity. In her case study of Zambian copper mines, Lee found that Chinese state-owned companies were more likely to agree to worker concessions than private companies of any nationality, because they sought to stabilize their labor force for the long term. Thus it was not the firm's "Chinese-ness" but its profit logic that determined outcomes.

In a study of the Chinese-built Mulungushi textile factory in Zambia, on the other hand, Andrew Brooks found that when a private Chinese company took over the socialist-era project and eliminated salaried positions, it used a distinctively Chinese management style. Managers were more likely than other investors in Zambia to eliminate salaried positions and replace them with casual or "day" labor—even when they were restructuring politically symbolic ex-socialist projects like Mulungushi. It seemed to many that post-socialist China had learned the harsh lessons of neoliberal capitalism all too well, and was now exporting these lessons to Africa.

Chinese investors enter into labor markets in Africa on many of the same terms as other foreign enterprises, and thus global factors such as neoliberalism, as well as the size and profit logic of the individual company, are critical to understanding relationships with workers. Any approach that seeks to identify a uniquely Chinese "way of work" in Africa will therefore fail to grasp the diversity of factors that shape workplace interactions over time, as well as their larger global context. Most important, such a narrow focus risks missing the critical ways that Africans themselves are profoundly shaping the labor situation in Africa, as they have done from the very beginnings of Afro-Asian engagement. Just as workers played a critical role in Africa's imperial, colonial, and decolonization eras, they continue today to shape their workplaces, their local and regional economies, and the global stage.

One major difference among Chinese enterprises is their ownership model, and whether it is largely public or private. The Chinese state-owned firms that bid on big construction projects do so through bilateral contracts that are made between the Chinese government and individual African governments. Competition for these contracts can be fierce, resulting in the driving down of costs, including wages. Private Chinese companies can also be quite large in scale—for example, the Huawei telecommunications giant. But the majority of private Chinese companies operating in Africa are small- and medium-scale enterprises (SMEs). These firms may receive some financial and other support from the Chinese government, including China's regional provincial governments, but in practice they have much more autonomy.

Chinese state-owned companies are important players in agriculture. In Zambia, there were six registered farms in 2009 owned by Chinese state-owned enterprises (SOEs), along with about a dozen owned by private individuals. The state-owned farms could be large in scale, up to twenty-six hundred hectares in size, though they were not among the largest commercial farms in Zambia. They followed a farm-management structure that was contract based—the same system used in rural China since the mid-1980s economic reforms. The Zambia-based farm managers worked under contracts to export profits back to their board of directors in China. Management–worker relations differed greatly, not only among the SOE farms but also among the private farms.

Chinese firms are subject not only to their own regulations but also to the labor laws governing employment in the countries where they operate. These are of course quite variable in their structure and implementation. During construction of the Bui Dam in Ghana, local labor law allowed workers for the hydroelectric company Sinohydro to organize through a trade union to negotiate their wages and working conditions. But Chinese firms have generally discouraged trade unions at their work sites. In African countries with strong political institutions and deep histories of union activity, African workers have been able to negotiate better terms. In cases like the Angolan oil and construction sectors, however, where there has been less historical stability and no strong trade-union tradition, workers are less likely to set the terms for their work.

While the large-scale, state-owned Chinese enterprises in Africa may still be the most visible, SMEs have increasingly shaped the work encounter. In these workplaces researchers find more conviviality and connection across class and ethnic lines, especially as joint ventures, African management, and even African ownership of firms hiring Chinese employees are emerging. Chinese firms are staying longer in Africa and making investments in training for their African staff, and these experienced workers are now rising through the management structure. In Kano, Nigeria, a small Chinese firm has employed three Nigerian college graduates for over ten years, and these employees have taken senior positions. Near Accra, a Chinese factory that has operated for more than thirty years has a Ghanaian manager who also oversees Chinese staff.

Tang Xiaoyang spent time in Ethiopia researching the experience of African workers in two different Chinese firms in the same sector—leather working. Ethiopia is an important leather producer, and the Chinese firms came to Ethiopia to develop factories where leather could be processed on-site into marketable products, rather than exported as a raw commodity. This was a priority for the Ethiopian government, which had passed legislation in 2011 to restrict the export of raw leather through tariff policies. The Chinese factories were therefore responding to the policy and needs of the Ethiopian government in addition to their own profit motives.

What Tang discovered is that the two firms he studied—both Chinese, both in the same African country, and both in the same industry—had set up very different conditions for workers. This in-depth story gives us a good example of how there may be something "Chinese" about work in these factories even though their employees had strikingly different experiences. The Friendship leather tannery and the China-Africa Overseas tannery were both established outside Addis Ababa in 2011. Of the two factories, the China-Africa Overseas factory was the largest, and its management invested heavily in fixed assets from the beginning. The company boasted that it had developed the best effluent treatment system in Ethiopia and could produce more varieties of leather than any other enterprise. The total investment made by the China-Africa Overseas tannery was 300 million Chinese yuan (US$48 million), of which 200 million yuan (US$36 million) was spent on fixed assets.

The Friendship leather tannery, on the other hand, set up a much more modest initial operation at around the same time. The Friendship factory built several rows of simple warehouses and brought only a small number of machines from China that could meet their immediate processing demand. The company's owner did not plan to build a factory following ISO standards for product quality, or to introduce advanced technology; his goal was to do basic leather treatment to meet the Ethiopian government's minimum export requirements. The Friendship factory followed a business model that we might call "Chinese," in the way that it initially started up the business with a low level of investment and did not wait for all of the buildings and other factory structures to be completed before beginning to train workers and start operations. This approach, sometimes known as "three simultaneous," aims to accelerate production by carrying out construction, training, and operations all at the same time.

Of the two private Chinese leather factories in Ethiopia, it was the smaller factory, Friendship, that paid higher wages to its workers. The Friendship management needed a strong and reliable workforce to keep production steady through the initial period of establishing the factory foundations and completing the infrastructure. Thus workers were paid nearly 1,000 birr (US$59) per month if they had no experience and were unskilled, while skilled and managerial staff were paid up to ten times more. The high wage level attracted quite a few employees from other tanneries in the country. Thus one "Chinese" way of setting up an enterprise—starting with a low level of investment and carrying out construction, training, and operations simultaneously—resulted in relatively high wages that were set to ensure the recruitment of a strong and loyal labor force.

In contrast, the high initial investment and the foundational technology assets at the China-Africa Overseas tannery were much more impressive than at Friendship. For workers, however, the low profit margins meant a lower wage scale than at Friendship. As a result, many workers did not stay long with the company. These examples from the leather industry demonstrate that there was not a single "Chinese" approach to work. Although the Friendship factory's gradual approach to plant construction was a variant of a typical Chinese practice, this business model was by no means confined to Chinese investors.

A perusal of the competitive bidding practices of Chinese enterprises seeking to invest in Africa suggests ways that Chinese investment can lead to outcomes for worker wages, and especially for worker training, that are in fact unique to the Chinese global context. Chinese companies—both state owned and private—are under intense pressure to win bids for projects in Africa by trying to underbid their competition. Even when company investments receive some government subsidies in the form of state-private cooperation, the bidding environment can be fiercely competitive. These low bids leave companies little room for bargaining with workers to meet their demands for higher wages. As a result, many companies working at low margins follow a strategy of hiring inexperienced, unskilled workers and then training them on the job. These trained workers, in turn, are most likely to leave their jobs when more promising positions open up elsewhere.

In Ethiopia, Tang Xiaoyang learned that the Huajian shoe factory had this experience. They initially recruited eighty-six local employees and sent them to China for a three-month training course. Once they returned to Ethiopia, however, more than 80 percent of the newly trained workers left the Huajian company. African workers at several enterprises interviewed by Tang Xiaoyang cited the low wages paid by Chinese companies as a main reason for their high turnover rate. Pinched by intense bidding competition on the one hand and by worker demands on the other, Chinese companies are searching for new solutions for employment and training in their African projects.

WORKPLACE ENCOUNTERS: LANGUAGE AND CULTURE

Our question—Is there a Chinese way of work in Africa?—is implicitly a question about work culture. Culture can be a slippery concept to deal with, because there are so many different definitions of what culture is and how it relates to work globally. And there is no single Chinese "culture" any more than there is a single African culture or language. It would be impossible to generalize based on a single understanding of "Chinese-ness" or "African-ness." Yet, cultural differences and language barriers have definitely played a role in employment relations when Chinese enterprises set up shop in African countries.

The Chinese-owned retail shops, or "China shops," that are springing up in African cities and small towns provide a useful example of ways that culture and language affect the work experience. We don't often think about the Chinese shopkeeper in Africa as an employer—yet many of the most up-close and everyday work relationships between Chinese and Africans take place in the small-scale commercial sector. Chinese and Africans encounter one another in markets and shops not only as buyer and seller, but also as employer and employee. Karsten Giese and Alena Thiel investigated the dynamics of these personal interactions in Ghana and found complex cultural realities and mutual misunderstandings on both the Chinese and the African sides. The Ghanaian employees expected their Chinese bosses not only to be employers, but also to play the role of respectable elders by showing a caring attitude toward junior employees. Ghanaians also expected their bosses to provide gifts and to promise future rewards in the form of job security or promotions. But the Chinese traders expected their African employees to behave more like casual wage laborers. They preferred to keep their distance through a wage-based relationship rather than to take on the more intimate relationship of elder patron. These different expectations of the employer-employee relationship led to a lack of mutual understanding between Chinese employers and Ghanaian employees, resulting ultimately in labor conflicts that reinforced cultural stereotypes.

Liu Shaonan found a very different workplace environment when he visited a Chinese trading enterprise in Lagos, Nigeria. The Chinese manager had a harmonious and intimate relationship with his Nigerian employees. His English was very fluent, and he enjoyed talking with his employees at all levels, including drivers, cleaners, and security workers. His wife even complained that he spent much more time talking to his Nigerian employees than talking to her. Moreover, every time his employees needed help due to family illness, funerals, or weddings, he offered financial support in the form of a gift. Therefore, his employees spoke very highly of him, treating him as a respectable elder who could help them to overcome difficult circumstances.

Cultures of work can differ greatly from one place to another within Africa. In Uganda there were conflicts related to the practice of *enjawulo,* a concept of reciprocity in which retail workers not only labor on behalf of their bosses but also seek to make personal gains by selling each item at the highest possible price. The Chinese shopkeepers tried to maximize their profits by selling the largest amount of goods possible at lower prices. But the African workers sought to increase their own personal gains by selling items at higher prices even when this resulted in a lower sales volume. Although Ugandan employees complained about the limited opportunities of performing *enjawulo* in Chinese-owned shops, they also complained about Ugandan shop owners. The conflicts over *enjawulo* were a part of existing employment relations in Uganda, where the acceptance or rejection of *enjawulo,* as much as the nationality or cultural background of the shop owner, was the key to mutual understanding between employers and employees.

CONCLUSION

There is not one single form of Chinese investment in Africa, just as there is no single African worker or work experience. African workers and their relationships with Chinese management vary greatly across the continent. They have deep historical dimensions that include not only work itself but the way it is imagined and narrated. Thus there may not be a single Chinese "way of work" in Africa, just as there is no single African "way of work." Yet we have found that there are specific Chinese characteristics that make a difference in the way Africans have experienced work in Chinese enterprises. Perhaps foremost among these are the ways that Chinese economic players have themselves responded to the significant and rapid changes of the neoliberal transition. As Chinese state companies combine their interests with those of private capital, these complex structures are also exported abroad. The managers who are asked to bring profits back home—whether from intense bidding competition in the construction sector or through complex contract-management demands in farming—face pressures to minimize outlays abroad, including payments to workers. Still, not all employers are equal: in the leatherworking factories of Ethiopia the smaller-scale investments of the Friendship factory allowed the management to pay workers higher wages and retain them, while the China-Africa Overseas factory paid less but invested more in infrastructure. In the Zambian copper mines the state-owned Chinese company paid better and tried to generate more worker loyalty for the long term, while private capital was less interested in sinking roots, preferring to stay mobile and therefore not worrying so much about retention of workers.

Culture and language also play a role in the workplace—in differing expectations about what it means to be a "boss" and an "employee," in the definition of assigned tasks, and in who gets to earn what kinds of benefits from the work process. Linguistic differences lead to less communication—or, worse, miscommunication—at all levels.

And Africans from the level of the state to the individual worker definitively shape the work encounter: states do this through wage and union regulations; workers do this through their work culture and expectations; and unions organize to make a difference.

ADDITIONAL RESOURCES

Akurang-Parry, Kwabena O. "We Cast About for a Remedy: Chinese Labor and African Opposition in the Gold Coast, 1874–1914." *International Journal of African Historical Studies* 34, no. 2 (2001): 365–84.

Giese, Karsten, and Alena Thiel. "The Vulnerable Other: Distorted Equity in Chinese-Ghanaian Employment Relations." *Ethnic and Racial Studies* 37, no. 6 (2014): 1101–20.

Lee, Ching Kwan. "Raw Encounters: Chinese Managers, African Workers and the Politics of Casualization in Africa's Chinese Enclaves." *China Quarterly* 199 (September 2009): 647–66.

Li, Anshan. *A History of Overseas Chinese in Africa to 1911.* New York: Diasporic African Press, 2012.

Mohan, Giles. "Beyond the Enclave: Towards a Critical Political Economy of China and Africa." *Development and Change* 44, no. 6 (2013): 1255–72.

Yun, Lisa. *The Coolie Speaks: Chinese Indentured Laborers and African Slaves in Cuba.* Philadelphia: Temple University Press, 2009.

. . .

JAMIE MONSON is a Professor of African History and Director of the African Studies Center at Michigan State University. She is a specialist on the history of the TAZARA railway, a development project built in Tanzania and Zambia with Chinese development cooperation in the 1970s. Her book *Africa's Freedom Railway: How a Chinese Development Project Changed Lives and Livelihoods in Tanzania* (Indiana University Press, 2009) has been recently published in Chinese (2015). Professor Monson's new research projects concern technology transfer, gender, and civil diplomacy in China–Africa engagement. She has also published widely on African environmental history and East African colonial history, including the history of the Maji Maji War in Tanzania. She speaks Swahili, German, French, and Chinese.

. . .

SHAONAN LIU is a PhD candidate in African history at Michigan State University. His dissertation research focus is on the history of Chinese migrants in Nigeria from the 1960s to the present. He speaks Chinese, Igbo, and Twi.

. . .

TANG XIAOYANG is an associate professor in the Department of International Relations at Tsinghua University and a resident scholar at the Carnegie-Tsinghua Center for Global Policy. His research interests include political philosophy, China's engagement in Africa, and modernization processes of the developing countries. He is the author of *China-Africa Economic Diplomacy and Its Implication to the Global Value Chain* (World Affairs Press, 2014) and has published extensively on Asia–Africa relations. He completed his PhD in the Department of Philosophy at the New School for Social Research in New York. He earned his MA in philosophy from Freiburg University in Germany and his BA in business management from Fudan University in Shanghai. He also worked as a consultant for the World Bank, USAID, and various research institutes and consulting companies. Before he came to Tsinghua, he worked at the International Food Policy Research Institute (IFPRI) in Washington, D.C.

2.8

The Radicalization of Environmental Justice in South Africa

Jacklyn Cock

Abstract: Although imported from the United States, the discourse of environmental justice has been radicalized in South Africa, as elsewhere in the Global South. Activists in South Africa go beyond symptoms to identify and challenge the structural causes of the current environmental crisis. The case of Steel Valley illustrates the power of the more radical concept of environmental justice by showing how a small, local environmental justice organization was able to challenge toxic pollution by the most powerful steel corporation in the world. The traveling and adaptive discourse of environmental justice has the capacity to connect local, particularistic struggles, generalize them, and forge global alliances.

Keywords: Environmental justice, activism, pollution, conservation, mining, South Africa

INTRODUCTION: THE STEEL VALLEY STRUGGLE

"Steel Valley" is the area around Vanderbjlpark, about one hundred miles from Johannesburg, in the industrial heartland of South Africa. It is the site of a struggle whereby a small environmental justice organization successfully challenged toxic pollution by the most powerful steel corporation in the world. The case of Steel Valley demonstrates both the power of the discourse of environmental justice and what has been called "the slow violence of ecological degradation." This is a violence that extends over time; it is insidious, undramatic, and relatively invisible. In Steel Valley the penetration of toxic pollution by a steel mill was extensive and largely invisible, permeating the landscape and moving slowly through the air and the groundwater. In many cases it was driven inward and embodied in the form of illness, genetic defects, cancers, and kidney failures among five hundred residents.

When the struggle began, one of the key actors, Lakshmi Mittal, was estimated to be the third-richest man in the world. He was chair of ArcelorMittal, a corporation that controlled 10 percent of global steel production and operated in twenty-seven different countries, including South Africa. One of his most profitable steel mills was situated in Steel Valley.

The second key actor was Strike Matsepo, one of the small farmers who lost his health and livelihood from the pollution of the air and groundwater around the steel mill. As he described in an interview in 2007, during the political transition, "at the time of Mandela when people could buy where they liked," he cashed his retirement pension to buy a farm in the area. He had heard that there were pollution problems but thought they were a myth created to keep black people out. He brought his large extended family to live with him. As he stated proudly, "A big sack of mealie meal [corn] was finished in two weeks." He claimed that Steel Valley "used to be a good place," but in the last years several of his animals had died, and many were born with birth defects. "In all thirty cows have died, as well as 9 calves, 5 sheep, 6 goats, 3 tortoises, 1 pig, 7 dogs, 30 chickens and 4 cats." Several family members also died. Strike himself was sickly and had spent several periods in hospital being treated for kidney failure associated with pollutants known to be in the groundwater. He became one of the founding members of a small local group, the Steel Valley Crisis Committee, formed to address local concerns about this spreading toxic pollution.

This was the context in which Samson Mokoena and several other local, young black activists were exposed to the discourse of environmental justice and formed the Vaal Environmental Justice Alliance (VEJA) "to stop the pollution." Many participants at the foundational workshop were excited by the concept of environmental justice. Some defined the concept very broadly: one participant maintained that "[e]nvironmental justice means the creation of jobs, the total eradication of poverty, the equal distribution of wealth, ending discrimination due to illness[,] and health protection." Most participants linked the concept to protecting livelihoods: "Environmental justice to us means the natural resources need to be used in a way that will preserve them for generations to come. The environment must provide the resources to live. You can't tell a hungry person not to kill an animal, or a cold person not to cut down a tree and make a fire to warm himself. We must not destroy the environment which is our source of life."

As the concept circulated in various township communities, activists decided to broaden the struggle against the steel mill to target other corporations in the area that were concerned with "profit at the expense of environmental and social justice" and whose emissions were creating severe air pollution. They formed VEJA in 2004. As Samson explained in a 2013 interview, when he was the chair of VEJA, "For me with environmental justice you become yourself .... [Y]ou engage with real issues that the community is faced with every day, like having water in your tap. It's a powerful concept because it links all the issues. It shows how everything is connected."

Over time the community engaged in many forms of collective action to stop the pollution and obtain compensation. Actions included three court cases, publicity, protest marches, picketing, participation in local forums, and appeals directly to Presidents Mandela and Mbeki. All these strategies failed as the steel mill denied the toxic nature of the pollution and so escaped liability for it. For instance, all requests to gain access to the secret 2002 environmental "master plan" of the steel mill, which documented the extent and liabilities of the pollution from the company's waste dumps and unlined dams, were refused. VEJA waged a ten-year battle to obtain the plan. Finally, a judge ruled in 2013 that the company had been "disingenuous" and that VEJA's monitoring of the pollution, as well as its mobilization and dissemination of information, proved "a vital collaboration between the state and private entities." He ordered the corporation to divulge the contents of its nine-thousand-page master plan. ArcelorMittal appealed. But the Supreme Court of South Africa confirmed the judgment in May 2015, ruling that "in relation to the environment ... there is no room for secrecy ... [and] constitutional values will be enforced." This judgment will be the grounds for a new series of campaigns to force the corporation to rehabilitate the area and pay compensation to the victims. "There must be a process whereby ArcelorMittal acknowledges it has done wrong. There must be compensation for residents," explained Samson.

ArcelorMittal has provoked globalized protests. At the same time, advocacy organizations have "upscaled"—from the small local organization that is the Steel Valley Crisis Committee, to the wider Vaal Environmental Justice Alliance, to the formation of Global Action on ArcelorMittal in 2008. Global Action involves environmental justice activists worldwide—from Kazakhstan to India, from Ohio to Luxembourg. Its formation and scope suggest the potential of resistance to environmental injustice that is locally rooted but globally connected.

The discourse of environmental justice originated in the Unites States in opposition to practices termed "environmental racism." It was radicalized in South Africa in a process of translation. The appropriation from the United States was not a passive transmission; the discourse changed dramatically in the process of translation from the North to the Global South. As it circulated it was extended beyond a concern with inequity in distributional impacts. The linkage of notions of rights, justice, power, and equality meant that the South African adaptation of the concept involved a commitment to radical, transformative change. Unlike in the United States, this change was driven by majority rather than minority interests. As such, the movement in South Africa frequently addresses the root causes of environmental degradation and processes rooted in neoliberalism, like privatization and deregulation—in contrast to the US movement's historical focus on symptoms.

The concept of environmental justice was first formally introduced in South Africa by an American sociologist at a conference of environmental activists in 1992. The concept resonated with the experience of black South Africans. As one participant said, "It was articulated as a black concept and a poor concept and it took root very well." This intervention came at a charged political moment; the transition to democracy was under way and, as Nadine Gordimer said at the time, "[p]rogressive forces in our country are pledged to one of the most extraordinary events in world social history, the complete reversal of everything that, for centuries, has ordered the lives of all our people." The "reversal" of environmental racism was central to the process of democratization, especially between 1990 and 1994.

The most dramatic outcome of the conference was the creation of the Environmental Justice Networking Forum (EJNF). The forum signaled a decisive break with the narrow, authoritarian conservationism that was dominant at the time. The EJNF described itself as a "democratic network, a shared resource, a forum which seeks to advance the interrelatedness of social, economic, environmental and political issues, and to reverse and prevent environmental injustices affecting the poor and the working class." It brought together over seven hundred organizations ranging from community-based organizations (CBOs) to nongovernmental organizations (NGOs), from churches to trade unions. Members took up grassroots issues such as the mercury poisoning of workers and communities, the toxic legacy of asbestos mining, illness as a result of working with poisonous substances, the absence of basic services such as access to water and sanitation, and waste dumps situated next to townships. The EJNF also did high-profile policy work, playing a leading role in post–apartheid environmental policy formulation such as in the National Environmental Policy Process (CONNEP), which formulated South Africa's progressive National Environmental Management Act, a framework law that laid down the principles for further legislation and also formulated Section 24 of the new constitution, the "environmental justice right."

RECONFIGURING ENVIRONMENTALISM

During both the colonial and the apartheid regimes, environmentalism operated effectively as an authoritarian conservation strategy that was mainly concerned with the protection of threatened plants, animals, and wilderness areas. As elsewhere, the conservation approach neglected urban, health, labor, and development issues. In the 1970s the mainstream environmental movement in the United States was subject to criticism of its "environmental elitism," and the establishment of many national parks involved displacement and dispossession. Similarly, for many black South Africans, dispossession was the other side of conservation. They were forcibly removed to create national parks and "protected areas," thereby losing their lands and undermining their livelihoods. The Makuleke people, for example, were evicted (their huts burned and their crops destroyed) from the northern area of the Kruger National Park in 1962. Although the new post-apartheid Board of the South African National Parks restored their land, many claims of land dispossession by indigenous communities have still not been resolved.

Under apartheid the national parks reflected the culture and practices of white exclusivity and domination. Until the 1980s, African visitors in Kruger National Park were allowed accommodation only at a tented camp with very rudimentary facilities. Since then the national parks have become more inclusive, and the value of cultural diversity as well as biodiversity has been made explicit through the promotion of local tourism and the development of cultural heritage sites such as Thulamela (the walled stone remains of a vital fifteenth-century trading center). Some progress has also been made in improving relations with neighboring communities, but community members continue to live in desperate poverty. Improvements in communication are largely due to environmental justice organizations demanding change from a "fortress and fines" model of conservation in which neighboring communities were perceived and treated as threats.

Fragments of the linkage of environmentalism with conservation remain in post-apartheid South Africa. The protection of biodiversity is often eclipsed by survivalist concerns with jobs and livelihoods. As a workshop participant recently commented, "White people must be mad to care so much about the poaching of rhinos when black children are going hungry." The concept of environmental justice provides a radical alternative to the discourse of "conservation and sustainable development," questioning the market's ability to bring about social or environmental sustainability. It affirms the value of all forms of life against the interests of the rich and powerful. It represents a powerful challenge to the anodyne concept of sustainable development, and the increasing commodification and financialization of nature packaged as "the green economy."

ENVIRONMENTAL JUSTICE ORGANIZATIONS AND STRUGGLES

Environmental injustice continues in post-apartheid South Africa as inequality deepens and the 65 percent of the population classified as "poor" bear the brunt of increasing environmental degradation. Black South Africans continue to live on the most damaged land, in the most polluted neighborhoods often adjoining mine dumps, waste sites, or polluting industries, without adequate services of refuse removal, water, electricity, and sanitation. In the province of Gauteng, in which Johannesburg is situated, some 1.6 million people live on mine dumps contaminated with uranium and toxic heavy metals including arsenic, aluminum, manganese, and mercury. Environmental injustice involves the externalization of the costs of production in the form of toxic pollution of the air and groundwater in many communities, and the enclosure of natural resources, such as land and water. Poor people (the majority of whom continue to be black) are also the most vulnerable to the impacts of climate change such as more extreme weather events, crop failures, rising food prices, and water shortages.

Established environmental justice organizations such as Earthlife Africa, Groundwork, VEJA, and the South Durban Community Environmental Alliance are bridging ecological and social justice issues. New environmental justice organizations are emerging such as the Highveld Environmental

Justice Alliance, Mining Affected Communities United in Action (MACUA), and WoMin. They are developing new alliances, new forms of power, and new narratives of "food sovereignty" and "energy democracy." These are vital steps toward achieving environmental justice. They are part of a growing emphasis on moving beyond denunciation to formulating alternative social forms. For example, several organizations are not only mobilizing opposition to fracking but also "exploring alternatives which will foster energy democracy and transformative development while protecting the natural resources and people of the Karoo." Other organizations are promoting concrete postcarbon alternatives such as the Earthlife's Sustainable Energy and Livelihoods Project, which combines water harvesting, food sovereignty, and clean energy through installing and maintaining biogas digesters and PVC solar-power units and training women on their use. These initiatives are generating demands that either challenge or cannot easily be accommodated by neoliberal capitalism.

Some of these new alliances or coalitions are between formerly antagonistic groupings, such as those concerned with the conservation of threatened plants, animals, and wilderness areas and those concerned with social needs. An example is the struggle against the proposed huge open-cast Fuleni coal mine near the border of Hluhluwe iMfolozi Park, one of Africa's oldest game reserves and central to rhino conservation. The mine is supported by Glencore and BHB Billiton, the world's largest commodity trader and mining house, respectively. Local women, however, have mobilized against the mine with the support of conservation organizations to form the iMfolozi Community and Wilderness Alliance. Similarly, the Save Mapungubwe Coalition was formed to safeguard the Mapungubwe National Park, a World Heritage Site, from an Australian–based mining company, Coal of Africa. The diverse coalition includes environmental NGOs such as World Wildlife Fund (WWF) and the Endangered Wildlife Trust (EWT) as well as local people. Such alliances are beginning to close a historic gap in the environmental movement between two (sometimes antagonistic) main streams: those organized around the discourse of conservation and those organized around the discourse of environmental justice.

New linkages exposing the false binary of "jobs" versus "environmental protection" are emerging between another set of distinct and often antagonistic groupings—labor and environmental justice activists. For example, the main trade-union federation, the Congress of South African Trade Unions (COSATU), established two committees consisting of representatives from all twenty-two affiliate unions and from key environmental organizations. These committees promoted shared research into coal mining, chemicals, and poultry farming. They have engaged in extensive popular education and formulated policy positions around a "just transition"—a shift away from fossil fuel energy to a renewable energy regime based on the principles of both justice and sustainability. Another example of collaborations between unions and environmental organizations is the Climate Jobs Campaign, which has collected one hundred thousand signatures in support of creating jobs to address both poverty and climate change. Based on meticulous research, the campaign has demonstrated that up to three million such jobs are possible, challenging capitalist ownership in favor of community-owned projects. Informal collaboration with the National Union of Metalworkers of South Africa (NUMSA) is strongly promoting the environmental justice notion of energy democracy as another building block toward an alternative future. Energy democracy resists the agenda of fossil-fuels corporations and reclaims the energy sector as part of "the commons" so that public resources are outside the market and democratically controlled. The idea was endorsed by fifty-one Africa countries in the Abuja Declaration of 2006.

Environmental justice struggles involve a range of mobilizing issues. The most common demands and claims relate to "rights" and health, drawing on the constitutional framing of the *human* right in the post-apartheid constitution, which proclaims the right of all "to live in an environment that is not harmful to health or wellbeing." The overall focus is on the "environmentalism of the poor," which flows from the recognition that it is the poor and the working class who are most burdened by environmental injury.

Nonetheless, much current popular mobilization is about access to services such as water and energy. The actions are localized, episodic, discontinuous, and not framed as "environmental struggles." Such a reframing could, however, provide an ideological basis for unified collective action. Clearly coal, as the main driver of the ecological crisis in the form of climate change, constitutes a powerful ground for unified action. Formal alliances in opposition to coal are growing to include human rights issues such as land dispossession, health impacts through water and air pollution, loss of livelihoods, corruption in the granting of mining licenses, inadequate consultation with frontline communities, and methods for increasing food security. Many of these "land grabs" are driven by multinational corporations. In a number of cases, there are serious allegations of Australian and Indian corporations fomenting violence in these communities to destroy any local opposition.

While coal is the main cause, food insecurity is acknowledged to be one of the most serious consequences of climate change. Popular mobilization against the present food regime in South Africa is growing. The coexistence of hunger (53 percent of the population is officially classified as experiencing hunger either regularly or intermittently) and food waste (a third of all food produced) is acknowledged as profoundly unjust. Like coal, food is an intensely political, connecting issue. One of the growing initiatives confronting the food regime in South Africa is the Food Sovereignty Campaign. The campaign is mobilizing grassroots communities, engaging in activist schools and study groups, establishing food gardens, and developing innovative strategies. In 2015, for example, they brought together grassroots experiences and "expert" evidence in the People's Tribunal on Hunger, Food Prices and Landlessness. The tribunal involved hearing accounts such as, "I fainted but I explained that I was not really sick. It was just not my turn to eat that day."

The linking of principles of social justice with ecological sustainability in the discourse of environmental justice is providing the impetus for many of these struggles. Collectively, all these initiatives confront different aspects of the ecological crisis. They demonstrate an alternative paradigm, a different relationship both among human beings and between human beings and nature. For some, these relationships draw on the traditional African notion of *ubuntu,* which in Xhosa asserts that "people are people through other people." *Ubuntu* emphasizes collective action, solidarity, and empowerment rather than individual advancement. Furthermore, the traditional African view that people, animals, and plants form an integral whole provides a strong contrast to the dualistic understanding of "nature" and "society" as separate entities that is widespread in the Global North.

CONCLUSION

All over the world the discourse of environmental justice is creating a form of "epistemic solidarity," both in forging alliances locally and globally between north and south, and in linking the principles of social justice and ecological sustainability. The radicalization of the concept in South Africa involves a direction to structural causes—the expansionist logic of extractivism in the case of mobilization around coal, for example. The South African case described in this chapter is not unique. Many of the environmental justice struggles on the African continent are against the dispossession and toxic pollution involved in extractivism. This "second scramble for Africa" involves the appropriation of Africa's profitable natural resources by powerful multinational corporations. Throughout the continent poor people are not passive victims of these processes. Much protest activity is directed against these corporations, such as that of the Ogoni, the Ijaw, and other groups in the Niger Delta against the damage from oil extraction by Shell. The hybridized discourse of environmental justice is critical in many of these struggles.

South Africa is a microcosm of the contemporary world order, a world marked by growing inequality and environmental degradation that is leading to environmental catastrophe. The traveling and adaptive discourse of environmental justice has the capacity to connect particularistic local struggles, generalize them, and forge global alliances. The current unprecedented global concentration of corporate power calls for these forms of transnational solidarity.

NOTE

The chapter draws from a review of the relevant primary and secondary literature, interviews, and the author's participation as an environmental justice activist in many of the events described.

ADDITIONAL RESOURCES

Cock, Jacklyn. *The War against Ourselves. Nature, Justice and Power in South Africa.* Braamfontein, South Africa: Wits University Press, 2007.

Hallowes, David. *Toxic Futures: South Africa in the Crises of Energy, Environment and Capital.* Scottsville, South Africa: University of KwaZulu-Natal Press, 2011.

Klein, Naomi. *This Changes Everything: Capitalism vs. the Climate.* New York: Simon and Shuster, 2014.

McDonald, David. *Environmental Justice in South Africa.* Cape Town: Oxford University Press, 2002.

Nixon, Rob. *Slow Violence and the Environmentalism of the Poor.* Cambridge, MA: Harvard University Press, 2011.

. . .

JACKLYN COCK is a professor emeritus at the University of the Witwatersrand in Johannesburg and is active in the environmental justice movement.

PART III

Circulations of Communities and Cultures

INTRODUCTION

Circulation connotes flow and movement. Africa is at the center of an immense, multidirectional circulation of communities, cultural practices, and innovations. The speed at which things move into and out of Africa and the transformations and innovations that accompany them can be dizzying and dazzling. Judith Byfield highlights the African, African-American, and Swedish cuisine at Marcus Samuelsson's Red Rooster restaurant in New York City. Samuelsson's multicultural turn in the kitchen is matched by the combination of indigenous athletic traditions and European form that shape African football/soccer on the field. Peter Alegi captures the innovations African players have introduced as well as the ways African societies have indigenized the cultural performance of this global pastime.

Circulation, however, is not a neutral process. What circulates, how, and why are steeped in overlapping histories with different proportions of adventure, ambition, and greed. Textiles provide a rich source for stories about the circulation of communities, cultural practices, and innovations. Wax-print cloths, as Victoria Rovine shows, weave together stories of cultural and economic interactions among northern Europe, Southeast Asia, and West Africa. Although wax prints did not originate in Africa, this quintessential "African" textile can be seen wherever African communities form.

Newly formed African communities have sprung up across the United States, Europe, and Asia, especially in recent decades. As Chinese migrants settle across the African continent on farms and in mines and marketplaces, Africans are migrating to China as traders, missionaries, and workers. Guangzhou, China, hosts many of these African migrants. Michaela Pelican and Li Dong capture the experiences of these African migrants in a vivid photo essay. Heidi Østebø Haugen reveals the fervent efforts of Nigerian evangelical missionaries in China, who conduct their spiritual work under the watchful eye of the Chinese government.

In the same way that some Africans made Christianity their own, some African writers made European languages their own. Ngũgĩ wa Thiong'o is one of the most famous novelists, essayists, playwrights, and scholars in African literature. In an interview with his son Mukoma wa Ngugi, Ngũgĩ reflects on how African literary traditions were shaped by and challenged European literary conventions, forms, and languages.

Music, like literature, circulates in broad, complicated pathways. In New York the confluence of African-inspired musical forms (a lasting legacy of the transatlantic slave trade), urban disinvestment, and youth protest created rap music. As rap filled the airwaves beyond the United States, it became a defining feature of a globalized youth culture. In a sense, an African-inspired musical form has come back to Africa. Zakia Salime shows that in Algeria and Morocco rap connects young people to their counterparts in Paris, London, and New York. Rap has become the preferred medium through which young people express their dissatisfaction with and alienation from the current politics of their countries. Thus, the circulation of communities and cultures reflects the optimism of collaboration and innovation as well as the messiness of unequal relations of power.

3 . 1

———————

Profile

A TASTE OF AFRICA IN HARLEM: RED ROOSTER

Judith A. Byfield

Abstract: Acclaimed chef Marcus Samuelsson opened his restaurant, Red Rooster, in Harlem in 2010. Since then it has become an icon of the resurgent food scene in Harlem. Samuelsson, born in Ethiopia, raised in Sweden, and trained in restaurants across Europe, brings an array of flavors to the African, American, and Swedish dishes that populate his menu. Moreover, he has helped to popularize African cuisine internationally.

Keywords: Harlem Renaissance, African-American culture, Ethiopia, migration.

WHEN WE EMERGED FROM THE subway, the rain had just begun to fall. As a result, the normally filled sidewalk tables were empty as we approached Red Rooster Harlem. (See figure 3.1.1.) We feared this meant that inside, the restaurant would be empty as well, but the wave of sounds that hit us as we opened the door made clear that business was bustling. A line of customers, many from Europe, waited for tables. A band playing jazz and gospel music accompanied an inspiring singer as the staff bobbed around chairs, tables, and laughing guests, carrying trays of tempting dishes. It was the best combination—a little church with your food.

Marcus Samuelsson, the Ethiopian-born chef, and his cocreator, Andrew Chapman, opened Red Rooster Harlem in 2010. Named after a famous Harlem speakeasy, the restaurant pays homage to an earlier generation of restaurateurs who helped to make this section of Manhattan world famous during the Harlem Renaissance. The period, roughly encompassing the interwar years, witnessed an explosion of creative expression in all avenues of African-American life and culture. Harlem became a hub for those who sought inspiration as they walked its streets, visited its clubs, and ate in its restaurants. It nurtured the creativity of writers such as Langston Hughes,

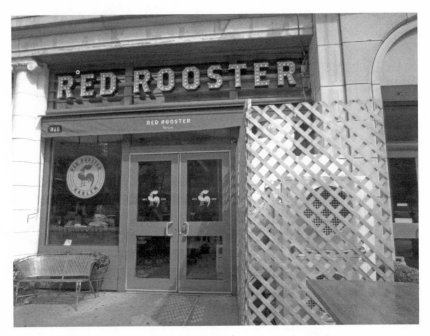

FIG. 3.1.1. Entrance to Red Rooster, 2014. Photo by Clarence Sheppard.

Zora Neale Hurston, and Claude McKay and the pioneering music of Duke Ellington and Bessie Smith. Many who flocked to Harlem were part of the "great migration" from the American South as African Americans sought relief from unencumbered racial violence. Harlem also welcomed migrants from the Caribbean like Arthur Schomburg, whose extensive collection of literature and art on Africa and the African diaspora became the basis of the Schomburg Center for Research in Black Culture, a branch of the New York Public Library. Harlem was also a hub of political activism as W. E. B. Du Bois published the *Crisis* magazine, Marcus Garvey's United Negro Improvement Association advocated a return to Africa, and the African Blood Brotherhood championed socialism and communism.

Red Rooster is located in the heart of Harlem, at 310 Lenox Avenue/ Malcolm X Boulevard, between 125th and 126th Streets. Today it is associated with the revitalization of a community that experienced decades of neglect, the withdrawal of government resources, massive unemployment, and several drug epidemics. Red Rooster is contributing to a resurgence of the cultural energy that characterized the Harlem Renaissance while also trying to address some of the economic and social challenges that residents encounter. They hire staff from within the community, host neighborhood cooking classes, and buy fresh produce and fruits from the farmers' markets in Harlem and Union Square. The walls of the restaurant display paintings, drawings, photographs, and sculptures by a new generation of artists. The five musical groups that take turns sharing the space with diners enliven the atmosphere as they play jazz, rhythm and blues, gospel, reggae, neo-soul, Latin, and hip-hop.

Nonetheless, the real star of Red Rooster Harlem is the cuisine. Samuelson was raised in Sweden by his adoptive parents from the time he was three years old. He credits his Swedish grandmother with inspiring his passion for cooking. He began his training as a professional chef in Sweden and augmented it with apprenticeships in Switzerland and Austria. An apprenticeship with the Swedish restaurant Aquavit brought him to the United States in 1991, and in 1995 he returned as a member of the kitchen staff. At Aquavit he pushed the boundaries of Swedish cuisine, incorporating elements of Ethiopian culture into their offerings or experimenting with new ingredients. His innovative styling in the kitchen helped him become the executive chef of Aquavit by the time he was twenty-four, as well as the youngest chef to win a three-star restaurant review from the *New York Times*. In 2003 the James Beard Foundation named him Best Chef: New York City, and in 2006 the foundation awarded his African-inspired cookbook *The Soul of a New Cuisine* the Best International Cookbook prize.

The menu at Red Rooster reflects Samuelsson's cosmopolitan palate. Diners can feast on Scandinavian standards such as gravlax or Helga's (Swedish) meatballs with lingonberries; Ethiopian-inspired Og chicken with injera (Ethiopian bread), sour collard greens, egg, and sauce Addis; or an African-American classic: chicken and waffles. The names of dishes are as playful and entertaining as the music. Shrimp, Hog and Grits comes with cheddar port grits, bird junk, and *piri piri,* the East African–inspired sauce, while Broadway St. Drunken Noodle has grilled octopus, short rib, fermented black beans, and cumin. If your stomach still has room after the main course, there are luscious desserts to tempt you (see figure 3.1.2), such as "Music Roots" pie ("music roots" is cowboy slang for sweet potato), filled with sweet potatoes and chocolate and topped with marshmallow ice cream; toasted coconut truffles; and Hot Java—walnuts, sour-cream sorbet, and glögg sauce.

Red Rooster is not the only restaurant integrating elements of African cuisine into Harlem's culinary landscape. Cecil's, an Afro-Asian-American restaurant, offers a fusion of dishes and cultures deeply inspired by African

FIG. 3.1.2. Dessert at Red Rooster, 2014. Photo by Clarence Sheppard.

spices, texture, and cooking techniques; it was named Best New Restaurant by *Esquire* magazine in 2014. Lenox Saphire combines French and Senegalese cuisine. Diners can also find several restaurants that concentrate on cuisine from different parts of Africa. Keur Sokhna and Africa Kine are considered among the best Senegalese restaurants in Harlem. Massawa has been serving Ethiopian and Eritrean dishes for twenty-five years and is now joined by Zoma and Abyssinia. African and African-fusion restaurants are not exclusive to Harlem. In 2013, Akin Akinsanya, a Wall Street consultant originally from Nigeria, launched New York African Restaurant Week. Participating restaurants from across the city offer a special menu at a fixed price and introduced many people to African restaurants in downtown Manhattan as well as Brooklyn.

Interest in African cuisine is growing by leaps and bounds. As African immigrants settle in New York City and other US cities, they help to consolidate demand for African food. Nonetheless, Marcus Samuelsson continues to play a central role in introducing African cuisine to the global palate. His frequent guest appearances on popular cooking shows such as *Top Chef, Chopped,* and *Iron Chef America* defuse the novelty of African dishes. He expands the spice vocabulary of ordinary cooks and foodies alike and encourages American consumers to step out of their food comfort zone as they experiment with African dishes and seasonings at home or in his restaurant. In the process, Samuelsson and the success of Red Rooster have played an instrumental role in cementing Harlem's and African cuisine's place in the global food scene.

ADDITIONAL RESOURCES

Hill, Laban Carrick. *Harlem Stomp! A Cultural History of the Harlem Renaissance.* New York: Little Brown, 2003.

Samuelsson, Marcus. *The Soul of a New Cuisine: A Discovery of the Foods and Flavors of Africa.* Hoboken, NJ: John Wiley & Sons, 2006.

Samuelsson, Marcus, with Veronica Chambers. *Yes, Chef: A Memoir.* New York: Random House, 2012.

Studio Museum. *Harlem: A Century in Images.* New York: Skira Rizzoli International Publishers and the Studio Museum of Harlem, 2010.

Wassenberg, Anya. "New York African Restaurant Week 2015: Akin Akinsanya on Building NYC'S African Culinary Empire," *OkayAfrica,* May 28, 2015. www.okayafrica.com/news/new-york-african-restaurant-week-june-2015-akin-akinsanya/.

• • •

JUDITH A. BYFIELD is Associate Professor of History at Cornell University, where she teaches African and Caribbean history. She is the author of *The Great Upheaval: Women, Taxes and Nationalist Politics in Nigeria, 1945–1951* (Ohio University Press, forthcoming); and *The Bluest Hands: A Social and Economic History of Women Indigo Dyers in Western Nigeria, 1890–1940* (Heinemann, 2002); a coeditor, with Carolyn Brown, Timothy Parsons, and Ahmad Sikainga, of *Africa and World War II* (Cambridge University Press, 2015); and a coeditor, with LaRay Denzer and Anthea Morrison, of *Gendering the African Diaspora: Women, Culture, and Historical Change in the Caribbean and Nigerian Hinterland* (Indiana University Press, 2010).

Networks of Threads

AFRICA, TEXTILES, AND ROUTES
OF EXCHANGE

Victoria Rovine

Abstract: Textiles have a long history of global circulation, moving readily as trade goods and as clothing worn by people who travel. African artists, merchants, and consumers skillfully adapt textiles drawn from beyond their cultural orbits, often transforming them to suit local tastes and social structures.

Keywords: textiles, wax print, pelete bite, Asafo, Ibrahim Njoya, Maki Oh

TEXTILES HAVE TRAVELED THE WORLD for centuries, gathering stories as they move. Many of these textiles originate in, pass through, or reach destinations in Africa. Cloth traverses oceans and deserts; it moves between average consumers and elite markets; it bridges technologies by spurring innovations. And textiles move in many forms: as clothing worn by travelers themselves; as trade goods carried or sent to markets; and as images, for nearly every image that includes people is also a depiction of clothing and textiles. Although they are inanimate, textiles, garments, and images are propelled into global circulation by the desires of the people who encounter them.

As they move, textiles are accompanied by a host of stories. These narratives are particularly vivid because cloth and clothing are highly visible and infinitely adaptable, and because they are closely connected to the people who wear them. They mark places, people, and histories, and they readily acquire new associations as they travel. An examination of Africa's participation in global networks of textiles and garments offers rich insights into the power of travel and exchange systems to shape material culture and inspire creativity. Through a series of stories—narratives that trace the journeys of textiles and garments across cultural, geographic, and chronological distances—we gain insights into connections, values, tensions, and innovations that may be evident in other records, but rarely are they as vivid.

This exploration of Africa's long-standing global networks of cloth and clothing has implications far beyond the fields of art and fashion. Textiles are on the leading edge of international exchange all over the world. For centuries—even millennia—cloth and clothing have constituted an important trade good that inspires new technologies as well as new dress styles. Textiles also exemplify the speed with which people bring the new into their repertoire, serving as highly visible markers of global connections. If they gain traction in their new contexts, these once-exotic styles are absorbed into the cultures of their new homes, their distant origins fading until they become thoroughly local.

STARTING WITH WAX: A WEB OF NETWORKS

The textiles widely known as "African print," "wax print," or simply "wax" offer an excellent starting point for this exploration. (See figure 3.2.1.) They illustrate the unexpected intersections by which textiles move around the world, transformed through the creativity of producers, merchants, and consumers. They are rooted in colonial connections on opposite sides of the globe. In fact, this textile genre was produced by interactions between three regions: northern Europe, Southeast Asia, and West Africa. Yet after all of their travels, these textiles have become thoroughly African. More effectively than any other cultural expression, these fabrics illustrate the intersecting networks of power and aesthetic innovation that link distant cultures, and they epitomize both the historical depth of the global circulation of textiles and the dynamism that continues to fuel textile innovations at the cutting edge of contemporary African art and fashion.

Textile factories in Europe have manufactured wax-print fabrics since the late nineteenth century, and today they are produced in African factories as well. Despite the immense variety of the motifs and images that adorn them, the cloths in this genre are immediately recognizable: they are industrially woven and printed cotton textiles, often in brilliant colors, with large patterns that may be abstract, figurative, or—most often—a combination of both. Whether they are produced in Europe, Asia, or Africa, these fabrics are intended for African consumers. This central element of African visual culture enlivens streets and social gatherings; wherever people wear them, wax prints make an impact. While its styles reflect regional variations and it is more common in some parts of Africa than in others, wax print still comes

FIG. 3.2.1. African wax-print fabrics for sale in Djenné, Mali, 2008. Photo by Victoria Rovine.

closer than any other single element of African dress to being truly continental. The fact that these cloths originated a world away from Africa is, then, all the more surprising. And their story has come full circle: today, factories in many African countries produce wax prints, and when these textiles are sold in Western markets, they are heralded as an authentic African art form—a category that often implies cultural purity, denying the cosmopolitanism of both people and things. Only by exploring this genre's history can we appreciate that wax prints—like so many African creative expressions—are both authentically African and authentically global.

Wax prints are rooted in what was arguably the first deliberately global trade system: the network established by the Dutch East India Company beginning in 1602. This private enterprise granted Dutch merchants special trade privileges in areas where Holland had established political influence. These regions included the Southeast Asian archipelago that later became the Dutch East Indies, and, after 1945, Indonesia. The Dutch also had forts and trading posts in Africa, located on the Gold Coast (now Ghana); in southern Nigeria, Benin, and Togo; and in South Africa. All of these locations gave Dutch traders ready access to African and Asian goods and consumers, and they encouraged traders to find goods that could be marketed between these sites, making the most of their network.

Textiles circulated readily among these world regions. Dutch traders found that Indonesian batik fabrics were popular in Europe, where these "exotic" textiles were highly valued. Batiks are lightweight cloths adorned with designs created by painting wax onto the cloth, which prevents dyes from permeating those areas. Removing the wax in some areas and re-dyeing the cloth enabled batik artists to create multicolored textiles with fine details—a very labor-intensive process. The cloth has a distinctive aesthetic: when immersed in dye, the wax-covered areas often crack, allowing thin rivulets of color to seep through. This creates fine lines in a random pattern—an unintended effect, but a crucial element of the success of batik as a trade good.

With the popularity of Southeast Asian batik in European markets, this textile's story takes a dramatic turn. In the mid–nineteenth century, the British textile industry was burgeoning. Both Dutch and British merchants sought to reproduce batik style using new technologies, so that they could both produce and market the cloth. Instead of painting by hand, manufacturers created the patterns with metal rollers, applying dye to the cloth more efficiently and thus more cheaply. This cloth was designed to imitate the key features of batik, including the "crackling" effects of the wax. Thus, the accidental became a key stylistic element that designers struggled to reproduce in a mechanized process. Although this fabric did not succeed in European markets, merchants found enthusiastic consumers in their African markets.

From their earliest development, the design of wax-print textiles was an indirect collaboration between European manufacturers and African consumers. European representatives of textile firms carefully recorded the color and pattern preferences of consumers in each region, consulted with African merchants (including many women), and even created fabrics with design elements that were aimed at specific markets, such as symbols of royalty from a particular chieftaincy or kingdom, and portraits of rulers. Wax prints were absorbed into African systems of value; specific patterns have long been given names that evoke local history and popular culture. And beginning in the mid–twentieth century, factories in Africa began to produce the cloth, so that boutiques and market stalls in African communities today might offer cloth produced in the United Kingdom or Holland, as well as styles produced in the consumer's home country or neighboring African nations. China has also become a leading producer, known for its speedy reproductions of popular patterns, underselling European producers.

Internationally renowned Anglo-Nigerian visual artist Yinka Shonibare MBE uses wax prints as his primary medium because they give him access to this history of complicated and multilayered influences. He is well known for his installations of life-size figures wearing Victorian-style tailored clothing made of brilliantly colored "African" fabrics. The pieces challenge conventional assumptions about the distance between Africa and Europe, alluding to the long history that has produced tightly interwoven cultures—as inseparable as warp and weft. While so many aspects of Europe's nineteenth- and twentieth-century involvement with Africa were negative, culminating in colonization and the use of Africa as a source of labor and raw materials, we can find through wax prints a glimmer of the productivity that might have flourished had relations between Europe and Africa maintained their early balance of power. Wax-print textiles express this history, along with its incongruities and complications, in a seductively colorful form.

DEEP HISTORY OF TEXTILES AND TRADE

Our exploration of African textiles and global networks can reach beyond the inception of wax prints in Indonesia, to find trade and travels that date back centuries earlier. Because textiles rarely survive in archaeological contexts, scholars have limited direct evidence of African weaving in past centuries. Even in Egypt, with its extensive excavations and dry climate, actual cloth from the early centuries of textile production is rare. However, representations of cloth in other media attest to the importance of textiles in Egypt from as early as 4000 BCE.

Written records provide another means of documenting the antiquity of both African textile production and the global networks in which textiles travel. For example, taxation records from ancient Rome indicate that cloth and clothing were among the goods traded from what is today Mauretania into Roman territories by 200 CE. Beginning in the eighth century, the writings of Muslim travelers from the Middle East and North Africa indicate that woven goods from south of the Sahara, such as woolen blankets, were being traded north. And in turn, textiles from Europe were traded into Africa across the Sahara. Textiles and clothing also crossed oceans; by the fifteenth century, Atlantic maritime trade along the west coast of Africa provided European merchants with direct access to sub-Saharan Africa.

On the other side of Africa, the Indian Ocean has been an active trade thoroughfare since the twelfth century or earlier, uniting producers and consumers from South Asia, the Arabian Peninsula, and the length of the Swahili coast of East Africa, and extending to inland African regions via longstanding trade routes. East Africa has its own variation of wax prints, which developed out of the South Asian trade in block-printed cotton fabrics. As in West and Central Africa, the desire to speed production and increase profits led new actors to enter the market, producing technological and stylistic innovations. By the late eighteenth century, Indian hand-woven fabrics with block-printed designs had long been popular in coastal East Africa. They were displaced in the early nineteenth century by industrially woven cotton from the United States, until the Civil War created a crisis in American manufacturing. By the 1870s, British textile producers had gained dominance in the market by creating factory-printed textiles that imitated the Indian block prints, just as they had imitated Indonesian batik for West African markets. The end product of this multinational innovation is the *kanga,* East Africa's most popular textile. Lengths of this cloth, sold in pairs for women who wear them as skirts and shawls, are today distinctively African. They are made in Tanzania and Kenya (as well as in India, Japan, and elsewhere), often adorned with proverbs in Swahili, and they depict objects and images that appeal to East African consumers. Yet their East African identity includes India, Britain, and the American Civil War.

MAKING IT LOCAL: WRAPPERS AND FLAGS

Like wax prints, two textiles from West Africa are the products of international networks and complicated histories. Unlike the industrial production that transformed wax prints, however, individual African textile artists produced these innovations. Also unlike wax prints, each of these textiles is associated with a specific region, where it is deeply embedded in local cultural practices. Both cloths have complicated stories, yet in their most essential characteristics both are definitively African. Pelete bite, a textile associated with the Kalabari Ijo ethnic group of the Niger Delta region, begins its life as an imported cloth, and it then becomes Nigerian through the removal of some of its threads. Asafo flags from coastal Ghana combine European iconography with Ghanaian modes of communication and social structure to create an entirely new form.

Pelete bite's story begins in the mid to late nineteenth century, when British merchants began to import light cotton textiles from India for sale in British West Africa, moving goods from one of their spheres of influence to another. Indeed, both India and Nigeria became British colonies, India in 1857 and Nigeria in 1914. In short, the movement of this cotton cloth from India to Nigeria was the result of connections created by the colonization of Africa and South Asia by a European power. The multilayered identity of this Indian cotton cloth, adorned with woven checks and plaid patterns, is evident in its names. It was called Madras by the British, a reference to the Indian city where many such textiles were produced, and George by the residents of the Niger Delta region, a reflection of the cloth's association with the British merchants who brought it to the region.

When Kalabari Ijo women acquired this patterned cloth, they developed a complex technique to adapt it to their dress styles. They used their understanding of the cloth's structure, the warp and weft that were its foundation, to selectively remove some threads without destroying the cloth. Using a razor blade or a knife, the makers of pelete bite—always women—cut and pull out sections of weft thread to create, for example, triangles that seem to emerge out of the stripes of a checkered or plaid fabric. This labor-intensive process requires that the women preserve the integrity of the cloth even as they weaken it. (See figure 3.2.2.)

Pelete bite has become a symbol of Kalabari Ijo identity. Despite its origins as an imported textile, the cloth is so deeply embedded in local culture that it has become a key element of funerals and baptisms—social rituals that are foundational to people's communal and individual personal identities. At funerals, pelete bite is used to adorn the room in which visitations take place, artfully draped on walls and layered on the bed where the body is laid out. At baptisms, the baby is wrapped in the cloth as he or she is presented to the community. Through the removal of threads, women augment the social significance of otherwise unremarkable plaid fabrics, transforming the British George into Kalabari Ijo pelete bite.

The transformation of imported forms into symbols of local culture can be viewed as an assertion of agency; rather than being transformed by imported styles, local cultures remake textiles to suit their social and aesthetic systems. The political nature of this transformation is particularly clear in the case of Ghana's Asafo flags, or *frankaa* in Akan. Unlike wax prints or pelete bite, these brightly colored banners are not worn but rather displayed in public contexts. (See figure 3.2.3.) Asafo flags are made of appliqué fabrics in bold colors, with

FIG. 3.2.2. The Kalabari pelete bite artist Amonia Akoko, in Abalama, Nigeria, displaying a red pelete bite that she designed and cut. She is wearing an indigo wrapper set of her own design and execution. Photo by Joanne B. Eicher.

patterns, figures, and words stitched onto their surfaces. The appliqué technique is deceptively simple: pieces of cotton cloth in solid colors are cut into abstract and figurative forms, which are stitched onto a background cloth, also a single color, to create a flag that can be hung from a pole or carried in a procession. These flags exemplify the globally networked nature of nongarment textiles, for they are the products of international sources of inspiration and iconography, yet their uses and meanings are distinctively local.

FIG. 3.2.3. Flag dancer of Dentsifo no. 2 Company, Gomoa Dago, July 25, 2015. Photo by Silvia Forni.

The flags are associated with the Fante ethnic group of coastal Ghana, one of several ethnic groups that make up the Akan culture. Their coastal location brought the Fante into early contact with European traders who sailed around the coast of West Africa in the late fifteenth century. Asafo are military units that were first created among the Fante in the eighteenth century, consisting of groups of men who could protect the town or neighborhood against other groups, though their role has long been more symbolic than actually military. Asafo units may perform community services such as cleaning public spaces and assisting police in emergencies. Asafo companies also appear at public events, parading in uniform and bearing flags as their insignia.

Skillful flag makers create images that evoke each group's history and its purported military prowess: the flag may commemorate a legendary battle, make a taunting reference to a neighboring unit or community, or simply declare the greatness of the company that bears it. Flag makers often use proverbs to communicate these complicated ideas in a single, readily decipherable image. Proverbs are central to Akan culture, used to communicate values and principles in entertaining, memorable forms. They often feature

animals as well as people, which flag makers skillfully depict using silhou-
ettes cut from cloth in bright colors, sometimes enhanced with embroidered
features. Text, in English or Akan, may be incorporated as well—large, block
letters appliquéd to the surface, often declaring the name of the Asafo unit.
The flags must communicate from afar, so that bold shapes on an empty field
are effective, while detail is unimportant.

Though their precise history is not known, the flags might have been inspired
by European flags and banners. The long familiarity of Fante people with
Western culture would have made flags a familiar sight, flying from a ship's mast
or a fort's towers, or carried in parades and battles. This influence is plainly evident in an important element of the flags' iconography, the sole aspect of their
design that remains consistent whatever the proverbial imagery: a small flag
appears on the upper left corner of each flag. In a reflection of the very long
history of Fante interaction with Europeans, and particularly with the British,
on Asafo flags that predate the mid–twentieth century, the flag in the corner is
the British Union Jack. Using strips of red, white, and blue fabric, flag makers
re-created the overlapping bands that are immediately recognizable as the insignia of the United Kingdom, and of its former colonies. The Union Jack might
have made its way onto Asafo flags as a means of emphasizing their "flag-ness,"
or as a way to affiliate the Asafo units with a powerful military force.

Flag makers adapted these visual statements of their Asafo units' might to
changing power dynamics: when Ghana became the first former European
colony in West Africa to gain independence, Asafo flags ceased to display the
British flag. Instead, with the establishment of Ghana as an independent
nation in 1957, Asafo flags began to feature the Ghanaian flag's bands of red,
yellow, and green, with a black star at its center. While the flag form has
continued to play an important role in Asafo symbology, its iconography was
quickly adjusted to reflect a new source of political power.

CLOTHING STYLES IN MOTION: *BOUBOUS* AND BEADED BRAIDS

Along with cloths that travel, transformed by African and non-African inno-
vators, garment styles may move as well. Garments may move from one
African region to another, as exemplified by the beautifully embroidered
gowns associated with an early-twentieth-century Central African ruler,
King Ibrahim Njoya of the Bamum Kingdom in Cameroon. This leader and

innovator in many realms will also lead us to an instance of garment innovation that reaches across continents.

Njoya was the ruler of the Bamum Kingdom between 1889 and 1933. His use of textiles is unusually well documented as a result of his fascination with photography. Beginning in 1902, Njoya and the members of his court posed for photographs taken by German missionaries, colonial agents, and merchants who visited the kingdom. A decade later, Njoya himself began to take photographs of the people and activities in his palace. In these images, Njoya and his subjects appear in a wide array of clothing styles, all of which are the products of global networks of textiles and people.

Many photographs depict residents of Bamum wearing long, flowing robes adorned with embroidered patterns on their yokes and chests. The untailored, dramatically large garments are of a type that is today worn by men and women in many parts of West and Central Africa, in regional variations that reflect local embroidery styles and fabric preferences. This garment goes by many names, including *boubou, agbada,* and *riga.* Whatever its name, the robe is associated with prestige and with Muslim piety. King Njoya's use of the *boubou* was not a reflection of long-standing practice, nor was it a symbol of his kingdom's deeply rooted embrace of Islam. Instead, the Bamum court's adaptation of these garments was the result of Njoya's successful bid for military assistance from a neighboring ruler, of the Muslim Fulani ethnic group, to suppress a rebellion. In gratitude for his aid, Njoya converted to Islam and adopted elements of Fulani culture, including dress. The style was absorbed into traditional attire in Bamum, and it is still worn today.

Other photographs by Njoya and visitors to his kingdom portray the king and his court wearing sharply tailored German-style military dress uniforms. These are more obvious products of globalization, indicating the king's fluency in the status symbols of the German traders and missionaries who were newly established in his domain. Rather than simply acquiring German garments, Njoya created his own, Bamum-style versions of the tightly fitted jackets, pants, and shirts. His tailors and embroiderers created innovative copies, using photographs of the German king and court as sources of inspiration. On some of the Bamum jackets, for example, the braided epaulets that appear on European uniforms have been translated into a Bamum emblem of power: beadwork. By transforming the braids into beads, re-created in a shape that resembles the original epaulets, King Njoya's uniform vividly illustrates the impact of globalization on African clothing and textiles, as well as the power of African innovation.

A final example of the global travels of African textiles demonstrates that their movements need not always cover geographical distances; within a single location, textiles and clothing styles may operate at multiple registers, aimed at distinct markets. The work of Amaka Osakwe, a Lagos-based fashion designer, illustrates this "globalization at home." Her brand, Maki Oh, employs the same design, production, and marketing strategies used by most Western designers, yet she adds a layer of distinctively African style through the subtle use of local materials. For example, a 2012 line of clothing included daringly brief women's shorts made of *adire,* a fabric adorned with indigo dye applied using a resist technique similar to batik. The cloth is closely associated with the Yoruba ethnic group, and women conventionally use it as wrappers, baby carriers, and head wraps. Osakwe's reinterpretation does not Westernize the textile, but rather globalizes it. Marketed in Lagos as well as in global cities the world over, Maki Oh garments circulate not as African attire but as contemporary fashion design. African textiles continue their journeys across cultural boundaries, places, markets, and meanings, sometimes experiencing dramatic transformations even in their places of origin.

ADDITIONAL RESOURCES

Erekosima, T. V., and J. B. Eicher. "Kalabari Cut Thread Cloth: An Example of Cultural Authentication." *African Arts* 14, no. 2 (1981): 48–51, 87.

Geary, Christraud. "Political Dress: German-Style Military Attire and Colonial Politics in Bamum." In *African Crossroads: Intersections between History and Anthropology in Cameroon,* edited by Ian Fowler and David Zeitlyn, 165–92. Providence, RI: Berghahn Books, 1996.

Kriger, Colleen E. *Cloth in West African History.* Lanham, MD: AltaMira, 2006.

Labi, Kwame A. "Fante *Asafo* Flags of Abandze and Kormantse: A Discourse between Rivals." *African Arts* 35, no. 4 (2002): 28–37, 92.

Mama Benz and the Taste of Money. Directed by Karin Junger. Produced by Carmen Cobos and Estelle Bovelander. New York: Filmakers Library, 2002.

Picton, John. *The Art of African Textiles: Technology, Tradition and Lurex.* London: Barbican Art Gallery, 1995.

Rovine, Victoria L. *African Fashion, Global Style: Histories, Innovations, and Ideas You Can Wear.* Bloomington: Indiana University Press, 2015.

Ryan, MacKenzie Moon. "Converging Trades and New Technologies: The Emergence of *Kanga* Textiles on the Swahili Coast in the Late Nineteenth Century."

In *An Ocean of Cloth: Textile Trades, Consumer Cultures and the Textile Worlds of the Indian Ocean,* edited by P. Machado, G. Campbell, and S. Fee. New York: Palgrave-Macmillan, forthcoming.

. . .

VICTORIA L. ROVINE is Associate Professor of Art History at the University of North Carolina at Chapel Hill. Her first book, *Bogolan: Shaping Culture through Cloth in Contemporary Mali* (Indiana University Press, 2008), examines the recent transformations of a Malian textile. Her second book, *African Fashion, Global Style: Histories, Innovations, and Ideas You Can Wear* (Indiana University Press, 2015), explores the innovations of designers from Africa, past and present, as well as Africa's presence in the Western fashion imaginary. Rovine is also a Research Associate with the Visual Identities in Art and Design Research Centre (VIAD) at the University of Johannesburg.

3.3

Sending Forth the Best

AFRICAN MISSIONS IN CHINA

Heidi Østbø Haugen

Abstract: The first African Pentecostal churches in China were founded by Nigerians two decades ago. The migrant-run ministries have a global and mission-oriented identity. Disappointed in how Christianity has developed in Europe, Nigerians in China have taken it upon themselves to conquer Asia for God.

Keywords: Nigeria, China, Pentecostalism, migrant, mission

CHRISTIAN NIGERIANS PRAISE EUROPEANS FOR bringing the Bible to Africa. But many think Europe has turned into a spiritual desert, placing Africans in charge of restoring God's kingdom on earth. To that end, they have planted dozens of churches in China.

Nigeria's most powerful Christian leader, Pastor E. A. Adeboye, made his first journey to China in 2014. He held sermons at a hotel surrounded by a French Renaissance–style garden, as lavish and eclectically global as the pastor's vision. Under Pastor Adeboye's leadership, the Redeemed Christian Church of God (RCCG) has set up branches across the world and relentlessly looks to extend its reach. The purpose of his visit to the city of Guangzhou, home to China's largest population of Africans, was to launch the "takeover of Asia for God." People came from Hong Kong, the Philippines, Malaysia, and beyond to meet the superstar preacher. Among the Chinese attendants, some were fervent believers, while others joined a charismatic service for the first time. But the audience primarily comprised African migrants, sharply dressed for the occasion. Suit-clad ushers led them to their seats, where they waited for the pastor's arrival. Next, a procession of black cars rushed up the driveway with flashing lights, resembling a presidential motorcade. Pastor Adeboye and his wife stepped out, followed by the pastoral couples in charge of the RCCG missions in Asia.

The RCCG has planted branches in over one hundred countries during Adeboye's time as its general overseer (he is affectionately nicknamed "Daddy G.O."). He travels around the world in a private airplane bought to "ease the stress of missionary assignments," as he has put it. Yet the visit to China proved difficult to organize. The pugnaciously secular Chinese state was not interested in receiving a foreign celebrity missionary with global ambitions. The visa and landing permit were denied. But laws go where dollars please, whether in Nigeria or China. The RCCG deployed a large Chinese entrepreneurial company as a go-between. The firm has been contracted by the RCCG to build a new "redemption camp": an enormous self-contained church city that will constitute one of Nigeria's largest urban construction projects. The pastor's bureaucratic problems were eventually resolved, and in September 2014, Daddy G.O.'s Gulfstream V jet was allowed to land at Guangzhou's Baiyun Airport.

The extravagant modes of transportation notwithstanding, the seventy-two-year-old pastor prides himself on a modest lifestyle. In a meeting with the African ministers based in China, he lectured about not eating too many portions of okra soup and keeping levelheaded when congregants flatter them. With a calm demeanor and baritone voice, he is known for his ability to put people at ease. At the same time, he called attention to his status in not-so-subtle ways, dropping references to his vast evangelical empire and close relationship with then-president of Nigeria Goodluck Jonathan. Pastor Adeboye's lectures were delivered in an accent that betrayed his Yoruba origins, and were translated into Mandarin for the benefit of the Chinese audience.

The Chinese government's concern that Pastor Adeboye intended to proselytize were not unfounded. He opened his four-day program in China by declaring that it was time for Asia to be handed over to Jesus. "I believe in God for China. I believe in God for Asia," he said. "Since we have set our feet on this land, the wind will blow and Asia will be saved. Every nation in Asia is held in bondage by forces of blackness. But deliverance will come." The speech elicited cheers, indicating that thousands of people were ready to take on the task.

Pastor Adeboye embodies wealth and uninhibited spatial mobility—assets that African migrants in China aspire to secure. Nobody knows how many Africans live in Guangzhou. The city authorities have registered sixteen thousand residents holding African passports, but the actual number of migrants staying there is probably much higher. The first African settlement in South China was formed by a group of Nigerians who had been deported from other parts of Asia to Hong Kong. The living costs in Hong Kong were exorbitant, and by moving across the border to mainland China, they could sustain themselves cheaply. They facilitated visits for itinerant African traders, who travel to Guangzhou several times a year to restock and keep abreast of the latest fashions. Migrants offer compatriots lodging, interpretation, and logistics services. There are also a number of African students selecting Chinese universities for their low tuition and easy visa procedures. In addition, a number of Africans enter China without much knowledge about the country and its employment structure, often encouraged by visa agents who exaggerate the opportunities China offers. These migrants typically arrive on a thirty-day business visa, and must return home empty-handed or stay on as undocumented migrants after the document expires. Many opt for the latter, hustling while hiding from the police. All of these groups may establish a church: there are examples of congregations in China lead by African businesspeople, students, and undocumented migrants.

Guangzhou has hosted African Christian and Muslim institutions for centuries. Most of the African-initiated churches in China today are Pentecostal: they emphasize direct experience with God and the working of the Holy Spirit in people's lives through glossolalia, divine healing, and other practices. Every Sunday, pulpits are raised and chairs set up in temporary preaching sites, rented in office buildings, hotels, and restaurants. The spaces of worship are undetectable from the outside, and newcomers find them through friends and business partners. Nigerians and Congolese were the first to establish ministries in China, and some of these are still active. Other churches have a fleeting presence: they are set up by newly arrived migrants who leave China quickly or fail to raise money to sustain their ministries. At any one time, there may be a choice of services in English, French, or Portuguese, as well as several Niger-Congo languages. The churches are financed by contributions from members in China: seed faith giving, offerings, tithes, and monetary gifts to fund specific projects.

The venue of the RCCG conference, while extravagant, was inconveniently located on former farmland under redevelopment to accommodate Guangzhou's sprawling growth. (As such, the venue's name was changed from Pasture Village to Evergrande Royal Scenic Peninsula.) There were no road signs to inform the public about the program and no mention in Chinese media of Pastor Adeboye's visit. This discretion contrasts with Nigeria, where churches and Christian messages are ubiquitous in the urban landscape. The RCCG uses physical infrastructure like the planned redemption camp to advertise its presence. The organization's vision is defined in spatial terms: to plant churches five minutes' travel time apart in every city and town in the world. Abroad as well as in Nigeria, the RCCG aspires to move into first-rate buildings that dominate the urban landscape, preferably owned rather than rented. The church buildings are signs of God's blessing. A favorite RCCG anecdote is that of young Daddy G.O. asking for a house in prayer, and the Lord answering by granting him a city.

. . .

China has exerted a special attraction on generations of Christian missionaries. At the beginning of the twentieth century, the country became a favorite destination for Pentecostal proselytizers. Demographics rendered the saving of the Chinese an urgent priority in missionary work: a third of the world's population lived in China at the time; a million Chinese passed into eternity every month, condemned to everlasting agony unless saved.

In any current attempt to forecast global religious developments, China represents a critical unknown. There is no reliable data on religious affiliation or conversion in the country. The Chinese Christian population is put at 68 million persons by the Pew Research Center's report *The Future of World Religions*. Population growth alone will only slightly elevate this number. However, the effects of religious conversion are potentially immense. If the current estimated conversion rates are maintained, Purdue University sociologist Fenggang Yang suggests, 734 million Christians will live in China by 2050. Meanwhile, Europe's Christian population will drop substantially, and Africa is poised to become the heartland of global Christianity. Four out of every ten Christians in the world will live in sub-Saharan Africa by 2050 according to the Pew projections. Pentecostals now represent 12 percent of Africa's population, and the share is growing.

While the Chinese population has halted its rapid growth, the economy has not. China's remarkable economic growth has become an added rationale for evangelization. In the view of many Nigerians in Guangzhou, it is time to place China's abundant material blessings under Christian leadership, and Africans must be the catalysts for this turnaround. As a Nigerian usher in a Guangzhou church explained, contrasting the resilience of Africans with the softness of white people: "Africans are the only ones who can bear China," he said. "The more Christians face persecution, the more stubborn they will become. Persecution is what is raising the Gospel. Hunger and harassment will raise it. But no white man can stand it." Converting China to Christianity has become the black man's burden.

China's colonial history provides impetus for the present-day suspicion against religion in general and foreign missionaries in particular. Missionary organizations were associated with British imperialism, including the opium trade and the enrollment of Chinese indentured laborers. When China came under communist rule in 1949, all foreign preachers were expelled. Paradoxically, during the Cultural Revolution (1966–76), when religious activities in China were more suppressed than ever, a Pentecostal-style Christianity gained a foothold. It manifested many of the same practices as African Pentecostalism: faith healing, spiritual warfare, exorcism. The assault on Chinese traditional religion and the removal of Christian authorities during the Cultural Revolution provided a fertile ground for Pentecostal practices to develop.

After the upheaval of the Cultural Revolution subsided, the Chinese government instituted state-sanctioned places of Christian worship. The Catholic Sacred Heart Cathedral in Guangzhou is one of them. The church organizes English-language services and hosts prayer meetings for Africans. But many African Catholics are unhappy with the austere ceremonies. They turn toward foreign-run Pentecostal churches, which operate illegally, without official approval. The Public Security Bureau, which enforces religious regulations in China, tacitly tolerates the African ministries as long as they operate discreetly. Above all, the churches should remain invisible and refrain from proselytizing among Chinese nationals.

. . .

The strict regulation of religious activities notwithstanding, Pastor Charles from Nigeria was very optimistic when he founded a church—The Tower of Salvation—in Guangzhou in 1998. (I am using pseudonyms for the church and pastor.) It was the advent of African migration to China, and the congregation grew as more migrants arrived. The Chinese proved receptive to Pastor Charles's preaching. He rented a swimming pool to baptize new followers, wedded Chinese couples, and coached a local pastor. For a while, the Tower of Salvation sustained a Chinese underground church that was managed on a day-to-day basis by the minister trained in its midst. "Before 2007, things were moving at an incredible pace," Pastor Charles recollected. "Now things are bad." He attributed the difficulties he has experienced to demonic forces. "Ultimately, everything bad can be attributed to the devil. He is the architect behind what has happened. But in the end, God will convert evil for good."

The laws concerning religious activities have remained unchanged since the 1990s, but they are gradually being implemented more strictly. The tolerance for preaching among Chinese citizens is particularly low because the subversive potential is seen as greater when Chinese believers assemble. Therefore, while religious gatherings outside the state-sanctioned places of worship are prohibited for foreigners and Chinese nationals alike, they elicit different responses. Most African churches therefore not only have stopped making efforts to attract Chinese congregants, but also turn away Chinese citizens unless they are very closely associated with their African members.

The understandings between the churches and the Chinese Public Security Bureau are usually worked out in quiet. However, one Nigerian church violated this norm a few years back by inviting an open confrontation. About twenty police officers entered a church service to interrupt it. "You are requested to stop these activities immediately," the operational leader ordered, reading from the Chinese law about foreign religious activities. The pastor responded with a shout ("Praise the Lord!"), and the congregation broke into song and prayer. Inevitably, the pastor was expelled from China. He settled in Hong Kong, from where he has continued to run churches in China and has established branches in Nigeria, Cameroon, the Philippines, and the United Kingdom.

The work of missionaries from developing countries to win converts in Europe, the traditional Christian heartland, is described by the term "reverse mission." It has been an effort of mixed success. The most remarkable achievement has been made in Ukraine, where two thriving megachurches were started by Nigerian and Zimbabwean former students in Eastern Europe. Both ministries are primarily filled with Ukrainian believers. By contrast, the African-initiated churches in western Europe mainly attract migrants from Africa and other parts of the world and struggle to appeal to the indigenous population.

Regardless of the ethnic composition of their ministries, the self-image of African Pentecostal churches is invariably global. With this identity comes the responsibility to conquer the world for Jesus. "Nigeria has released to the world more missionaries, more missions, and more ministers than any other nation," Pastor Charles said. "Most of the greatest and thriving churches that truly understand the counsel and purpose of God today come from Nigeria.

And they are spread all over, from Ukraine, right up through Europe, right up through South and North America."

Pastor Charles and his followers believe that God has made a covenant with Africans: when promulgating Christianity in its true form, they will receive material rewards. The pastor understands that evangelization and economic advancement to go hand in hand, and encourages people to make migration decisions accordingly. "Whenever you see a nation receiving a spiritual awakening, mark that nation! If you have something to invest, run towards there because that is where to sow the seed. When the spiritual finishes, the physical begins to manifest," he said. It was based on this idea that he first set course for China, where he has enjoyed some success as a businessman and preacher.

· · ·

The origin of the Pentecostal movement is identified as the Azusa Street Revival in Los Angeles. In 1906, an African-American preacher baptized in the Holy Spirit led an interracial congregation in vivid worship. Dozens of missionaries were sent out of the Azusa Street ministry, and within its first two years the movement reached fifty countries, including China. The lack of formal authorization procedures for Pentecostal clergy means that anyone who is called upon by God can run a church, and leaders from the Azusa Street Revival spun off to form other congregations. Pastors who break out of the ministries they are trained in to form their own churches remain a common phenomenon in the Nigerian Pentecostal movement today.

Nigerian churches have incorporated some elements of their American Pentecostal counterparts. Praise songs, literature, and tales originating in the United States are adopted by African ministries, and pastoral exchanges take place across the Atlantic. But the Nigerian-founded churches are above all African, and proudly so. Nigerian pastors are happy to accommodate conservative US preachers in search of new affiliations to escape liberal interpretations of the Bible at home, but they will not take orders from foreigners. An exchange between Coca-Cola's marketing department and Pastor Adeboye illustrates how Pentecostalism goes hand in hand with national pride in Nigeria, as in the United States. Coca-Cola sent a customized gift to the pastor. "Thank you Coca-Cola NBC for sending me my own personal bottle. Shame I don't drink Coke. I drink Chivita Ice Tea lemon and Grand Malt though," Pastor Adeboye responded on Twitter, providing publicity for his preferred Nigerian soft drinks instead.

. . .

The global expansion of Pentecostalism is facilitated by its remarkable ability to adapt to local circumstances. In Africa, the Pentecostal churches have neither ignored nor incorporated traditional beliefs. Rather, local spirits are confronted and ferociously combatted. The spiritual entities in African religious traditions are fused with the Christian image of the devil. During church services, believers name their afflictions as a first step toward overcoming them. Examples of problems Nigerian traders experience in China include goods stuck in customs, business partners who embezzle money, and orders that run dry. These difficulties are perceived to originate in personal relations, play out in the spiritual realm, and require the remedy of prayers. Prayers thus sustain beliefs in a universe where attacks by witches and wizards loom.

The Pentecostal practices transported from Africa to China have undergone change. For Nigerian migrants, the remoteness of their relatives and hometowns creates a sense of distance from demonic influences—forces that churches are vehicles for combatting. Pastor Charles complained that African Christians become much less committed to their religion when they go abroad. "People do not want to miss church for anything in Africa. When in Africa, there are witches and wizards everywhere. A rich man will be the first to come. He has to protect his blessings when they send demons after him," he said to explain why running a migrant church in China is difficult.

The rich spiritual universe of the African Pentecostal churches has been subject to exoticization and misrepresentation. The tendency for mass media to caricature African spirituality has been particularly strong in Europe. Tragedies such as murder, child abuse, and sex trafficking have been portrayed as the consequence of exotic ritualism, the details of which are often meticulously outlined in the media. Such reporting conceals the structural basis for the violence, such as stringent immigration policies that separate children from guardians, and the inadequate protection offered for undocumented migrants. African religious leaders in Europe have attempted to counter the negative public perception of their churches through engaging in community services and by responding directly to adverse media coverage. In reaction to the reporting concerning the murder of a Nigerian boy in London, whose dismembered body was soon dubbed "the Thames Torso," a church leader felt the need to stress that "murder is not a part of African religious practices." His indignation was evident when he argued that the crime "should be treated the same way as any other murder, not as a cultural persecution through invented 'cultural profiling.'"

In China, African missionaries have two advantages over their compatriots in Europe: Their theology will not be compared with a "pure" or "original" form of Christian worship. And many potential followers already recognize various spiritual forces as part of their everyday lives. The prosperity gospel—the belief that God rewards his followers with material riches—also seems to sit comfortably with many Chinese. The city of Wenzhou, which spearheaded China's manufacturing growth, is known for its "boss Christians," for whom getting rich and serving God are flip sides of the same coin.

The young Nigerian men in the Tower of Salvation do indeed find it easy to get Chinese youth interested in the Gospel. They introduce Jesus to people they meet in trading malls, on buses, and in parks. But the momentum is hard to sustain without institutions where converts' initial fascination can be nurtured. While Pastor Charles continues to think of himself as a missionary, he turns most Chinese believers away from the main church to appease the local government. He aspires to establish eight more underground churches for Chinese followers and, when conditions in China are more conducive, to start a Pentecostal televangelism channel. For now, he finds consolation in his early achievements. "One of my greatest joys is to think of all the Chinese I have converted and the churches that may have been planted by them," he says.

On the last day of the RCCG festival in Guangzhou, attendance dropped. The services led by Pastor Adeboye had been subdued and bland compared with those of the African churches that have been initiated in China. Above all, people were disappointed that he had not produced any miracles, which he does at gatherings in Nigeria. The China chapter of RCCG counted only a few dozen members after Pastor Adeboye left Guangzhou. Yet the young usher who had invited me to their festival was undeterred. "Of course everyone likes to see miracles," he said. "But taking over Asia will be hard work."

ADDITIONAL RESOURCES

Adogame, Afe. "Engaging the Rhetoric of Spiritual Warfare: The Public Face of Aladura in Diaspora." *Journal of Religion in Africa* 34 (2004): 493–522.

————, ed. *The Public Face of African New Religious Movements in Diaspora: Imagining the Religious "Other."* Farnham, UK: Ashgate Publishing, 2014.

Haugen, Heidi Østbø. "Destination China: The Country Adjusts to Its New Migration Reality." Migration Policy Institute, Migration Information Source, 2015. www.migrationpolicy.org/article/destination-china-country-adjusts-its-new-migration-reality.

Marshall, Ruth. *Political Spiritualities: The Pentecostal Revolution in Nigeria.* Chicago: University of Chicago Press, 2009.

My Father's House. Directed by David L. Bandurski and Dayong Zhao. dGenerate Films, 2012. Documentary.

. . .

HEIDI ØSTBØ HAUGEN is a postdoctoral researcher at the Department of Sociology and Human Geography, University of Oslo. She has done research on migration and trade between West Africa and China since 2003. Between 2009 and 2016, she carried out sixteen months of fieldwork among Africans living in Guangzhou, South China, during which she followed several persons over a five-year period. She was a visiting scholar at Sun Yat-sen University in 2014 and has studied Chinese at Beijing Normal University. Prior to starting her PhD, she worked at the United Nations World Food Programme's West Africa Bureau.

3 · 4

Photo Essay

BAOHAN STREET: AN AFRICAN COMMUNITY IN GUANGZHOU, CHINA

Michaela Pelican and Li Dong

Abstract: Over the past two decades, China has become a new and attractive destination for migrants from all over the world, including Africa. The city of Guangzhou, with its long history of international trade, has attracted tens of thousands of Africans, primarily to do business. Here we focus on Baohan Street, an area frequented by African traders.

Keywords: Africans in China, Guangzhou, globalization, trade

WE ARE IN THE HEART of Guangzhou, a megacity in southeastern China with an estimated fourteen million inhabitants. Amid the many high-rise buildings that characterize the city's developed zones, we look down on one of the many "urban villages" where Baohan Street is located. Urban villages are areas still owned and managed by the town's original residents, who have turned their properties into cheap, low-class accommodations rented out to Chinese rural migrants or, as in the case of Baohan Street, to foreign traders, often from Africa, South Asia, and the Middle East.

In the past ten to fifteen years, the People's Republic of China has attracted many visitors and migrants from different parts of the globe. In particular, the city of Guangzhou, being an ancient center of commerce and global connections, has experienced the arrival of tens of thousands of traders and migrants from many parts of Africa, including Nigeria, Ghana, Guinea, Senegal, Mali, Niger, Cameroon, Uganda, Kenya, Tanzania, Somalia, Mozambique, and South Africa. Many have been attracted by the Canton Fair, held in spring and autumn every year. The majority are visiting traders and short-term residents who frequent local markets and factories to purchase manufactured goods to be shipped in bulk to Africa. Many reside in the Baiyun or Yuexiu District, where Baohan Street is located. Besides these temporary visitors, there are also more-established migrants, mostly businesspeople, professionals, and students who have lived in Guangzhou for a number of years and who prefer to reside in other, often better-off, parts of the city.

Determining the number of Africans in Guangzhou is a challenge. There have been estimates of two hundred thousand temporary visitors from Africa, and in October 2014 the Guangzhou administration announced that sixteen thousand Africans were registered as permanent residents. While their number in any case accounts for less than 1.5 percent of Guangzhou's population, it is their conspicuous presence in the city's commercial life that has made them stand out.

Coverage in the national media and discussions in Chinese social forums have shaped the diverse opinions of the Chinese public about the presence of Africans in Guangzhou. These range from commentaries highlighting the economic and social benefits of China's opening to the world, to remarks with a nationalist undertone that emphasize the disruptive influence of foreigners. It is to this ongoing debate that the documentary photographer Li Dong wanted to make a critical but constructive contribution. With his photographs of "the new Guangzhou residents," he wishes to draw attention to the globalizing and multiethnic character of urban spaces in China and to some of the associated but neglected social issues.

Li Dong's perspective is necessarily partial and focuses on particular groups of migrants in a specific social environment. Baohan Street is a low-end commercial and residential area, frequented by traders from Africa, the Middle East, and South Asia. It is the place to start out, and to build up social and economic capital so as to venture into Guangzhou's countless markets. It is popular not only among African traders but also among Chinese migrants from other parts of the country. Of the latter, many belong to the Hui and Uyghur ethnic minorities and are Muslims. They run food shops and restaurants, offer money exchange, transport facilities, phone booths, and numerous other services in demand by visiting traders. Many of their customers are also Muslims, and their joint presence contributes to the neighborhood's transnational Muslim atmosphere.

Most of the houses on Baohan Street belong to local Chinese, and the rental market is firmly in Cantonese hands. Ms. Liu, for example, has been in the business since 2002, managing hundreds of rooms in the area. Like most house owners, she originally lived in this urban village but later moved to the city's outskirts, where housing is less crowded and of a higher standard. In the beginning, many people did not like to rent out apartments to Africans, but as money started to flow, it was no longer a problem. By 2014 about 10 percent of Ms. Liu's rooms were rented out to Africans. She explained that she had no problem renting rooms to anyone and that nationality or religious affiliation did not matter as long as her client's visa was in order and the rent was being paid. However, this situation changed in early 2015, when the Guangzhou city administration decided to tighten the registration requirements for foreigners wanting to reside in the Yuexiu District. As a result, many African traders were no longer able to rent a room on Baohan Street and were obliged to lodge in a hotel or move to a different area. The new regulations thus caused substantial annoyances and economic losses, both for Cantonese landlords and for their African clients.

The tightening of administrative measures and police control in the Yuexiu District preceded numerous other interventions to curb irregular migration. Although the Chinese government has welcomed foreigners as temporary visitors who come for leisure, studies, or business or as professionals with a timed work contract, it seldom grants long-term residency to foreigners. So while entering China is relatively easy and affordable, extending and regularizing one's stay have become increasingly difficult. As a result, several migrants have inadvertently or knowingly become overstayers—a situation the local administration is attempting to control through stricter policing.

The recent measures on Baohan Street have engendered diverse responses within both Chinese and African publics. Some of the well-established African migrants condone the tighter policing as a measure to ensure a safer business environment. Others sympathize with their suffering compatriots and see their own businesses negatively affected. Johnny, for example, started off as a broker for visiting African traders and later ran a small restaurant together with his Chinese wife. Eventually, they decided to open a bar next to Baohan Street, mainly catering to the needs of an African clientele. Johnny was worried about the sudden slump in customers; in the meantime, business activities have recuperated. And while life on Baohan Street has gradually been restored, the street's lively character has transformed lastingly, giving way to a more regulated and tidy environment.

NOTE

Research for this chapter was supported by the Global South Studies Center of the University of Cologne and the German Research Foundation (DFG, project AH 210/1–1).

FIG. 3.4.1. Guangzhou, Yuexiu District, 2013. Photo by Li Dong.

FIG. 3.4.2. Guangzhou, Baohan Street, 2013. Photo by Li Dong.

FIG. 3.4.3. Baohan Street, business life, 2013. Photo by Li Dong.

FIG. 3.4.4. Baohan Street, phone booth, 2013. Photo by Li Dong.

FIG. 3.4.5. Baohan Street, Chinese Muslim migrants, 2013. Photo by Li Dong.

FIG. 3.4.6. Baohan Street, Chinese and African Muslims, 2013. Photo by Li Dong.

FIG. 3.4.7. Baohan street, landlady with customers, 2013. Photo by Li Dong.

FIG. 3.4.8. Baohan Street, police patrol, 2015. Photo by Li Dong.

FIG. 3.4.9. Johnny's former restaurant, 2014. Photo by Li Dong.

FIG. 3.4.10. Baohan Street, August 2015. Photo by Li Dong.

Castillo, Roberto. *Africans in China: Cultural Research about Africans in China, and Beyond* (blog). Accessed October 18, 2015. http://africansinchina.net/.

China Remix. Directed by Dorian Carli-Jones and Melissa Lefkowitz 2015. Documentary film. Accessed October 18, 2015. Documentary. www.chinaremixmovie.com.

Haugen, Heidi Østbø. "Destination China: The Country Adjusts to Its New Migration Reality." Migration Policy Institute, Migration Information Source, 2015. Accessed October 18, 2015. www.migrationpolicy.org/article/destination-china-country-adjusts-its-new-migration-reality.

Li, Zhigang, Michael Lyons, and Alison Brown. "China's 'Chocolate City': An Ethnic Enclave in a Changing Landscape." *African Diaspora* 5 (2012): 51–72.

Pelican, Michaela, ed. *BAOHAN Street: An African Community in Guangzhou; Documentary Photographs by Li Dong.* Kölner Arbeitspapiere zur Ethnologie 4. Cologne: Department of Cultural and Social Anthropology, University of Cologne, 2014. http://kups.ub.uni-koeln.de/5782/.

Traub, Daniel. "Little North Road." Photographic project. Accessed October 18, 2015. www.xiaobeilu.org/.

Uturn Asia. Website by Heidi Østbø Haugen and Manon Diederich in collaboration with Gambian migrants who have been to China. https://uturnasia.com/

. . .

MICHAELA PELICAN is a Junior Professor of Cultural and Social Anthropology at the University of Cologne. Her current research focuses on migration from Africa to the Arab Gulf States and China. In her latest project, she has collaborated with the Chinese documentary photographer Li Dong, who spent two years on Baohan Street documenting the lives of domestic and foreign migrants. His exhibition *The African Street* was shown in Guangzhou, Paris, Cologne, and Brussels in 2014, while another exhibition, *The Other's Home* (focusing on Chinese rural migrants), had its premiere in Guangzhou in June 2015.

3.5

The African Literary Tradition

INTERVIEW WITH NGŨGĨ WA THIONG'O

Mukoma Wa Ngugi

Abstract: In this interview, celebrated Kenyan writer and activist Ngũgĩ wa Thiong'o ponders how histories of European imperial power shaped publishing and language, and thus the African literary tradition.

Keywords: language, literature, imperialism, translation, diaspora, publishing industry

NGŨGĨ WA THIONG'O, CURRENTLY DISTINGUISHED Professor of English and Comparative Literature at the University of California, Irvine, is a novelist, essayist, playwright, journalist, editor, academic, and social activist from Kenya. His early works include *Weep Not Child* (1964), *The River Between* (1965), *A Grain of Wheat* (1967), *Secret Lives* (1969), and *Petals of Blood* (1977). The year 1977 forced dramatic turns in Ngũgĩ's life and career. *Petals of Blood* painted a harsh and unsparing picture of life in neocolonial Kenya. That same year Ngũgĩ's controversial play *Ngaahika Ndeenda* ("I Will Marry When I Want"), written with Ngugi wa Mirii, was performed at the Kamirithu Educational and Cultural Center, Limuru, in an open-air theater. Sharply critical of the inequalities and injustices of Kenyan society, Ngũgĩ was arrested and imprisoned without charge at Kamiti Maximum Security Prison (see *Detained: A Writer's Prison Diary,* 1981). After Amnesty International named him a Prisoner of Conscience, an international campaign secured his release a year later, in December 1978. It was at Kamiti Maximum Prison that Ngũgĩ made the decision to abandon English as his primary language of creative writing and committed himself to writing in Gikuyu, his mother tongue. In prison, and following that decision, he wrote, on toilet paper, the novel, *Caitani Mutharabaini* (1981), translated into English as *Devil on the Cross* (1982). While in Britain for the launch and promotion of *Devil on the Cross,* he learned about the Moi regime's plot to eliminate him on his return. This forced him into exile, first in Britain (1982–89) and then the United States (1989–2002). He remained in exile for the duration of the Moi dictatorship. When he and his wife, Njeeri, returned to Kenya in 2004 after twenty-two years in exile, they were attacked by four hired gunmen and narrowly escaped with their lives. His later works include *Murogi wa Kagogo* (2004), published in English as *Wizard of the Crow* (2006); *Something Torn and New: An African Renaissance* (2009); *Dreams in a Time of War: A Childhood Memoir* (2010); *Globalectics: Theory and the Politics of Knowing* (2012); and *In the House of the Interpreter* (2012).

ON THE AFRICAN LITERARY TRADITION

In his autobiography, Allan Hill, the founder of the Heinemann African Writers series, says he wanted to change the way books were published in Africa by big Western publishers, whose sole interest he saw as profit while "putting nothing back in the way of investment in local publishing and encouragement of local authors." He therefore felt that the African Writers Series (AWS), published by Heinemann Educational Books, could provide a "publishing service for African authors." To what extent did AWS fulfill this vision? What have been some of the pitfalls?

Allan Hill was among those that I describe as practical visionaries. By this I mean people who have a vision but also a tactical sense of how to realize it. People who see the possibility in a moment, seize the time, and unlock the possibility. Good practice produced good profit, and all the stakeholders—writer, publisher, and reader—gained from it. The African Writers Series was born at the moment of transition of the African continent from colonial imperialism to independent status. The series acted as a ready venue for emerging African writers, most of them products of English or French departments of universities in Africa or abroad. And through translations, the series brought together most of the then-existing works in Arabic, English, French, and Portuguese. By putting all African writers together, the AWS gave us the nearest thing to a common Pan-African cultural product. That was the good side. The negative side was that this fit very well with the neocolonial character of the emergent independent states who flew the flag and sang a national anthem, but whose economic tunes were still composed from the metropolises of the West. Africa still provided raw materials that were processed in those metropolises and then resold to the [African] continent. So African writers provided the raw materials, which were processed in England and then resold for the expanding school market in Africa. The series also cemented, for the Anglophone, the centrality of European languages in the definition of what constituted African literature.

But on the positive side of that intervention, the series spawned other series including the Caribbean Writers Series and the Asian Writers Series, and also inspired competing centers of African publishing. Some branches of the Heinemann literary empire declared their independence. And that was how the former Heinemann branch in Kenya became the giant, Kenya-based East Africa Educational Publishers.

The watershed 1962 Makerere Conference, "African Writers of an English Expression," excluded writers working in African languages. What historically was the norm for other cultures—writing in their languages and then getting translated—became the abnormal for African writers. Can you take us back to 1962 and describe for us your relationship to the English language and literature then?

I talk about this moment, and my relationship to it, in my forthcoming memoir, *Birth of a Dreamweaver.* As for my relationship to English, it forms the cornerstone of my 1984 book, *Decolonizing the Mind.* But quite briefly, what went for the cultural norms, or even economic norms, of the newly independent African countries was a normalization of abnormality. The colonial armies that were literally hunting down the nationalists fighting for independence overnight became national armies, defenders of the very independence they fought tooth and nail to prevent! As for the economy, Western corporations continued their game with Africa's natural resources. The normalization of English, French, and Portuguese was in the same vein. My entire school education from middle school, high school, to college, was in English. English had in fact become the central criterion of one's intelligence and educational worth. When I started writing, I never agonized about the language issue: whether or not to write in English. To intellectualize in English had become an axiomatic norm.

Michael Beach has argued that Samuel Johnson [who created an authoritative dictionary of standard English in 1755] and others hoped that English culture "would become the building block of . . . a metaphysical empire, an empire of language and literature that would outlive the actual British Empire." You, however, have been emphatic that English is not an African language. Can you elaborate on why English is not an African language?

One can use a language, for whatever reason or purpose, without having to claim that its national origins is other than it was. African writers have used English with innovative mastery, and that has never been the issue. They have even added to the possibilities of English! But English does not need African writers! African languages need African writers.

By the way, the concept of metaphysical empire is very apt in describing the state of power relationship between languages in the world today, particularly in those countries and nations that were once colonies. You once drew my attention to it, and it has really helped me in further understanding the politics of the colony of the mind.

What is your response to writers and critics who have argued that English is a unifying language? Or to those who argue that English is a Pan-African language that can, ironically, help in decolonization? Is it possible for decolonization to contribute to the English metaphysical empire?

Unifying whom? The middle class? In *Decolonizing the Mind,* I have talked of languages as carriers of cultures and as means of communication. For purely historical reasons, English and other European languages have become the languages of power in Africa. Mastery of the languages of power, whatever they are, is a matter of economic and political survival. But there is nothing inherent in any language that makes it occupy the position of power broker. It is matter of history. In our case that history is colonialism. I say, use English to enable but not to disable. Enable without disabling.

There is the principle of all languages being created equal and the pragmatics of it where English writing gets all the resources and writing in African languages very little in terms of publishing, literary prizes, and governmental support. What should writers and literary critics be doing in order to democratize languages? What is the role of the state? Can you speak more about how the pragmatics can be democratized?

There has to be equal distribution of resources between African [languages] and the "European" languages of power. I advocate a three-language policy for every African child. Mother tongue plus the language of intracommunity communication plus English (or whatever the language of power is). In the case of East Africa it would be mother tongue plus Kiswahili plus English, in that order. But for African languages to occupy their rightful place in the sun, state policies must change. African languages need governments plus publishers plus writers and finally readers.

Literary critics have somehow remained above the language debate. But writing in African languages cannot be complete without an accompanying literary criticism in African languages. Can you discuss the philosophical questions around literary criticism and language? And some of the pragmatics?

We are really in a vicious circle: there are no positive government policies on African languages. There are very few readers of African-language books. Therefore, very few publishers in African languages. Therefore, very few books in African languages. Therefore, no readers and buyers, no publishers, no books for use in schools, and so on. And because there are so few books in African languages, there is virtually no critical tradition in African languages. Somewhere, somehow, this vicious circle has to be broken. This includes intellectualizing and conceptualizing in African languages.

When my novel *Murogi wa Kagogo/Wizard of the Crow* came out in 2006, one African/Mūgīkūyū critic wrote a review of it in English for an English newspaper in Kenya, and complained bitterly that I had not written it in pure Gīkūyū. I checked on the Internet and elsewhere to see if this critic had ever written anything in Gīkūyū, and I could not find a thing!

Chinua Achebe's Things Fall Apart *has been translated into over fifty languages, making it the most-translated African novel. But even now, almost sixty years after it was first published, it has yet to be translated into Igbo, his language. What is the role of translation in African writing?*

Translation has always been the key in the development of languages. All major western European languages gained from translations from Greek, Latin, and Italian. The translations of the Bible have had a big impact on the development of the languages into which it has been translated. I would like to see translation become a subject in schools and colleges, and I would like to see translations between and among African languages; and from world languages into African languages. Call it translations every which way possible!

How is translating between African languages such as Kiswahili and Zulu different from translating from African languages into Western languages, or translating from Western languages into African languages?

I have no experience in this area, but I would assume that many African languages, particularly the ones grouped under the term "Bantu," have similar grammatical structures. They are natural allies!

The African literary clock often starts with the authors who attended the 1962 Makerere Conference, including Chinua Achebe, Ngũgĩ wa Thiong'o, Wole Soyinka, and Bessie Head. The myth has become so pervasive that almost without exception, critics generally herald Achebe as "the father of African Literature," a title that he himself was uncomfortable with, saying that "there were many fathers and mothers." For example, there is Thomas Mofolo's Moeti oa Bochabela, *published in 1907, later translated into English as* Traveller to the East *in 1934; and* Chaka, *written in 1909 but published only in 1931; and* Samuel Mqhayi's isiXhosa book, Ityala Lamawele (The Lawsuit of the Twins), *published in 1912. Why are they absent from both popular and literary imaginations? And what does that mean for the African literary tradition?*

This omission has everything to do with the politics of periodization in Africa. There are those who like to believe that Europhone African literature begins with the African Writers Series in the sixties! It is literary and critical nonsense, and African critics should and must correct this myopic view!

The question of where we start the African literary tradition becomes interesting when we consider that earlier literary critics understood early slave writing such as [Olaudah] Equiano's memoir/narrative as part of African literature. Why don't we read early slave writings, especially the ones whose imaginative power relies on memory of Africa?

All this is part of our heritage. Perhaps we should be teaching Africana. Africana would have two main branches: continental and diasporic. These main branches can further be split into smaller branches, depending on the needs of any particular nation and university. See my book *Something Torn and New!*

ON SOUTH-TO-SOUTH LITERARY NETWORKS

In 1963, Langston Hughes edited an anthology of African poetry, Poems from Black Africa. *Can you talk about the early African and African-American literary networks?*

Our links to the diaspora are as deep and continuous as our history since the sixteenth century. After all, the slave trade, slavery, and plantation slavery at the dawn of capitalist modernity meant the African body. And since those momentous events, our struggles on the continent and the struggles in the diaspora have mirrored each other. Even the brief period of reconstruction in America mirrors the brief period in Africa between the end of the slave trade and the scramble for Africa. Colonialism corresponds to Jim Crowism in America. The Civil Rights Act of 1964 corresponds to African people on the continent earning the right to vote.

These links are also reflected in cultural links. We share the slave narratives—but also cultural, intellectual, and political workers like Edward Blyden, Marcus Garvey, W. E. B. Du Bois, and Paul Robeson. The Harlem Renaissance impacted the Négritude movement.

In 1982 you met C. L. R James in London, who in turn advised you that exile is better than dying. Kamau Braithwaite—I have vague memories of this as a child—got the name Kamau in a ceremony held in our home in Limuru. Starting with a personal recollection of the renaming, can you talk a little about him and African and Caribbean literary connections?

My own connections with Caribbean writers begin with my discovery of the novels of George Lamming in Makerere. *In the Castle of My Skin,* in particular, made a strong impression on me. Professor Cherry Gertzel, of the history department, lent me the books. At Leeds in 1965, I chose to work on the Caribbean writers, in particular the work of George Lamming. It was during my Leeds years that I came into contact with John La Rose, Kamau Braithwaite (then Edward), and Andrew Salkey. I attended the second meeting of the Caribbean Arts Movement at Orlando Patterson's place in London. Later, when we changed the English department at Nairobi into the Department of Literature, I invited Kamau Braithwaite and George Lamming, at different times, into the department. Nyambura (your mom) and I gave a reception for Braithwaite at our rented home in Tigoni. Many women singers (mostly from the Njiriri family) sang for him. My mother gave him the name Kamau. "Edward" was gone forever.

How has the role of the writer in society changed over the years as we have moved from colonialism, to an incomplete decolonization, to unequal globalization?

With all the differences in ideological nuances, Europhone African literature has been socially engaged. Chimamanda Ngozi Adichie's *Half of a Yellow Sun* embodies the history of Nigeria and by extension Africa better than any historical work about the 1960s, or, generally, the immediate postcolonial era. I think the role of writers and writing remains the same across centuries: the use of the imagination to paint images of society that capture the contradictions in society, but hopefully on the side of change and hope.

You teach Adichie, NoViolet [Bulawayo], and other post-Makerere African writers. What are some of the continuities and discontinuities?

For me, the big division is between the Europhone literary tradition and the African-languages literary tradition.

For both Western and African literary critics, African writers are not often understood as artists working with words to create an aesthetic. What is the role of beauty in your writing?

We aspire to beauty. But the beautiful is not abstracted from the reality out of which it grows. Think of a flower. It is so beautiful. But it grows out of a plant with roots and trunks and branches. But the flower, so beautiful, also contains the seeds for the tomorrow of that plant.

ADDITIONAL RESOURCES

Thiong'o, Ngũgĩ wa. *Decolonizing the Mind: The Politics of Language in African Literature*. London: J. Currey, 1986.

———. *Devil on the Cross*. London: Heinemann, 1982.

———. *Dreams in a Time of War: A Childhood Memoir*. London: Harvill Secker, 2010.

———. *Globalectics: Theory and the Politics of Knowing*. New York: Columbia University Press, 2012.

———. *A Grain of Wheat*. London: Penguin in Association with Heinemann African Writers Series, 2002.

———. *In the House of the Interpreter: A Memoir*. New York: Pantheon, 2012.

———. *Something Torn and New: An African Renaissance*. New York: BasicCivitas, 2009.

· · ·

MUKOMA WA NGUGI is an Assistant Professor of English at Cornell University and the author of the novels *Mrs. Shaw* (Ohio University Press, 2015), *Black Star Nairobi* (Melville, 2013), *Nairobi Heat* (Melville, 2011), and two books of poetry, *Logotherapy* (University of Nebraska Press, 2016) and *Hurling Words at Consciousness* (Africa World Press, 2006). He is the cofounder of the Mabati-Cornell Kiswahili Prize for African Literature and codirector of the Global South Project (GSP)—Cornell. The goal of GSP is to facilitate public conversations among writers and scholars from Africa, Latin America, and Asia as well as minority groups in the West. In 2013, *New African* magazine named him one of the one hundred most Influential Africans. In 2015 he was a juror for the Writivism Short Story Prize and the Neustadt International Prize for Literature. Mukoma holds a PhD in English from the University of Wisconsin, Madison, and an MA in creative writing from Boston University. His father is Ngũgĩ wa Thiong'o.

African Soccer's Global Story

Peter Alegi

Abstract: African soccer has a complicated social, cultural, political, and economic history. Examining such issues as its involvement in FIFA, the migration of African players overseas, and the transformation of African fans into consumers of European football casts light on the contradictory effects of globalization.

Keywords: soccer (football), history, colonialism, globalization, Africa

THE STORY OF AFRICAN SOCCER (football) is a global tale. The modern game arrived in Africa in the late nineteenth century much as it did around the world: in the wake of Britain's assertion of commercial and imperial power. The earliest documented African matches were played in 1862—a year before the rules of the game were written down in London—by white colonial bureaucrats and soldiers in Port Elizabeth and Cape Town, South Africa. Coastal towns elsewhere in Africa were crucial to the game's first steps, as African boys and men congregated to watch European teams divided along national lines play formal and informal matches. By the 1920s, the sport had begun to spread from the coasts into the interior of the continent, precisely following the development of mission schools, railway lines, and colonial military outposts.

Western-style education brought football, alongside the Bible, collared shirts, and Shakespeare, into African boys' lives. In the British colonies, Victorian men and women carried with them a belief that sport forged physically fit young men of sound moral character. The French and other imperialists soon warmed to modern sport's potential to advance the self-ascribed "civilizing mission"—that is, to teach Africans the virtues of Christianity, capitalist commerce, and Western civilization. In the 1890s, students attending the school in Kiungani, Zanzibar, founded by the Universities' Mission to Central Africa already enjoyed football as a daily activity. By that time, in Natal, South Africa, black students at the US Congregationalist American

Board of Foreign Missions schools were already participating in interscholastic football matches. In West Africa, formal schooling was just as important in spreading the gospel of football. In the Gold Coast (Ghana), for example, the first organized team was founded in 1903 at Cape Coast's Government Boys' School. In Calabar, Nigeria, in 1904 black students at the Hope Waddell Institute held their own in a match against visiting British sailors.

Football grew rapidly in the interwar period as African cities exploded in size. "We played football there with mango seeds, limes or oranges or old tennis balls," recalled Nnamdi Azikiwe, Nigeria's first president. "Any collection of boys would be divided into two sides and a spirited game would ensure. We made and altered our rules to suit each game and so we emerged to become self-made soccerists." The rise of organized clubs embodied social connections forged in neighborhoods, schools, religious institutions, workplaces, and rural villages. Several of Africa's most successful and historic clubs still active today emerged during this period, such as Al Ahly (Cairo, 1907), Hearts of Oak (Accra, 1911), Espérance (Tunis, 1919), Canon and Tonnerre (Yaoundé, 1930 and 1934), Young Africans and Simba (Dar es Salaam, 1935 and 1936), Orlando Pirates (Soweto, 1937), and TP Mazembe (Lubumbashi, 1939).

While the forces of colonialism, urbanization, and demographics drove football to the heart of African popular culture, it is important to remember that local players, officials, and fans were never passive dupes of European cultural hegemony. Indigenous athletic traditions that predated European conquest (such as wrestling, stick fighting, running, and canoe racing) shaped Africans' enthusiastic appropriation of football and other modern sports. The game's rhythm, flow, and democratic accessibility in terms of rules, space, and cost immediately made it a crowd favorite. It also helped that football (like boxing, track and field, and other sports) carved a space for expressing vernacular cultures and forging relationships.

Participation in football came to symbolize the changing cultural practices, worldviews, identities, and aspirations of an increasingly cosmopolitan urban African population. How the game was played revealed aspects of African agency. For example, oral interviews with former players, coaches, officials, and fans along with news reports, scraps of film footage, and educated guesswork point to the past existence of many different playing styles and approaches on the continent. The general pattern was for teams to initially adopt English "kick-and-rush" and the "pyramid" formation (two defenders, three midfielders, five forwards). Then, as competition stiffened among African clubs and as visiting European teams ignited the imaginations of observers, many local teams shifted to more elaborate formations and hybrid styles of play. Another aspect of the localization of this global cultural form is the presence of magicians, healers, diviners, and sorcerers in the game. Since the earliest competitions of the colonial era, religious specialists have joined the coaching staff to prepare teams for important matches. They deploy occult means (at a price) to ritually and psychologically embolden players and boost their chance of victory. In addition, the coining of player nicknames by fans seems inspired by the oral literary tradition of griots and praise poets of agrarian times.

Finally, African newspapers—a powerful expression of modernity that often mobilized for black rights—cultivated audiences by assiduously reporting on football. The *West African Pilot* in Nigeria, the *Daily Graphic* in Ghana, and *Bantu World* in South Africa, among others, fed their readers' ravenous appetite for sport news with regular accounts of matches, reports of organizational meetings, commentary, announcements, and commercial advertisements. In the context of colonial capitalism, soccer created new needs and demands among African consumers, as well as new markets for sports merchandise—to the delight of European manufacturers and distributors and some local retailers. Teachers, clergymen, clerks, entrepreneurs, miners, policemen, railway men, and other wage earners exercised their right to spend their limited disposable income any way they wanted, and this included purchasing cleats, jerseys, footballs, and other equipment.

By the Second World War, the football craze had spread into the countryside. In a telling contemporary observation, an ethnographer in Lesotho noted that "the game was universal" and that "herd-boys spent any spare moments kicking a tennis-ball around." The game's constituency expanded and diversified not only in terms of geography, but also in terms of gender. One of the earliest documented women's football activities in Africa dates back to 1943 in the Nigerian market town of Onitsha, where a "ladies' football match which so thrilled the township" reportedly took place. The number of African women participating in football would grow significantly in the 1980s and 1990s, when women's soccer took off internationally. The female game is most developed in Nigeria, Ghana, South Africa, Cameroon, and Ivory Coast, though many other countries are catching up thanks in part to new continental and regional tournaments at senior and junior level backed by FIFA, world soccer's governing body. Numerous sport-for-development initiatives by NGOs and community-based groups are also expanding access to football for girls and women. Still, women's leagues are underdeveloped, funding is scarce, and men's lack of support and tight grip on administration and management means that there are limited opportunities for even the most talented and passionate female footballers.

The struggle for equal rights in football is not a new phenomenon. Going back to the late colonial period, increasingly militant anticolonial movements recognized the game's massive popularity and absorbed it into a broader quest for political and cultural liberation. "We started football clubs as social clubs where we would talk the principles of civics to the masses—that this is their country and that they have the right to independence," said Abdel Halim Mohamed, a prominent soccer administrator from Sudan. "This helped to show that while it was we, the intelligentsia, who were the architects of the independence movement, we were backed by the people." This moderate approach applied to other anticolonial movements, though Algerian and South African sportsmen and -women challenged white minority rule in a more directly confrontational manner.

During the war of independence against France, the National Liberation Front (FLN) of Algeria formed a "national team" in exile in 1958 comprising Algerian professional players based in French clubs. For the next three years, the FLN team played nearly one hundred matches in North Africa, the Middle East, eastern Europe, and East Asia. Putting patriotism before profit and showcasing an emerging national identity to the world, the FLN footballers symbolized the Algerian people's struggle for equality and freedom. "What I got out of that FLN team," said Rachid Mekhloufi, a young star in France at the time he joined the revolutionary team, "couldn't have been bought with all the gold in the world." In apartheid South Africa the link between sport and human rights was also dramatic. Antiapartheid activists spearheaded an international campaign that led to the country's exclusion from FIFA from 1961 to 1992 (with a one-year reprieve in 1963). It was the first time that a major international organization had imposed sanctions on the apartheid regime. This raised awareness of the injustices of apartheid among sports fans around the world and instilled hope among South African liberation movements at a time of draconian government repression. Within the country, the black-led South African Soccer Federation and South African Soccer League opposed apartheid in sport and regularly drew large crowds to their ramshackle grounds. Pretoria's heavy-handed clampdown of these leagues helped sway many South Africans, as well as the world community, to support the sport boycott.

To the north, after independence, an almost exclusively male political leadership turned to football as a culturally sanctioned and vigorously masculine form of national identity. Football featured prominently in the independence celebrations of Ghana, Nigeria, Togo, Zambia, Uganda, and Kenya, among others. Kwame Nkrumah, Nnamdi Azikiwe, and Kenneth Kaunda were among the notable African leaders who fully appreciated how "the imagined community of millions seems more real as a team of eleven named people," in Eric Hobsbawm's words, and that "the individual, even one who cheers, becomes a symbol of his nation himself." Often having played football themselves, African leaders invested financially (and ideologically) in the game by constructing large modern stadiums and subsidizing national teams and domestic competitions. Their main aims were to unify linguistically diverse territories arbitrarily created by the European scramble for Africa, raise the global visibility of their new nations, and consolidate their personal and partisan lock on political power.

African governments, despite tangible investments, had enormous difficulty in compelling fans to prioritize allegiance to the nation over local clubs. While national teams, especially successful ones, produced ninety-minute patriots, well into the 1990s it was clubs that captured fans' strongest emotional attachments. Clubs with ethnic connotations posed special challenges to nationalist parties and to one-party rule. As popular vehicles for ethnic chauvinism, certain clubs came to express (and often garnered support for) alternative conceptions of nationhood, such as Ghana's Asante Kotoko (symbol of Asante identity), Nigeria's Enugu Rangers (Ibo), Algeria's JSK Tizi Ouzou (Kabylie), Cameroon's Canon Yaoundé (Beti), Kenya's Gor Mahia (Luo), Zimbabwe's Bulawayo Highlanders (Ndebele), and South Africa's Amazulu (Zulu). This trend was not unique to Africa, as the evidence from Europe and beyond clearly shows. FC Barcelona, for example, is closely identified with Catalan nationalism, just as Athletic Bilbao is linked to Basque nationalism. In Scotland, Glasgow's divisions between Protestant Scots and Irish Catholics inform one of the oldest and most bitter rivalries in sports: Rangers versus Celtic.

Internal tensions aside, African nation-states asserted their sovereignty and global citizenship by joining transnational institutions like the United Nations, the International Olympic Committee, and FIFA. By the mid-1960s, members of the Confederation of African Football (CAF), the Pan-African organization founded in 1957, made up nearly half of FIFA's membership and formed its largest voting bloc. CAF made world soccer more inclusive and democratic, and did so in a number of ways: It ostracized apartheid South Africa from world football for three decades. In partnership with Asian and Eastern Bloc allies, Africans introduced an antiracist clause into FIFA's constitution. African members flexed their political muscle in 1974 when their votes propelled Brazilian businessman João Havelange to the FIFA presidency in a close race against the incumbent, Stanley Rous, an English school headmaster unsympathetic to apartheid's critics. Once at the helm, Havelange shrewdly stuck to his pledge to keep South Africa out of world football until apartheid's demise.

At FIFA, Africans fought for guaranteed berths in the World Cup finals. FIFA allots a different number of places in the tournament to each continental confederation based on multiple rounds of qualifying matches—but to begin with did not do so for CAF. African nations boycotted the 1966 tournament in England over this issue. Finally, the Eurocentric world body awarded Africa a place at Mexico 1970 (taken up by Morocco). With Havelange's blessing, and with the FIFA Executive Committee's African members pressing, the number of African teams in the World Cup gradually increased, reaching five in 1998, when the final tournament expanded to thirty-two teams. In the 1980s and 1990s, FIFA's youth and women's World Cups came to prominently feature an adequate number of African finalists.

In 2010, South Africa became the first African nation to host the FIFA World Cup. Widely hailed as a success, the tournament showcased the country's efficient organization, glossy stadiums, tight security, comfortable hotels, glitzy malls, and functional transportation and telecommunication networks. The World Cup, in essence, was a global marketing campaign for "Brand South Africa"—the image of the country as a modern, democratic, business-friendly, and exotic tourist destination. It challenged frequently negative portrayals of the continent and its people in international media. Within South Africa, the World Cup fostered patriotic unity and reawakened Pan-Africanist sentiments at a time of rising xenophobia. These emotional returns were undeniably real, but also fleeting and difficult to quantify.

The financial rewards, however, accrued to FIFA rather than South Africa. The host nation did not recover the $6.5 billion (and possibly more) in public funds for stadium construction, security arrangements, and other hosting costs, while FIFA earned around $2.3 billion in tax-free profits. In addition, several of the ten World Cup stadiums are not used regularly now and are at risk of becoming white elephants. Also, FIFA compelled the South African government to sign agreements and enact laws (e.g., Special Measures Acts in

2006) that temporarily surrendered sovereignty and constitutional rights to FIFA and its corporate partners. Finally, long-term benefits have not trickled down to soccer in the poorest urban communities, schools, and rural areas.

With FIFA currently in the throes of a major leadership and governance crisis, what about the evolving economics of the African game? Until the 1980s, clubs and leagues were legally amateur organizations. Most of their income came in the form of sponsorships from government departments and private companies, registration fees, fund-raising events, and ticket sales. Even so, top players since at least the 1930s were known to receive small cash payments under the table from clubs keen to retain their services. But in these conditions very few players made a dignified living from football wages alone, relying on day jobs to make ends meet. The only alternative was to leave to play professionally in Europe.

West Africa and North Africa have for decades supplied football labor to Europe. The first player to sign a professional contract was a tall Senegalese defender named Raoul Diagne—the son of Blaise Diagne, the first African representative in the French National Assembly—who put ink to paper in 1931 for Racing Club Paris. Diagne earned a place in the heart of France's national team (he played in the 1938 World Cup), which also featured Larbi Ben Barek, a superbly prolific Moroccan striker. The postwar era saw a number of Africans reach the highest levels of football in Europe. Some of the most prominent players were Matateu, Coluña, and 1965 European Player of the Year Eusébio (Mozambique); Steve "Kalamazoo" Mokone and Albert Johanneson (South Africa); Rachid Mekhloufi (Algeria); Charles Kumi Gyamfi (Ghana); Paul Bonga (Congo); and Salif Keita (Mali)—who in 1970 became the first African Player of the Year. Until the 1980s, African football migration centered on France and Portugal, but it then widened to Belgium, Germany, England, and elsewhere in Europe.

Cameroon's outstanding performance in the 1990 World Cup in Italy accelerated the outflow of talent from the continent. Hundreds of millions of viewers around the world watched live satellite television broadcasts of Cameroon's stunning run in the tournament. The Indomitable Lions, as the team is affectionately known, began with an upset win over defending champions Argentina and reached the quarterfinals, losing to England in extra time: the best World Cup finish in history for an African team. (Senegal and Ghana equaled the feat in 2002 and 2010, respectively.) Thirty-eight-year-old Roger Milla's goals and dancing celebrations made Cameroon an unforgettable side. Nigeria and Ghana each won two junior world championships in the 1990s, adding luster to the African game's global reputation. By the year 2000, more than one thousand Africans were playing professionally in European clubs, and more signed for clubs in the United States, the Persian Gulf, India, Vietnam, South Korea, and China. The rise of superstars like Abedi Ayew "Pelé" (Ghana), George Weah (1995 World Player of the Year, Liberia), Nwankwo Kanu (Nigeria), Samuel Eto'o (Cameroon), and Didier Drogba and Yaya Touré (Ivory Coast), together with hundreds of lesser-known athletes in minor European clubs and in peripheral leagues, consolidated Africa's position in world soccer and made the sport a more inclusively representative form of global culture.

In strictly economic terms, outward football migration has had contradictory effects on the African game. For individuals who sign lucrative contracts with well-endowed clubs in glamorous European leagues, the massive financial rewards are life changing. Some material benefits also accrue to African coaches, scouts, agents, and other stakeholders who ably insert themselves into this global commodity chain, particularly through their involvement in a huge number of youth football academies in West Africa. But stark inequalities remain between the Global North and South. European clubs reap most of the rewards in the relationship. They buy young African players at low prices and then turn a profit by reselling them later in the international market. European leagues also become more attractive forms of entertainment thanks to the added value brought by many of Africa's best footballers. Finally, national teams in Europe (and beyond) benefit from fielding players of African origin in international competitions.

This history of unequal global relations has multiple implications for the contemporary African game. First, the popularity (and often the quality) of national leagues has tended to decline due to the talent drain and to poor management, inadequate facilities, and limited finances. Second, national teams (South Africa, Egypt, and Tunisia excepted) now rely heavily on overseas-based players. In the last three World Cup tournaments (2006, 2010, and 2014), approximately one in five national-team players were based in African clubs. (Some observers believe Europe-based players raised the performance standard of national teams.) The third consequence is that African football has taken on a more thoroughly commercial character. CAF earns substantial revenue from the sale of broadcasting rights to the CAF Champions League and African Nations Cup and from awarding sponsorship rights to transnational corporations. Some domestic leagues (e.g., South Africa, Nigeria) have similar arrangements in place. Fourth, the satellite-television and Internet revolution of the 1990s revolutionized African fandom. The large followings of local clubs that into the 1980s sustained vibrant African leagues were gradually replaced by loyalty to and passion for European teams.

The shifting nature of African fandom has ushered in a new phase in the historical relationship between globalization and football. Most fans today watch live football not at the stadium but in bars, restaurants, and public viewing centers, as well as in the more affluent private homes. In Ouagadougou, Burkina Faso, more than fifty "video clubs" show the English Premier League (EPL), Spanish Liga, Italian Serie A, French Ligue 1, German Bundesliga, and the UEFA Champions League. In rural southwestern Uganda, anthropologist Richard Vokes noted how in shops and bars "one today hears not only the more usual talk of crop yields, school fees and the like, but also conversations about the past week's EPL results, movements in its transfer market, and its various teams' chances over the months ahead." While based in Kenya, the English journalist Steve Bloomfield was struck by the lack of interest there in the broadcast of the 2008 African Nations Cup final because "Ghana versus Egypt clashed with Arsenal versus Manchester United in the English Premier League. Nairobi's bars were full with Kenyan football fans, but all the screens were switched to the English game."

Indeed, many African fans today are insatiable consumers of European football brands and products. From sprawling cities to rural hamlets, the club colors of Manchester United, Arsenal, Barcelona, Real Madrid, and other big European clubs are visible almost everywhere. Motor vehicles, shops, and homes are adorned with flags, scarves, badges, photographs, posters, and slogans. Men of all ages (and not a few women) can be seen wearing European club jerseys, either costly originals or cheap knockoffs. While such consumption has undeniably neocolonial overtones, African audiences (stratified along age, gender, and economic lines) are far from powerless in shaping and interpreting the global flow of goods, information, images, and ideas.

Nigerian scholars Senayon Olaoluwa and Adewole Adejayan, for example, discuss how Igbo fans in the 2000s bestowed the royal title of *Igwe* on Thierry Henry, Arsenal's all-time leading scorer. By doing so, these fans culturally marked, even appropriated, the North London club's Frenchman of Antillean heritage. Working in Kenya, Solomon Waliaula has shown that Swahili-language radio announcers of EPL matches hark back to the style of precolonial bards. They connect with the audience by inserting greetings, proverbs, metaphors, abrupt changes in rhythm and tone, songs, player nicknames, and humor. The role of Facebook, Twitter, and other social media is important, too, compressing time and space and encouraging African participation in global football's online communities. According to a 2014 study by Portland Communications, football was the most-discussed topic on Twitter in Africa.

And so football has changed Africa and Africa has changed football. The political, economic, social, and cultural entanglements of the game continue to evolve. In the wake of decades of austerity, privatization, and state disinvestment from sport, "big men" use football to launch political careers, as seen in George Weah's election to the Liberian senate in 2014 and the ongoing presidential campaign in the Democratic Republic of Congo launched by Moise Katumbi—the Lubumbashi businessman, politician, and owner of glamor club TP Mazembe. More than fifty new stadiums have been built in Africa in the past two decades with Chinese government support—part of China's soft-power thrust into the continent. African soccer's ongoing changes illustrate how and why, in the words of anthropologist James Ferguson, "specific forms of 'global' integration on the continent coexist with specific—and equally 'global'—forms of exclusion, marginalization, and disconnection."

ADDITIONAL RESOURCES

Akindes, Gerard A. "Football Bars: Urban Sub-Saharan Africa's Trans-Local 'Stadiums.'" *International Journal of the History of Sport* 28, no. 15 (2011): 2176–90.
Alegi, Peter. *African Soccerscapes: How a Continent Changed the World's Game.* Athens: Ohio University Press, 2010.
Chipande, Hikabwa Decius. "Episode 92: Football, Power, and Identity in Zambia." *Africa Past and Present: The Podcast about African History, Culture, and Politics,* episode 92 (May 21, 2015). http://afripod.aodl.org/2015/05/afripod-92/.
Ligon, Nisha. "Twiga Stars: Tanzania's Soccer Sisters." 2010. https://www.youtube.com/watch?v=kEh2I8FYH_g.
Vokes, Richard. "Arsenal in Bugamba: The Rise of English Premier League Football in Uganda." *Anthropology Today* 26, no. 3 (2010): 10–15.
Waliaula, Solomon. "Envisioning and Visualizing English Football in East Africa: The Case of a Kenyan Radio Football Commentator." *Soccer & Society* 13, no. 2 (2012): 239–49.

• • •

PETER ALEGI is Professor of History at Michigan State University and Research Associate at the University of KwaZulu-Natal in South Africa. His books include

Laduma! Soccer, Politics and Society in South Africa (University of KwaZulu-Natal Press, 2004), *African Soccerscapes: How a Continent Changed the World's Game* (Ohio University Press, 2010), and (coedited with Chris Bolsmann) *Africa's World Cup: Critical Reflections on Play, Patriotism, Spectatorship, and Space* (University of Michigan Press, 2013). He hosts the *Africa Past and Present* podcast with Peter Limb (afripod.aodl.org) and blogs at *footballiscominghome.info.* He is Founding Editor of Michigan State University Press's new African History and Culture book series and serves on the editorial boards of the *International Journal of African Historical Studies* and *African Studies.*

Art, Identity, and Autobiography

SENZENI MARASELA AND LALLA ESSAYDI

Christa Clarke

Abstract: Senzeni Marasela (from South Africa) and Lalla Essaydi (from Morocco) are two internationally renowned African artists whose artistic practice draws upon autobiography. The nuanced personal narratives explored in their work challenge essentialist ideas about the singular identity of the "African artist." Their stories instead illuminate how individuals embrace both the local and the global, providing insights into cultural specificity and context while connecting more universally to broader questions of lived experience.

Keywords: Senzeni Marasela, Lalla Essaydi, South Africa, apartheid, Morocco, calligraphy, harem, autobiography, global contemporary

> In the twenty-first century, the voices of women artists have also joined in insisting on their multiple identities. I insist on multiple identities and demand that all of my identities be respected— be they geographic, cultural, faith-based, or artistic—since they demonstrate that I am part of a cosmopolitan world with its joyous and sorrowful aspects.
>
> —LALLA ESSAYDI, 2006

INTRODUCTION

Globalization—the increasing interconnectedness of people, places, and cultures—has had a major impact on the contemporary art world. Over the past two decades or so, artists from Africa and its diaspora, along with others in centers all too recently considered peripheral, are increasingly visible on the world stage. But while the umbrella of the "global contemporary" may appear to be all-embracing, the inclusion of artists from Africa remains selective, often based on criteria established through Western art historical practices. Artists from this vast and complex continent are often subsumed under a monolithic and essentialized notion of "African" cultural identity, one that overlooks their rich individuality as artists. Given that the visual vocabulary and artistic concerns of its artists transcend cultural, national, or geographic boundaries and reflect personal experiences and multifaceted identities, "Africanness" is clearly not a viable lens for interpreting and under-standing the contemporary arts of the continent.

Considering autobiographical practices, in which individual experience is privileged, offers an ideal antidote and an approach to artistic practice that can both engage and transcend ethnicity and nationality. This essay explores the use of autobiography in the work of two artists—Senzeni Marasela and Lalla Essaydi—considering how personal experience has informed and ani-mated their artistic practice. While there are many artists from Africa and its diaspora who engage autobiographical content, these artists speak to the range of ways personal history can be visualized and inflected through gen-der. Both artists revisit and reframe childhood memories, processing those experiences in different ways to seek transformation and empowerment. They both adopt media and techniques—such as sewing and henna—and engage subject matter associated with the domain of women while at the same time subverting such associations. Using distinct visual languages, they speak of their own sense of displacement, familial and geographic, and explore the interface between the public and domestic spheres.

SENZENI MARASELA

Senzeni Marasela's artistic practice engages autobiography as a means to investigate and reclaim gaps in her personal history and as a lens through which to consider the larger cultural and political history of South Africa. She was born in 1977 in Boksburg, South Africa, an industrial and mining center just east of Johannesburg. Her father served on the police force during apartheid, an unwilling enforcer of the policies of a racist government. Her mother was a domestic worker who suffered from schizophrenia and was periodically institutionalized. She was largely absent during Marasela's childhood, both physically away from home as a migrant laborer and psychologically distant due to illness. Marasela's sense of alienation as a child was compounded by her Catholic school education in a white Afrikaans suburb, where she was sent because policemen's homes were targets for attacks. This move effectively shielded her from the atrocities of apartheid and, as she describes, also deprived her of a sense of identity as a black South African.

In 1996, Marasela was a student in fine arts at the University of Witswatersrand, during the Truth and Reconciliation Commission (TRC) hearings that followed the dismantling of apartheid two years before. At the hearings, which were often publicly broadcast, victims of and witnesses to human rights violations (along with their perpetrators) shared their recollections of apartheid-era atrocities. The memories of pain, loss, and trauma emerging from these testimonies led Marasela to grapple with her personal history and the compromises of her upbringing outside the townships, unaware of the struggles of other blacks in South Africa. Driven by a desire to reclaim her history and identity, Marasela did so through her artistic practice, which may be seen within this larger national context.

Art historian Colin Richards describes a "strong restorative impulse in Marasela's work," in which memories are recovered and reframed to work through feelings of loss and trauma and create a space of belonging. Her childhood experiences and self-stated "indifference" to history, as well as the constant absence of her mother, have been a sustained focus of her work since she received her BFA in 1998. *Our Mother* (1997), an early mixed-media work created while she was still a student, in many ways sets the stage for Marasela's later, autobiographically based practice. (See figure 3.7.1.) An old and stained housecoat, once worn by her mother, is set against a background featuring a montage of photographs of Marasela and her siblings and friends. While the emptiness of the dress reinforces absence, the physicality of the dress itself serves as an index of her mother's presence. Around the bodice, Marasela has clustered pins—a gesture that replaces the comfort and sustenance typically associated with a mother's breast with the pain and trauma of absence. The needles also provide a suggestion of violence, reinforced by the presence of her father's police baton below. Together, the dress and police baton—emblems of her parents—contrast sharply with the photographic images of smiling young faces, emphasizing, as Annie Coombes has suggested, the "tension between the lived experience of two generations." The contrast also speaks to the artist's self-described obliviousness to South Africa's turbulent history as a child who grew up in an environment away from the violence of political struggle.

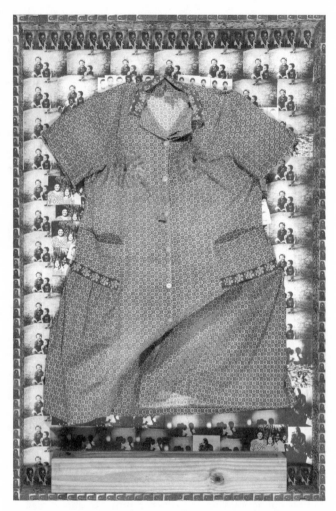

FIG. 3.7.1. Senzeni Marasela, *Our Mother,* 1997. Mixed media, 60 x 40 x 6 in. Axis Gallery.

Marasela's experience of maternal absence and desire to reembody personal history also informs a photographic triptych produced in 2000, similarly titled *Our Mother.* (See figures 3.7.2a, 3.7.2b, and 3.7.2c.) In these works, she moves away from the use of appropriated images and constructs her own, with her mother as subject. In this case, it is an indirect representation: the photographs capture the shadow of Marasela's mother, who is shown sweeping a yard as she carries on her back her grandson, the artist's young son, Ikwezi. The mother is represented by absence, her corporeal presence only suggested

FIG. 3.7.2a. (*left*) Senzeni Marasela, *Our Mother*, 2000. Photographic triptych. Axis Gallery.

by the shadow she casts, which shifts in size and perspective, and—in two of the photographs—by the broom she holds. The inclusion of Marasela's own son in these images, snuggly tucked on the back of her mother, provides an alternate reading of childhood memories, one that seeks to replace feelings of neglect with a sense of comfort the artist long sought after as a child.

The staged nature of these photographs is inherently performative, and in 2004, Marasela began to incorporate performance more directly into her practice. The performances, which have been done in both local and

FIG. 3.7.2.b. (*center*) Senzeni Marasela, *Our Mother,* 2000. Photographic triptych. Axis Gallery.

international settings, always feature the artist as the protagonist, accompanied by a professional photographer whom she hires as a "witness" to the performance. These performances are documented or represented in other media, most directly in photography, but also in linocut prints and, more recently, embroidered textiles. In many of these performances, the artist takes on the persona of Theodorah, who is created in the image of her mother. An ongoing series, *Theodorah Comes to Johannesburg,* begun in 2004, features Marasela performing in the guise of her mother. Wearing one of her mother's cast-off dresses, she

FIG. 3.7.2.c. (*right*) Senzeni Marasela, *Our Mother,* 2000. Photographic triptych. Axis Gallery.

enacts the confusion and alienation that her mother felt coming into the city from the rural eastern Cape as a migrant domestic worker. The photographic series based on these performances tracks Theodora, often depicted with her back to the camera, as she retraces her way through contemporary Johannesburg—a lone figure navigating the urban landscape. The various locations of her journey include the Apartheid Museum, where she contemplates a memorial to Hector Pieterson (a thirteen-year-old boy killed by police during the 1976 student uprising in Soweto), the now-abandoned site of one of Soweto's

FIG. 3.7.3. Senzeni Marasela, *Our Mother III*, 2006. Worn uniform, lace, tulle, beads, embroidery, 46 ½ x 37 in. Collection of the Newark Museum, Purchase 2006 Helen McMahon Brady Cutting Fund 2006.49a-f. By permission of the Newark Museum, NJ.

exclusively black shopping centers, a sidewalk outside a suburban home, and finally, a well-known store, frequented by diviners and their clients, that sells materials used in ritual and healing contexts. Marasela explains, "It was my way of inserting my own mother into the ever-changing landscape of Johannesburg." At the same time, in revisiting her mother's history by embodying lived experience, Marasela is also able to better understand and come to terms with the absence and neglect of her personal history.

In 2006, Marasela developed a new body of work using a group of old domestic uniforms once worn and given to the artist by her mother, along with her psychiatric records. In *Our Mother III,* as in earlier works, maternal absence is suggested by a disembodied dress. (See figure 3.7.3.) The artist implicates herself within her mother's history by adorning the dress with beadwork, tulle ribbon flowers, and a lace collar as well as embroidered images that reconstruct her mother's history, both real and imagined. The disturbing scenes, which include a lynching, express feelings of persecution and fear and are drawn from thoughts and memories recorded in her mother's therapy sessions. For the artist, the process of hand-stitching evokes remembrances of her mother obsessively sewing and mending clothes. The repetitious and labor-intensive nature of the stitches is also therapeutic for Marasela, helping her reconcile with her difficult past. "Sewing, I believe, is a form of meditation. For me it offers redemption for the disruptive anger I felt towards my mother as a young woman."

It is through the lens of redemption that we might see Marasela's *Confessions for Another Day,* created the same year and in many ways a companion work to *Our Mother III.* (See figure 3.7.4.) Here, Marasela uses the dress of her young daughter, Nikelwa, as a canvas for an embroidered narrative of the artist's own childhood memories. Stitched in light gold thread, the text appears merely decorative from a distance, reinforcing the sense of fragility conveyed by the small girl's dress and contrasting with its message of shame and isolation. It reads:

> I wonder if she knew anything about my suffering. The lost dreams I hated going to school because they would all talk about their mothers talk about their mischievous revelry frolicking freeing in shopping malls purchasing their fantasies. They wished for futures filled with fortune where their currency was happiness and they used that to buy into some future while we were shell-shocked hiding behind veils of lies and shame and anger and fear I could not converse about my mother in girlish giggles nor be engulfed in giddy feelings in anticipation of our weekends I was afraid they would find out about her and laugh at us and wonder if when we made mistakes it would be a confirmation that our mother was mad.

Through this poignant narrative, the artist revisits the anguish of her personal history as a daughter, coming to terms with the memories in a restorative attempt to stop the cycle of pain and trauma passed down from generation to generation.

FIG. 3.7.4. Senzeni Marasela, *Confessions for Another Day*, 2006. Textile, thread, beads, tulle, lace, 11 ½ x 14 in. Collection of the Newark Museum, Purchase 2006 Helen McMahon Brady Cutting Fund 2007.3. By permission of the Newark Museum, NJ.

LALLA ESSAYDI

Like Marasela, Lalla Essaydi in her work also draws upon childhood experiences, which she returns to with a similar sense of being an outsider, and with the intention of creating a sense of belonging. Essaydi is nearly a generation older than Marasela, having focused on her artistic practice largely in the last decade, after raising two children. Born in 1956 in Tamesloht, a town outside of Marrakech, Essaydi was raised in Morocco and moved to Saudi Arabia in her early twenties. More recently, she has lived in the United States—first in Boston, where she received her MFA in 2003 from the School of the Museum of Fine Arts at Tufts University, and now in New York. Essaydi describes herself as being shaped by two cultures—East and West—and by the multiple dimensions of her identity as an African, as an Arab, and as a Muslim, as well as as a woman and a mother. These multiple identities—or "converging territories," as she phrases it—have informed her photographic practice as an artist. According to Essaydi, her work creates and provides a space and sense of belonging not found elsewhere.

In an early body of work from 2003, entitled *Silences of Thought,* Essaydi literally returns to a particular space of personal history and memory—the interior of a house in which women and girls from her family were placed in isolation, sometimes for weeks, for transgressing the rules of Islam. Photographed within the actual interior of the artist's childhood home, the women in Essaydi's images are covered with Arabic calligraphy. The text, written by the artist using pigment derived from henna, praises the owner of the house for its beauty. A literal reading of the text emphasizes the decorative role of the women, equating them with their material surroundings and evoking conservative Moroccan views that women are objects to be owned and controlled by men. Essaydi obliquely critiques this perspective through her use of calligraphy, co-opting an exclusively male art form used primarily for writing religious texts and transforming it into a statement of female empowerment. The feminist critic Fatema Mernissi associates Essaydi's use of Arabic calligraphy with the ninth-century Islamic tradition of *washi,* in which "women wrote electrifying messages on their clothing in order to destabilize" religious authorities. The use of henna as a medium in the calligraphy reinforces its subversive message with its female associations: henna was traditionally used by Berber and Arab women in northern Africa to inscribe symbolic motifs upon their bodies during significant stages of their lives: puberty, marriage, conception, and the birth of a child.

Essaydi's 2004 series of photographs, *Converging Territories,* is similarly set within the interior of this house of her childhood, but here, the specificity of place—as evidenced through the architecture of the rooms and their decor—is erased. Instead, calligraphy attains prominence, and the act of writing itself becomes the subject of many of the photographs. (See figure 3.7.5.) The text transforms Essaydi's childhood home from a literal space—a space of confinement and isolation—to a psychological and cultural space, in

FIG. 3.7.5. Lalla Essaydi, *Converging Territories #9*, 2003. Chromogenic print, 48 x 58 ½ inches. Collection of the Newark Museum, Purchase 2011 Helen McMahon Brady Cutting Fund 2011.7.2. By permission of the Newark Museum, NJ.

which women can speak to one another freely. "I am writing. I am writing on me, I am writing on her. The story began to be written the moment the present began. I am asking, how can I be simultaneously inside and outside? I didn't even know this world existed, I thought it existed only in my head, in my dreams. And now here I am, an open book: Inside the book cover, chapters are chaotic and confusing." Through her writing on every imaginable surface, the artist implicates herself—her thoughts and experiences—in her work and links her personal history to that of the women who are represented in the photographs. Essaydi's fluid and poetic words reveal an internal narrative that suggests the complexity of her identity and presents identity itself as a work in progress, constantly revisited and renegotiated.

As with Marasela, the staging of these photographs is performative and the process of creating them labor-intensive. The women who participate in her photographic scenes are often family acquaintances, women who have had a similar relationship to the physical space of confinement as the artist. She describes them as "willing participants in the emancipation of Moroccan women and their freedom to revise, edit, and rewrite the complex narratives of their own Arab/African identities after generations of translations." Essaydi (who was initially trained as a painter) painstakingly applies the henna, a process that can take as long as nine hours and must be uninterrupted. To facilitate the process, she creates an atmosphere of conviviality, with food and drink, the playing of music and the telling of stories. For Essaydi, this process is an essential part of the work itself, and the photographs ultimately embody the shared experiences of their creation, the literal enactment of memories. The artist's past is thus reworked, as a place of isolation and silence becomes a space of empowerment for the renegotiation and revision of complex identities.

Essaydi's 2007 series of photographs, *Les Femmes du Maroc,* extends from previous explorations of personal history, revisiting the concept of private space through the lens of history by borrowing and subverting Orientalist conventions of representation. The staging is based on specific nineteenth-century American and European paintings that depict, or—more accurately—imagine, the interior world of the North African harem with its objectified and sexualized women. As a student, Essaydi found herself drawn to the exquisite beauty seen in works by artists such as Eugène Delacroix, Jean-Léon Gerôme, and John Singer Sargent, but also disturbed by the racialized and sexualized depictions of women in their paintings. For her series, Essaydi staged the images in her Boston studio, working with Moroccan women who live in the West but also identify as Arab or Islamic. The images confront and deflect the Western lens, replacing the nudity of the antecedent compositions with subjects whose bodies are concealed and covered, and eliminating the social stratification and seductive settings. The calligraphy similarly disrupts the gaze, painted in a deliberately expressive manner that cannot be easily interpreted by Arabic readers—thus preserving the deeply personal nature of the text itself.

The harem itself as a physical and psychological space is the subject of a recent series begun in 2009, entitled *Harem,* which shifts from a staged setting to an actual harem. (See figure 3.7.6.) Essaydi based the series inside the harem rooms of an opulent palace near Marrakesh that once belonged to Pasha Thami El Glaoui. The palace was a place Essaydi found herself repeatedly drawn to as an adult, eventually finding out from family members that she had a direct and personal connection to it. The pasha had become her grandmother's guardian after the death of her grandmother's father and brought the grandmother (whom he divorced from her husband) and her young son (the artist's father) to live in the palace. "She was like a prisoner,"

FIG. 3.7.6. Lalla Essaydi, *Harem #1*, 2009. Chromongenic prints (triptych), 40 x 30 in. each. Collection of the Newark Museum, Purchase 2011 Helen McMahon Brady Cutting Fund 2011.7.1A-C. By permission of the Newark Museum, NJ.

Essaydi notes, "no matter how luxurious the surroundings are, and it became something direct to me."

In the photographs, the women are almost undistinguishable from the background, dressed in clothing with the same patterns as those of the surrounding tiles. As with her previous work, the process of producing the photographs was long and meticulous, including photographing the tiles, printing the designs on fabric, and then stitching dresses made from the fabric. The resulting images speak, on one hand, of confinement and the role of women within the interior rooms of the harem, where they are literally identified with their surroundings. As Essaydi asks, "How do we separate the beauty of the rooms, fabrics, and so forth, from that of the women themselves, so seemingly passive and receptive, rather like the furniture or the welcoming spaces." At the same time, although objects of the gaze, the women suggest resistance in their direct stare back, offering a knowing and somewhat mocking gaze. Their faces are inscribed with the artist's thoughts and poetry written with henna—an artistic medium that Essaydi has consistently used as a statement of female empowerment.

CONCLUSION

The art historian and artist Olu Oguibe has argued that the Western world is primarily interested in constructing the African "essence" of the contemporary artist. He states, "Autonomy. Self-articulation. Autography. These are contested territories where the contemporary African artist is locked in a struggle for survival, a struggle against displacement by the numerous strategies of regulation and surveillance that characterize Western attitudes toward African art today." Autobiography may offer an ideal framework for considering artists beyond an essential identity of African, one that embraces both the local and the global, allowing personal experience to guide insights into cultural specificity and context while connecting more universally to broader questions of lived experience. The different strategies of self-representation in the work of Senzeni Marasela and Lalla Essaydi resist any monolithic notions of African identity, demonstrating instead the complexities of personal identity while suggesting the interconnectedness of individual experience to larger national, and world, histories.

ADDITIONAL RESOURCES

Bedford, Emma, ed. *A Decade of Democracy: South African Art, 1994–2004*. Cape Town: South African National Gallery, 2004.

Carlson, Amanda. "Leaving One's Mark." In *Converging Territories,* by Lalla Essaydi and Amanda Carlson. New York: Powerhouse Books, 2005

Coombes, Annie. "On Secrets and Lies: Embodying the Past/Envisioning the Future." In *A Decade of Democracy: South African Art, 1994–2004*, edited by Emma Bedford. Cape Town: South African National Gallery, 2004.

Mernissi, Fatema. *Les Femmes du Maroc.* New York: Powerhouse Books, 2009.

Oguibe, Olu. *The Culture Game.* Minneapolis: University of Minnesota Press, 2004.

Richards, Colin. "Senzeni Marasela." In *10 Years/100 Artists: Art in a Democratic South Africa,* edited by Sophie Perryer. Cape Town: Bell-Roberts Publishing, 2004.

Thompson, Barbara. *Black Womanhood: Images, Icons and Ideologies of the African Body.* Seattle: University of Washington Press, 2008

Waterhouse, Ray. "Lalla Essaydi: An Interview." *Nka: Journal of Contemporary African Art* 24, no. 1: (2009): 144–49.

· · ·

CHRISTA CLARKE, a specialist in historic and contemporary African art, is Senior Curator, Arts of Global Africa, at the Newark Museum. Clarke's publications include *Representing Africa in American Art Museums: A Century of Collecting* *and Display* (University of Washington Press, 2010), which examines the impact of museum practice on the formation of meaning and public perception of African art. Her recent book *African Art in the Barnes Foundation* (Barnes Foundation, 2015), received the James A. Porter and David C. Driskell Book Award for African American Art History and an Award for Excellence from the Association of Art Museum Curators in 2016.

3.8

Raï and Rap

GLOBALIZATION AND THE SOUNDTRACK OF YOUTH
RESISTANCE IN NORTHERN AFRICA

Zakia Salime

Abstract: The emergence of raï music in the 1980s and hip-hop/rap in the mid-1990s, in northern Africa, challenged the predominance of Europe and North America as platforms for the production and circulation of resistant global sound tracks. This chapter locates the production of raï and hip-hop in histories of colonization, displacement, geopolitical orders of securitization, and the fight against Muslim youth radicalization. The international circulation of both genres also demonstrates local artists' struggles over redefining the dominant maps of music circulation as they continue to produce northern Africa as a global performance scene.

Keywords: raï, hip-hop, music, youth, political activism

INTRODUCTION

Northern Africa and its diasporic communities in Europe are vibrant sites in the global circulation of music. The region's geographical location facilitated the incorporation of musical influences from other parts of Africa, and from Europe and the Middle East, into an already-rich musical repertoire in the region. Contemporary raï and hip-hop reflect this long history of mixing and incorporation. Both music genres are now transforming the place of northern Africa in the international music scene by challenging the predominance of Europe and North America in the production and circulation of global soundtracks. *Raï* is the Arabic term for "opinion" or "perspective," and it has become integrally connected to a genre of music associated with popular resistance that emerged in the city of Oran during the French colonization of Algeria. Rap/hip-hop is a global music genre that emerged in New York City's South Bronx in the early 1970s, and was appropriated by Moroccan artists in the aftermath of 9/11.

This chapter calls attention to the critical roles played by Algerian and Moroccan performers in the development and circulation of music, at home and in the diaspora. I will discuss the development of raï through the role played by the emblematic figure of Algerian Khaled, who transformed raï music from a regional genre into a globally recognized sound. Moroccan hip-hop is discussed through the efforts of young artists to transform the city of Casablanca into a central meeting point of global hip-hop. The annual Festival of Urban Music, Le Boulevard des Jeunes Musiciens, is an international hip-hop event entirely conceived and organized by young artists from Casablanca. The festival brings to Morocco hundreds of artists and thousands of fans who engage in a four-day musical exchange and performances before an ever-growing audience. My analysis of northern African rap and hip-hop reveals different phases of youth political engagement with the global music industry, the cosmopolitan audience of "urban" music, and the business opportunities this presents in a region overwhelmed by youth unemployment. The analysis also highlights the larger economic and political context in which raï and rap music are evolving into a global force. Contemporary raï and hip-hop music have to be read against histories of migration, displacement, and urban marginality at home, and in the African diaspora in Europe—notably in France. The production of these soundtracks should also be linked to geopolitical orders of securitization and the fight against Muslim youth radicalization, as well as struggles over redefining the hegemonic maps of music circulation.

A BRIEF HISTORY

Northern Africa (or the Maghreb) is the site of multiple cultural, ethnic, and linguistic influences. The Maghreb region—stretching from Libya on the east (east of Tunisia) to Mauritania on the southwest (south of Morocco and Algeria)—with its Amazigh Berber origin and African roots, is historically tied to the Arab world, Andalusian glory, and a history of Spanish, French, and Italian conquests and domination in the nineteenth and twentieth centuries. The strategic location of northern Africa as a bordering region and a crossroads to the heart of Africa, the Middle East, and Europe has enabled the circulation of bodies, monies, labor, and merchandise in ways that have not always disturbed old colonial orders of racialized oppression and domination.

In the 1970s my generation of North African teens was tuned in to European rock, Afro-Caribbean reggae, and Egyptian and Lebanese legends. The parallel economy of tape-recording enabled the diffusion of an even wider range of world music, including American pop. But listening followed a one-directional mode in which soundtracks were mostly circulating south of the Mediterranean and only occasionally moving back north. The advent of the satellite dish and the Internet in the first half of the 1990s enabled the production of American rap as a global sound track. Its circulation among African youth and expatriates made sense since it echoed their own frustrations. As a scream against multiple faces of oppression, rap inspired millions to reclaim neighborhoods, vocalize frustrations, and denounce political and economic marginality across the continent. The attacks on the World Trade Center in 2001 and the 2005 riots in the suburbs of Paris brought rap to center stage in geopolitical controversies over its importance as a diplomatic tool versus its impact in increasing urban unrest.

RAÏ AND EXILE

Raï music first entered into global consumption in the 1990s, when a group of raï singers, including Khaled, king of raï, fled Algeria to France to escape civil war and persecution of artists by Islamist militants. Before even the physical displacement of artists to France, raï was already the music of youth and diasporic North Africans who were looking for a new musical form to express the banality of everyday life, love, nostalgia, economic hardship, hope, and departure during the 1980s.

Raï originated in the city of Oran in the early 1930s. As the second-largest city in Algeria, Oran had been a site for varied musical influences because of its specific history of conquests by Spain between the sixteenth and eighteenth centuries, and by France in the second half of the nineteenth century. Raï emerged as a cry against French colonialism by women who suffered the most from the loss of livelihood, economic hardship, and the detention and disappearances of male relatives. As a women's music genre, raï also became linked to the new nightlife that offered peasant women their only means of subsistence in the city through performing for men in bars and burgeoning bordellos. The singers, known as *cheikhat*, were the first to give raï its romantic-nostalgic, gloomy, and blues-like mourning style. Cheikha Remitti is considered the founder of raï. She used improvisation in her melodies and dared to sing about love, sexuality, poverty, and the desperation of women as a disenfranchised population in colonized cities.

In the 1950s men appropriated raï by introducing new instruments and hiring professional composers. The rebellious roots of raï crystalized around the cause of national liberation, with some singers fleeing French-controlled Algeria to Tunisia or Morocco and providing raï with a Maghrebi character. Starting as a mix of rural and cabaret-style music mostly about farmers and peasants who had lost their land to French settlers, raï is now a global sound track.

KHALED, "KING OF RAÏ"

Cheb Khaled, an Algerian performer, first introduced raï to an international audience with his first album, *Kutché,* released in 1988. His first performance in France followed the release of his second album in 1992. As an international legend, Khaled transformed raï by incorporating a wide range of musical styles and genres including Hindi, funk, hip-hop, salsa, reggae, and the French chanson. The fusion of Arabic and French in his songs introduces Arabic sonic forms into the soundscapes of his fans.

The growing appeal of raï to the music industry was clear from the collaboration of Khaled with the world-renowned music firm Barclay in 1992. By the late 1990s raï was a dominant form in the world music market after achieving major successes throughout Africa, Asia, and Europe. Khaled's 1999 greatest hit, "Lharba Wine" ("to flee, but where?"), presents us with a fusion of several musical styles and genres featuring Khaled and the Hindi film-music star Amar. In 2005, Khaled was the Mideast and North Africa winner of the R3 BBC Award for World Music.

GLOBALIZING NORTHERN AFRICAN HIP-HOP

Moroccan rapper SiSimo defines rap as lyrics accompanied with music. He suggests that the lyrics take control of the music, and it is this combination of rhythmic music with rhyming speech that gives rap its distinctive feature. Although often used interchangeably, the "Master of Records," American DJ Afrika Bambaataa, notes that rap is one part of the hip-hop subculture that includes emceein, deejayin, B-boying, and graffiti. It emerged in New York

City's South Bronx, which was home to African-American, Afro-Caribbean, and Latino communities. Rap called attention to racial discrimination, advocated Pan-Africanism, and incorporated Islamic referents and black icons, including Malcolm X, into its symbols and iconography. As hip-hop and rap spread across the Atlantic, its symbols continued as sites of identification for rappers, and its critique of racial discrimination had a tremendous impact on diasporic Africans. For Moroccan rapper Ould Shaab, hip-hop culture created a "global blackness." Global blackness became a symbolic site of struggle for disenchanted African youth at home and in the European diaspora.

In spite of the similarities of their social and economic conditions, each region developed its own distinctive form of hip-hop. For example, the marginal suburbs, *banlieues,* of French cities generated their own specific styles of rapping that have continued to draw on histories of slavery, colonial legacies, economic inequalities, ethnic identities, and imagined geographies of liberation. Senegalese-born MC Solaar initiated the first big rap hit in 1992 in France, *Bouge de là* ("Get Out of There"). The song went platinum in France and became number five on the national charts. France is now a major site of hip-hop, representing the second-largest market, after the United States. A brief inventory of French hip-hop reveals a preponderance of French MCs of Maghrebi origin. The colonial origins of these performers were often reflected in their lyrics as French rappers of Maghrebi origin mixed Arabic dialects and French, subverting the grammar structures of French and making Arabic expressions and words part of the public acoustic in French songs. Though these artists spoke to and for a global blackness, their performances, as well as the production and diffusion of their music, were until the end of the 1990s mostly taking place in European and North American cities.

REVERSING THE TRENDS

Morocco's hip-hop scene is one of the most vibrant on the continent. Morocco became an international platform for hip-hop after the creation of the annual festival L'Boulevard (formally, Le Boulevard des Jeunes Musiciens) in 1999 by two young artists, Mohamed Merhari and Hicham Bahou. They both wanted to validate local creativity by building a platform from which local artists would shine internationally. Now L'Boulevard enables local artists to perform and innovate while engaging in a cross-continental mixing of styles, as evident from several collaborations among African artists, including

Moroccan Steph Ragga Man Feat and Senegalese-Italian-based King Barra. Their collaboration *Mama Africa* is an expression of Pan-African identities and perception of Africa as a motherland. In *Mama Africa,* they express their allegiance to Africa and their love and respect for the dignity of Africans in an African ragga style, and by alternating African national flags and languages. Their video condenses histories of suffering, wars, and imperialist interventions and oppression of Africans, denouncing their common sources and stressing common destiny.

Mama Africa is one example from Morocco's thriving hip-hop subculture as captured in the documentary *Casanayda.* The film shows the importance of L'Boulevard as an international platform and documents the important ways in which Moroccan hip-hop is distinctive from its North American antecedents. Throughout the 1990s Moroccan artists found in American rap a place for crafting notions of subalternity, urban marginality, and injured masculinities. American rap is now viewed as spectacle where urban desires, consumerism, and hypermasculinity are expressed. MrHatem, Ragga Man, from the city of Fez, was initially taken by the rage expressed in American rap, but later became disenchanted by its cooptation by the music industry of sex, money, and power. Though the Moroccan hip-hop scene had already developed its own spheres of wealth and power, it is still heavily carried by a street identity and documents daily struggles in poor urban neighborhoods.

Thus, instead of turning to American rap for identification, Moroccan rappers prefer to trace the genealogy of their own music to four legendary men, founders of the music band Nas El Ghiwane. This music troupe originated from Hay Mohammadi, a large working-class neighborhood of Casablanca, in the late 1960s. When Nas El Ghiwane first appeared on national television in the early 1970s, they were *shockingly* dressed in the hippie style—undisciplined hair, loose embroidered shirts, jeans—and strange gadgets hung from their drums and musical instruments. Their music, first perceived as a joke, was very quickly taken seriously. The popularity of Nas El Ghiwane stemmed from more than the familiar Moroccan rhythms and musical instruments. The group drew on popular common sense and wisdom, found inspiration in saints, and revitalized Sufi trance music and mysticism, while using popular prose and the mythical figures of marabouts, in both direct and metaphorical senses.

Operating in a political culture in which Moroccan plural music sceneries and genres were dubbed "folklore" during the colonial era, and where culture has been fixed within the symbolic counters of Pan-Arabism in postcolonial

Morocco, Nas El Ghiwane responded with lyrics and rhythms that brought to life the very rich repertoire of African spiritualities and drumming, rural sensibilities, women's wisdom, and the Moroccan Darija dialect. Nas El Ghiwane engaged in musical translations, gaining more ground among the young and authorizing a cross-generational, cross-cultural, and cross-regional exchange of tastes, imaginaries, histories, and rhythms. Within one decade, Nas El Ghiwane became the first northern African pop group to cross the national borders to perform in Europe and at the World Music Institute in New York.

Nas El Ghiwane's lyrics first spoke about the mundane. Slowly they started to use metaphors to document and portray the multiple faces of oppression, dispossession, and marginality under the rule of King Hassan II of Morocco. Their music was dubbed "Morocco's revolutionary song," "Morocco's soul music," and "Morocco's mythical song." Three generations later, Nas El Ghiwane are still remembered, their lyrics borrowed and spirituality revitalized through hip-hop and the lyrics of rap. Their revolutionary songs continue to make sense among the younger generations of urban dwellers who witnessed the riots of the 1990s and the state militarized response. The generation of Nas El Ghiwane couched protest in music in the same way this generation does with hip-hop.

The real turning point in youth awareness about the importance of hip-hop took place during the trial of the heavy metal band Reborn, from Casablanca. In February 2003 the fourteen band members were charged with being a satanic cult. Their trial, however, occasioned the first Moroccan conflation of politics and music when protestors carried the sign "I Vote I Sing" to contest the trial. This sign indicated a new shift in the discourse of citizenship rights, which, the protesters maintained, had to encompass musical forms of expression. Activist mobilization against the trial led to a wider awareness of the birth of a new musical scene in Morocco, and the release of the artists. Debates raging on the Internet and in the media brought about new notions of cosmopolitanism that crystalized around the individual citizen as a modern subject with acoustic and lifestyle "rights."

GOVERNANCE, RISK, AND YOUTH-NESS

Political elites' involvement with hip-hop entered a new phase after the Casablanca attacks of May 2003. Fourteen young men from the same shantytown, Sidi Moumen, blew themselves up in various places in the city, killing and injuring hundreds. Their motives were unclear. Could it be the American war on Iraq, and the rumors that Morocco would participate in the coalition? Rumor was already circulating about Morocco as the host country of USAFRICOM, the United States African Command, in charge of military operations in Africa. There was also the audiotaped speech attributed to Osama bin Laden putting Morocco on his blacklist.

Motives notwithstanding, the attacks increased the political tensions and uncertainties about Moroccan "exceptionalism," bringing the "war on terror" and its *global patriot act* to the heart of domestic politics. Moreover, the attacks pointed to the vulnerability of the Moroccan economy as represented by the cosmopolitan and industrial aspirations of Casablanca. It is worth noting that the state response to the first Casablanca attacks in 2003 (there were others in 2006 and 2007) was through passing the Antiterrorism Law. The forceful intervention to cleanse and pacify poor neighborhoods in Casablanca and across the country led to a criminalization of poverty, with certain neighborhoods falling under Islamist control. The state response was also entangled with the competing security agendas of the European and American governments, which located North African youth at the crossroads of global techniques of governance, surveillance, and also normalization.

Music is at the center of these policies. As North Africa was becoming a geopolitical center of fighting terror, the Moroccan state responded by creating music events and international music festivals to counter the Islamization of youth politics. High-profile politicians are now heading "associations" for the organization of yearly festivals in most major cities in Morocco. The point is to portray an image of political openness, religious tolerance, and economic liberalization and to put Moroccan cities on the global investment map. The Fes Festival of World Sacred Music, the Essaouira Gnaoua Jazz Festival, and the Mawazine Festival, in Rabat, are now on the agenda of multinational touring companies, allowing Morocco to become a privileged destination for pop stars and their fans from all over the world.

While local authorities market Moroccan cities as a locus of musical exchange, and pour money into the bank accounts of foreign artists and superstars, they have not been able to co-opt Moroccan youth. Young men in poor neighborhoods have created alternative spaces by producing their own music, their own stars, their own festival, and their local competitions and awards. L'Boulevard is their rendezvous. And in sharp contrast to the "verticality" of state-sponsored festivals, and their privileged international audience, L'Boulevard is entirely imagined and managed by young Moroccan artists, who are reversing the trends about musical production and diffusion.

CONCLUSION

Raï and hip-hop have certainly put northern Africa on the global circuits of musical production and diffusion. They have allowed artists to engage in unique forms of sampling, mixing, and performing that show the centrality of Pan-African identities, cosmopolitanism, and diasporic sensibilities. In fact, since the second half of the twentieth century, North African pop stars and expatriates started to impact global audiences through the mixing of styles, languages, and rhythms. Increasing migration from northern Africa to western Europe enabled sound to travel north in search of new audiences. Now both raï and hip-hop are an integral part of the European soundscape.

Equally important, hip-hop might be playing a similar role as that played by jazz in the 1950s. If the US State Department–sponsored jazz tours were the instrument for American cultural hegemony during the Cold War, hip-hop might be playing that role in the post-9/11 era. This genre became relevant to many governments after the 9/11 attacks in the United States, the attacks in Casablanca (2003), Madrid (2004), and London (2005), and also the Paris riots in the *banlieue* (2005). The 2008 Brookings Institution report entitled "Mightier than the Sword: Arts and Culture in the U.S.-Muslim World Relationship" noted the importance of hip-hop as "an African-American Muslim tradition of protest against authority, most powerfully represented by Malcolm X." In many parts of the world, US embassies embarked on what political scientist Hisham Aidi calls "hip hop diplomacy" as a main tool for earning hearts and minds across the African continent, Europe, and the Muslim world.

But regardless of the questions of co-optation, the rise of northern African hip-hop and raï as global tracks can still be read against histories of slavery, colonialism, and imperialist orders. While northern African immigrants and expatriates in Europe drew on soundscapes from home as they crafted a sense of belonging, remembering, nostalgia, and rebellion, European and non-European audiences have espoused these soundtracks through playing music, singing in Arabic lyrics, and dancing in the multiple scenes of performances created by artists from within and without the continent. The rebellious roots of raï and rap will forever connect their global audiences to the social movements and the cultural and political currents generated on the continent.

ADDITIONAL RESOURCES

Aidi, Hisham. *Rebel Music: Race, Empire, and the New Muslim Youth Culture.* New York and Toronto: Pantheon Books, 2014.

Al-Deen, Hana Noor. "The Evolution of Rai Music." *Journal of Black Studies* 35, no. 5 (May 2005): 597–611.

LeVine, Mark. *Heavy Metal Islam: Rock Resistance and the Struggles for the Soul of Islam.* New York: Random House, 2008.

Salime, Zakia. "I Vote, I Sing": The Rise of Aesthetic Citizenship in Morocco. *International Journal of Middle East Studies.* (2015) 47: 36–139

Van Nieuwkerk, Karin, ed. *Muslim Rap, Halal Soaps, and Revolutionary Theater: Artistic Developments in the Muslim World.* Austin: University of Texas Press, 2011.

. . .

ZAKIA SALIME is Associate Professor of Sociology and Women's and Gender Studies at Rutgers University, and Visiting Associate Professor of Women's, Gender and Sexuality Studies at Yale. She publishes in the area of gender, social movements, and the political economy of the "war on terror," with a focus on contemporary northern Africa and the Middle East. She wrote *Between Feminism and Islam: Human Rights and Sharia Law in Morocco* (University of Minnesota Press, 2011). Together with with Frances Hasso, she coedited *Freedom without Permission: Bodies and Space in the Arab Revolutions* (Duke University Press, 2016).

PART IV

Science, Technology, and Health

INTRODUCTION

Africa is a space of contradictions: the site of brilliant scientific discoveries and technological innovations, but also of long histories of resource extractions and devastating epidemics. Such contradictions can be understood only through the lens of history, politics, and economics: the legacies of slavery and colonialism, the opportunities for education and engagement, the enduring inequalities that perpetuate poverty for many and promote possibilities for some, the capacity for resilience and creativity, and the need for new ways of listening, learning, and knowing.

Renowned Cameroonian microbiologist Dr. Sara Eyangoh examines some of these contradictions—and the challenges she has faced as an African, a woman, and a scientist—in her interview by Tamara Giles-Vernick. Readers will be impressed by her Dr. Eyangoh's extraordinary accomplishments and passion for science, but dismayed by the lack of funding, training, and opportunities for African scientists. These inequities inform Douglas Webb's powerful assessment of the lessons learned (and not learned) from efforts by global organizations to quell epidemics like HIV/AIDS and Ebola in Africa. As a social scientist who has worked for various United Nations agencies leading these efforts, Webb demonstrates how politics, inequalities of resources and power, and failure to learn from HIV/AIDS interventions hampered the success of containing Ebola. He argues forcefully for the need for *people-centered responses* that engage, listen to, learn from, and invest in affected communities.

Despite these troubling histories and enduring inequities, Africa and Africans have also developed path-breaking scientific innovations. Ron

Eglash's provocative article showcases the contributions of African architectural ideas and fractal geometries to current generative technologies such as "makerspace" and "do-it-yourself." The circles within circles within circles of traditional households within homesteads promotes an egalitarian ethos, one now mirrored in current architectural marvels such as a stunning contemporary shopping center in Addis Ababa. Similarly, Kenyans have long been able to use their cell phones for sophisticated financial transactions, in ways that should be the envy of readers in the Global North. Dillon Mahoney explores how these proudly African forms of mobile money, called M-PESA, have reshaped the lives of everyday Kenyans.

Africa's extraordinary wealth of resources has spurred innovations and developments within and beyond the continent. But these resources have also been the site of pillage, plunder, and politics since long ago. Cell phones—those ubiquitous icons of "modernity" and connectedness throughout the globe—depend on coltan, a rare material found only in the Democratic Republic of Congo and a few other places in the world. "The Machine" is one of the many men and women who dig with their hands through the dirt to mine coltan and similar minerals. His story, as relayed by James H. Smith, offers readers a rare portrait of the lives of artisanal miners who struggle to produce the conditions of possibility for the digital age in the face of limited options, recurring conflicts, and misguided international policies.

Hoodia, a medicinal plant used by San peoples to suppress their appetites, is another African resource desired by global industries (in this case, pharmaceuticals). The efforts by international companies to discover, patent, and market indigenous plants like hoodia is often called "bio-prospecting" or even "bio-piracy." Rachel Wynberg uses the case of hoodia to document the dilemmas and politics of these confrontations between capitalists and indigenous peoples. Fortunately, new partnerships have emerged recently in southern Africa that might serve as models of more equitable ways to share the benefits.

But, as Siad Darwish argues, the drive for resource extraction and economic progress often comes at a cost, especially for former colonies like Tunisia. Garbage, waste, and pollution are all by-products of colonial and capitalist exploitation, their spread and stink fueled by the lackluster environmental policies of the long-term authoritarian government. Sadly, the "Jasmine Revolution" for which Tunisia is rightly celebrated also made visible how the nation had become, in part because of its global connections, a "country of rubbish." Garbage and pollution became vivid metaphors for powerfully felt political and economic inequities, sparking strikes and protests.

Together, these chapters will surprise, inform, and perhaps even infuriate readers. The contrasts and contradictions are stark: a continent of astonishing resource wealth and suffocating poverty, of startling innovations and enduring exploitation, of remarkable resilience and sometimes gloomy despair. But, as the essays show, these contrasts are actually connections, built on and produced by historical and contemporary relations of power both within Africa and between Africa and the rest of the world.

4 . 1

Profile

A CONVERSATION WITH MICROBIOLOGIST
DR. SARA EYANGOH

Tamara Giles-Vernick

Abstract: In this interview, leading Cameroonian microbiologist Dr. Sarah Eyangoh reflects on her contributions to the fields of tuberculosis and Buruli ulcer, on the nature of biomedical research in Africa, on being a woman and a scientist, and on the challenges facing the next generation of African scientific researchers.

Keywords: biomedical research, science, gender, Cameroon, tuberculosis, Buruli ulcer

DR. SARA EYANGOH IS A MICROBIOLOGIST specializing in two closely related bacteria—the tuberculosis bacillus (*Mycobacterium tuberculosis*) and *Mycobacterium ulcerans*. (*M. ulcerans,* the cause of Buruli ulcer, destroys skin and subcutaneous tissue and can lead to chronic, disfiguring ulcers and long-term disability; it occurs in some thirty-two countries worldwide.) Dr. Eyangoh, the longtime head of the Mycobacteriology Service at the Centre Pasteur du Cameroun (CPC), has since 2012 served as the center's scientific director. In this capacity, she oversees all research and public-health activities, evaluates the institution's scientific strengths, weaknesses, and opportunities, and sets new priorities and strategies for its current and future biomedical research. Dr. Eyangoh is an important figure in global health circles: she was recently nominated to the Scientific and Technical Advisory Committee to the Special Programme for Research and Training in Tropical Diseases, a program cosponsored by UNICEF, UNDP (United Nations Development Programme), and the World Health Organization.

The CPC is one of sub-Saharan Africa's leading biomedical research institutions, with active, globally linked laboratories in virology, epidemiology, and microbiology, as well as other services. Created in 1959, the CPC is a

Cameroonian public research institution, but also a member of the Institut Pasteur's international network of thirty-two research institutes. The creation of this international network had its beginnings in the 1887 founding of the Institut Pasteur (Paris), a private biomedical research institution, and its subsequent expansion throughout the colonial and postcolonial world, with institutes in Africa, Asia, and Latin America, as well as in Europe and North America.

In a wide-ranging conversation in French one afternoon in her Yaoundé office, Dr. Eyangoh reflected on her contributions to studies of tuberculosis and Buruli ulcer, the nature of African biomedical research, what it means to be a woman scientist, and the challenges facing young African researchers. She insisted on the need to pursue biomedical research in Cameroon and Africa that leads to appropriate public health applications and spoke eloquently about the professional and gendered dimensions of biomedical research that transcend specific locations.

In the interests of full disclosure, I should add here the Institut Pasteur (IP) is my employer. But my knowledge of the complex historical and contemporary relations between the IP and its network institutions offered me insights that are not evident to those outside the institution. I have also worked with Dr. Eyangoh on a large Buruli ulcer study, and thus have witnessed her in action—her analytical incisiveness and extraordinary capacity to lead a (sometimes unruly) international scientific research team.

· · ·

You began your research on tuberculosis, characterizing different strains of tuberculosis found in Cameroon. Could you explain for readers the importance of tuberculosis in Cameroon and in Africa, and the significance of your own research on it?

In Cameroon and the rest of the world, tuberculosis is a huge problem. The prevalence of TB in Cameroon is high, about twenty thousand cases every year. At the CPC, we serve as the national reference laboratory for tuberculosis. That entails, for instance, the surveillance of multiresistant strains [bacterial strains resistant to available therapies] and the implementation of tools that allow us to detect resistant cases and to report them. In our lab, we have put into place all WHO-approved tools. We assist Cameroon's national program by developing training, defining its strategies, supervising activities on the ground, and organizing everything that involves the laboratory.

In my doctoral work, I examined the profiles of resistant strains and collected data on multiresistance in Cameroon. We undertook this study in a pilot region of Cameroon because we couldn't carry it out in the entire country. We were able to genetically characterize the strains circulating in Cameroon. At that time, there wasn't a lot of work of this kind here. When I did the genotyping, I discovered that in Cameroon, about half of the circulating strains are quite diverse, but the rest is pretty homogeneous. This is what defines the tuberculosis family in Cameroon. Studies in Nigeria, Benin, and Côte d'Ivoire have shown that this family is dominant elsewhere as well. We didn't really know why. The BCG vaccine [against tuberculosis; given at birth in Africa] played a role: *Mycobacterium africanum* was a very dominant strain during the 1970s, and there was a subsequent shift. Perhaps it was also the advent of HIV that allowed for an evolution, a change that affected the fitness of the bacteria that accounted for more and more cases.

We're also interested in evaluating diagnostic tools that are better adapted to our context here in Cameroon. Working on TB requires strict biosafety measures because it's highly transmissible, and not all laboratory and clinical structures can accommodate such measures. So I have been involved in developing tools that we can implement here.

I'm also interested in childhood TB, which can be exceptionally complex to diagnose. We don't have good diagnostic tools for children. We've been participating in a study on tuberculosis in children co-infected with HIV. TB in children is very complicated, and when they are also infected with HIV, it's terrible. We're finishing up this study, but it was so interesting that we realized there was scope to develop another study in collaboration with the Pasteur network solely in Africa. We've just received funding to explore tuberculosis among children in three different countries: Cameroon, Côte d'Ivoire, and Madagascar.

I've heard you say that "Buruli ulcer is my baby." Could you explain to those who know very little about this disease why it is important? And why BU is "your baby"?

I joked at a recent Buruli ulcer meeting that BU was my baby and tuberculosis was my husband. I carried this baby, I pushed it [to grow], and I almost abandoned my husband to tuberculosis, because the baby needed to grow up. I now believe that the baby has grown up and taken flight. So I'm returning to my husband, [because] tuberculosis remains a huge problem. It still needs my expertise. In the coming years, the research projects that I lead will focus on tuberculosis. But I'll always support work on BU.

Buruli ulcer is important because it's a disease that . . . how can I explain it? You could say that it is a horror. It's true that when I was looking for funding, people would say, "So how many cases are there?" [About five to six thousand cases are reported worldwide each year.] They would insist, "But from a public-health standpoint, it isn't important!" But it is a horror. You cannot close your eyes to this horror, even if it afflicts just one person. There aren't many cases in Cameroon, and they have diminished recently. But cases are often concentrated in a single village, or a single region. So even for a small village or regional population, one hundred cases is enormous, even though for Cameroon as a whole and for the rest of the world these numbers don't seem important. But it is a horror, and you cannot close your eyes to it.

It's very important for research teams to continue this work because BU is truly a neglected disease. We don't understand transmission, [and] we don't really have a means of preventing it, because existing prevention strategies are so hard to implement. If we stopped doing this research, people whom the disease afflicts would be completely forgotten.

You've observed that you now supervise research, but you're less involved in its day-to-day practice. This distancing from the laboratory seems to be the curse of successful scientists: the more you succeed, the further you are from actual research.

I think it's a little sad, because we could give so much more to research if we could continue doing research. But at the same time, I realize you have to quit laboratory bench work, because this is how you invest in others. You use your experience to support other researchers, to evaluate them, to help them to start new projects. You discover that you're now serving on commissions, on advisory committees, to define research objectives, to obtain research funding. So I don't think we should call it a curse. To put it more positively, it is how a scientific career evolves. But you're never prepared for this change.

It seems to me that this shift from the laboratory bench to advising and supervision is quite common among successful biomedical researchers around the world.

Exactly. But it's hard to let go of the lab work. You have to, because otherwise you'll exhaust yourself.

I found it striking that all the research you've conducted has an applied, public-health dimension—something that seems to be a common feature among African biomedical researchers. But elsewhere in the world, it isn't hard to find biologists working on basic, fundamental questions. How did you make the decision to pursue biomedical research with public-health applications? Would you say that this feature characterizes biomedical sciences in Africa?

I don't think that I made a conscious decision from the beginning. In reality, this is a dimension of biomedical research in Africa that *must* exist. Basic research is absolutely essential, but given our needs, our capacities in Africa, translational, operational research will yield the most fruit. When I talk to young students who want to do doctoral dissertations, I tell them, "Be really careful about your research question. I know basic research is essential, but it cannot exist by itself in our context. When you do only basic research, you risk evolving in a different way." Sometimes adapting [to a local context] can be very difficult, because basic research requires very specific tools that don't exist here. And even if they do exist, the maintenance, the costs, are prohibitive and the materials are difficult to get. But at a good research center like the CPC, you need some basic research to elevate the overall level of research. You also have to be able to communicate why it's important, because otherwise, when you go to the Ministry of Health, they'll say that you're wasting money on research that doesn't accomplish anything.

I want to ask a somewhat provocative question. At times, some observers have caricatured African science, saying that it lags globally because African laboratories lack resources, because scientists aren't well trained, and because the most cutting-edge technologies aren't available. How do you react to this characterization?

It's too easy to caricature [African research]. You have to understand that doing research in Africa is already extremely complex. I'm always encountering people who ask, about one African researcher or another, "So what did he do this year? He only published one paper!" But what you accomplish in a single month [of lab work] in Paris will take you a year to do here. You might have the equipment, but it breaks down, and then you have to wait three months for repairs, even in the best institutions. So I would say to African researchers, "Hats off to those of you who dare, to those of you who don't have the tools, to those of you who aren't so well trained, to those of you who—despite everything that we lack—still dare to do this work."

How did you decide to become a scientist?

I really think it was my husband, not me. I was always interested in the sciences, and it's true that I always imagined myself in a lab coat, maybe a doctor. When I say that it was my husband, it was at a moment when I was struggling to get funding for my thesis in biochemistry at the University of Yaoundé I in Cameroon, and I told myself it wasn't worth it. If I became a middle school or high school teacher, I could easily make a living. But he was always telling me, "You're brilliant, you'll get there! If you become a teacher, you'll be bored." So I hung in there, and thanks to my husband, I applied for and received a fellowship to do another masters-level training in tropical diseases with the Francophone University Association [AUF].

As part of this training, I decided to work on tuberculosis, although I don't exactly remember why. I came to the CPC, and this was the first time that a woman worked in the TB lab here, manipulating salivary specimens. I must have made a good impression, because the lab chief at the time decided that he had found his successor—and it was me.

For this master's degree in tropical diseases, I followed three months of lectures in Gabon [at the International Center for Medical Research in Franceville, or CIRMF], six months of training at the CPC, and then nine months at the University of Bordeaux [France] to finish up my training. I simultaneously pursued a DEA [Diploma of Advanced Studies], and saved up money from my fellowship to spend a month in a lab at the Pitié-Salpêtrière Hospital to do genetic characterization of apolipoprotein E [biochemical analysis of lipid-transport proteins]. This was the last part of my lab research for my PhD in biochemistry at the University of Yaoundé I. I returned here in 1999 and finished up my manuscript to graduate with my PhD. The following year, I received another fellowship—to do a doctoral thesis in microbiology to work on the molecular epidemiology of tuberculosis in Cameroon, at the Institut Pasteur [Paris] and Paris Diderot University. I defended my dissertation in 2003, but by then I was already heading a laboratory at the CPC.

Let me follow up with another slightly provocative question. From time to time I encounter colleagues insisting that the Institut Pasteur is nothing more than a neocolonial institution. How do you respond to those who insist that the Centre Pasteur du Cameroun, as part of the Pasteur network, isn't a Cameroonian institution but a French neocolonial one?

This is part of my daily life! There are people who say, "It's a French institution." But it's a public Cameroonian institution, and we do a lot of work with the [Cameroonian] Ministry of Public Health to assist in surveillance. In fact, we've never implemented a single research project that did not reflect the priorities of the Ministry of Public Health. Whatever work we do, we make certain that it is first and foremost part of Cameroon's health strategy. We remind people daily that this is a public institution: it fits within the organizational chart of the Ministry of Public Health, and we work together to put public health into practice. But we are also members of the Institut Pasteur international network, because this membership opens us up to outside institutions and brings us funding. The Pasteur network offers undeniable support that allows us to improve the quality of our research.

As a woman, what do you bring to scientific research? Have you experienced being a woman as an advantage? A challenge? Does it figure into your work at all?

Clearly, in our context, it is a challenge. Because research doesn't just mean time spent in the lab. Research implies investing more of yourself. So it's really a challenge, and even more so in Africa. We want to claim that we have evolved. But in Africa, being a woman means being available. Even when a couple can accept [the demands on a woman scientist], sometimes it's everyone else who complains, "You're never here, you're never available, you never come to social events!" I think it's a permanent challenge. You have to tell yourself constantly, "I'm not going to complain. Oh, I'm pregnant, but no matter, I have to be at the lab tomorrow. I'm nauseous, but I don't care."

I see my male colleagues who leave the lab at 9 p.m. without it being a problem. Me, when I'm still sitting here at 7 p.m., I start to feel guilty. I've never experienced being a woman as an advantage, because you have to reconcile your family life with your daily work, which has no fixed hours. When you do research, you also have to present it, which means you're obliged to travel. So you're not only preoccupied with work; you are also absent from your family.

But I don't think about it every day. When I wake up, I don't think, "Oh, I'm a woman, I'm going to do this." Of course, there are always children around to remind you: "Mama, you aren't listening. Mama, it's a holiday but you've just been on your computer."

"Well, dear, I was at home all day."

"But you didn't talk to me!"

Even from time to time, your husband will say, "You need to stop. All you're doing is consulting your mail."

So love, family, and all the rest do exist. You hope that your children will grow up quickly, before you're too old. You tell yourself that they'll be more independent, but I don't know. The worst is that we don't take care of ourselves. Some people, they make themselves beautiful—they do their nails, they take care of their skin, and you want to as well! [*laughs*].

What advice would you give to the next generations of Cameroonian and African scientists? And to women scientists?

I'd like to say something first to our universities. We need to find a way to train our young people better. We have to improve training, to avoid refresher courses that bring people from everywhere but don't select the best people. We have to target smart young people. If we start with ten good people every year, the impact will be substantial.

To young, upcoming scientists, I would say, "Ask yourselves questions that are most appropriate to your context." That could be limiting, but I don't think so. "You young scientists are best integrated into your own context. You are most motivated to pursue this kind of research, because you live our challenges here on a daily basis." I tell them to ask questions that speak to our problems, because then we'll come up with answers that are best adapted to our concerns.

And if you are a woman, forget that you are a woman. If you're always thinking first and foremost that you're a woman, you're going to impose limits on yourself. But you need to learn to explain to your partner what you do, so that he understands and supports you. Because it's much harder if you have a partner who doesn't understand anything, who blocks everything. That must be hell. If you're always thinking that you're a woman, you're just going to say, "I shouldn't, I can't." And you'll limit yourself.

ADDITIONAL RESOURCES

Farmer, Paul. "Social Scientists and the New Tuberculosis." *Social Science & Medicine* 44, no. 3 (1997): 347–58.

Giles-Vernick, Tamara, and James L. A. Webb Jr., eds. *Global Health in Africa: Historical Perspectives on Disease Control*. Athens: Ohio University Press, 2013.

Kitetu, Catherine Wawasi, ed. *Gender, Science and Technology: Perspectives from Africa*. CODESRIA Gender Series 6. Dakar: Council for the Development of Social Science Research in Africa, 2008.

Marion, E., J. Landier, P. Boisier, L. Marsollier, A. Fontanet, P. LeGall, J. Aubry, B. Noumen-Djeungo, A. Umboock, and S. Eyangoh. "Expansion of Buruli Ulcer Disease in Cameroon." *Emerging Infectious Disease* 17, no. 3 (2011): 551–53.

Prince, Ruth J., and Rebecca Marsland, eds. *Making and Unmaking Public Health in Africa: Ethnographic and Historical Perspectives*. Athens: Ohio University Press, 2014.

. . .

TAMARA GILES-VERNICK is a Director of Research in the Emerging Diseases Epidemiology Unit at the Institut Pasteur in Paris. She has conducted medical anthropological and historical research in Central and West Africa, publishing on viral hepatitis, Buruli ulcer, the historical emergence of HIV in Africa, global health in Africa, the history of influenza pandemics, and environmental history. She is currently leading a three-country study on the history and anthropology of human–nonhuman primate contact and emerging diseases in Central Africa.

The Politics, Perils, and Possibilities of Epidemics in Africa

Douglas Webb

Abstract: Epidemics are social events, and as new health threats emerge in Africa we are repeatedly faced with the need to learn lessons from the past. AIDS has been the great teacher as we look forward to face the complex health environment of today, which is characterized by overlapping epidemics of infectious and noncommunicable diseases. Countries now grapple with the need to increase their accountability and make difficult choices over the use of financial and political capital. AIDS taught us again that addressing all types of threats to health relies on engaging with affected communities while placing human rights above the institutional prejudices and failures that allow epidemics to thrive. The lessons of the past, however, seem quickly forgotten.

Keywords: health, epidemics, AIDS, Ebola, Zika

HUMAN DEVELOPMENT IN AFRICA REQUIRES a healthy population. Economic growth, the same. Yet ill health and its causes continue to present a significant paradox. Technological advances should have made many common health problems obsolete or at least very rare: HIV, TB, water-borne illnesses, malnutrition, preventable childhood infections, and so on. The list is as long as it is unnecessary. So why do we tolerate ill health on a wide scale? Have we learned anything from prior experiences, especially the responses to the HIV pandemic?

EPIDEMICS AS POLITICAL EVENTS

Nearly twenty years ago my book *HIV and AIDS in Africa* was released into a research community that was desperate for any good news about the HIV pandemic. Rates globally were rising, and prospects of an affordable treatment were some years away. The book described the socioeconomic environment of southern Africa, in which the virus was rapidly spreading. The conclusion was as simple as it was unwelcome—that the epidemic was as much a political event as it was a biological one. Political transition, combined with the fallout of structural adjustment, occupied the minds and pockets of both the powers that be and ordinary citizens. In the two decades since then, little has changed, and arguably the future of the HIV epidemic in Africa, as well as of other existing or emerging epidemics, will remain determined by political and social forces.

When confronting epidemics we need to consider two major groups. The first group is infectious diseases—characterized by, first, the continued presence and transmission of familiar bacteria and parasites such as tuberculosis, malaria, and schistosomiasis; and by, second, the outbreaks of new infectious agents such as HIV, Ebola, and Zika. The second group consists of noncommunicable diseases (NCDs) such as diabetes, cancer, and cardiovascular diseases. Populations experience both groups, all the time, even though attention flits between specific conditions and the spotlight rests on one condition, potentially to the detriment of combating others. Responses to diseases have become just that: *disease responses,* as opposed to public health and *people-centered* responses. Societies shift attention from one malaise to another even as overlapping epidemics actually define the health landscape and people's experience of ill health. Political processes and those that govern resource allocations have preferred to categorize health into defined and specific conditions and experiences. Financial streams and the associated building of skills and assets in health systems have thus tended to favor certain diseases and subsequently *discriminate* between diseases burdens. After all, in a context of finite resources, prioritization is inevitable, is administratively expedient, and allows greater accountability in health system governance, no?

But making choices has its downsides; people experience ill health and insults to well-being through immediate and visceral means, irrespective of preferred health financing trends or projections. I learned this early on. Even when conducting field research for my book in 1992–93, it was clear that HIV was a secondary concern for both urban and rural South Africans, at a time when the "West" was prioritizing AIDS in health discourse above all else. Top of the list of concerns of hundreds of citizens I interviewed were TB, gastroenteritis, and "hi-hi," or hypertension. AIDS was ninth on the list overall. AIDS was yet to hit hard, and even though adult HIV prevalence rates were already over 1 percent, it had yet to infect people's consciousness in a meaningful way. While HIV is now, rightly, a regular feature in the health-risk landscape, it is part of a double epidemiologic burden currently confronting much of sub-Saharan Africa—that of overlapping and concurrent infectious and NCD epidemics. Cardiovascular disease, diabetes, chronic lung disease, and cancers now vie with HIV, malaria, TB, and water-borne diseases, as well as a nefarious host of other infectious ailments, for financial and political attention.

NCDs, of course, have not suddenly appeared in Africa. However, attention has been focused elsewhere. But their presence is inexorably on the rise, all the while shadowed by preexisting health commitments. One in four African adults are now hypertensive, with a further one-fifth at high risk of becoming so. The stage is set for a growing pandemic of cardiovascular diseases, including stroke, as well as diabetes and renal failure, among other associated conditions. In confronting a new pandemic of NCDs, what lessons can responses to AIDS and other epidemics teach us?

UNDERSTANDING THE "COMMUNITY"

Epidemics happen in social spaces. The ongoing experience in responding to HIV helps us to understand this insight. Pragmatism dictates that when deliberately confronting new (or previously ignored) epidemics, it is wise to strategize with the assets that you have in place. A collective analytical effort is ongoing to assess how the considerable infrastructure assembled and dedicated to HIV prevention and control over the last three decades, worth billions of dollars, can be utilized, built on, or repurposed for a range of health conditions. This "learning from HIV" process incorporates both the physical infrastructure dedicated to screening, diagnostics, and treatment, and also the significant human-resource capacity generated by the demands HIV has placed on health systems.

Perhaps the most significant contribution of tackling HIV in Africa as a rapidly emerging threat to health has been the huge body of experience that has accrued through engaging with people within their communities—examining their health-seeking behaviors, beliefs, and habits as well as their complex interactions with the formal and informal health sectors. Mistakes were inevitably made. Early health-education campaigns on the perils of HIV looked to instill fear into the susceptible populations. Health authorities utilized scare tactics and dread-laden images that succeeded only in inducing further fear among affected populations. Billboards were dominated by images of graves and skeletal patients. Some early messages were misguided altogether. I recall seeing written signs on combi-taxis (share taxis) in Soweto in 1992 that unhelpfully advised residents, "You cannot get AIDS from swimming pools." We have, thankfully, come a long way since then. Normative standards of HIV prevention now include education and information campaigns developed with and for the target groups concerned, and people living with HIV are routinely engaged in HIV program design and performance accountability. The widespread engagement of civil society has proved crucial, providing services to the unreached, technical know-how, policy advocacy, and the essential role of witnessing the response to ensure that those in power are held accountable.

In regard to HIV care also, community engagement was a feature of some of the earliest responses. The health system had very little to offer AIDS patients for around two decades into the epidemic, until the advent of affordable antiretroviral therapy (ART). Through outreach programs that were pioneered in heavily impacted countries like Uganda, Zambia, and Zimbabwe, patients were supported by home-based care programs that forced communities to confront and tackle the disease and associated stigmas head-on. Faith-based health-care providers and civil-society organizations spearheaded these programs, which have helped countless patients, perhaps numbering in the millions, to bridge the gap between health-sector services and dignified care outside of a clinical setting.

Charges of AIDS exceptionalism have pushed a more comprehensive health agenda in recent years. Efforts to combat HIV and the funding they have received have garnered envious looks from other disease "constituencies." From a human rights–based perspective, the charge is unjustified. Everyone, including people living with HIV and those susceptible to it, has the right to health. The achievements of the AIDS community to generate high levels of political will and subsequent resources is a major public health success story. The precedent set by the multi-institutional and -dimensional response to AIDS provides a solid platform on which to build, especially in regard to combating NCDs and their co-morbidities—which, for example, link ART administration to increasing rates of cardiovascular disease and diabetes. People living with HIV have a far higher incidence rate for NCDs. Thus the HIV service platform is the obvious place to develop further community-based NCD prevention and control interventions. Indeed, voluntary counseling and testing services established for HIV now include blood-pressure tests and screening for hypertension and diabetes across Africa, led by good pilot experiences, and have been adopted in countries like Lesotho and Uganda. Stigmas increasingly experienced by those with cancer can be addressed by the same counseling and community-engagement capacity previously devoted to HIV. Global institutions are starting to recognize the links. The Global Fund for AIDS, TB, and Malaria is opening up the possibility of financing co-infection and co-morbidity prevention and control, which could directly impact the speed and direction of scaling up tobacco-control legislation, for example, and addressing the ominous interaction of diabetes and tuberculosis.

RESPONDING TO EBOLA—LESSONS NOT LEARNED

But such advances and insights, accelerated by HIV responses, are far from universal when other pathogens enter the arena. The 2014–15 Ebola crisis in West Africa that claimed over eleven thousand lives in Sierra Leone, Liberia, and Guinea demonstrated that lessons from HIV are not yet institutionalized in emerging epidemic management. Lacking confidence in health-care providers, families hid patients, believing that clinics, hospitals, or rapidly assembled Ebola treatment units (ETUs) could provide no help or indeed would guarantee that a patient's chances of recovery were zero. This deep level of distrust, exacerbated by misguided messaging from the health services that "Ebola has no cure," prevented patients from being isolated in clinical centers, thus spreading the infection further in households and communities. The imperative of understanding belief systems regarding the etiology, transmission, and implicit *meaning* of this new infection in a naive population was recognized too late by responding agencies. In an epidemic where over half and perhaps as many as two-thirds of transmissions occurred during body preparation for burial, the scoping of the nature and extent of health-determining rituals and their variations that affect public health should be a starting point, not an afterthought. High-level orders that mandated cremation, for example, overruled community preferences for ritualized burial, and so insulted notions of spiritual travel to the afterlife. As a result, the phenomenon of "night burials" became a feature of the epidemic, spreading infection further as families sought to adhere to traditions and avoid the stigma and practical challenges of sanctioned quarantining. HIV responders taught institutions that understanding the ways that communities vary in their interpretation of and negotiation of behaviors within a belief system, and the ways they respond to disease (especially emerging ones), is a principal duty of those charged with ameliorating public health threats.

MONEY MATTERS

The second major lesson relates to money: who provides it matters. With so much international financing (in relative terms) being directing at combating HIV and AIDS—epitomized by the largest bilateral health interventions ever, including the US government's President's Emergency Plan for AIDS Relief (PEPFAR) initiative, begun in 2003, and the Global Fund to Fight AIDS, TB, and Malaria—the imperative for sustainable domestic financing of AIDS responses in the most heavily impacted countries has been slow coming. Under the narrative of "global solidarity and shared responsibility," the international community is increasingly anxious to see HIV and AIDS responses financed by the high-burden countries themselves, starting with the middle-income countries. Lower-income countries have had a longer notice period, but the message is the same: "We can't keep paying forever." Countries most affected by HIV in sub-Saharan Africa are rapidly moving toward or have already reached middle-income status. Overall levels of wealth are increasing, allowing a greater flexibility of governments to increase spending on public health. Indeed, as gross national income rises, the proportion of government budget allocated to health tends to increase. We are seeing a movement of financing burden toward the taxpayers of affected countries. National AIDS levies and trust funds are starting to appear. The prototype was the AIDS levy instituted in Zimbabwe, necessitated by declines in politically conditioned aid flows from outside. Later variants, such as that in Kenya, incorporate funding meant to tackle both HIV and NCDs. Kenya is one example of health financing in transition, as nearly half of the national health budget is from development partners.

But herein lies the challenge, and the reality: economic and political capital are intertwined. A major lesson from AIDS was that national governments must own and manage the response. The search for who is to blame, combined with denial of the scale of the problem, presents crucial delays in the required response. Governance mechanisms, or the way that institutions and constituencies are convened, empowered, and interact, need to be sufficient to respond to the public health threat at hand. The emergence over time of national coordination bodies, policies, strategies, and operational frameworks dedicated to overcoming HIV was a significant achievement. Central to this success was the surge in financing—rising from several hundred thousand US dollars of international support in the mid-1990s to about $16 billion in 2014, with a projected "fast-tracking" requirement of over $30 billion from all sources by 2020. As countries transition and struggle to finance responses to existing health threats, it is no surprise that the planning, costing, resourcing, and coordination of efforts to prevent and control NCDs have barely begun. As with HIV, delays now guarantee higher impacts and greater costs later. This is one lesson that should not have to be relearned.

While there are many options for increasing financing for health, not least through revenue-raising strategies such as levies on private-sector transactions or revenue, or increasing taxes on tobacco and sugar, the issue is more complex. The transition of financing implies a transition of accountabilities for HIV responses, and along with it a reassessment of the political capital attached to HIV prevention and treatment. HIV itself, of course, does not discriminate, but since the beginning of the pandemic, and over sixty million infections later, we have seen that HIV is effective at highlighting fault lines in society, and any institutional and social prejudices. These serve to shape the epidemic at all levels and determine its trajectories. The economic and legal environments are perhaps the most significant. Failure to address these social and structural determinants of HIV serves to nurture the epidemic and its impacts at the fringes of society. Where the right to health is fragile for the majority, it can be highly precarious for those on the margins.

THE CENTRALITY OF HUMAN RIGHTS

Respecting, protecting, and fulfilling human rights has rightly dominated the HIV and AIDS discourse and policy debate throughout. This has not been a static discussion. Over the past three decades, the framing and interpretations of AIDS have shifted. In the 1980s, AIDS in the African context was a platform for interpretations and counternarratives of racism, directed at Africa and its perceived (and externally constructed) sexualities. Imbued with colonial interpretations of sexual proclivity, early commentaries on the emerging pandemic in sub-Saharan Africa created a political backlash from within Africa itself against research and initial attempts to understand the behavioral dynamics of the condition. Indeed, the anti-Western rhetoric was strongest and most persistent in South Africa, which came to epitomize the denialism that impeded so many anti-HIV efforts and inevitably cost so many lives. Conspiracy theories regarding HIV origins and its causal links to AIDS are now almost entirely confined to the dustbin of history, and the efficacy of ARTs is proven. This fact is testified by the over fifteen million people who are benefiting directly from life-saving treatments (and countless more indirectly). Given the predominance of the medical model in treating HIV (and contributing to its prevention), the battle lines have shifted. Debate has moved from the nature of African "sexuality" in general toward the presence and rights of the LGBTI (lesbian, gay, bisexual, trans, and/or intersex) communities within Africa. Recent years have witnessed inflamed discrimination and increasing incidents of violence against LGBTI individuals and structural violence toward their communities. These incidents are not confined to the arena of HIV alone; reports of violence against gay people in Liberia during the Ebola outbreak confirm the precept that any society seeks to blame the marginalized in the midst of an epidemic. Such a stigma and its malevolence comprehensively obstruct attempts to achieve universal access to HIV prevention and treatment services, which any holistic, human rights–based response demands. The net result of the active persecution of service providers supporting sexual minorities will only strengthen the presence of the virus in LGBTI communities. In extreme situations we are witnessing active attempts to deny services to those most in need. Irrationally, one part of government is spending resources on expanding HIV services and treatments to all segments of society while another part is allocating resources to ensure that such services are beyond reach. Human rights violations, combined with wasting money, is the price of political expedience. As long as institutional discrimination continues, this will be an unfortunate but common feature, especially while HIV financing has both international and domestic dimensions.

ACCOUNTABILITY FOR HEALTH LIES BEYOND THE HEALTH SECTOR

AIDS responses also taught us that powerful tools in the fight against diseases, and in the mitigation of their impacts, lie in the hands of those beyond the health sector. A good example is the opportunity presented by the rapid acceleration of investments in programs devised to reduce extreme poverty and economic inequities. This is typified by social protection, particularly the emergence of social cash transfers in Africa. These have been demonstrated as having multiple benefits, including poverty reduction (their principle aim) as well as increased uptake of other social services—notably, education and health. Beneficiaries tend to have improved diets, better schooling outcomes, improved uptake of health services, sufficient assets for agriculture, and the maintenance of other livelihoods and savings. In the context of this discussion, cash transfers have triggered changes in sexual behavior. From trials in Malawi, Tanzania, Kenya, and South Africa, it is clear that cash transfers reduce HIV and HSV2 (herpes simplex virus type 2) transmission (by up to two-thirds in the case of HIV) and teenage pregnancy rates. The exact mechanisms through which cash mediates sexual networking and the differential impact of cash by age and gender are not yet fully understood. But the evidence indicates again that HIV is a not simply a disease of poverty, but more accurately reflects patterns of *economic and social inequities.*

The data derived from impact assessments of social-protection interventions that target the most vulnerable raises some important questions. First, who pays for an intervention that has demonstrable benefits for more than one sector? If impacts and their associated benefits and cost savings are spread across the health, education, and agricultural sectors, for example, who should bear the cost? Second, when resources are limited, even when the benefits are recognized and valued in economic terms, how will such a cost-sharing arrangement be determined and negotiated? Siloed financing by sector is the entrenched norm, and breaking this mold will require some political and administrative bravery. As it stands, social-protection programs are undervalued and thus underfinanced. In addition, much of the financing for social protection is in the form of international aid or loans. The capital—both economic and political, such as financing for HIV responses and health services beyond—is yet to be domesticated.

HEALTH RECONFIGURED IN THE GLOBAL AGENDA 2030

The politics of health has two distinct and interacting time frames. The medium term is that of the global development agenda, which now follows a fifteen-year pattern. We are now entering the 2016–30 cycle. The second time frame refers to national electoral cycles and the democratic terms of office that rearrange national political priorities, institutions, and personnel. The global cycle beginning in January 2016 allows us to reposition epidemic responses, with the premise that resources allocated to epidemic prevention and response ought to be determined by the political priorities as they are realigned and updated in the new Global Agenda for Sustainable Development 2030.

While the Millennium Development Goals had three out of eight goals dedicated to health, their sustainable successors—the Sustainable Development Goals (SDGs)—have only one health-specific goal: to "ensure healthy lives and promote well-being for all at all ages." Looking across all seventeen goals, we could ascertain that achieving twenty-three targets would have direct impacts on health. The new development agenda is thus diverse, wide ranging, and all-inclusive, which creates new challenges. As we move into the 2030 Agenda period, the ambition in relation to HIV has reached the ultimate level—the ending of the AIDS epidemic (represented by Target 3.3). This technically feasible but herculean challenge, however, is *one subpart of one target,* among 168 other targets.

Target 3.8 requires that countries move toward *universal health coverage.* This means the provision, to all, of quality health services without creating financial hardship for patients or their families. Citizens should be able to demand their right to health irrespective of who they are, where they live, or what necessitates the access, and to the use of a preventive, curative, or rehabilitative service. The *person* is predominant in this model, not that person's affliction. And with the person comes his or her belief system, culture, and life world. It's a simple idea, but it could revolutionize the way health is portrayed, maintained, and managed by governments. The political discourse needs to mature from blame and discrimination to ownership and accountability. While the health landscape and burden of disease evolve, and new development commitments are made, we are running out of excuses for not keeping up.

NOTE

The views expressed in this article are the author's and do not necessarily reflect those of the United Nations Development Programme.

ADDITIONAL RESOURCES

DeWaal, Alex. *AIDS and Power: Why There Is No Political Crisis—Yet.* London and New York: Zed Books, 2006.

Farmer, Paul. *Pathologies of Power: Health, Human Rights and the New War on the Poor.* Berkeley: University of California Press, 2004.

UNDP. "Discussion Paper: Addressing the Social Determinants of Non-Communicable Diseases." New York: United Nations Development Programme, 2013. www.undp.org/content/dam/undp/library/hivaids/English/Discussion_Paper_Addressing_the_Social_Determinants_of_NCDs_UNDP_2013.pdf.

UNDP. "Discussion Paper: Cash Transfers and HIV Prevention." New York: United Nations Development Programme, 2014. www.undp.org/content/undp/en/home/librarypage/hiv-aids/discussion-paper—cash-transfers-and-hiv-prevention.html.

Webb, Douglas. *HIV and AIDS in Africa.* London: Pluto Press, 1997.

· · ·

Douglas Webb is a social scientist in New York with the United Nations Development Programme (UNDP), in the HIV, Health, and Development Group. Between September 2014 and February 2015 he was seconded to be Deputy Director of Essential Services within the UN Mission for the Ebola Emergency Response (UNMEER) in Ghana and Senegal. From 2008 to 2011 he was with UNICEF in Ethiopia, managing UNICEF's response on child-focused social protection and social welfare systems development, HIV prevention, and AIDS impact mitigation. He was a member of the Joint Learning Initiative on Children and AIDS (JLICA) in 2006–8. He was the Chief of the Children and AIDS Section in the UNICEF Regional Office in Kenya (2004–8), where he developed and provided technical support to the regional program in eastern and southern Africa on orphans and vulnerable children. He was the HIV/AIDS Adviser for Save the Children UK (2000–2004) in London as well as the vice chair of the UK Consortium on AIDS and International Development. Previous appointments were to UNICEF Zambia (1995–97) and UNICEF Mozambique (1998). His doctoral thesis examined social responses to HIV and AIDS in South Africa and Namibia in contexts of political transition (University of London, 1995). He has written over fifty published articles and book chapters covering issues such as children affected by AIDS, adolescent sexual and reproductive health, HIV and AIDS, and development. He is the author of *HIV and AIDS in Africa* (Pluto Press, 1997) and a coeditor (with Sudhanshu Handa and Stephen Devereux) of *Social Protection for Africa's Children* (Routledge, 2010).

Generative Technologies from Africa

Ron Eglash

Abstract: Bottom-up technosocial innovations such as open-source software, makerspaces, DIY bio, urban agriculture, commons-based governance, and other forms in which value is circulated in unalienated form, rather than extracted and alienated from its generators, have created new possibilities for social justice and sustainability. This essay explores African cultural contributions to the history and future of these generative technologies.

Keywords: Fractals, sustainability, indigenous knowledge, commons-based production, computing

THE DISASTERS CURRENTLY FACED by the world—global warming, poverty, health inequality, environmental toxins, and so on—are all linked to the operations of large corporations, most under a free-market economy. But the historical record of communism shows little difference: USSR pollution was worse than that of the United States, and although some success is undeniable—for example, literacy rates under Mao Zedong or health care under Castro—issues such as human rights abuse and continued poverty make it hard to say which political economy is worse. While the discussion has been dominated by these horizontal ends of the left/right political spectrum, an orthogonal axis of bottom-up versus top-down has come into focus. Bottom-up technosocial innovations such as open-source software, makerspaces, DIY bio, urban agriculture, commons-based governance, and other forms in which value is circulated in unalienated form rather than extracted and alienated from its generators have created new possibilities for social justice and sustainability. We refer to this ethical domain as "generative justice," and thus the technologies that make it possible as "generative technologies." This essay explores African cultural contributions to the history and future of generative technologies.

Almost all of the geometry we learn in school is Euclidean geometry—the world of circles, squares, and triangles that was the standard in Europe since the ancient Greeks. But nature is full of rough textures like that of bark, bushy structures like trees, wiggly edges like coastlines, and so on. Fractal geometry, which was fully understood only in the 1970s, can describe these irregular forms. A good way to understand fractals is with the concept of symmetry. For most of us, the word *symmetry* means the similarity between each side of a mirror reflection: the way one side of the face is similar to another, or one side of a car looks like the other side. There is just one scale to consider. Fractal geometry, in contrast, is based on similarity *between* scales; a fractal will show similar patterns as you "zoom in" to smaller sizes. Trees are composed of branches of branches; clouds are puffs of puffs—even your own skin shows crinkles within crinkles. While infinite fractals are only a mathematical abstraction, many natural objects exhibit fractal characteristics within a limited range of scales. These "self-similar" patterns are the result of the bottom-up process of self-organization.

Typically the word *organize* means there is an organizer: the general in an army; the composer of music for an orchestra; the school custodian who arranges the desks for students in a rectangular grid of rows and columns. It is no surprise that systems organized from the top down tend to create Euclidean shapes: if the custodian just left desks strewn around the room randomly, he might get fired. But some of the most beautiful forms of organization in nature have no leader. The swooping shapes of a flock of birds in flight; the buzz of activity that generates a beehive; the cells of a growing embryo that results in a plant or animal: none of these has a boss calling out orders to each bird, bee, or cell, telling it what to do. Rather, these structures are self-organized from the bottom up, and they often result in the self-similar patterns of fractal geometry.

In the book *African Fractals* I detailed the evidence that fractal structures, similar to those of natural self-organization, were used extensively in traditional African village architectures. For example, in this aerial view of a Karamajong village in Uganda we can see that there are circular houses grouped into circular clusters; circular clusters grouped together to form a subvillage; and clusters of clusters of clusters that form the village as a whole. (See figure 4.3.1.) Rather than the artificial grids typical of American cities,

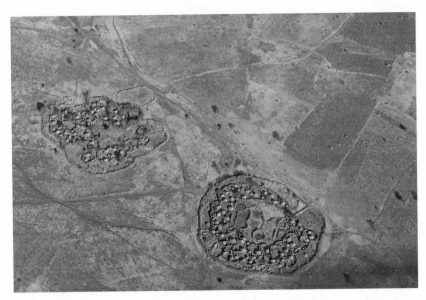

FIG. 4.3.1. Karamajong village in Uganda. Photo by Robert Harding.

imposing order from above without regard to landscape or history, these villages organically grow to fit both the natural and social environments. This flexibility tends to be not only more ecologically sustainable, but more socially equitable as well. For example, anthropologist Pat Caplan described how women in a Tanzanian village were able to divorce or make room for other changes in family structure by building their own houses. Land in such villages is not "owned" like a commodity you buy at Walmart, but is rather a part of a *commons*—that is, a common pool of resources that are available to anyone in the community as long as you fulfill your obligations to use and sustain them.

This flexibility in land use is just one of many traditional African social mechanisms for maintaining an egalitarian society. These were not universal to all groups; and they often degraded as colonialism pushed people onto each other's lands; created rivalries in a divide-and-conquer strategy; invented hierarchies where none existed before; or created wealth inequality and its tyranny through commerce (the slave trade, the ivory trade, etc.). Nonetheless, the survivals of these traditions were so striking that anthropologists in the twentieth century coined the term *acephalous*—meaning a society with no authority in charge—to describe the "bottom-up" organization in groups such as the Igbo, Tiv, Fulani, Dagaaba, !Kung, Hadza, Mbuti, and Batek, to name but a few. Many civil wars in Africa—for example, the Nigerian Civil War of Igbo secession in 1967—can be better understood once we take into account the bottom-up tradition of animists. (For example, a common name in Igbo is Ezebuillo, which means "a king is an enemy.")

Closely related to these egalitarian political traditions is the concept of gift culture. Among hunter-gatherer groups in the Kalahari Desert for example, the *hxaro* gift-exchange system stipulates that meat belongs to the maker of the arrow, not the one who shot it. Thus those who do not hunt—such as women and elders—can still be credited with a kill. Even then, such status comes with the responsibility to "gift" shares to others. Such emphasis on equality is also related to fractal architecture. In the United States we might call the fancy mansion inhabited by a bank president or state governor a "house," but it looks nothing like my little home in the suburbs; the architectural difference symbolizes our economic class difference. In most African villages, on the other hand, all houses look pretty much the same; the chief's house is just a bigger version of an ordinary person's home, symbolizing the lack of class distinctions. The self-similarity of fractal geometry is both a cause and effect of egalitarian social structure.

First disregarded as a "primitive" form of living, contemporary architects have rediscovered the advantages of fractal, bottom-up architectural forms. Working in Ethiopia, Xavier Vilalta leveraged the fractal African tradition to design a new vocational school (the Melaku Center) in which the clusters of clusters allowed a more humane, welcoming campus where nooks and crannies could be spontaneous meeting places or outdoor spaces for workshops. His shopping center in Addis Ababa was restrained by a much more limited footprint, so it had to conform to the usual boxy shape. (See figure 4.3.2.) But even here he was able to show how fractals could make a difference. He noted that the glass exterior of these buildings created a heat-trapping effect that required massive air conditioning, making it more expensive, and its climate control unreliable due to occasional power blackouts. He replaced that exterior with fractal perforations in concrete, thus creating a breathable skin that reduces energy needs. A fractal array of solar cells on the rooftop turns a potentially alienating space into a pleasant outdoor meeting spot, and generates enough electricity to keep the building powered during blackouts, making it more attractive to local merchants.

FIG. 4.3.2. Vilata's fractal shopping center in Addis Ababa, Ethiopia. Photo by Gonzalo Guajardo.

AFRICAN TRADITIONS AND BOTTOM-UP
SOFTWARE DEVELOPMENT

In the 1960s, when MIT engineers were looking for new directions in machine architecture, they were trying to move away from the top-down, centralization approach, such as how a single central processor—the "Von Neumann bottleneck"—had to issue every command and receive every input in computers of that era. In his book *The Media Lab,* Stewart Brand describes a defining moment for them: "A book that inspired [Nicholas] Negroponte and the Architecture Machine Group was called Architecture Without Architects, a provocative collection of photographs of beautiful vernacular— native—buildings from all over the world. Arch Mac was following that thread wherever it might lead—books without authors, films without scripts or directors. A grander scale of research, something like a Media Laboratory, seemed worth attempting" (p. 142). The best examples of truly bottom-up architecture in that book were all from Africa.

A similar reevaluation of bottom-up information design arose when software developers such as Eric Raymond made a connection between the concept of free exchange of software source code and the exchange of material goods in African and other indigenous societies. For example, his 1998 manifesto includes a section titled "The Hacker Milieu as Gift Culture," where he notes, "We can observe gift cultures in action among aboriginal cultures living in ecozones with mild climates and abundant food." The analogy has sparked an exciting exchange of ideas between the areas of indigenous-culture research and technological development. Scholars such as Elinor Ostrom began to apply their studies of "the commons" style of resource sharing in indigenous societies to the question of how to create a similar "innovation commons." In 2002 a group of legal scholars and computer scientists launched the Creative Commons licensing platform, which today hosts over 880 million works ranging from software to photos to music.

That is not to say that this was a one-way flow, from Africa to software designers. Rather it has been a gradual two-way exchange: as open-source information technology has become more popular, it has had a profound effect on how information technology has developed, including that in Africa. Above we looked at how Negroponte's MIT media lab was inspired by images of African fractal architecture; in 2005 he returned the favor by attempting to develop an open source, low-cost laptop. The "OLPC" ("one laptop per child") has been undergoing evaluations in a dozen different African nations, as well as elsewhere in the world. Coming from the other direction, software designers in Kenya created an open-source information-reporting platform called Ushahidi (Swahili for "testimony") to collect eyewitness reports of violence during the 2007 election. The open-source status allowed it to be modified for other purposes: the system has been used to track pharmacy "stockouts" in several East African countries; to monitor elections in Mexico and India; and to map the Gulf of Mexico oil spill in the United States, forest fires in Italy, and many other "geosocial" events around the world.

AFRICAN PARTICIPATION IN THE GLOBAL DIY MOVEMENT

The DIY ("do it yourself") movement (sometimes renamed "DIT," for "do it together") encompasses a wide range of bottom-up activities. These include the *maker movement,* where lay enthusiasts share code, circuits, and physical construction techniques in an open-source commons (such as the Creative Commons described above; more often sites such as Instructables, Hackaday, and Makezine); *upcycling*, in which discarded materials are changed into new ones rather than destroyed for recycling or waste disposal; and *urban gardens,* where food-justice movements intersect civic "greening" efforts. The usual account of such activities in Africa emphasizes their external influences—the donation of equipment from a development agency or volunteers from a foreign university exchange program, for example. But just as self-organizing African traditions laid the groundwork for contemporary fractal architecture, contemporary DIY projects in Africa also draw on older practices.

Perhaps the best known of these are toy models made from scrap wire and tin—in particular, wire cars. Art historian Aneta Pawlowska notes that our fascination with such "transitional art" (mixing indigenous tradition with contemporary materials and subjects) cannot avoid the self-deluding wish to have it perform some form of "invisible mending" by which cultural catastrophes such as slavery and colonialism magically vanish. But transitional arts are also forms of resistance and rebirth. Art historian John Peffer documents how transitional art was used in the South African resistance to apartheid, such as coded symbolism in the combination of modern house paints and traditional Ndebele and Sotho-Tswana design created during that time. (For example, anti-apartheid activist Gary Van Wyk reported that one design, which he calls "the Cosmic Flower," used fractals to invoke the idea of infinite creativity in a bounded space.) Peffer suggests that toy wire models of APCs (armored personnel carriers used by the South African police to patrol the black townships) had a more complex relationship, creating a space in which this deadly force could be playfully mocked at the same time it was feared. Wire car toys have become iconic tourist items throughout Africa, but as we will see below, they also played a "transitional" role in the ways they were embraced by contemporary DIY groups.

Tracking how these wire constructions gradually emerged to become part of the global maker community can be helpful in illuminating the ways that generative technologies can avoid the isolation and elitism that proprietary technologies entail. Recall that software developers in Kenya created the open-source information-reporting platform Ushahidi in 2007. One of the founders, Erik Hersman, had also been documenting the wire toys on his Afrigadget website, which had already amassed a huge number of DIY innovations in Africa. Thanks to this exposure, in 2008 African wire toys became featured on the website for *Make* magazine, a flagship publication of the maker movement. Another route to greater exposure occurred when artist Chido Johnson, who was familiar with the toys from his childhood in

Zimbabwe, moved to the famed "motor city" of Detroit to teach sculpture. His 2009 wire "cruise car" in Detroit inspired an "Instructables" webpage for the toy. Johnson's work grew into a series of wire-car workshops held across the city, and to cultural exchanges between Zimbabwe and Detroit artists that included their mutual struggles around labor movements. (For example, Johnson had workshop participants join an imaginary Wire Car Workers Union.) The first "maker faire" (public exposition of DIY works) occurred in California in 2006, and, because of the exchanges described above, maker faires began to appear in Africa as early as 2009. One of the widely publicized highlights—it made the BBC, the *Guardian,* and so on—was fifteen-year-old Nigerian Odo Gerald's toy trucks created from scraps, in which he had modified the traditional form to include electronics and even a hydraulic system using syringes.

While the whimsical wire toys helped to bring African DIY traditions into global "maker" circulation, other technologies had a more complex relation to local culture. Social scientist Tolu Odumosu carried out research on cell phones in Nigeria around this same time period (2006–9), and found an extraordinary range of "appropriations" in which cell phones were adapted to local needs. This was made possible in part by the Nigerian Telecommunications Consumer Parliament (TCP), which allowed ordinary citizens a venue in which they could directly question corporate representatives, who would then be held accountable for issues in quality of service. Odumosu found that many of the TCP staff were citizens from the Ibo community—an ethnic group who were renowned for their bottom-up, egalitarian cultural practices. Thanks to that indigenous tradition, Nigerian mobile phones enjoyed strong technical support, which helped to enable innovations ranging from "flashing" (contacting someone and then disconnecting, just to send a free "thinking of you" message) to DIY fund transfers (buying and selling phone minutes as if it were currency). Since then mobile phone banking has become formally institutionalized (e.g., the Kenyan M-PESA), and African mobiles have become a broad innovation platform for many professional efforts in Africa. But we should not forget that its origins are in this grassroots form of DIY development.

Other African generative technologies link the biological and technical worlds. Urban agriculture is a new movement in the United States, but it has long been the established norm in Africa. In contrast to the seed-based agriculture typical of the United States, which requires enormous space, irrigation, and machines or a mass labor force (slavery in the past and migrant exploitation today), African traditional food gardens were typically based on "vegeculture" in which one root is cut up and propagated into many plants. With different plants at each height, and the vines of beans, gourds, and other vegetables climbing up taller plants like bananas, the 3-D density of African vegeculture is perfect for small spaces in populated areas; inherently more supportive of biodiversity and therefore of better health; and often linked to better gender equity. Some evidence suggests that the prevalence of vegeculture in African-American gardens of the American South was influenced by this tradition; the ties are even stronger in the case of the Caribbean. In 2004 the United Nations Food and Agricultural Organization worked with the Venezuelan government to bring urban gardening to its largest cities. Rather than import experts from Harvard and Cornell, it brought in urban gardeners from Senegal and Cuba. This is not simply a "retention" of African tradition, but rather an ongoing innovation for generative technologies that combines indigenous practices from both Africa and the Americas with contemporary developments like an organic nutrient solution delivered to raised trays.

Perhaps the most profound case of bio/techno DIY can be found in the efforts of Agbogbloshie Makerspace Platform (AMP) in Ghana. Located in an area that is part e-waste dump and part recycling/repair shops, this makerspace program is run by the architect D. K. Asare-Osseo. In a recent interview with my students and me, D. K. remarked that as soon as he first heard of makerspaces he immediately thought of the African scrap yards, their associated fabricators and fixers, and the ways that prior traditions might lend themselves to a DIY effort. He frames this reuse as simultaneously an opportunity for cross-class collaborations (he has both low-income and middle-class participants) and for human/nonhuman collaborations—for example, ways to reduce the toxic waste leaching into the soil such that both low-income communities and natural communities benefit. Asare-Osseo's group activities include creating a DIY drone from waste for mapping the area, exploring techniques for "upcycling," and soil bioremediation—all with the goal of reclaiming the land as a productive biosocial ecology.

CONCLUSION

Dismissed by colonialists as merely "primitive" ways of life, African traditions of generative technologies are in fact harbingers of an alternative sustainable future. While capitalist or socialist economies tend to extract value and thus alienate both people and nature from the sources of their vitality, generative technologies such as open-source software and ecologically sustainable agriculture allow value to retain its unalienated form and circulate in "bottom-up" fashion among those who created it, benefiting human and nonhuman alike.

ADDITIONAL RESOURCES

Benkler, Yochai. *The Penguin and the Leviathan: How Cooperation Triumphs over Self-Interest.* New York: Crown Business, 2011.

Eglash, Ron. *African Fractals: Modern Computing and Indigenous Design.* New Brunswick, NJ: Rutgers University Press, 1999.

Eglash, Ron, and Colin Garvey. "Basins of Attraction for Generative Justice." In *Chaos Theory in Politics,* edited by Santo Banerjee, Şefika Şule Erçetin, and Ali Tekin, 75–88. Dordrecht: Springer Netherlands, 2014.

Odumosu, Toluwalogo B. "Making Mobiles African." In *What Do Science, Technology, and Innovation Mean from Africa?,* edited by Clapperton Chakanetsa Mavhunga. Cambridge, MA: MIT Press, 2016.

Peffer, John. *Art and the End of Apartheid.* Minneapolis: University of Minnesota Press, 2009.

.   .   .

RON EGLASH is a Professor of Science and Technology Studies at Rensselaer Polytechnic Institute, with a secondary appointment in Computer Science. He received his BS in Cybernetics, his MS in Systems Engineering, and his PhD in History of Consciousness, all from the University of California. His work as a Fulbright scholar was published as *African Fractals: Modern Computing and Indigenous Design* (Rutgers University Press, 1999) and featured in his 2007 TED talk. His NSF-funded Culturally Situated Design Tools software, offering math and computing education from indigenous and vernacular arts, is available for free at www.csdt.rpi.edu. Recently funded work includes his NSF "Triple Helix" project, which brings graduate fellows in science and engineering together with local community activists and K–12 educators to seek new approaches to putting science and innovation in the service of underserved populations, and to develop the theoretical framework for "generative justice."

4·4

"Money in Your Hand"

M-PESA AND MOBILE MONEY
IN KENYA

Dillon Mahoney

Abstract: The mobile-money transfer system M-PESA has allowed new types of financial inclusion, flexibility, risks, and challenges in modern Kenya. Cellular provider Safaricom has succeeded in creating a sense of transparency, helping Kenyans circumvent risks that had previously been a major hindrance to business development and financial stability.

Keywords: Mobile money, banking, trust, risk, transparency

> Digital technologies have grown a lot in Kenya. We came from phone booths until now everyone has a cell phone. You can find anyone, anywhere, anytime, anyplace. These days there is even M-PESA [mobile money]. You can send money and you don't even have to be there physically. You can have businesses, or you can have transactions, all through M-PESA.
>
> —YOUNG NAIROBI *Entrepreneur, 2014*

> We used to deal with a lot of risk, you know. And now you don't have to, and if I trust you, I can send you the money, get me that something. Immediately you will see that the money is in your account. Or let's say something has happened to you and you don't have any money. You can call your friend and tell him, "I'm stuck here, please send whatever you can." If he can, he will send it to you, to your phone, and then I can return the money later.
>
> —MOMBASA-BASED *Exporter, 2014*

These two quotes capture the revolutionary impact of M-PESA, a form of mobile money, on the everyday lives of Kenyans. Indeed, the success of M-PESA in Kenya has made it a model for banking in many other parts of the world. Rural and urban Kenyans can now perform more financial functions with their phones than wealthy urbanites in the United States: withdraw money from ATMs, buy gas and other goods, and send money internationally. Not only is Africa globally connected, but the continent continues to play a central role in developing and spreading new technologies related to media, banking, and economic development. M-PESA has become a proudly African product that is a model of technological innovation only now being replicated in countries off the continent.

Most first-time users of M-PESA are struck by how simple it is to sign up for an account and immediately start depositing, sending, and withdrawing money with their cell phone. The M-PESA system comes already loaded on a SIM card, so there is no need to download a special app. Safaricom, the dominant cellular provider in Kenya, has invested heavily in training agents, who are responsible for helping customers deposit and withdraw cash. By 2013, the government estimated that there were over ninety-three thousand mobile-money agents in Kenya working for several different emergent mobile-money services in towns, shopping centers, and even small roadside kiosks in rural areas. The M-PESA logo has become a regular part of the Kenyan landscape.

To open an M-PESA account or to withdraw funds, a customer needs to provide three items: a Safaricom SIM card, an official form of identification (a Kenyan ID or an international passport), and a personal identification number (PIN). If I were to, for example, arrive in Kenya on an international flight with only a few dollars, I could quickly and cheaply purchase a SIM card, register my M-PESA account for free, and call any friend in Kenya to ask them to send me up to 70,000 shillings (US$700 in 2015). After the instantaneous transfer, I would receive a text saying that I had received the money. With my ID and my PIN, I could receive cash from an agent. My account balance would be automatically updated.

While there have been fears of fraud and the use of M-PESA in money laundering, most Kenyans I interviewed raved about the safety that comes with using M-PESA. As one man explained: "They give you a PIN. You know, even if somebody steals your phone or takes it, there's nothing they can do with it." "The best thing about M-PESA," said another man, "is that you don't have to carry cash. If you need to withdraw money it is very easy. You see everywhere, M-PESA, M-PESA."

Cellular phones and the new applications they enable have, in the minds of many analysts, revolutionized the ways Kenyans communicate, exchange information, conduct business, manage livelihoods, pay for things, and bank their profits. But M-PESA has accomplished much more than simply "banking the unbanked." Most (but not all) businesspeople I interviewed in Mombasa and Nairobi had bank accounts in addition to M-PESA. As a struggling businessman in his forties told me, "So let's say I have cash. The first thing I do, instead of going to the bank and putting it in the bank, I put it in my phone [via an agent]. I think even now the banks are being hurt by it. And then, you can use M-PESA for, actually an account. Some banks, they have access for M-PESA to transact your money directly from your account to M-PESA. Let's say now you pay me some money, like twenty thousand or whatever. Instead of risking walking with it, I put it in M-PESA directly [via an agent]. It is very accurate actually. Safaricom is like a bank. That is what they are coming to. They are their own bank now."

M-PESA is currently used by Kenyans of all classes as a mobile bank. As a young and struggling Nairobi entrepreneur expressed it to me, "M-PESA is a bank. It is a bank. You know they say *pesa mkononi* ["money in your hand"]. They are trying to make it official. That's a Safaricom line, *pesa mkononi*. They are trying to get you money wherever you are. If you are in the rural areas, it doesn't matter where you go, you can still be paid using M-PESA. That's what they are trying to do. Everything, *lipa na M-PESA* ["pay with M-PESA"]."

DEVELOPING TRUST

M-PESA was not the first mobile-money service in the world to be developed, but it has undeniably become the most successful. While the World Bank supports any initiative that connects poor people to new financial services, most attempts at creating mobile-money systems in the Global South have failed, either due to poor design or because of resistance from the formal banking sector. M-PESA was originally conceived by Nick Hughes and Susie Lonie, both of whom worked for London-based Vodafone, a partial owner of Safaricom. The original idea was to create a mobile-money transfer system that would allow borrowers to repay microfinance loans more easily. But Kenyans quickly started using M-PESA for much more than simply repaying micro–credit loans. Kenyans desperately needed more reliable and cheaper ways of transferring money, both within Kenya and from abroad. In fall 2014, the *Daily Nation* estimated that 120 billion shillings (US$1.2 billion) were remitted to Kenya annually from overseas. Western Union, which charges large percentage-based fees (usually around 10 percent), had long dominated the money transfer business, especially remittances from abroad.

A 2010 study of M-PESA by the Gates Foundation found that most early users of M-PESA were wealthier men living in urban areas. But as competition increased, Safaricom consistently dropped prices and introduced a variety of services to make cellular phones more accessible and useful for Kenyans of all classes. Kenya's 2014 Economic Survey found that mobile penetration had stabilized by 2013, with 75 percent of Kenyans owning mobile phones. Services like M-PESA, originally launched in 2007, were adapted to Kenyans' need for communicative and financial flexibility. The service would later launch through other Vodafone or Vodacom operations in Tanzania (2008), Fiji (2010), South Africa (2010), the Democratic Republic of the Congo (2012), India (2013), Mozambique (2013), Egypt (2013), Lesotho (2013), and Romania (2014).

Kenyans, at the same time, have a great deal of confidence in Safaricom, which has long dominated the Kenyan cellular market and has consistently lowered its prices. Though partially owned by Vodafone, Kenyans take great pride in the fact that Safaricom is a Kenyan and an African company. This reality has helped increase customers' trust in the company and its services. Every Kenyan I interviewed in 2014 and 2015 told me they trusted Safaricom more than they trusted the commercial banks or the government.

Kenyans' extensive trust in M-PESA and Safaricom rather than government or commercial banks is ironic, since Safaricom makes M-PESA and its other financial services possible only by partnering with regulators and commercial banks. There is hardly a bank or micro-credit system in Kenya today that does not partner with M-PESA, including Western Union and MoneyGram. Several commercial banks have created their own mobile apps that allow customers to directly transfer funds from bank accounts to M-PESA with the click of a button. For Kenya's middle class, this makes M-PESA like a mobile wallet, or a debit card, with the added benefit of being able to, say, transfer the equivalent of five dollars directly to another person.

Safaricom's success has also had much to do with Kenya's historical context. During the postelection violence in early 2008, new digital technologies were desperately needed for opening lines of communication and passing along reliable information. In the first few days of the crisis, one of the major challenges facing Kenyans was a lack of access to phone credit to verify the safety of friends and loved ones. This risky environment created a need for better services, especially for transferring money and phone credit.

In the aftermath of the crisis, Kenyans increasingly adopted new services that allowed them to manage such challenges. Mobile money transfers opened up new opportunities for financial inclusion and gave M-PESA users the ability to buy credit directly from Safaricom using their phones. By 2013, there were twenty-six million mobile-money subscribers. According to the government's economic reports, the total amount of money transferred via mobile phones increased from 90 billion shillings in 2010 to 914 billion (US$9.14 billion) in 2013.

Safaricom's marketing strategy has been central to M-PESA's success. The initial strategy invited the public to "send money home," clearly identifying the need by many Kenyans to remit money from urban centers and foreign countries back to rural homes without having to travel on dangerous roads in person with cash. While other transfer methods were more expensive and calculated charges based on percentages, M-PESA charges flat, understandable fees. The percentage a customer pays declines the more money one sends. In 2015, the fees ranged from one shilling (US$0.01) for transactions up to 1,000 shillings (US$10) to 110 shillings (US$1.10) for transactions between 15,001 shillings (US$150) and 70,000 shillings (US$700, the maximum that can be transferred). Daily transfers are capped at 140,000 shillings (US$1,400). These fees are much less than those charged by Western Union and commercial banks. The agents are not paid by customers, but receive a flat fee for every transaction from Safaricom. (Kenyan Safaricom agents are estimated to make about US$70 per month.) The fee for conducting the transaction is paid to Safaricom directly from the customer's M-PESA account. Safaricom monitors transactions closely, which is easy because all transactions have an electronic footprint.

According to the 2010 Gates Foundation study, 98 percent of M-PESA users said it was safer and faster than other options for transferring money, while 96 percent said it was more convenient and cheaper. Much of this convenience is due to the fact that Safaricom has been quick to create partnerships with other banks and companies. In July 2008, Safaricom partnered with PesaPoint, a company that supplies ATMs throughout Kenya. With PesaPoint, a customer can withdraw money from M-PESA by simply selecting "ATM Transaction" on their phone's menu. He or she would input a code number into the ATM, and the ATM emits the cash. To further increase convenience, Safaricom introduced its "Lipa na M-PESA" ("Pay with M-PESA") service in June 2013, which provides merchants with a six-digit account number that customers can use to make payments at no extra cost. Most businesses signed up, making it possible to pay for almost anything, from gas to food, using M-PESA. Other apps allow customers to pay rent, electric bills, and school fees using M-PESA. Of course, a customer can always still transfer money to an individual directly, including to police. At least one individual I interviewed reported paying a bribe using M-PESA, which she found risky because the electronic receipt both she and the officer received included their full names. Nonetheless, she was grateful for the opportunity because she would otherwise have had to pay a substantial fine for talking on the phone while driving, which is illegal in Kenya.

Kenyans of all classes and backgrounds raved about these new technologies and the services they offer. As one businessman in his thirties described M-PESA's impact, "For phones, it helps the most because you can be someplace and you have no money, and the banks are closed. But you can go to M-PESA. You can use it anytime. When it comes to mobile phones, M-PESA has helped more than everything else."

As another Mombasa-based businessman who works with clients throughout East Africa put it, "M-PESA is my life, bwana. It's my life. A lot of my customers, they pay me with M-PESA. . . . The best thing about M-PESA is that a person cannot be scammed. If someone sends you money, you see that it has been sent. If he doesn't send money, you tell him, 'We cannot continue with business until you send it.' It has helped a lot. Even when I travel I can pay for my bus ticket with M-PESA. Everything you can pay with it."

NEW OPPORTUNITIES, NEW RISKS

The Kenyans I interviewed found mobile money to be particularly advantageous because it made expensive, dangerous, and time-consuming physical travel unnecessary. Thomas Molony has described mobile phones in East Africa as "travel-saving technologies." But they are also risk-reducing technologies that allow Kenyans to avoid the dangers of traveling in person with cash. Kenyans doing business between Mombasa and Nairobi previously had to buy goods using cash, which had to be either delivered in person or sent using innovative means. M-PESA has nearly eliminated this risky aspect of doing long-distance business.

Much more than a means for banking the unbanked, M-PESA has revolutionized many daily practices in Kenya by providing convenience and a way to minimize risks. Safaricom and M-PESA have succeeded in creating a sense of trust and transparency around the financial system at a time when such values are hard to come by. Yet through services like M-PESA, Safaricom has placed much of the onus of risk management onto individual customers, few of whom have training in financial management.

Some of the new applications associated with M-PESA have, however, had negative consequences. In 2012, Safaricom launched M-Shwari, an application that enables Safaricom users to access a savings account and to take small loans. Deemed "revolutionary" by Safaricom, M-Shwari works through M-PESA but is a product of the Commercial Bank of Africa. Unfortunately, M-Shwari also caused many of my research participants to go into debt.

"Oooh! It has bankrupted me," complained one man. "It gives you a loan, then you pay it within a month. If you don't pay it within a month, they send you a warning. If you don't pay it within that second month, they send you another warning. But me, I've been blocked! I can't get M-Shwari anymore. I still have an outstanding loan [*laughing*]. I'm a very stubborn guy.... I have a loan of two thousand [shillings], but you can get as much as seventy-five thousand from M-Shwari."

For all the promise of transferring money and accessing new financial services, many Kenyans immediately took loans that they could not possibly repay, putting them nearly permanently in debt. As another man put it, "This is Kenya. If you are not in debt you are not a real Kenyan [*laughing*]." Indeed, M-PESA has been heralded as a means to an end but not an end in itself. Financial education is inadequate, allowing these systems to become predatory. Safaricom and other development analysts tend to place the blame on the individual users. M-PESA is about access, not necessarily inclusion. As one Mombasa entrepreneur with a business degree told me in 2014, what Safaricom has succeeded in doing with M-PESA is putting all of the liability on the individual customer: "They are passing that liability and risk back to you."

It is also important to remember that Safaricom and Vodafone are for-profit companies. As one interviewee expressed to me in 2014, "At Safaricom, they are making money, and a lot of it. Because, you know, if you put your money in a bank, you are given interest. With M-PESA, you are actually paying them. So who's fooling who?"

There are important lessons to be learned from Safaricom's and Vodafone's success with M-PESA. Many commercial banks, whether in Kenya or western Europe, are uninterested in banking with poor people, because they offer little profit to banks whose economic model is based on interest from loans and large deposits. M-PESA's success reveals not just the need for low-cost financial-transaction tools, but also the value of using mobile tech to make financial services accessible to the poor. Because it is designed to make money from usage and not the interest made from accounts, it makes sense to include the poor.

The social and economic impacts of M-PESA are complicated. Kenya is continually referred to as the "Silicon Savannah," and researchers and analysts must ask about the technopolitics of these developments. Development has continued to be uneven in Kenya. Mobile money, with its credit, lending, and development angles, plays a role in enabling certain individuals and their networks. For them, M-PESA has become a trusted anchor for risk management and a sense of security. Safaricom has succeeded in winning the trust game. However, there is also new risk of falling further into debt. New forms of mobility come with new risks, and even accentuate old risks. This is becoming clear with M-PESA, as with new digital technologies more generally. At the same time, M-PESA's success and popularity have taught banking experts and tech developers around the world new lessons about the possibilities for financial inclusion of the poor and the importance of risk reduction in enabling businesses to develop. The story of M-PESA in Kenya is just one case of Africans' needs and desires having an important global impact.

ADDITIONAL SUGGESTIONS

Jack, William, and Tavneet Suri. "The Economics of M-PESA." 2016. Unpublished research article commissioned by the Central Bank of Kenya. http://oneapi.gsma. com/mobilefordevelopment/wp-content/. uploads/2012/06/mpesa_d_1540.pdf.

Mas, Ignacio, and Dan Radcliffe. "Mobile Payments go Viral: M-PESA in Kenya." Bill and Melinda Gates Foundation, 2010. http://52.16.200.48/uploads/article-files/261/file_0_1420722663.pdf #page = 171.

Maurer, Bill. "Mobile Money: Communication, Consumption and Change in the Payments Space." *Journal of Development Studies* 48, no. 5 (2012): 589–604.

Molony, Thomas. 2009. "Trading Places in Tanzania: Mobility and Marginalisation at a Time of Travel-Saving Technologies." In *Mobile Phones: The New Talking Drums of Everyday Africa*, edited by Mirjam de Bruijn, Francis Nyamnjoh, and Inge Brinkman, 92–109. Leiden: African Studies Centre, 2009.

· · ·

DILLON MAHONEY is an urban anthropologist specializing in globalization, informal economies, and digital technology in East Africa. He has conducted more than two years of fieldwork during seven trips to Kenya since 2001. Contributing to the study of globalization and development as well as the anthropology of media, art, and communication, his research explores the emergent strategies of Kenyan traders, especially those working in the shadow of the country's international tourism industry. His focus is on the lived experiences of ups and downs, risk, precariousness, and the importance of a sense of trust and transparency in long-distance connections.

4 · 5

What's in Your Cell Phone?

James H. Smith

Abstract: Congolese coltan is a mineral critical to digital devices and the digital age. Coltan provides insights into Africa's relationship to the world economy, global governance, and "modernity" (or postmodernity) broadly conceived. Tracing the movement of coltan from the soil and forests of Africa to various markets around the world, and finally into computer chips, changes the way we see Africa and the world.

Keywords: coltan, Congolese wars, digital age, regulation, artisanal mining

ANYONE WHO'S EVER WATCHED A TED talk, any of the four different movies about Steve Jobs, or the popular television show *Silicon Valley* is well versed in the alluring American narrative regarding how techno-savvy individuals have changed the world by mobilizing their indomitable wills against outmoded cultural and political traditions. Linked to this romance is the notion that we can "save everything" by "clicking here" on our devices, as Evgeny Morozov reminds us in his similarly named book (*To Save Everything, Click Here*). But this mythology about how virtuoso minds invent technologies that liberate the world from the past's cumbersome materiality—things like paper, stone, timber, and concrete—conceals an even more compelling and revealing set of truths. By focusing on how these devices are made, we can see how far-flung places connect to one another, what the "digital age" amounts to, and how the technological worlds we inhabit are produced. One crucial though perhaps less visible example is that of the Congolese artisanal miners who actually get down in the mud and, through extremely laborious and highly organized work, unearth the materials that make this seemingly futuristic world possible in the first place. If you want to understand Africa's relationship to the world economy, global governance, and "modernity" (or postmodernity) broadly conceived, the dark metallic mineral called coltan would be an excellent place to start. When we unpack this mineral, and its movement from the soil and forests of Africa to various markets around the world, and finally into computer chips, it changes the way we see Africa and the world.

Coltan ore is important to engineers because tantalum and niobium can be extracted from it; tantalum's density makes it highly sought after for its capacity to hold a high electrical charge. Coltan is found in all electronics devices, including mobile phones and laptops, though not all of it is from the Democratic Republic of the Congo (DR Congo). While at one point the Australian company Sons of Gwalia was thought to control half of the world's coltan production (it closed in 2004 and suffered from ongoing strikes before that), these days most coltan is mined artisanally in diverse parts of the world, especially in Africa and, increasingly, South America. According to the US Geological Survey, the DR Congo has 80 percent of the world's coltan. The dark, metallic silicate is similar in appearance to, and often found alongside, other minerals that are equally crucial for digital technologies—especially wolframite, the ore from which tungsten is derived; and cassiterite, from which tin is derived. Tungsten is used to make computer screens and also enables cell phones to vibrate; tin is used in wiring, among many other processes. International NGOs working in Congo refer to coltan, tin, and tungsten as the "three T's," a phrase that has become prominent in the policy literature, gradually replacing the earlier emphasis on the single mineral "coltan." Congolese involved in the trade refer to these minerals as "black minerals" (*mineraux noirs*). Miners tend not to specialize in one mineral or the other, but to move between these and other minerals depending on price, security, and accessibility.

Congolese coltan and the other "digital minerals" are found in forests and in hillsides on what would otherwise be agricultural land. To say that these minerals are mined "artisanally" means that they are dug by small groups of diggers using mainly hand tools, like picks and shovels. Sometimes these diggers have to dig into shafts and end up underground in what can be perilous circumstances. There are about two million artisanal miners in the DR Congo and ten million people dependent on mining. Many of these people became miners during the First and Second Congolese Wars, when they lost their access to agricultural land, their livestock, or other property. This kind of mining is typically done by relatively young men, though women sift and clean the ore that is dug, leaving it to dry in the sun. They also sell things to the miners. There are many other kinds of workers involved in this trade, including the porters who are hired to carry the minerals on their head out of the forest.

Each mine is different—miners often say that each mine is its own "universe"—with divergent political and social systems, and principles of taxation and land ownership. That said, at any given mine there are also a number of people on-site whose job it is to make sure that the work is organized and that it begins at a certain hour (say, 8 a.m.) and ends at another (say, 6 p.m.)—unless the mine is under militia control and/or the price is running high, for then diggers will work in shifts day and night. Artisanal miners have borrowed job titles from the days of Belgian-controlled factory mining to create a division of labor and a sense of historical continuity: at any mine one is likely to find a *chef de colline* ("chief of the hill") serving as the mine manager or representing the mine owner. A *chef de group* collects fees and tax from groups of workers, and organizes the distribution of food and other things, while a *chef de camp* may be in charge of social relations and civic peace in the camp. The *chef de chantier* is likely to be the foreman in charge of making sure a group of workers have whatever it is they need. According to the Congolese mining code, each mine also has a diggers' cooperative made up of middlemen and diggers, whose job it is to ensure that workers have the food and materials they need and that there is order in the mine. This cooperative also keeps track of workers and their debts and may impose other rules (regarding sex or alcohol consumption, for example). Despite artisanal mining's reputation for being criminal or dangerous, it is also highly organized. Diggers are usually proud of the sophistication and efficiency of the social and cultural forms that they generate artisanally.

So how do the people who dig these minerals understand the work they do, and their contribution to a global economy that is at once increasingly interconnected and radically disconnected?

CONVERSING WITH "THE MACHINE"

"The Machine" smokes a lot, that's for sure. He assures me that the smoke from the cigarette doesn't have time to linger in his body and cause harm, and warns me that I shouldn't follow his example because the warnings on cigarette boxes were made for the likes of me, not the likes of him. He dramatically enacts breathing and digging for me, blowing in and out with great force while moving his arms, as if to prove his point. "The Machine" explains that the smoke from the cigarette fills the hole in which he works and makes it feel like home, almost like a kitchen, so he forgets his worries and is comfortable in the darkness. All diggers smoke, he says, because they're always in the dark. This idea is one that comes up often among miners, in different ways and contexts: diggers are often said to be "in the dark" or "in a hole," unable to "see ahead," because they lack knowledge about forces that affect them, such as the prices for the substances they dig up from the ground, or what the stuff is for in the first place. They are often said to be unwilling to plan or save for the future, but the truth is they must be ready to move and change tactics at a moment's notice.

My new friend isn't the first "Machine" I've met while studying the artisanal mining trade of the eastern DR Congo; it's a fairly common name, suggesting the capacity of the person to work vigorously without stopping. Sometimes the term "machine" is also used to talk about the highly organized and productive nature of artisanal mining itself—the complex division of labor among miners, and the multiple committees and subcommittees that work to mitigate conflict—as in the oft-repeated phrase "We are better than a machine!" It's just one of the ways in which people assert the value of themselves, their social networks, and their work—with an implicit comparison to some of the things they help to produce. Miners also desire the phones and other technologies they help to make because, through these devices, they can acquire some measure of control over their situation, and some predictability in their work lives. They will use these phones to call their friends in the city to find out the price that coltan or other minerals are fetching at any given time, for example.

The Machine drinks a strong stout beer called Tembo, or "elephant." Many of the other miners at this bar use a sobriquet as well, usually one that speaks to and also helps to make a global social imaginary. At our table at the bar alone we have a Chuck Norris, a Rambo, a Snoop Dogg, and a P-Diddy. "Have you ever met an Obama?" I ask the Machine with a laugh. "Obama?!" The Machine points to a small house. "He's right over there! He works real hard but he smokes too much pot!" On the one hand, these names symbolize the fact that miners' work connects them to a social field that is global in scale: they help to produce this interconnected world, and they draw their identities from this interconnection. On the other hand, such names are also designed to help these workers avoid creditors. There is simply no such thing as an artisanal miner who doesn't have a debt to someone, since this work cannot take place without a regular flow of money from middlemen to diggers. But an array of unpredictable and uncontrollable factors can make it so that these debts don't get repaid in a timely fashion. And so diggers like the

Machine have to come up with adaptive strategies for dealing with people who could bring them harm. "We are like snakes in the ground, always looking for a hole to crawl into," he says, expanding upon his original theme about being in a hole.

The Machine didn't start out as a digger. Like many, he got into this work during the Second Congolese War (officially, 1998–2003), when all of his things were taken by the Rwandan-backed Rally for Congolese Democracy. Before that, the Machine sold miscellaneous wares. After those were gone, he heard about the price that coltan ore was fetching and so went into the forest to make a living for his family. But he has never been able to return home. The Machine had no idea that, in late 2000, Sony had run out of the tantalum it needed to meet the Christmas demand for Sony Playstation 2. This shortage fueled already existing on-line speculation that led to a dramatic price bubble: coltan prices rapidly rose tenfold, only to drop down to close to its original price in 2001. Among miners and traders, the price hike for coltan is still remembered as a miraculous and dangerous time; in some places it is known simply as the *fois deux* (the doubling), and in others it is recalled as the time of *bisikatike,* or "may it never end." Today, the Machine calls coltan the "mother of all minerals" because of its incredible density; it draws in multitudes of workers and vast divisions of labor—all of whom get to "touch money," as Congolese put it. Because it puts so many people to work and feeds so many other businesses, coltan and the other "black minerals" are more likely to generate real, enduring peace than gold or diamonds, which can be easily smuggled to foreign countries and individually possessed.

This price hike for coltan happened during the middle of the Second Congolese War, which is often described as Africa's "First World War" because it involved at least nine African countries, as well as international corporations. This horrible war, in which more than six million people died, had complex causes, including the overflow from the Rwandan genocide and the long history of kleptocratic governance under Mobutu. The value of minerals in the Congo incentivized neighboring countries and international corporate players to get involved, and minerals were used to purchase arms, which allowed some groups to continue to make a living through armed violence. These neighboring African countries were responding to a budgetary crisis brought about by the structural-adjustment programs of the 1980s and 1990s, which bankrupted African treasuries. During the war, occupying armies, especially the Rwandan-backed Rally for Congolese Democracy, bought Congolese minerals and mined for them, often forcing civilian populations to dig coltan at the "barrel of a gun"—to echo one NGO report. According to a 2002 UN report, eighty-five firms from twenty countries—including Anglo American, Barclays, Bayer, Cabot, HC Stark, and Standard Chartered Bank—collaborated with occupying armies or illegal militias during the war. The UN recommended economic sanctions on twenty-nine firms from Britain, the United States, Germany, Malaysia, Hong Kong, and Belgium, but they were never implemented. The demand for minerals by foreign armies also helped fuel the dollarization of the Congolese economy, and had many dramatic ramifications that continue to affect people to this day.

For a while, the Machine was able to make enough money from his own sweat to become a middleman himself. But when the price fell from one hundred dollars a kilo to ten dollars a kilo, it left thousands of people in the forest holding worthless sand. The resulting indebtedness on the part of those, like the Machine, who financed their enterprise using different sorts of "loans" (often interest-bearing ones) affected the entire region. It impacted everyone, from urban entrepreneurs to low-level diggers, many of whom continued to stay in the mining business to pay their debts or escape debts while living in the forest far from home. Several people have told me that this was the moment when eastern Congolese became "addicted" to mining, because their debts made it so they had to look for other minerals in the forest in order to return home. The Machine also had debts that he needed to pay off to various financial backers, so he couldn't return to the city of Goma, his original home. Instead he hung around in the forest, digging to make ends meet, while waiting for something to happen. When the Machine heard that Bakumu trappers had discovered cassiterite and bauxite in the middle of the rainforest at a place that came to be called Bisie (Bakumu for "it will never end"), he went there to work, along with what soon turned out to be nearly twenty thousand others. During that time (roughly 2003–10), the Machine says, he ate and drank like a king. But these days, a foreign company has taken advantage of the work of these artisanal miners and secured a contract from the government to drill. The Machine and his friends have been evacuated by the government from the site they discovered and developed. A small fraction of them now work for the foreign company, building a road for a pittance.

His physique no longer allows the Machine to live up to that name. Before, when the Machine's boot touched the ground, it left behind a major imprint, but now he treads lightly on the earth. He is not alone. The closure of the artisanal mine at Bisie has put thousands of people out of work, and tied up millions of dollars' worth of minerals for businessmen who have taken loans from buyers back in the towns. The situation is dangerous, for those miners who were once working are now stealing from people on the roads: "Bisie was our security," the Machine laments, because the work of mining kept people from more violent ways of making a living. The Machine is lucky because he works for the company, but they feed their workers only twice a day. For the Machine and others, coltan was a peace-building mineral because it kept them fed and allowed them to build sustainable futures. The closure of artisanal mines in 2010, and an effective embargo on Congolese minerals since that time, have inaugurated a new kind of conflict and a new sort of violence.

CONFLICT MINERAL OR PEACE-BUILDING MINERAL?

Despite the complex histories of the Congolese conflicts, NGOs have argued to the international community that there is a direct relationship between coltan and conflict.

Unfortunately, the simple argument that some minerals *cause* violent conflict has had immediate and ironic effects. It has allowed international actors to secure a de facto international embargo on Congolese minerals, with devastating effects for Congolese. June 2, 2014, saw the deadline for US companies that purchase minerals sourced from the DR Congo to submit their "conflict minerals report" documentation to the Securities and Exchange Commission in accordance with Section 1502 of the Dodd-Frank Act. The law, which was promoted by prominent international NGOs like the Enough Project and Global Witness, compels American companies to reveal whether the minerals in their products originated in the DRC or any adjoining country, to report on the "due diligence" undertaken to examine the supply chain, and to take measures if the minerals are not "conflict free." In 2010, President Kabila responded to such legislation by abruptly shutting down artisanal mining in the eastern DR Congo, which led to an epic social crisis in those places dependent on mining. In the area around Bisie, the largest artisanal mine in the east, reported malnutrition cases have increased more than tenfold in the last five years.

The new legislation has also made it easier for companies to tighten their grip on miners, using the concept of "conflict minerals" and the association of conflict with artisanal mining to legitimate their claims to artisanally mined land. In Rubaya, North Kivu, the company that purchased rights to the coltan mine there works with an international NGO to track minerals from designated "conflict free" sites. They are the only company that miners can legally sell to, although miners can also smuggle illegally through willing government agents by paying them fees. This company has bought coltan from middlemen on credit, in accordance with a contract that stipulates that the middlemen be paid within two weeks. As of November 2015, the company had held onto these minerals for months because they had not yet received money from their buyer in Asia. Meanwhile, interest-bearing debts are accumulating, and many middlemen have been compelled to sell their homes and take their children out of school—a situation that promises to promote violent conflict between middlemen and the company on the one hand, and middlemen and the diggers on the other. As of September 2015, the middlemen had surrounded the company's office in Goma in an effort to prevent the company from moving those minerals before they were paid; these same middlemen are unable to return to Rubaya for fear of losing their lives, because they owe money to the diggers. It is a clear case of an outside organization—here an NGO working alongside high-tech companies from the United States—unwittingly helping to produce conflict while trying to generate peace because of a narrow and decontextualized understanding of what "conflict" is in the first place.

THE MATERIALITY OF THE DIGITAL AGE

Those who work to extract the minerals used in digital devices produce the conditions of possibility for the so-called digital age. The social forms they generate are as much part of this new world as the "incubators" of Silicon Valley. In some ways, these miners also represent a new category of Congolese—dispossessed people who have lost whatever land they had and for the most part no longer practice agriculture. These miners depend on these minerals and are subject to instabilities in price and various forms of violence—from debt to war. But their dependence is also the source of new forms of sociality, movement, and belonging that didn't exist before. The technologies they make also help to enable these new connections, as well as new ideas about what the future might look like. Miners embrace their incomplete "global citizenship" in a number of ways, including the names they give to themselves. Their work is not merely "material," in the sense of being physical, nor does their occupation merely engage them in the dirty work of extracting things from the ground. It also allows them to communicate with deceased ancestors who live in the ground or follow workers through the forests. Mining is as much about rebuilding social worlds across space and time in the wake of war as it is about extracting substances used in digital devices.

ADDITIONAL RESOURCES

Autesserre, Severine. *The Trouble with the Congo: Local Violence and the Failure of International Peacebuilding.* New York: Cambridge University Press, 2010.

Jackson, Stephen. "Making a Killing: Criminality and Coping in the Kivu War Economy." *Review of African Political Economy* 29, nos. 93–94 (2002): 517–36.

Mantz, Jeffrey. "Improvisational Economies: Coltan Production in the Eastern Congo." *Social Anthropology* 16, no. 1 (2008): 34–50.

Morozov, Evgeny, *To Save Everything Click Here.* New York: Perseus Books, 2013.

Nest, Michael. *Coltan.* Cambridge: Polity Press, 2011.

Smith, James H. "Tantalus in the Digital Age: Coltan Ore, Temporal Dispossession, and "Movement" in the Eastern Democratic Republic of the Congo." *American Ethnologist,* 38, no. 1 (2011): 17–35.

. . .

JAMES H. SMITH is a Professor in the Department of Anthropology at the University of California Davis. His research interests include the politics of temporality, vernacular development narratives, and practices of artisanal mining and resource extraction. He is the author of *Bewitching Development: Witchcraft and the Reinvention of Development in Kenya* (University of Chicago Press, 2008) and (with Ngeti Mwadimi) *Email from Ngeti: An Ethnography of Sorcery, Redemption, and Friendship in Global Africa* (University of California Press, 2014). His journal articles include "Tantalus in the Digital Age: Coltan Ore, Temporal Dispossession and 'Movement' in the Eastern Democratic Republic of the Congo" (*American Ethnologist,* 2011) and "'May It Never End': Price Wars, Networks, and Temporality in the '3 Ts' Mining Trade of the Eastern DR Congo" (*Journal of Ethnographic Theory,* 2015).

Bioprospecting

MOVING BEYOND BENEFIT SHARING

Rachel Wynberg

Abstract: *Hoodia gordonii*, an indigenous plant used by San peoples in southern Africa to suppress their appetites, is just one of many indigenous plants that corporations and other organizations have sought to discover, patent, and market. Such efforts to co-opt and commercialize the traditional medicinal knowledge of indigenous peoples have been called "bioprospecting" and even "biopiracy." The case of hoodia and other plants in South Africa suggests the problems with such arrangements, and the emergence of new, more equitable forms of benefit sharing.

Keywords: traditional knowledge, indigenous peoples, hoodia, southern Africa, Nagoya Protocol

HOODIA SETS THE STAGE

Light green in color, snarled, prickly, bursting with promise when watered, withered and shriveled when not—who could have imagined that this unassuming plant would become so emblematic of indigenous peoples' struggles and the fight for fair reparation?

The story emerges from the arid regions of southern Africa, where the succulent plant *Hoodia gordonii*, or hoodia, has long been used to stave off hunger and thirst by the indigenous San peoples. This knowledge was published by colonial botanists and was later used by the South African–based Council for Scientific and Industrial Research (CSIR), one of the largest research organizations in Africa, to investigate the plant's potential as an appetite suppressant. In 1997, after a lengthy period of development, the CSIR patented use of the active constituents of the plant that are responsible for suppressing appetite. Deals were subsequently struck with the UK-based company Phytopharm and pharmaceutical giant Pfizer to develop an antiobesity drug. When these fell through, another agreement was negotiated—this time with Unilever, one of the largest consumer companies in the world, to develop a diet drink.

Up until 2001, San communities had no idea that their knowledge of hoodia had commercial application, and that this knowledge had led to research, scientific validation, and the filing of international patents by the CSIR. They were, moreover, excluded from lucrative deals being struck to develop commercial products. In 2001, the South African San Council was alerted to the use of San knowledge without consent. Astonishingly, the CSIR had told Phytopharm that the hundred-thousand-strong San "no longer existed"—a statement later defended by the CSIR as a response on their part to avoid raising expectations.

Political pressure and intense media coverage forced the CSIR to negotiate with the South African San Council, leading to the adoption of a benefit-sharing agreement in 2003. The agreement stated that San would obtain 6 percent of all royalties received by the CSIR from Phytopharm for products, and 8 percent of income received by the CSIR when certain product-development targets were reached. Money was to be paid into a trust set up jointly by the CSIR and the South African San Council, "to raise the standard of living and well-being of San peoples of southern Africa." Strict rules were developed to distribute the funds. San representatives recognized that the San community held knowledge about the plant collectively, and therefore an agreement was reached to share the money among all southern African San.

The involvement of the indigenous San peoples, and the intrigue of a plant that may simultaneously tackle the Western affliction of obesity and the social and economic developmental challenges of San communities, triggered the public's imagination at a time when disparities between rich and poor have never been greater. For some, the case illustrated the possibilities of *bioprospecting*—the search for biological material with commercially valuable genetic and biochemical properties—and a final, albeit tenuous and equivocal, delivery on the long-standing promises of equitable benefit sharing in the Convention on Biological Diversity (CBD) and its Nagoya Protocol. For others, it typified the problems of *biopiracy*, where traditional knowledge is appropriated without the consent of the holders of that knowledge.

The agreement was hailed initially as a significant breakthrough in the access and benefit-sharing impasse. Here was an example of how the CBD could work in practice to benefit both indigenous communities and those seeking to reap profit from traditional knowledge and biodiversity. The global weight-loss and weight-management market is currently estimated at a massive $148 billion; thus, returns were expected to be high. But very soon the cracks began to show. Further analysis revealed that although the San Council might receive a considerable amount of money, this would be minuscule in comparison with the profits gleaned. Monies received by the San Council would be extracted from royalties received by the CSIR, but profits of Pfizer and Phytopharm were to remain untouched. Was this equitable benefit sharing? The requirement for the San Council to have an exclusive agreement with the CSIR was also troubling, since it would reduce any other opportunities that might arise for the San Council to benefit from use of hoodia. What if the Pfizer deal fell through?

These concerns were to some extent prophetic. In 2003, Pfizer merged with Pharmacia and closed its Natureceuticals group, which had been responsible for developing hoodia. Pfizer discontinued clinical development of the drug and handed the rights back to Phytopharm. In 2004, the consumer giant Unilever stepped in through a joint-development agreement with Phytopharm and began investigating hoodia as an ingredient for its line of SlimFast drinks. A massive cultivation program was launched, involving over three hundred hectares of hoodia in South Africa and Namibia, clinical safety trials, manufacturing, and an agreement to develop a $75-million extraction facility.

Caught up in the hoodia frenzy, a swathe of opportunistic hoodia growers and traders emerged. The CSIR patent was focused on the hoodia extract, and nothing prevented other companies from simply selling raw hoodia material for incorporation into herbal supplements. Unregulated collection from the wild soared, and by 2004 concerns about the threats posed to natural populations had led to the inclusion of hoodia species in Appendix II of the Convention on International Trade in Endangered Species (CITES), an international agreement that aims to ensure that trade in wild animals and plants does not threaten their survival. Dozens of hoodia products were being advertised on the Internet and sold in drugstores and pharmacies as diet bars, pills, creams, and drinks, traded by a myriad of companies using the publicity and clinical trials of Phytopharm and Unilever. San were receiving no benefits from these products, many of which were also of dubious authenticity and quality. Rising concerns about environmental impacts and quality led to a more regulated industry based on cultivated material. Those involved in growing hoodia for the herbal and dietary supplement market also negotiated another benefit-sharing agreement with the San Council. As the hoodia industry became more organized, it was dealt a blow by the sudden withdrawal of Unilever in 2008, which announced that it was abandoning plans to develop hoodia as a functional food because of safety and efficacy concerns. Although some hoodia herbal products remain on the market today, the multi-million-dollar projections of profit remain elusive.

DEVELOPING WORKABLE MODELS FOR BENEFIT SHARING

Despite these disappointments, the effect of the hoodia case has been catalytic. Although commercialization has generated relatively insignificant monetary benefits for San communities (about $50,000 to date), more importantly, the case has demonstrated a "workable" model for benefit sharing with indigenous peoples—a feat long considered unachievable by industry skeptics. At the same time, capacity has been built within San communities to negotiate with industry and leverage benefits. Claiming to be primary traditional knowledge holders of all southern African biodiversity, San communities are now at the frontline of any deals proposed to commercialize the region's biological resources. This has paid rich dividends. South Africa's Biodiversity Act, for example, requires any company wishing to exploit the country's indigenous biological resources—or traditional knowledge associated with these resources—to demonstrate that it has both received prior informed consent of affected communities and negotiated a benefit-sharing agreement.

With the precedent set through hoodia, the South African San Council has since negotiated a suite of such agreements. *Sceletium tortuosum,* for example, a succulent plant well known for its mood-enhancing properties, is the subject of a 2010 benefit-sharing agreement between the San Council and HG&H Pharmaceuticals. This led to HG&H securing the first bioprospecting permit ever issued under South Africa's Biodiversity Act. San Council benefits include 5 percent of net proceeds received by HG&H and an annual exclusivity payment of 1 percent on sales. In return, the San Council is expected to exclusively endorse products, allow the use of their logo, and assist with marketing and branding. The patented product, dubbed Zembrin, has secured GRAS (generally regarded as safe) status in the United States and is marketed as an evidence-based botanical supplement to treat stress and anxiety. To date about $50,000 has been received by the San Council from this agreement.

In a similar example, an agreement between the South African San Council, the National Khoisan Council, and a local pharmaceutical company, Cape Kingdom Nutraceuticals, gives San and Khoi communities 3 percent of the profits from products emerging from the use of buchu leaves (*Agathosma betulina* and *Agathosma crenulata*), from which an essential oil is extracted that is used widely in the international flavor and fragrance industries and that is also an important tonic, anti-inflammatory, antiseptic, and diuretic. As for plants of the *Sceletium* genus, the agreement stipulates that the San and Khoi communities will "offer their cooperation and collaboration" to provide endorsement and marketing assistance, although financial benefits to date have been scant.

A third agreement, founded on the back of the highly successful rooibos (*Aspalathus linearis*) tea industry, involves the San Council in an agreement with Nestlé, the world's largest food company, based on the development of a novel tea product. Ironically, the agreement emerged following, and perhaps because of, a highly controversial case. Nestlé had previously filed several rooibos patents without first securing permits from the South African government. Negative media publicity and biopiracy accusations led to the subsequent withdrawal of these patents by Nestlé. While implementation of the agreement is still embryonic, it represents one of the first in an industry that, in contrast to the pharmaceutical sector, has very low levels of awareness about the contested arena of access and benefit sharing.

WHOSE KNOWLEDGE COUNTS?

Such initiatives, on the face of it, signal a sea change in the way in which biodiversity business is conducted. Companies and researchers now have a legal obligation to "do the right thing." Indigenous peoples are now duly included as beneficiaries in ventures exploiting their knowledge. Governments can now proudly assert their adherence to international agreements and their commitment to addressing poverty and inequality.

But amid this optimism there is some cause for concern. San remain among the most marginalized peoples in southern Africa, with a long history of dispossession, persecution, and relocation. Most live in remote, harsh, and arid environments, eking out a living through agriculture, livestock, wage labor, and the harvesting of nontimber forest products on land to which they have no rights or traditional claim. Many San live below the poverty line and face extreme hardship in terms of access to social services, employment, and income-generating opportunities. Introducing large sums of money into such communities could have potentially divisive and even catastrophic impacts, especially since local San institutions are extremely fragile and weak. The wide distribution of San outside of South Africa and across very remote parts of southern Africa makes the situation particularly fraught. Ensuring the equitable distribution of funds to such communities is a very hard task indeed.

Further complicating matters is the fact that several groups hold traditional knowledge about the same plants to which San communities lay claim. Almost all of such groups have, to varying degrees, San as their progenitors. The most significant of these include Khoi communities, originally pastoralists but today often urbanized, "hybridized," and, more and more, politicized. Although absent from hoodia negotiations, the National Khoi-San Council, established by former president Nelson Mandela in 1999 to accommodate San and Khoi historical leadership within South Africa's constitutional framework, has increasingly become a partner in various benefit-sharing agreements, in collaboration with the South African San Council.

What this means in practice is ambiguous, and is often embroiled in the politics of identity and representation, a lack of clarity about who exactly "qualifies" for being San or Khoi, and a concern that benefits will flow to an elite leadership. A further complication is that many contemporary San and Khoi have been dislocated and resettled over millennia and are today seldom found in areas where the plants over which they claim traditional knowledge grow. In contrast, present-day communities who reside in such areas have customary rights and ownership over these plant resources but do not easily identify themselves as "indigenous." Increasingly, this speaks to a disconnect between, on the one hand, the realism of contemporary biodiversity custodians and knowledge holders, and on the other, a worldview, supported to a large extent by international agreements and global movements, that essentializes indigenous peoples. As a result, emphasis is given to priority, or "who was first," without acknowledging either the wide distribution of herbal knowledge and resources, or the long chain of rural communities, healers, researchers, and drug companies that contribute in different ways toward product development.

The *Sceletium* case, for example, lauded by some as a gold standard in benefit sharing, had less illustrious beginnings than is commonly believed. In the 1990s, research took place with traditional healers of the indigenous Nama, a group within the Khoi. Patents were filed in 2000 based on this knowledge but without securing prior informed consent or agreeing on benefit sharing. The 2010 agreement with HG&H Pharmaceuticals thus recognizes San peoples as "primary knowledge holders" but also recognizes the contribution of Nama peoples. This has resulted in the allocation of 50 percent of royalties to the villages of Nourivier and Paulshoek—where the research was initially conducted, in the Northern Cape province of South Africa.

Elsewhere in the region, identities are even more ambiguous. Mountain communities in the Western Cape, for example, which include some of the only areas where buchu and rooibos grow naturally and are wild-harvested, comprise largely so-called coloured residents. These groups are typically mixed-race descendants of settlers, former slaves, and Khoi people. Nonetheless, the harvesting and use of these plants have formed a central part of the livelihoods and cultures of such communities for decades. Paradoxically, while the benefit-sharing agreements described have to some degree safeguarded the rights of traditional knowledge holders associated with contemporary San and Khoi political structures, they have not adequately integrated other communities into the trade to allow for a share of commercial benefits. In fact, most of these harvesters and small-scale farmers—who are also often traditional-knowledge holders—remain completely unaware of the access and benefit-sharing regulations that protect their rights.

The natural-product companies that purchase material from these communities are also skeptical. Faced with an edict from the South African government to negotiate benefit-sharing agreements with San and Khoi communities, companies trading buchu have expressed concern about the fact that they already engage with harvester communities (who do not readily identify themselves as San or Khoi) and would prefer to develop benefit-sharing agreements with these communities, where they have established relationships. As one such trader remarked, "We are already making such small profits but we have to do this whole bioprospecting process and there is just so much red tape that gets involved . . . and we have people who have been here for one hundred years but we can't make a contribution to them, we have to give our money to somebody [the San and Khoi councils] in Kimberley, far away."

In the politically contested spaces of the rooibos tea industry, small-scale producers have voiced similar concerns. Despite twenty years of democracy in South Africa, the rooibos industry remains largely untransformed, continuing to enjoy the benefits of having been propped up by the apartheid system. In 1954, the government established the Rooibos Tea Control Board, a government-controlled monopoly rights system that served as the sole buyer from producers and the sole seller to approved exporters and tea processors. The board also had the authority to prohibit producers from selling rooibos to any party without its approval. As a result of the establishment of the control board, the rooibos industry could be assured of direct government protection and support, including subsidies for affiliated producers and research, and the provision of extension services. The rooibos industry expanded, entering a period of substantial growth and development. But, in apartheid South Africa, the board system excluded the mostly coloured farmers of mountain areas such as Wupperthal and the Suid Bokkeveld, who had traditionally gathered rooibos tea from the wild.

Together with apartheid, the Rooibos Tea Control Board was abolished in 1993, and over the past two decades the democratic government has provided increasing support to small-scale black and coloured rooibos farmers. Nonetheless, most of these farmers remain marginalized, and will continue to be so—physically, because of their remote location; environmentally, because of the harsh, drought-prone conditions under which they farm; and economically, in terms of their limited marketing capacity and continued struggles to gain access to extension services, markets, credit, and land. Whether access and benefit sharing can help with their plight is questionable, especially in the context of the wider development challenges that are faced. As one rooibos farmer from the Suid Bokkeveld remarked, in response to the information that San were claiming benefits from rooibos, "Our people are the ones who collect seed. Are we going back to the old South Africa where people are classed by race? I don't know where I belong—black, white, coloured?"

TOWARD A BROADER VISION FOR ACCESS AND BENEFIT SHARING

Learning from these experiences is perhaps the biggest challenge of all, in the context of government systems and approaches that are typically highly managerial, siloed, and territorial in their individual mandates. Despite their good intentions, African regulations dealing with access and benefit sharing are characteristically marred by insufficient human capacity, limited experience with community dynamics, and poor knowledge of the rapidly changing scientific and technological environment in which bioprospecting is located. The ability to make good decisions is often compromised in such circumstances. A persistent backdrop is the politically charged nature of bioprospecting and the often-competing directives of neoliberal governments to commoditize biodiversity and traditional knowledge and to get a cut for the state of what are perceived to be profitable activities. The concern, as evidenced in the South African example, is that governments react to these complexities and to the imperative of the Nagoya Protocol by entangling themselves in unworkable laws and by adopting a somewhat mechanical "tick-box approach" that aims to ensure regulatory compliance rather than creating a climate that is conducive to ensuring social justice and stimulating economic development.

Experiences emerging from southern Africa provide rich fodder not only for the emerging regime of the Nagoya Protocol but also for wider initiatives focused on reducing the profound inequalities that exist in our society today. While building on the impetus and goodwill to address these injustices, we should not forget the priorities faced by indigenous peoples and local communities throughout the world. Establishing greater benefits for communities or traditional-knowledge holders is essential, but this goal won't be achieved by benefit-sharing agreements alone. Equal attention should be given to building the long-term financial and technical capacity of communities to engage in commercialization; transferring technology to African countries and adding value to raw material; facilitating market access; and interrogating the unequal power relations of African natural-product value chains, which often continue to be monopolized by a handful of corporations. Realizing such changes will not be possible without securing rights to the resources, knowledge, and land that have been trampled upon over centuries and challenging the broader threats that are causing rampant biodiversity and cultural loss—such as logging, mining, and commercial agriculture. Greater integration of these issues is vital if the dual objectives of achieving both equity and biodiversity conservation are to be achieved.

ADDITIONAL RESOURCES

Dutfield, G. "Traditional Knowledge, Intellectual Property and Pharmaceutical Innovation: What's Left to Discuss?" In *The SAGE Handbook of Intellectual*

Property, edited by M. David and D. Halbert, 649–65. London: SAGE Publications, 2015.

"Responsible, Inclusive Innovation—The Buchu Plant." https://www.youtube.com/watch?v=Nk_Tl7dK5Oo. (This video features interviews about the buchu plant and its wide range of possible uses to improve health and well-being. Its purpose is to show how traditional knowledge holders can collaborate with responsible entrepreneurs and scientists to drive inclusive innovation.)

Wynberg, R. 2016. Making Sense of Access and Benefit Sharing in the Rooibos Industry: Towards a Holistic, Just and Sustainable Framing. *South African Journal of Botany.* http://dx.doi.org/10.1016/j.sajb.2016.09.015

Wynberg, R., D. Schroeder, and R. Chennells, eds. *Indigenous Peoples, Consent and Benefit-Sharing: Learning from the San-Hoodia Case.* Berlin: Springer, 2009.

The following websites providing further information about access and benefit sharing:

www.abs-initiative.info

www.bioeconomy.org.za

www.cbd.int

. . .

RACHEL WYNBERG is an academic, activist, and policy analyst with a special interest in biodiversity use and benefit sharing, community rights, social justice, and environmental governance. She holds a Research Chair on Social and Environmental Dimensions of the Bio-Economy at the University of Cape Town, where she is associate professor in the Department of Environmental and Geographical Science. With a background in the natural and social sciences, she has a strong interest in interdisciplinarity and policy engagement across the humanities, arts, and sciences. Bridging the gap between the theoretical dimensions of academia and the real world of environmental, social inequality, and poverty challenges is her central passion.

Of Waste and Revolutions

ENVIRONMENTAL LEGACIES OF AUTHORITARIANISM IN TUNISIA

Siad Darwish

Abstract: The Tunisian revolution unveiled an environmental catastrophe that had been festering under the country's dictatorship for decades. Hidden behind a facade of environmentalism, vast amounts of waste were dumped into the environment, and the legacies of authoritarianism still prevent a clear image of Tunisia's environmental health from emerging.

Keywords: waste, pollution, authoritarianism, inequality, revolution, Tunisia

REVOLUTIONS LEND EXPRESSION TO PUBLIC secrets, and sometimes they do so in the most visceral of ways. Weeks after the Tunisian revolution of 2011, piles of rotting garbage filled the streets, sewage was running in the rivers, and toxic waste was being pumped into the Mediterranean in unprecedented amounts. The uprising unveiled, and in part created, an environmental health crisis—one that had been festering under dictatorships for decades. During the reign of Zine Abedinne Ben Ali (1987–2011), the Bretton Woods Institutions (World Bank and International Monetary Fund) hailed Tunisia as North Africa's poster child of economic development—and, like elsewhere in the world, this growth was fueled by the creation of waste. In the heyday of structural adjustment, industrial parks burgeoned; plastic bags and packaging appeared, enveloping an ever-increasing amount of consumer products; but the nascent waste-management system could not keep up. The situation was similar across the African continent, of course; however, in Tunisia this reality was hidden by a facade of democratization and environmentalism kept in place through censorship of the media, tight state control over research, and torture and imprisonment of activists. From the early 1990s a "Boulevard de l'Environnement" was designated in each village, and a desert fox wearing a blue unitard—Labib, Tunisia's environmental mascot—

populated public squares and roundabouts throughout the country. Meanwhile, over 75 percent of Tunisia's industrial waste was being dumped into the natural habitat with near impunity, according to World Bank estimates. This facade of environmentalism makes the underlying health impacts of the waste crisis on humans and ecology today only vaguely apparent. However, what can be ascertained is that Tunisia's poor are disproportionally affected as the distribution of waste is shaped by deep-seated social, economic, and geographical inequalities throughout the world.

Waste—disposable matter—is the underbelly of modern consumer lifestyles. Dangerous for environmental health or not, it pollutes physically, aesthetically, and morally, dividing people, cities, regions, and countries into the clean and the unclean. Waste therefore both underlines and creates economic disparities locally, regionally, and globally, with the richest consuming the most and the poorest often receiving the majority of the waste. At least since the times of colonization, Africa has served as a sink for European economic activity. Colonial entrepreneurs extracted natural resources in their race to create new commodities for Western markets, but the waste associated with that extraction remained. Tunisia's phosphate industry, established by the French in 1885 and today the most polluting in the country, is a case in point. The acceleration of economic globalization increased this unequal trend exponentially in Africa, where multinational companies sought out cheap labor, tax reductions, and arguably laxer environmental regulations. While this so-called race to the bottom, or pollution haven theory, is disputed, the very international financial system, with its single-mined focus on economic growth, has pushed governments across Africa into unsustainable economic practices. In order to attract foreign investment and to borrow and repay international debts, governments relax or turn a blind eye to the environmental crimes of national and international corporations. This is particularly true in the context of authoritarian political systems, like the one in Tunisia before the revolution, in which those most affected by waste have little or no power to address the issue. In the postrevolutionary hierarchy of needs, calls for a clean and healthy environment have been marginal on the national agenda. Locally, however, the issue has rekindled a myriad of environmental conflicts that are now starting to surface, and in the immediate aftermath of the revolution waste has been pushed into the public imagination.

Few public-service strikes impact the lives of citizens like those in waste management. Quite suddenly, the revolution allowed Tunisians to make their grievances heard publicly, and among the first groups to exercise this right with a general strike were municipal garbage workers. Now all workers demanded civil-service contracts, along with better pay and working conditions, which had been intolerable under the former regime. Rumors surfaced that the deposed authorities actively disrupted public services in order to stem the tide of the revolution, as was the case in Egypt; but the grievances were real. Within days, the streets of all major cities were flooded with loosely sealed red, black, and blue garbage bags. Like a leaky display of household consumption, broken eggshells, empty plastic bottles, tuna and beer cans, cigarette buds, fish carcasses, stale baguettes, coffee grounds, and a farrago of fruits and vegetables spilled into the public arena, where they decomposed in the heat of the North African spring. Here and there images of the former dictator were visible among the refuse. A sweet, rotten odor took hold of the country as illegal dumps sprang up wherever they couldn't be prevented, and waste distribution stations, often located centrally in residential areas, turned into the final resting places for consumed goods. As the philosopher Greg Kennedy explains, garbage denotes finitude, violence, and chaos—chaos that is intrinsic to revolutions through the refashioning of the social order. But this unexpected extension of public disorder now displayed the cost of transition too blatantly. What was dubbed the Jasmine Revolution by outsiders started to reek in Tunisia, and the phrase *balad al-zibleh* ("country of rubbish") was employed in discussions about corruption, traffic, and the seemingly slow pace of political transition. Garbage became a metaphor for everything that was wrong with Tunisia, and it threatened to pollute revolutionary promises. Worried and disgusted, Tunisians started to react. A series of graffiti appeared in every neighborhood that read: "God will not have mercy on the parents of those that dump garbage here." On Facebook, first the garbage selfie and then the garbage-bucket challenge, mirroring the global meme of the ice-bucket challenge, expressed citizens' outcries. Tunisians quickly created organizations to address the issue.

Although in large parts of Tunisia municipal garbage collection has always been poor, especially on the periphery of urban centers and in the country's interior, the strike brought waste to the heart of the cities, even the most affluent areas, and thereby into the consciousness of the elites. Morched, a tall, brisk environmental engineer with degrees from Canada, founded one of Tunisia's first postrevolutionary environmental NGOs to get to the bottom of the problem. "It was with the garbage crisis that we realized that the whole system was rotten and corrupt. . . . We thought we were Sweden when it comes to waste management, and now after the revolution, we find we work more like Somalia," he said. What he and his colleagues discovered were completely inadequate and sometimes dangerous waste-management systems, with landfills at their terminus that threatened local communities and habitats.

Tunisia's largest landfill, Jbel Borj Chakir, is surrounded by barbed-wire barricades that rise from wheat fields, vegetable gardens, and olive and almond groves in the hinterlands fourteen kilometers west of Tunis. Trucks and tractor-drawn carriages that wind their way up through working-class neighborhoods and clog the streets deliver about three thousand tons of waste each day. Ordinarily, landfills are designed to lock refuse away impermeably. They are "dry graves" whose geographical location depends on solid bedrock underneath to prevent groundwater pollution by leachate—a garbage juice that ranges from mildly toxic to biohazardous depending on its composition. Morched and his NGO, SOS BIAA (Save the Environment), however, have proven that Borj Chakir and many other landfills in the northeast either are permeable or deliberately dump leachate into waterways. They contaminate drinking water and the wells of farmers with organic compounds—the only pollutants the organization has tested for so far due to financial constraints—but the fact that these compounds are present suggests that there is worse to be discovered. SOS BIAA also uncovered evidence that hospital and industrial hard wastes have made their way into municipal garbage dumps (at least after the revolution), which makes the leachate of these landfills potentially very dangerous. These allegations have been confirmed by local officials. Thus, like garbage itself, landfills have become contentious across the country, not only because of their potential danger for human health and the environment, but also because of the dictatorial force by which they were imposed on local populations.

Often, if not always, landfills and other waste-management stations are located in poorer areas where people have limited means to resist their creation and are intimidated by authorities, and to which they are lured with jobs. Tunisia's poor, the *zawaali,* eat meat only on holidays, as a popular proverb proclaims. They can't afford bottled water, which is seen as part of a healthy lifestyle, and therefore rely on the quality of the water beneath their feet. Their sons and daughters are likely to be out of work, despite having university diplomas. Sometimes they can escape their neighborhoods and villages to bring the whole family for a long picnic to one of the public beaches, avoiding the waste and pollution that so often mar their everyday experience. The revolution was initially a revolt of the *zawaali,* not of the urban middle classes. It was their cry for freedom and dignity, as the slogan of the revolution proclaimed. Locally, a clean and healthy environment free of waste and pollution has in many parts of the country become integral to that dignity and has led to the convergence of environmentalism and social struggles across Tunisia.

The island of Djerba, one of Tunisia's prime tourist destinations, was the backdrop to another waste crisis that hit the media in 2014–15. The island's only landfill was located in the smallest and poorest of its three municipalities, Gelalla. While the two larger municipalities on the island received the taxes from many hundreds of high-end tourist resorts, Gelalla received only their waste. After the revolution this inequality converged with residents' worries about garbage burning, smoke, stench, and the effects on the local water table, which is already overexploited. When the company that managed the landfill wasn't responsive to their grievances, like in the old days, residents took matters into their own hands. They stormed the barricades of the landfill, burned down offices, infrastructure, and equipment, and shut the landfill down by civil force. In the aftermath of this closure, the tourist paradise was gripped by a garbage crisis, which, because of its high-profile location, couldn't be ignored and has now been temporarily resolved. While this was one of hundreds of local expressions of the waste-management crisis, at its heart lies a structural conflict within the body that governs waste and pollution: the Ministry of the Environment.

"The main problem with environmental pollution in Tunisia is structural," explains Wahed Ferchichi, a professor of law at the University of Tunis specializing in the environment. The Ministry of the Environment, established in 1991, actually delivers public services rather than serving only as an adviser and watchdog. Waste management, sanitation, and even the treatment of hazardous waste is essentially the responsibility of the ministry, presented through its various agencies. Paradoxically, this in turn makes the Ministry of the Environment one of the major polluters in the country. For example, Tunisia's wastewater agency, ONAS, is plagued by underfunding, inefficiencies, mismanagement, and corruption and has been implicated in several environmental disasters. In 2012, a report of the Court of Auditors, a Tunisian oversight body, found that "75.8 million cubic meters of untreated sewage are released into the Tunisian environment each year." Water-borne diseases, such as hepatitis A and C, have made their return to Tunisia—or their discovery is now being publicized. Even a strain of cholera was found in the summer of 2013 in the country's second-largest river, the Meliane, which is little more than a stream of sewage where it reaches the sea just south of the capital. The term "water-borne" is of course misleading, as these diseases are really borne in sewage and are transmitted through the mixing of waste and drinking water.

In the summer of 2013, more dead fish than usual washed up on the Bay of Monastir near the town of Ksibet Mediouni. The bay was the site of a major toxic spill from nearby factories in 2006, which flooded the waters with untreated sewage from two ONAS wastewater plants. On Wednesday, September 18, the entire town went on a general strike to protest decades of environmental marginalization. Roads were blocked by boulders, administrations were sometimes forcefully closed, and inhabitants demonstrated in front of one of the plants with banners that read "Marginalization, Exclusion, Unemployment and Now Ruin through Environmental Pollution." Protesters and a local representative of the Tunisian Forum for Economic and Social Rights (FTDES), a renowned and well-respected Tunisian NGO, made the links between the town's social, economic, and environmental marginalization explicit. More important, as the ONAS stations discharged sewage and industrial wastewater, locals came to recognize the link between their marginalization and Tunisia's position in the global economy. Mounir Hassine, a professor of geography and the head of FTDES in Monastir, explains: "With the structural-adjustment programs of the 1980s, we encouraged investors to come to Tunisia who had no consideration for the environment, which resulted in major environmental catastrophes in the region. In this period, the textile industry was established here—an industry that was cast out of Western countries because of its detrimental effects on the ecology." In early 1990s, to attract foreign investment, Tunisia created free economic zones in which industries manufactured exclusively for an overseas market. Thus again, while Tunisians built car parts, textiles, and agricultural products supplied to global and particularly European markets, the "byproducts," or industrial pollution, of that production remained behind. Pollution in Tunisia is therefore part of an uneven environmental, social, and economic cost of industries and global markets, but it is also enmeshed in the corrupt practices of the former regime.

There are over 5,000 industrial units in Tunisia, and as of 2013 over 3,000 of those were European owned or partnerships with European companies. Only about 600 factories use any type of hazardous-waste treatment; another 180 were signed up with the country's only hazardous-waste treatment station, but that facility operated only between 2009 and 2011, having been closed after the revolution because of popular protest. The environmental and health effects of an emerging industrial economy discarding nearly all its hazardous waste into local landfills and waterways are completely unpredictable and understudied. And while this broad-scale dumping of industrial waste has not attracted much attention in the media, pollution by larger public companies is increasingly being addressed.

In the city of Gabes—particularly on the northern side of town, where the Tunisian Chemical Group has its headquarters—coffee-colored waves rhythmically hit the beaches, where they leave thick black sludge behind. Chimneys that emit bright yellow smoke—not white, not gray, not black, but bright yellow—seem to rise from the sea at the end of the bay. The Gulf of Gabes, in southern Tunisia, is one of the most polluted stretches of the Mediterranean. Fishermen from the nearby port protest in front of the chemical plant continuously, as their livelihoods have been poisoned and their hope for a job outside of the industry destroyed. Every day, seventy-five thousand tons of phosphogypsum, a lightly radioactive and potentially cancerous by-product of fertilizer manufacturing, are dumped into the sea. Mountain ranges of the yellow dust pile up around its processing stations in the country's interior, close to the cities of Gafsa and Medhilla.

Since the revolution a few studies have traced the environmental effects of such dumping, and they are damning, but so far no study has systematically looked at the health implications of phosphate manufacturing for local populations. Anecdotally, however, people complain about respiratory diseases, allergies, heart defects, cancer, and issues with their teeth and bone density. Inhabitants of the Gafsa mining basin are clearly distinguished by their yellow, decayed teeth, apparently brought about by excessive amounts of fluoride that leach into the groundwater during an industrial washing process. Comparative data from phosphate plants in the United States lend some support to the link between some of those diseases and phosphogypsum, but the composition of the original resource here is slightly different. Similar situations of broad-scale dumping of industrial waste by public companies can be observed in the Kasserine paper mill and the Beja sugar factory, both part of industries established in the 1960s to bring much-needed employment to the underdeveloped regions of Tunisia. But with jobs they also brought waste. How all this waste and pollution was hidden in plain sight is one of the most bewildering aspects of the former political order. And the regime's simultaneous projection of environmental concern delivers much insight in the workings of the Ben Ali regime.

A report by the German development corporation GIZ that looked at the environmental management of Tunisia from independence to the revolution concluded: "The development of environmental policy in Tunisia may in many respects be regarded as exemplary for a Southern country." Policies and practice here are clearly divergent, and what the report is referring to is the overall image the international community had of Tunisia. NGOs existed, but they were hardly independent, having to be funded by the state, and were relegated to cosmetic forms of environmental work, like the cleaning of beaches and planting of trees. This, and the near total control of the press, allowed the government to project its own form of state environmentalism relatively free from critique. When arriving at the airport of Tunis-Carthage, foreigners were greeted by the environmental mascot Labib. They would drive past wind turbines and solar panels that were carefully displayed at the Tunis International Center for Environmental Technologies (CITET).

The ANPE, Tunisia's environmental-protection agency tasked with enforcing international environmental standards, was understaffed and underpaid, and was blocked from effectuating any real reform by the country's notoriously corrupt courts. In 2004, the ANPE, which has about thirty staff members to monitor factories all over Tunisia, handed out over 600 environmental fines. Of these, 150 were actually enforced; however, the actual fines, which the ANPE only suggests, were often reduced by judges to the nominal amount of 50 dinars (US$30). In the absence of any independent organizations, the state was the only check on the environmental crimes of public and private companies, and the Ben Ali regime had a vested interest in not only ignoring but also actively hiding them to bolster foreign investment. Any critiques that surfaced were suppressed with brute force.

In the fall of 2009, Zouheir Makhlouf was beaten, intimidated, and imprisoned for posting videos on Facebook that showed the dumping of hazardous waste by several industrial zones in his hometown of Nabeul. Now one of the country's most prominent human rights activists, he looks like a man who has fought all his life, with small, wet eyes that emit empathy, passion, and pain in equal measures. He explains that environmental activism was particularly dangerous before the revolution: "Criticizing Ben Ali's politics and human rights record wasn't so much of a problem; there was room for that. But if you threatened his development plan and economic policy, you were in real trouble because he was hailed as an economic champion all over the world." Environmental activism threatened the dictatorship since it highlighted the cost of the very economic miracle that sheltered Ben Ali's authoritarianism from international critique.

Several recent observers of Tunisia have established that Ben Ali's rule depended crucially on the governing myths of the economic miracle, democratic gradualism, and secularism, which prevented a clearer understanding of the political and socioeconomic situation of Tunisia to emerge. Similarly, a myth of environmentalism enabled the government to present an image of ecological concern while simultaneously hiding the harmful effects of its economic model—the broad-scale dumping of waste—behind it. Like the facades of democratic gradualism and state feminism, this projection of environmental concern wasn't completely empty. In fact, much environmental administration was established, and useful legislation was passed, but what it primarily did was allow the regime to silence any critique while breaking the very same rights it was ostensibly upholding. These myths then do much harm to the revolutionary project, since postrevolutionary realities always lag behind the authoritarian mirage, not only because a new social and economic order has to be established, but also because citizens have to be disabused of a reality that never actually existed. Ask any Tunisian, and they will tell you that the country was cleaner before the revolution. While again partly true, primarily this assumption inspires a sense of nostalgia for the former regime and frames the revolution as a period that was "unclean" and somewhat a failure. The international community, of course, needs such champions as Ben Ali, and positive examples like Tunisia that seem to thrive under their development plans, to lend legitimacy to the very same. In that way, international organizations were complicit in the environmental crimes of the regime, as they uncritically bought or even helped perpetuate a reality that hardly matched that of ordinary Tunisians. While a recent study found no hard evidence that Tunisia was a pollution haven for European companies, many companies did profit from the lax environmental regulations in its immediate neighborhood. As new trade talks between the EU and Tunisia are on the horizon, accountability by these companies will have to be addressed, but once again the underlying economic model of neoliberalism and the shortsighted politics of growth are not going to be challenged.

The revolution has radically transformed the political landscape in Tunisia. It has rewritten the very principles of government with an inspiring new constitution that guarantees all citizens a "healthy and balanced environment." But what revolutionaries throughout the ages have learned is that governance exists beyond political systems and legal documents, that it is engrained in an unequal international order and its local manifestations. The specters of authoritarianism in Tunisia still haunt people's minds, but they also dwell in their bodies and landscapes in real, tangible ways through the scars of torture, hunger, poverty, illness, and the impacts of waste and pollution. Environmental NGOs are therefore not merely concerned with the ecology; they do the work of truth finding in Tunisia. And slowly, as environmental crimes are uncovered, the call for a clean and healthy environment is being heard.

ADDITIONAL RESOURCES

Clapp, Jennifer. "Distancing of Waste: Overconsumption in a Global Economy." In *Confronting Consumption,* edited by Thomas Princen, Michael Maniates, and Ken Conca. Cambridge, MA: MIT Press, 2002.

Cohen, William A., and Ryan Johnson. *Filth Dirt, Disgust, and Modern Life.* Minneapolis: University of Minnesota Press, 2005.

Dauvergne, Peter. *The Shadows of Consumption: Consequences for the Global Environment.* Cambridge, MA: MIT Press, 2008.

Dürr, Eveline, and Rivke Jaffe. *Urban Pollution: Cultural Meanings, Social Practices.* New York: Berghahn Books, 2014.

Hibou, Béatrice. 2011. *Force of Obedience: The Political Economy of Repression in Tunisia.* Cambridge: Polity Press.

. . .

SIAD DARWISH is a Doctoral Candidate in the Anthropology program at Rutgers University. His dissertation examines the environmental legacies of authoritarianism in postrevolutionary Tunisia. He holds an MA in the Anthropology of Development from the University of Sussex and has worked as an activist across the Middle East and North Africa.

PART V

——————

Africa in the World Today

INTRODUCTION

Africans—and their ideas, innovations, and insights—are central to many contemporary conversations throughout the globe. We profiled some of these key figures in earlier sections: eminent philosopher Ibn Khaldun, Noble Prize–winning activist Leymah Gbowee, renowned former Tanzanian president Julius Nyerere, and award-winning chef Marcus Samuelsson. Here we showcase the pathways and contributions of some other notable Africans. Mo Ibrahim is one of the wealthiest people in the world—an extraordinarily successful entrepreneur and committed philanthropist. In his interview with Stuart Reid, he shares his thoughts about business, success, the role of government, the importance of education, and the future of the African continent. Keiso Matashane-Marite is perhaps less well known, but her story about her remarkable personal journey from a humble village in rural Lesotho to the formidable corridors of the United Nations is quite compelling. Readers will also learn how and why she became a fierce advocate for gender justice. Meschac Gaba is a much-admired artist from Benin who has displayed his work around the globe. Kerryn Greenberg explores his signature work, *Museum of Contemporary African Art*—a twelve-room installation that challenged presumed boundaries between art and life, public and private, and observation and participation.

Other key contributions of Africa and Africans to the contemporary world are more collective—the product of numerous people, actions, and initiatives. Nollywood, an extraordinarily popular genre of films produced in Nigeria, has become one of the most recognized African art forms in the world today. Onookome Okome examines the genesis and genius of Nollywood, in part through a study of one of its earliest and most famous films, *Living in Bondage*. African religious practices have also circulated across the globe, surfacing in sometimes unexpected places—like Philadelphia. Cheikh Anta Babou explains the mystery of how and why African forms of Sufi Islam have circulated—and resonated—far beyond their origins on the African continent. He recounts the lives and travels of two Senegalese Sufi masters, the late Murid and Tijani shaykhs Abdoulaye Dieye and Hassan Cisse, both of whom eventually became renowned proselytizers in the United States.

As readers will be aware of from earlier chapters, Africans have long traveled as individuals and in groups around the world, both forcibly and voluntarily. In some parts of the world, the size and similarities among certain African migrants have produced common ways of being in and seeing the world. "Afropolitanism" is a term coined just a few years ago to describe wealthy, cosmopolitan Africans who traverse the world for business and pleasure. Obadias Ndaba met with some self-identified Afropolitans in New York, who explain that Afropolitanism is at once a celebration of their African identity and a challenge to enduring derogative representations of Africa and Africans.

The section—and the volume—concludes with a photo essay by Salem Mekuria, of Awra Amba, a model "utopian" community in Ethiopia. Despite the many accomplishments and contributions of Africans past and present to the work documented in this book, the negative stories of crisis, conflict, and utter hopelessness still dominate media and popular images of the continent. Such being the case, it seems fitting to end on a note of hope—a reminder that Africa can also be a source of inspiration for models of more generous, equitable, and peaceful ways to live in the world.

Profile

AFRICA CALLING: A CONVERSATION
WITH MO IBRAHIM

Stuart Reid

Abstract: In this interview, Sudanese entrepreneur and philanthropist Mo Ibrahim reflects on the pathways of his extraordinary success and the challenges to economic growth on the continent.

Keywords: entrepreneurship, state policies, corruption, infrastructure

BORN IN NORTHERN SUDAN IN 1946, Mo Ibrahim received a scholarship to Alexandria University, in Egypt, and graduated with a degree in electrical engineering in 1968. After several years working for Sudan's state telecommunications company in Khartoum, he left for the United Kingdom to study mobile communications, first at the University of Bradford, for his master's degree, and then at the University of Birmingham, for his PhD. He spent several years at British Telecom before quitting in frustration, and in 1989 he founded his first company, Mobile Systems International, or MSI, which provided software and advice for cellular networks. His second company, Celtel, created its own cellular networks across sub-Saharan Africa and eventually served twenty-four million customers in fourteen countries. After selling Celtel in 2005, he established the Mo Ibrahim Foundation, which publishes an index of African governance and awards cash prizes to African leaders who leave office peacefully. Ibrahim spoke to *Foreign Affairs* deputy managing editor Stuart Reid in November 2014.

What are the most important qualities for an entrepreneur to have?
The initiative to try to do something that other people shied away from. That self-belief, that can-do spirit—that nothing is impossible. Then there's focus: if you start the mission, you need to eat, drink, and sleep it.

Are entrepreneurs successful because of their own personal qualities or the context they find themselves in?

They complement each other. I left Sudan when I was twenty-five or twenty-six years old. If I had stayed, I would never have ended up being an entrepreneur. You can have the qualities, but if you don't have the environment, you just wither away. It's like a fish: take it out of water, it will not survive.

Why would things not have worked out had you stayed in Sudan?

It was a stifling society, with government controlling all aspects of life. You could not get funding for any sort of project. There was no infrastructure to support you. And there were a lot of social pressures to just take a government job and have some babies, and that's it.

Were there times in your career when you thought you would fail?

Many times. There were times when we really ran out of money. Our problem was always funding, because all our operations were growing at a breakneck speed. We needed to double our investments almost every year, because that's the way that growth would happen. The financial markets were not very friendly to Africa or to telecom. Remember, 2000 was the year of the dot-com bust. The telecom industry lost about $2 trillion in market capital at that time. We had the double whammy: being a telephone company and being African.

Are there Africa-specific inhibitions to entrepreneurs?

The picture varies from country to country, but in general, there is a lack of infrastructure—good roads or power, for example. This can be an impediment. We had so many radio sites, these stations you have to have everywhere for mobile. The vast majority of them didn't have power, so we had to put in generators. And if you put in generators, you need backups for these generators. You also need batteries. And you need somebody to go every morning to each one of those sites to supply fuel and put in the batteries. These are not very accessible locations. Imagine the huge effort you have to put in just to keep your services on. So lack of infrastructure is a problem. It can be overcome; we overcame it. But what is interesting is that it generated a lot of other businesses around us in each country, where we dealt with supplying the generators or maintaining them.

Did it help that you didn't need much infrastructure?

What mattered was the extreme need for this service. Africa is a huge continent. When we started, there were about three million fixed lines serving over 950 million people. Congo had three thousand fixed lines but

55 million people. Postal service doesn't work, unless you're happy to wait for a month to get the message. Roads are not practical in Africa. If you want to get the message from A to B, it's a real pain in the neck. So a phone call is worth a lot, because of the lack of alternatives. But it's terribly expensive to lay fiber or copper over these expanses and connect it to every home. If you put up a mobile station, immediately you can service every single house within one hundred square miles. In a few months, you can cover the capital city—every home and every single road in that city. That's why we were able to leapfrog: because the technology met the need.

What can Africa and the developing world more broadly do to create a climate that's friendly to economic growth?

Rule of law is the most important element in any civil society. To build a successful country, we need to have rule of law. And rule of law is not just about writing a beautiful constitution or set of laws. It is also about the independence of the judiciary. It's about institutions. It's about respect for rights—human rights, social, economic rights, and so forth.

Were there times in your own career when you had difficulty operating in a certain country without a strong rule of law?

Absolutely. We operated during the civil wars in Sierra Leone and Congo. What helped us was that all competing parties perceived a benefit: they really needed mobile communications. So they left us alone. Our infrastructure was never damaged or looted.

In other countries, where telecom was a monopoly of the government when we came in, problems originated from a lack of appreciation for the role of the private sector. You end up with a regulator who comes from the incumbent, and they perceive us as a competitor. But it's interesting: we had three situations in three countries where we had to take the government to local courts for infringement of our contract. In all three cases, we won. If anything, that shows that there can be reasonable rule of law in a country even when administrations sometimes misbehave.

What did you do when government officials asked your employees for bribes?

We had a discussion with the board when we started. We said, "It's not enough for the board sitting in its nice, cozy headquarters in Europe to make statements about anticorruption. What is needed is to offer support to our local people." Because who comes under pressure for bribes? It's not the guys at the top of the company but the people operating in the country. And each operation is actually a local company headed by a CEO. The scheme we came up with was very simple. We said that the CEO and the local management did not have the power to sign any check in excess of $30,000. It was intentionally quite low to make sure that when a minister or a senior official came to put pressure on the CEO, he could say, "You're asking for two million? I need to write to the board to ask for permission." No president or prime minister would dare to submit a request to ask for a bribe.

Your background is in electrical engineering. How did having that scientific expertise affect the way you ran your companies?

My first company, MSI, was a consulting company. I didn't even know how to read a balance sheet. I was an engineer. I just wanted my freedom. British Telecom was a huge bureaucracy and failed to see the future of communications, and I just got fed up working there. So I said, "OK, what I know is how to grow a network, and I am going to do that."

Then I had too much work. I couldn't handle it by myself, so I brought on some more engineers. I didn't have a marketing department, I didn't have an HR department, and I didn't have a finance department. We were just a bunch of engineers selling our services. In a short time, I had a major operation. I knew I didn't have the business background, and I did seek help. But in the first years, I managed the company's cash flow, which was easy for me. I found this was just common sense. And I made every engineer in my company a shareholder. That was something I felt strongly about—that we needed to build a committed team. That proved to be a great thing, because we had a high retention rate and complete devotion from our work force.

I'm on the board of London Business School, and sometimes they ask me to give a lecture here or there about how to run businesses—when I didn't have any business training other than common sense and learning on the job. But it seems to me that's the essential thing. We do not need to trouble our heads with too much Harvard Business School or London Business School teaching.

Do founders make good executives?

It depends. I'm not really the dictatorial type. I don't have a big ego. If you don't have a big ego as a founder, you can be a wonderful executive because you are willing to listen. Once you listen to everybody, and then decisions are made, then all of us need to row in that direction. That's how companies move forward. Provided you don't let your ego stand between you and common sense or suggestions, then founders can be good executives.

How important is entrepreneurship, not just for firms and industries but for the economy as a whole?

It is vital. Where will jobs come from? The government won't produce jobs. Governments in Africa are bloated and need to shed jobs, and most of the jobs are created by small businesses. Everywhere, even now in Germany and Europe and all developed economies, it is small companies that are creating the jobs. Look at some of the greatest champions of business in America: your tech companies. All those firms were start-up companies twenty years ago or so. These would provide innovative solutions, jobs, wealth, and so on.

What, if anything, can governments do to increase the scale and quality of entrepreneurship in their countries?

To be honest, I think government cannot do much other than trying to help develop the atmosphere. Africa is a little bit different from the United States, because you're at a different stage of development. Entrepreneurship is already deeply rooted in your society. You have a massive community of venture-capital angels; this thing is lacking in Africa. We don't have strong private-equity or venture-capital funds, which look for investors, and mentor and finance and help pick winners. The government cannot play that role, frankly, because the government is not qualified to do that. Otherwise, you're going to end up with massive nepotism and corruption, unfortunately.

The education system is also important. We have a problem in Africa with our education system. It is a relic from the past. The education system was meant to create clerks to help the administrative role of the colonial power. So the emphasis was on neat handwriting and how to write good reports and things like that, and if you move further, then you study Shakespeare and Molière. But we don't have enough engineers and scientists. Two percent of African university graduates study agriculture, when 70 percent of our people are living off the land. Obviously, we have a problem. How many engineers and scientists do we produce? Very few. Something like 30 percent of our graduates just study literature, which is interesting, but how do you build power stations, build roads, build dams, build the continent unless you have the skills?

Some of the funding for what became Celtel came from governments in the form of development funds. Can the government play a role as an early-stage investor?

No, because the state has no money and so many demands. Look, if you're running a country like Burkina Faso or Mali, you have demands for health, education, roads, power. How much capacity do you have to support entrepreneurs there? Financially, it's difficult.

Don't forget that those guys gave up the licenses to use telecom because they couldn't do it themselves. The telecom industry had a terrible time because they were government-run departments and the largest customers were [other] government departments. The government departments never paid their bills, because if you're the minister of education, you need to build schools, you need to publish books, and you need to pay teachers. You know that the telecoms cannot cut off your service. That meant that the telecom department was starved for cash, so it could not invest in new technology, like mobile communication. Remember, at the beginning, everybody thought mobile communication was something for the elite, not for the people. So it was very convenient for the government to say, "OK, I'm going to focus on basic services and let that crazy investor have a go at this. And if he succeeds, I'm going to charge him a lot of taxes and licenses and make some money out of him."

You've operated in many different countries. Is it easier being an entrepreneur in some of them as opposed to others?

Yes, of course. For me, it has always been about the rule of law. When things are clear, and you have a process of bidding and licensing that is open and clean, it's important. When you're not wrapped up in red tape—that's really important. In some countries, it was very straightforward, and the governments understood exactly what we were trying to do and gave us support. And in some countries, we were met with suspicion—that any businessman coming here is essentially a thief and has to be watched very carefully, and if we can squeeze him, why not? It takes time to build an understanding that you're not really a thief and that what you are doing is an essential service. Then they end up falling in love with you, which is terrific.

Ethnic minorities can sometimes be the most prominent entrepreneurs in certain parts of Africa: South Asians in East Africa and Lebanese and Syrians in West Africa. Have these groups been constrained by governments that are suspicious of outsiders?

Not really. Most of those minorities are involved in trade, manufacturing, transport, services, and so forth. They are entrepreneurial, and they helped a lot to kick off economies. I think immigrants are a wonderful resource for any country, because by their nature they are entrepreneurial. I mean, you leave your village and jump on a ship and go somewhere else to start a new life away from your family and friends—it shows character. Immigrants everywhere have been a wonderful bonus for the host countries. Sometimes it amazes me how anti-immigration feelings arise in Europe or the United States, when immigration has been wonderful for business.

The only difference in Africa is that many of those immigrants did not necessarily integrate themselves completely in the country. They kept their passports. Very few of them acquired the local nationality. You'll find third-generation or fourth-generation families still with the Lebanese or the Indian passport. That's what produced the issue of whether you are part of the country. It's understandable; some of those people are not sure about the political situation going forward. What Idi Amin did with the Indians [expelling them from Uganda in 1972] was not helpful. But it's a mutual problem.

Is it fair to say that Africa has a democratic deficit?

I don't think so. Actually, participation has been one of the most improved parameters in our index. A lot of Africans actually live in a much better society now. Still, we have quite a handful of countries where some presidents just do not go away.

Power is very seductive. If you control a country for some time, then there comes a point where you feel indispensable. You become part of the landscape. Some leaders, of course, have also committed crimes, and they have blood on their hands. Or they have secret accounts with stolen money. And so if they leave, people will come after them. So they just don't leave. Like in Sudan: if you leave, you end up at the International Criminal Court. Staying in power is a form of insurance policy against the long arm of the law.

How can leaders be convinced to leave office? Both Rwanda and Congo, for example, have presidents who have hinted that they might change the constitution to stay in office.

They are two different cases. I know there's some criticism against President [Paul] Kagame, but one has to accept that he really managed to steer his country and was successful in the development of Rwanda. People admire that. That should be his legacy, and I hope he makes the right decision. Congo is a bit different, because I don't think the president there has succeeded in building his nation. Congo is dysfunctional. It's a very fragile state. I think it's very important for the sake of his own people that the president there just leaves peacefully. We'll hope to find better leadership. Somehow, that country needs to be put together again.

How much is the colonial era a factor at this point?

The colonial factor complicated matters, because it created a number of bogus borders. Many of the borders of the current African states don't necessarily follow demographic lines or natural land features; they're just compromises between various colonial powers in the race for colonization. These sorts of deals sometimes happened between two drunk pinheads in a tent in the evening, sipping gin and getting a map out and drawing lines across a map. So when independent Africa was born in the fifties, it was born with that big problem. One of the worst things was the lack of the natural development of a democratic movement. When people left, they left in a hurry and did not pay much attention to what they left behind.

Is creative destruction always a net plus for the economy, society, and employment?

It ought to be that way. I know the current debate now is about whether new technology is destroying jobs or not, and maybe the jury is still out on that. But if you look at all the major disruptions in the past, yes, there was upheaval at the beginning, but then, somehow, we managed to create more jobs once we adapted to the new disruptive technology. But I think we're now going into some uncharted waters, with intelligent machines coming. Are we ending up with a society where a few of us who are well equipped to work with and develop these new intelligent machines will end up rich while the majority of people will be out of work? I really don't know. But I am anxious.

NOTE

This interview has been edited and condensed. It was originally published in *Foreign Affairs*, January/February 2015. Reprinted with the kind permission of the publisher.

ADDITIONAL RESOURCES

Auletta, Ken. "The Dictator Index." *New Yorker,* March 7, 2011.

French, Howard W. *A Continent for the Taking: The Tragedy and Hope of Africa.* New York: Knopf, 2007.

Meredith, Martin. *The Fate of Africa: A History of the Continent since Independence.* New York: Public Affairs, 2011.

Radelet, Steven. *Emerging Africa: How 17 Countries Are Leading the Way.* Baltimore, MD: Center for Global Development, 2010.

. . .

STUART REID is a deputy managing editor at *Foreign Affairs* magazine, where he edits essays and reviews on a wide range of topics. In his freelance capacity, he has written for a number of publications, including *The Atlantic, Bloomberg Businessweek, Politico Magazine, Washington Monthly,* the *New Republic,* and *Slate.* He received his bachelor's degree in government from Dartmouth College.

From Lesotho to the United Nations

THE JOURNEY OF A
GENDER JUSTICE ADVOCATE

Keiso Matashane-Marite

Abstract: Injustices leveled against women and girls in Africa are deeply rooted in the social, economic, and political landscape of the continent and are often justified in the name of culture. The fight for gender equality and women's rights has been a personal call for one woman whose journey for social change began in a small village in the mountain kingdom of Lesotho. The journey takes the author through the streets of the capital to the corridors of the United Nations in a quest for gender justice.

Keywords: Gender justice, women's empowerment, development, human rights, child marriage

MY EARLY YEARS

Looking back on my life, I realize that the spark for gender justice was ignited early on, in my formative years. My life as a young girl in the 1970s in a village in Lesotho was a mixed bag of fun and challenges. Lesotho, home to approximately 1.9 million people, is one of the three remaining African kingdoms recognized as sovereign and independent states (the other two being Swaziland and Morocco). It is a mountainous country, landlocked within the Republic of South Africa, with about 80 percent of its population residing in rural and remote areas that have minimal infrastructural access. As a result, the availability and quality of services are limited. The economy depends on subsistence farming and remittances from migrant laborers in the neighboring South African mining and agricultural sector.

In the village where I grew up, we made do with what was available. On a good day, I played with friends from morning to late afternoon without giving a care to what was going on around us. This risked our getting a good hiding from the adults for extending our playing and not performing our assigned daily chores. Village life required that adults and children carry out a range of chores that were assigned along lines of gender, age, ability, and, to some extent, talent. Somehow everyone knew what was expected of them to fulfill their household and communal responsibilities. Occasionally delinquent adults "forgot" to do their part, failing to provide resources for the maintenance of their families. As a girl, I was expected to collect the household water, gather fuel for cooking (dried cow dung or firewood), and pick wild vegetables for dinnertime relish (my favorite chore, since I would perform it in the company of my female age mates). We seldom picked wild vegetables in solitude, since they grew in remote places away from the village. With the wisdom of hindsight I now realize that adults were protecting us young girls from "boogeymen" who preyed on and molested children, and also from possible abduction by delinquent young men. These men never made an age distinction in their pursuit of "mischief"—later to be defended as an attempt to marry a wife. How ten-year-old girls could be perceived as candidates for marriage beats anyone's imagination. Our parents frantically shielded us from these realities by insisting that we perform certain chores as a group.

Challenges of poverty, alcohol abuse, wife battery, child molestation, poor health facilities, lack of transportation, and scarcity of energy, clean water, and sanitation were the order of the day. At the time, I was young and arguably a bit too naive to understand the extent of these challenges and the effects they had on members of my community. It was not until I was twelve years old that I began to be aware of the anomalies of life around me. Notwithstanding, for a good part of my childhood I stayed with an aunt—a true matriarch, who in my eyes could do no wrong. My aunt's husband was a migrant laborer who worked in the mines in South Africa, but he rarely if ever sent money home for household upkeep. My aunt had to make do with selling homemade beer and vegetables to make a living. The beer-brewing business opened our home to all sorts of village gossip mongers and entertaining characters. Some of these characters would try to make passes at young female members of the family when my aunt was not looking; others were sources of useful information; and still others were "criminals waiting to happen."

It was through her customers that I overheard anecdotes about all sorts of injustices happening in our village. I heard many such stories, including one involving a fifteen-year-old girl whose parents, "under a guise of poverty," arranged for her to marry an elderly widower against her will. As the narration continued, it became clear that the girl's relatives and her friends had tricked her into submission. Sadly, she was doomed to a lifetime of unhappiness, since she never recovered from the trauma of her family's betrayal. Other stories were told by customers who were known as "village court lizards." These men often hung around the local courts to "listen" to cases of interest. As they enjoyed my aunt's beer, they would describe cases brought to the courts for adjudication. Some of these cases involved families who were ordered to pay damages as a compensation for the deeds of sons of theirs who had been found guilty of abducting young girls.

I would also hear stories of women being beaten because they resisted men's advances. Sadly, many of these stories involved women and girls who got maimed in these encounters, while others dealt with women who ended up losing their lives. When considered carefully and with the benefit of hindsight, these stories became cases of defilement and of early and forced marriage—criminal in nature and clearly a violation of the human rights of the victims. Why the cases were being heard in the local courts instead of in the higher-jurisdiction magistrates' courts was beyond anyone's comprehension. Nonetheless, all these tragic stories, as well as the hardships my aunt endured as a result of her husband's economic neglect, sowed a seed in me that later determined my career choice.

THE ONSET OF GENDER EQUALITY ACTIVISM

In my early teens I left the village for the capital city to pursue my high school education. Although my parents' preferred choice was a coeducational school, I opted, much to their disappointment, for an all-girls boarding school that was highly recommended by a teacher for its good discipline and impeccable results. (Needless to say, my parents were not amused.) My experience in high school was eye-opening: I was exposed for the first time to electricity and running water, as well as a few "luxuries," like three-course meals, that were unknown in my village. I came face-to-face with "girl power" and realized that girls were as smart, courageous, and heroic as boys, if not more so.

High school taught me the value of justice, of speaking up against abusive situations, and, best of all, of standing up and defending my rights as necessary. By the time I started my tertiary education, I was fully aware of the social inequalities in my community and the helplessness surrounding the girls of my own age, who continued to be victims of unwanted and forced marriages, without recourse to the justice system. Furthermore, understanding the complexities of growing up in an environment of absentee men—with women having to make so many decisions on a number of issues, including their children's education—opened a new world to me. I had never really understood why spousal consent (to be precise, the husband's consent) was sought. Later on I realized that this was made necessary because of my country's dual legal system, in which customary and common law operated side by side. In this system, women were regarded legally as minors, incapable of entering into contractual agreements without the consent of the male figures in their lives (fathers, brothers, and, if they were married, husbands). I also became conscious of the impunity with which violence against women was committed. It was shocking for me to hear stories of wife battering justified, of young girls being abducted and gang-raped and being forced into early marriages without so much as a revolt from the community. I was filled with anger and frustration at the helplessness of the situation of women and girls in Lesotho in the 1980s.

JOINING THE GENDER EQUALITY MOVEMENT

In 1993, I joined Women and Law in Southern Africa (WLSA), a regional NGO, as a researcher and later as a national coordinator for the organization's Lesotho chapter. WLSA was set up to improve the social and legal status of women in southern Africa through research, training, and education. At the time, global, regional, and national human rights consciousness was at its peak, questioning the low status of women and bringing attention to the discrimination they faced in society. This consciousness sparked activism in addressing the lack of constitutional, legal, and policy protection for women and girls. That same year, the United Nations Conference on Human Rights, in Vienna, reaffirmed women's rights as human rights, thus giving women more legitimacy globally to fight for an end to discrimination on the basis of gender.

In 1995, when I attended the fourth World Conference on Women, in Beijing, I was fully charged and inspired to make changes in Lesotho so that women could enjoy their rights, be accorded dignity, and be protected against gender discrimination. The opportunity for me to contribute to change presented itself when the government invited me to provide input for a draft bill intended to change the legal status of married women so that they enjoyed the same rights as their spouses. Through countless consultations and the lobbying of influential community figures for support, the Legal Capacity of Married Persons Bill became law. It was a moment of celebration and indeed of great achievement for me, for this was the first step toward the bigger changes that were needed to restore women's dignity.

Following the enactment of the bill into law, the biggest task before us was to intensify advocacy programs to educate women, and the general public, about the new law and the changes it would bring to their lives. This lengthy process required continuous dialogue with judicial officers, whose mind-sets and attitudes needed to be changed in order for them to administer the new law effectively.

I also worked on two research projects that examined the administration and delivery of justice and how that affected women's needs and rights. We were especially concerned about the court's administration of cases of sexual violence against women and girls. Court officials perceived our endless questions about these issues, which they considered sensitive, to be invasive. Needless to say, our questions were often met with resistance and hostility as we inquired about processes, procedures, and systems that would be followed to deliver justice to women. Our findings were disturbing. We discovered that sentences were not always commensurate with offenses: often sentences were so lenient as to trivialize the crimes committed. Throughout the research process, WLSA embraced the activist methodology—one in which we combined research methodology with consciousness-raising and advocacy. We did this with the aim of changing the mind-sets of court officials so that they would deal with sexual offenses against women with the seriousness they deserve and hand down heavy sentences as appropriate.

As one of the public faces of the organization, I gave interviews to the media about the high volume of cases of violence against women and about the lack of counseling and other facilities for the survivors. I also spoke out about a number of other issues, including a lack of sensitivity, the overly complex procedures that were being followed, and the endless delays in women's cases—delays that gave credence to a mantra that "justice delayed is justice denied."

Our speaking out against the injustice being meted out on women caused several things to happen: Our offices became flooded with cases of women who were poorly served by the justice system. We became a target of criticism from people who felt that women's rights were being pushed at the expense of men's. Our organization was now labeled an institution of "frustrated women who have nothing better to do with their time but to stir trouble." I took courage from this reaction: Our work was beginning to bear fruit! A revolution was looming, and there was no going back. As a result of the heightened activism, Lesotho enacted the Sexual Offences Act of 2003, which tightened the administration of justice regarding sexual offences and increased sentences of offenders while improving facilities and expanding recourse options for survivors.

JOINING THE ECONOMIC COMMISSION FOR AFRICA

I joined the international civil service in 2007 when I began working for the United Nations Economic Commission for Africa (ECA). The ECA provided me with a golden opportunity to influence African policies to implement regional and international commitments on gender issues. The commission's work is guided by the Continent-Wide Initiative for Gender Equality and Women's Empowerment. The initiative was endorsed at the joint meeting of the ECA Conference of African Ministers of Finance, Planning, and Economic Development and the African Union Conference of Ministers of Economy and Finance in 2013. The initiative aims to ensure that the work of the commission has a cascading and meaningful effect on the life of every woman and girl in Africa, irrespective of geographical location, socioeconomic and cultural status, ethnic affiliation, or any other personal classification, while building on the positive link between promoting women's human rights and attaining the continent's economic development.

The initiative addresses three interlinked components: economic empowerment, women's human rights, and promoting women's full involvement in and benefits from the social sector. The underlying assumption is that there are persisting inequalities in these areas that require targeted policy response and robust program intervention. The initiative takes into account and articulates Africa's development agenda and suggests breakthrough program approaches to address persisting as well as emerging challenges facing the continent in terms of gender issues and social inequality. In developing its strategic focus, the commission takes a firm stand in support of African member states' implementation of international and regional norms and standards on gender equality.

I work to ensure that the initiative reaches women on the ground. For example, I am involved in a program that supports African member states in the implementation of UN Resolution 67/146, which calls for ending female genital mutilation (FGM) and all other harmful traditional practices against women. The program affords protection to African girls against FGM, abduction, and early marriage through the development of policies and laws that are intended to ensure an end to harmful traditional practices, including violence against women. Out of the twenty-seven African countries where FGM is practiced, only eight— Ethiopia, Eritrea, the Gambia, Guinea-Bissau, Liberia, Sierra Leone, Somalia, and Sudan—do not have legislation prohibiting the practice. Nonetheless, the momentum created by UN Resolution 67/146 has resulted in resounding action plans to create awareness of these harmful practices and to influence related policy. The goal is for African girls to be able to exercise their human rights fully, so that they can, for example, freely go to school without fear of being whisked off to an early marriage.

On its part, the commission has designed a women's rights observatory—a Web-based platform to facilitate early warning systems for threats to women's rights, and to provide a place for women (and men) to share information on a wide variety of issues. The observatory enables the discussion of strategies for ending women's rights violations and injurious cultural practices, and supports the exchange of information about ongoing initiatives on women's land rights and political empowerment. Thus far the observatory is being used consistently and is showing potential for an entrenched women's rights culture. For instance, two high-level policy dialogues—one on the eradication of FGM and the other on assessing both the Ninth African Regional Conference on Women (Beijing + 20) and the fifty-ninth session of the UN Commission on the Status of Women—took place, with member states providing concrete suggestions for improving the implementation of human rights norms and standards in Africa. Thirteen African countries participated in the first dialogue, whereas the second dialogue attracted participation from nine countries.

CONCLUSIONS AND LESSONS FOR OTHER REGIONS

The Economic Commission for Africa has consistently underscored the importance of bringing gender equality to the center of continental development. This resonated profoundly with my own beliefs as a development and gender activist. To achieve this goal, strong political commitment is vital, and must be focused on programs that can effectively manage a shift from a culture of impunity to one of respect for human rights and of positive actions that improve the livelihoods of all. While I acknowledge the nobility of acceding to international norms and standards, this should not be an end in itself but rather a pathway to facilitate establishing appropriate policies, good legislative frameworks, and targeted programs to bridge the gender gap and instill a culture of respect for human rights.

By developing the Continent-Wide Initiative for Gender Equality and Women's Empowerment, the ECA is not proposing a one-size-fits-all solution for Africa, for this would clearly not work, given the cultural, religious, and social diversity that characterizes the fifty-four member states, as well as the different levels of economic development across the continent's five regions. The initiative has provided hope to young girls across Africa who wish to live a life of peace, free of threats of early marriage and genital mutilation, looking to the future with optimism and enthusiasm. The initiative also provides lessons in setting coherent agendas and in identifying appropriate strategies to stimulate dialogue and action. The commission's work on gender has instilled in me a degree of confidence that Africa is on course to achieving gender equality and thereby changing people's lives.

ADDITIONAL RESOURCES

Nthunya, Mpho 'M'atsepo. *Singing Away the Hunger: The Autobiography of an African Woman*. Bloomington: Indiana University Press, 1997.

Sethunya, Victoria. *How It Was Growing Up in a Village in Lesotho*. 2015. https://www.linkedin.com/pulse/how-living-village-lesotho-victoria-sethunya.

Tripp, Aili Mari, Isabel Casimiro, Joy Kwesiga, and Alice Mungwa, eds. *African Women's Movements: Transforming Political Landscapes*. Cambridge: Cambridge University Press, 2008.

United Nations Economic Commission for Africa. *African Women's Report: Measuring Gender Inequality in Africa; Experiences and Lessons from the African Gender and Development Index*. 2009. www.uneca.org/publications/african-women%E2%80%99s-report-2009.

———. *Putting Africa First: A Summary of the ECA Reform to Support Transformative Development in a Renascent Africa*. 2013. www.uneca.org/publications/putting-africa-first.

· · ·

KEISO MATASHANE-MARITE is Social Affairs Officer for the United Nations Economic Commission for Africa (ECA), in Addis Ababa, Ethiopia, at the African

Centre for Gender. Her background is in sociology and public administration, public health, and gender and development. She joined the ECA in 2007 after working for the regional women's rights organization Women and Law in Southern Africa Research and Education Trust, in Lesotho. Since 1993 she has contributed to research, advocacy, training, and debates on women's legal rights, gender perspectives on HIV and AIDS, and governance and elections in Africa.

5·3

Meschac Gaba

MUSEUM OF CONTEMPORARY AFRICAN ART

Kerryn Greenberg

Abstract: Museum of Contemporary African Art is Meschac Gaba's signature work. Frustrated by the lack of spaces for contemporary African art, Gaba set out to create his own. The resulting immersive twelve-room installation blurs the boundaries between everyday life and art, public and private, and observation and participation.

Keywords: Meschac Gaba; museum; contemporary art; Africa

> You don't need four walls to define your place, to decide who you are.... I am not a director of a museum or the Minister for Culture. I am just an artist. I was interested in creating a frame for my work within the museum, at the same time within another museum; although you know yourself, there is no room, you know yourself you are never going to be there. My job at [that] time was to push people to look and take it seriously.
>
> —MESCHAC GABA, 2012

MESCHAC GABA'S MUSEUM OF CONTEMPORARY AFRICAN ART is the largest acquisition Tate has ever made. Produced over a five-year period, from 1997 to 2002, the work is both physically immense and conceptually ambitious. While preparing to display the twelve rooms that make up the *Museum of Contemporary African Art* at Tate Modern in 2013, I realized how few people had seen the entire work and how elusive it was to those who had not. Colleagues across the institution kept saying more or less the same thing: "We understand it is important, but what is it?" After weeks of trying to translate long lists of objects and multiple installation images into something tangible, while attempting to avoid explaining the work in terms of the space it would occupy since each room can expand or contract, the answer I kept returning to is the same one Gaba originally offered in a 2001 interview with Chris

Dercon: "The *Museum of Contemporary African Art* is not a model to imitate ... it's only a question." It is temporary and mutable, a conceptual space more than a physical one, a provocation to the Western art establishment not only to attend to contemporary African art, but to question why the boundaries existed in the first place. The *Museum* is also Gaba's answer to the problem he encountered on arriving in Amsterdam: that he could not find a museum in Europe where he could show the type of work he wanted to make.

In the early 1980s, when Gaba stumbled across a bag of decommissioned banknotes cut into small circles on the streets of Cotonou, Benin, he had no idea where it would lead him, but he realized his discovery was important. A few years later he began to experiment with the banknote dots, creating painted collages that he initially framed behind glass and later made into three-dimensional reliefs. It was these works that first attracted international attention in 1992.

By the time Gaba was offered a residency at the Rijksakademie van Beeldende Kunsten in Amsterdam in 1996, he had been using decommissioned banknotes as a medium for several years, but it was in the Netherlands that his approach radically changed. In the Dercon interview, Gaba describes finding "another reality" when visiting European museums with considerable holdings of traditional objects from Africa: "I needed a space for my work, because this place did not exist. Amsterdam was the first place I began to crave a museum of contemporary African art. Because I say I do something, but the thing is not in the [same] reality as the place I am."

Before completing his residency at the Rijksakademie in 1997, Gaba presented the first room of his *Museum of Contemporary African Art*. The *Draft Room* (see figure 5.3.1) contained an unusual assortment of handmade, found, and altered objects: a piece of fabric on the floor with carefully arranged cylinders of shredded banknotes and plastic bags filled with banknote dots; a four-tiered white metal shelving unit with chicken pieces and circular breads made out of ceramic and glazed gold; a bamboo fishing rod and glass fish tank with a mirrored base, containing a fish skeleton underneath a sand-encrusted lid; a fridge-freezer filled with whole ceramic chickens; an enamel platter with a mound of ceramic chicken feet balanced on a white bucket; three large abstract monochrome paintings; a pile of fruit and vegetables cast in ceramic and glazed red, heaped on the floor in the corner; and *Swiss Bank 1997*, an old, simple wooden table with golden pebbles arranged on the lower shelf and stacks of coins and banknotes, weighed down with little stones, on the table top.

FIG. 5.3.1. *Draft Room* from *Museum of Contemporary African Art*. Installation shot of Meschac Gaba exhibition, Tate Modern, 2013. By permission of the Tate Gallery, UK.

At this first exhibition visitors were invited to support Gaba's *Museum* by purchasing a small brooch made from a banknote dot and safety pin. This action served two purposes: first, it symbolized the fund-raising activity one might expect with the establishment of a real museum; and second, perhaps inadvertently, these brooches became a marketing device for the project, with visitors to the exhibition taking a piece of the work out into the world with them. It is significant that these pins were made from West African CFA franc banknote dots, which for Gaba symbolize some of his key concerns: the circulation of ideas and objects, power structures, and value systems. The West and Central African CFA francs were created in 1945 for use in the former French colonies in the wake of World War II when the French economy was in ruin. In 1994 the CFA franc, which had been fixed at the same exchange rate to the French franc since 1948, was devalued. This precipitated a wave of price increases, labor disputes, and demonstrations across the region and is the reason why bags of decommissioned banknote dots could be found on the streets of Cotonou at the time. When asked by Dercon why money features so extensively in this work, Gaba responded, "I wanted to confront society with devaluation. Because money is what people like best. . . . Money is the sinew of war; it's the chief. You see, I don't like talking about colonization, but at the same time money can colonize. Maybe that's why I use money, because I refuse to use the word *colonization*. Besides, money travels." One might argue that money, like art, has value in exchange, but little value in use. When devaluation or extensive usage leads to the decommissioning and shredding of a banknote, it has neither use nor exchange value. A banknote dot is the ultimate worthless object, but it is also an ideal medium, laden with meaning.

When Gaba first exhibited the *Draft Room* he had not yet decided which rooms he would make next, but he was unequivocal that his *Museum* would consist of twelve sections. The *Draft Room* prefigures many of the artist's conceptual concerns and the aesthetic approach he developed in later rooms, with several objects from the initial presentation forming the basis of future sections. Some of the rooms are grounded in familiar concepts: the *Library, Museum Restaurant,* and *Museum Shop,* for example, are all recognizable aspects of the contemporary Western art museum. We are even accustomed to seeing architectural models in public institutions that are planning expansion and renovation projects. However, while these divisions are undoubtedly an important part of any major art museum, their activities are seldom seen as core. By placing these aspects at the center of his *Museum,* Gaba calls into question the nature and function of the museum and our relationship to it. By supplementing these sections with others, such as the *Humanist Space, Marriage Room,* and *Music Room,* which are well beyond most museum remits, Gaba creates a space not only for the contemplation of objects, but for sociability, study, and play, in which the boundaries between everyday life and art, the private and public, and observation and participation are blurred.

When Gaba first began working on his *Museum,* the legacy and backlash of the now-landmark exhibition *Magiciens de la Terre* at the Centre Georges Pompidou and the Grande Halle at the Parc de la Villette in 1989 were still fresh. On a grand scale, *Magiciens de la Terre* sought to depart from the hegemonic cultural perspectives of Western European and American institutions and their exhibition projects by looking beyond the so-called centers of artistic practice. However, even before the exhibition opened, critics like Benjamin Buchloh and Rasheed Araeen questioned the curators' treatment of the relationship between "center" and "margin" and noted the exhibition's potential neocolonialist subtext. Several reviews, including one by Eleanor Heartney, highlighted the absence of politically charged work from Africa, Southeast Asia, Oceania, and Australia and argued that this resulted in the exhibition further romanticizing the "Other." Unfortunately, by ignoring the dynamic practices of urban artists in Africa and the diaspora, the exhibition—rather than opening up international art discourse, as the curators had hoped—reinforced perceptions of the African continent as unchanging, remote, and exotic. It is nevertheless remembered as a seminal exhibition that marked a paradigm shift in curatorial practice.

Chinua Achebe famously argued in 1975 in his "An Image of Africa" speech that the propagation of such stereotypes is due to "the desire—one might indeed say the need—in Western psychology to set Africa up as a foil to Europe, as a place of negations at once remote and vaguely familiar, in comparison with which Europe's own state of spiritual grace will be manifest." In a similar vein Gaba talks about addressing "the new day, the new, the now of Africa, an Africa that is not in books," and he does so while referencing the interconnectedness between Europe and Africa. In the interview with Dercon he notably said, "If I create a *Museum of Contemporary African Art,* it's because I say that the people who gave me that kind of education didn't give us everything. They shut me up inside tradition." During the colonial era many educators, missionaries, and anthropologists advocated the preservation of tradition-based practices and railed against the "contamination" of the African artist—attitudes that were further entrenched by the collecting and exhibition practices of most Western museums and private collectors until recently. Today projections of artists working in Africa as isolated, untutored, and expressionistic, their art connected with folk or religious activities rather than a distinctive and self-conscious art practice, have been completely discredited and the important contribution of artists in the diaspora acknowledged.

Gaba takes inspiration from daily life and explains that it is there that "you find new things, you find traditional things, you find everything." In insisting on the here and now and by appropriating everyday objects in his work, irrespective of their origin, Gaba's project acts as a corrective to the history of past centuries.

In the *Art and Religion Room* (see figure 5.3.2) a Jewish prayer shawl, a silver horseshoe, simple wooden crosses, a metal padlock, sculptures of Hindu goddesses, a plastic human skull, boxes of incense, traditional wooden African sculptures, reliefs of the Virgin Mary, a dream catcher, and empty perfume bottles, among other things, are arranged side by side on a large, cross-shaped wooden structure. The museum (or *Museum* within a museum) is one of the few places where this kind of juxtaposition would be possible. It is also a place where looking, questioning, and dialogue are encouraged, and although governed by its own set of behavioral mores, it aims to be a relatively safe space in which visitors can consider their own positions and explore that of others. In the *Art and Religion Room,* hierarchies are further destabilized

FIG. 5.3.2. *Art and Religion Room* from *Museum of Contemporary African Art*. Installation shot of Meschac Gaba exhibition, Tate Modern, 2013. By permission of the Tate Gallery, UK.

by the presence of a tarot card reader in the center of the structure. Referencing the long relationship between art and religion across cultures, this room also mimics contemporary Benin, where Gaba explains most people are poly-religious: "Catholics brought Christianity, but for my ancestors Catholicism and Voodoo are not different. It's just the new religion.... I cannot be a fetishist, but my fetish protects me. You will see sculptures of angels, of Jesus Christ and the Mami Wata, all in the same house."

By removing these items from their original contexts and presenting them as art in his imaginary museum—an action that recalls the historical treatment of objects from Africa by Western museology—Gaba calls into question definitions of art and highlights the subjective nature of selection. We are reminded that a thing is valuable only because value has been ascribed to it and that the positioning of an object in a museum is the ultimate signifier of this.

While Gaba broaches many serious questions in his *Museum of Contemporary African Art,* his approach is in equal parts sincere and playful. When invited to propose a work for the exhibition *For Real,* at the Stedelijk Museum in Amsterdam in 2000, Gaba suggested the ninth room of his *Museum* project. On October 6, invited guests and ordinary museum visitors witnessed the marriage of Meschac Gaba to Alexandra van Dongen. Well-wishers brought

FIG. 5.3.3. *Marriage Room* from Mu*seum of Contemporary African Art.* Installation shot of Meschac Gaba exhibition, Tate Modern, 2013. By permission of the Tate Gallery, UK.

presents, which—together with the bride's wedding dress, shoes, and handbag, and their marriage certificate, guest book, and wedding photographs and video—feature in the resultant installation: the *Marriage Room* (see figure 5.3.3). In this room art and life are indistinguishable, and the relationship between viewer, art object, and artist is reappraised.

The artist's desire to share his fantasy continues throughout many of the twelve rooms. In the *Salon* visitors are invited to play the Adji computer game, an adaptation of Awélé, a game commonly played in Benin (and elsewhere in Africa) using stones and pitted boards or holes in the ground. In the *Architecture Room* the public can build their own imaginary museum using wooden blocks, and in the *Game Room* gallery goers are able to play with sliding puzzle tables, reconfiguring the flags of Chad, Angola, Algeria, Senegal, Seychelles, and Morocco.

While interactivity is a crucial part of this project, collaboration is equally so. Other artists have contributed objects to the *Museum Shop* and their time to activating the *Museum Restaurant;* the role of curators is enshrined in the *Library* (see figure 5.3.4) with a "curators' table," and in the *Architecture Room* there is a ladder with colorful Plexiglas treads inscribed with the names of the institutions and organizers who have presented the project. In the *Humanist Space* the branding on the gold bicycles declares that they were

FIG. 5.3.4. *Library* from Mu*seum of Contemporary African Art.* Installation shot of Meschac Gaba exhibition, Tate Modern, 2013. By permission of the Tate Gallery, UK.

produced for the *Museum of Contemporary African Art* presentation in Kassel for *Documenta 11,* the exhibition that firmly established Gaba's career internationally. While the realization of the *Humanist Space* marked the culmination of Gaba's *Museum,* it was also the beginning of his long-term interest in intervening in the public realm. In Kassel visitors were able to use the bicycles to navigate the city, and with this simple gesture Gaba extended the reach of his project out of the museum and into the street.

Gaba is conscious that context alters both the meaning and reception of his work. Along with a desire to participate in the Beninese art scene and economy, this is one of the main reasons he has remained committed to both producing and exhibiting in Cotonou, moving back and forth between Benin and the Netherlands. Conceptually and logistically he needs both places—Africa and the West—to realize his projects, which results in a hybridity that is evident across his practice.

The task Gaba set for himself during his residency at the Rijksakademie in 1996–97 was completed in 2002, but his interest in exploring social structures and value systems continues as he repeatedly reveals the site of art making and appreciation to be dispersed, fragmented, and difficult to locate. Time and again he challenges the canon, presenting and framing objects that are important in his life, in the hope that they may have meaning for other people's lives, too.

Gaba, Meschac. "I Use Money, Because I Refuse to Use the Word Colonisation." Interview by Chris Dercon. In *Museum of Contemporary African Art,* edited by Bert Steevensz and Gijs Stork. Vol. 1., *Library of the Museum.* Amsterdam: Artimo Foundation, 2001.

Greenberg, Kerryn, ed. *Meschac Gaba: Museum of Contemporary African Art.* London: Tate Publishing, 2013.

Steevensz, Bert, and Gijs Stork, eds. *Museum of Contemporary African Art.* Vol. 1., *Library of the Museum.* Amsterdam: Artimo Foundation, 2001.

Wolfs, Rein, Macha Roesink, and Bianca Visser, eds. *Meschac Gaba: Museum of Contemporary African Art & More.* Cologne: Walther König, 2010.

• • •

MESCHAC GABA was born in 1961 in Cotonou, Benin. He began his career as a visual artist in Benin before moving to the Netherlands in 1996 to study at the Rijksakademie voor Beeldende Kunsten in Amsterdam. It was at the Rijksakademie that Gaba first conceived his major work, *Museum of Contemporary African Art,* a twelve-room installation, which culminated with his presentation of the *Humanist Space* at *Documenta 11. Museum of Contemporary African Art* was acquired by Tate and exhibited at Tate Modern, London, in 2013. The *Library* of the *Museum* was donated by Gaba to the city of Cotonou as part of his project *Musée de l'Art de la Vie Active (MAVA).* Gaba lives in Rotterdam and Cotonou.

• • •

KERRYN GREENBERG is Curator (International Art) at Tate Modern. She leads Tate's Africa Acquisitions Committee and is responsible for formulating Tate's strategy in the region. She has curated solo exhibitions of Marlene Dumas, Meschac Gaba, Francis Alÿs, Nicholas Hlobo, and Steven Cohen and group exhibitions including Kader Attia, Sammy Baloji, Michael MacGarry, and Adolphus Opara, among others. At Tate Modern she has also organized large-scale retrospectives of Joan Miró, Mark Rothko, John Baldessari and Juan Muñoz and curated displays of Jane Alexander, William Kentridge, Santu Mofokeng, Ibrahim El-Salahi, Frédéric Bruly Bouabré, and Guy Tillim. She regularly publishes and lectures on contemporary art.

5 . 4

Africa in Nollywood, Nollywood in Africa

Onookome Okome

Abstract: Nigeria's popular cinema genre Nollywood emerged in the early 1990s and became a global sensation in a little over twenty years. Using *Living in Bondage* (1992), one of the earliest and most popular of Nollywood films, as an example, I describe the essence of this film genre as local and transnational at the same time, showing why choices of subject matter, narrative styles, and themes have endeared Nollywood to the hearts of the local audience.

Keywords: Nollywood, film, Nigeria

POPULAR NOLLYWOOD

By all accounts an African cinematic phenomenon, Nollywood—the name given to the popular Nigerian cinema genre—emerged in the 1990s. Its social milieu is as interesting as the content of the Nollywood film itself. The industry grew out of nothing and has managed to stay afloat for little over twenty years. Lagos, "the city by the lagoon," provided the cultural atmosphere for this growth, while the entrepreneurial spirit of local merchants provided the initial financial impetus. But it was a *New York Times* reporter, Norimitsu Onishi, who coined the word *Nollywood* in 2012 to describe the boisterous cinema industry that was then known locally as the "home-video film industry." The name stuck despite protests from some in the industry who argued that the word was foreign and had nothing to do with what the industry stood for. All that controversy is gone now, and the name itself has become part of the culture of this cinema genre. In the twenty-plus years of its operation, the Nollywood industry has produced a number of memorable films, challenged the dominant idea of *the* African cinema, and formulated a system of distribution that has undermined the presence of powerful American and European distribution companies operating in Africa. In this way, Nollywood changed the discussion about the availability of African films to Africans living in Africa and elsewhere in the world. With the advent of Nollywood, discussions about American and Indian cartels hindering the exhibition of African films have been put to rest. In a little over twenty years, the industry created a popular cinema, defined its practice outside what Nollywood filmmakers call "embassy films" (Francophone African films that are seen only at embassies outside Africa), and inaugurated a new African cinematic register the like which have never been seen anywhere on the continent.

Emerging out of the cultural and political exigencies of post-civil-war Nigerian society in the 1970s, the industry has so far defied the pundit who predicted its early demise, describing it as a "flash in the pan." Between the release of its first box-office "wonder," Kenneth Nnebue's *Living in Bondage* (1992), and Jeta Amata's *Amazing Grace* (2006), two distinct modes of Nollywood filmmaking were established: the old and new. The differences are noticeable in the modes of exhibition, distribution, and finance, and in the way stories are told. Narrative style in old Nollywood is often stagey and wordy; narrative pacing is slow, uncinematic in many respects—more like television drama, especially the soap opera; and acting is more akin to that of the stage. On the other hand, storytelling in new Nollywood is sophisticated and consciously follows the rules of the established cinematic language. But by and large the local audience does not see these contrasts as shortcomings. Both modes of Nollywood film are popular with the audience.

With a population of well over 170 million people, Nigeria sustains the industry by the enthusiastic patronage of this audience, who see the Nollywood film as a Nigerian commodity—a vision that comes with pride and, at times, unease. The Nigerian pidgin-English phrase "This na our cinema," meaning "This is our cinema," sums this up very well. Made from start to finish by Nigerians with the local audience in mind, Nollywood films explore the everyday life of everyday people. Members of the audience are familiar with the stories, which are taken from the "bottom of the street." *Living in Bondage,* for example, replays the fear of what Nigerians call the "the world of the occult," and *Glamour Girls* examines the scandal surrounding Nigerian girls working as prostitutes in Italy in the late 1990s. The Nollywood film *Nneka the Pretty Serpents* reinscribes the place of the Mami Wata spirit, a mythical mermaid, who in Christian-influenced Nollywood films like *Highway to the Grave* is depicted as the Antichrist.

Experts also agree that the success of the industry is accounted for in part by the low budget of the films, which makes it possible for many films to be made. The portability of the video CD and DVD is also an advantage. Easily transportable, Nollywood films circulate quickly throughout Africa and the African diaspora, traveling with Africans, especially Nigerians, as they criss-cross the continent and the globe for different reasons. There is also the unexpected advantage of piracy. Nollywood films are pirated quickly and cheaply in Nigeria and in the African diaspora. Although producers in the industry have been vocal about the dangers of piracy, there is little doubt that this clandestine economy has helped the popularity of the Nollywood film. Distribution is also a big factor: CDs and DVDs are sold directly to consumers on the streets of Lagos and elsewhere in the country. Exhibitions of Nollywood films also take place in "video parlors" in poor neighborhoods of cities and in rural areas of the country.

Typically, making a Nollywood film takes a couple of days and costs approximately US$30,000. The film is made directly on video CD, a poor cousin of the DVD. In the early days, films were made directly, and even more cheaply, on VHS cassettes. Kenneth Nnebue, the father of Nollywood, was said to have imported a cache of VHS tapes for sale and soon found another use for them. Collaborating with the director of a Yoruba traveling theater troupe, he recorded the troupe's performance directly on VHS tape and then mass-dubbed the original for sales to the public. The film, *Aje Ni Iya Mi* (1991), was one of the first in the industry. At first, actors were not paid; instead, they took turns acting in each other's films. But now the industry is more professional. The star system has also developed fully, making differential acting fees for actors and actresses possible. Eucharia Anunobi, Jennifer Okere, and Francis Agu became instant (and more expensive) stars after the release of *Living in Bondage* in 1992. Nkem Owoh, Richard Mofe Damijo, Genevieve Nnaji, Ramsey Nouah, Monalisa Chinda, and Desmond Elliot are household names not just in Nigeria, but all over Africa. Nollywood stars have been guests of heads of state and presidents.

Although the data is somewhat unreliable, Nollywood churns out over 1,000 films yearly, making it the biggest film industry in terms of volume after Bollywood. Data collected by UNESCO in 2006, the most comprehensive to date, put the annual output at 2,500 films, which surpasses the output from Bollywood by 1,091 films. Recognition from the Nigerian government came late, but when it did, the industry was rewarded with US$200 million to help build capacity. Today the revenue from Nollywood and from the booming music and sound-recording industries makes up 1.4 percent of the country's annual gross earnings.

It did not take long before the popularity of the Nollywood film was felt all over Africa, thanks in part to the South African satellite broadcasting company M-Net. About ten years into the operation of the industry, M-Net began a twenty-four-hour broadcast of Nollywood films, dedicating four channels to this purpose. Today, the Nollywood film is popular across the continent, bringing with it the popular perception of Nigerian cultures both urban and traditional. This is also true for the African diasporas in North America, Europe, and the Caribbean. A small number of Nollywood films are now on Netflix, making this popularity even more pervasive. It is not uncommon to hear people in South Africa call out *"Igue"* once they know that the subject of address is Nigerian. No "African shop" in the African diasporic communities in Europe and North America is complete without a small shelf reserved for the sale of films from Ghana and Nollywood. Preference is often for the Nollywood film, with all the sex, violence, and fetish practices that draw the audience into its world. Yaya Jammeh, the president of the Gambia, is a big fan of Nollywood and has hosted a number of Nollywood actors and producers. Increasingly, many Nollywood directors and producers have their films released in African countries. Emem Isong, one of the few female directors in the industry, premiered one of her latest films in the Gambia. Kunle Afolayan's film *October 1* premiered in New York before it was released in Nigeria last year. Coproduction is also common between filmmakers in Ghana and Nigeria, making the market for the Nollywood film in Africa larger than ever before. In the southern part of Africa, especially South Africa and Namibia, the Nollywood film has been appropriated and is now the rallying point for declaring a sense of popular Africanity. Created outside the control of global corporate capital and of the state, the increasingly numerous coproductions among African nations over the last ten years may have given birth to a grassroots type of Pan-Africanism. This is a new direction in cultural Pan-Africanism and may prove to be enduring.

Reaction to Nollywood's continental success has led to the desire by some African countries to create similar film industries, and the idea of the low-budget film is one of many selling points. Uganda and Kenya have at different points called upon Nollywood producers to help with setting up their film industries. In Tanzania, the popularity of the Nollywood film has led to the formation of a cultural institution, the videodisc jockey (VJ), which

Professor Matthias Krings, of the University of Mainz, describes as a key mediator in the consumption of the Nollywood film in Swahili. The VJ mediates the content of the Nollywood film by acting as a compere, much like the *benshi* in presound Japanese cinema. Congolese Pentecostal pastors use Nollywood films as a learning tool for preaching. In Haiti and many other parts of the Caribbean, the Nollywood film is loved for its cultural content. But there have also been moments of disquiet about the popularity of the Nollywood film, both in these places and in Africa. A couple of years ago, a riot broke out in Accra when it was discovered that, in what appeared to be an act inspired by the plot of a Nollywood film, a baby was murdered and its body parts stolen. The crime was blamed on Nigerians, who were subsequently attacked.

THE NOLLYWOOD FILM: *LIVING IN BONDAGE* (1992)

The appeal of Nollywood films is predicated mostly on the themes they deal with, many of them inseparable from the experiences and worldviews of the local audiences. Briefly examining the story of *Living in Bondage,* which has since assumed a mythical status in the pantheon of Nollywood films, will reveal the essence of this appeal. Made in 1992, in Igbo, the language of the ethnic Igbo of eastern Nigeria, it was subtitled in English when it became obvious that it was becoming popular beyond the confines of the Igbo culture, primarily because the story is essentially urban Nigerian. Set in Lagos in the early 1990s, it tells the story of Andy Okeke, who desires to live the fast life of the upwardly mobile class. As in many of the Nollywood films, his life is told as an integral part of the "highlife" modernity that this city encourages—a variety of the African modernity that particularly wishes to shun all that is traditional. But it is a modernity that is at best deceitful. Andy Okeke knows little of what this modernity actually means, and as he wades into the murky waters of the world of the nouveau riche, he soon realizes the danger of acquiring what Nigerians refer to as "blood money." Deeply concerned about the lofty ambitions of her husband, his wife, Merit, cautions against any reckless behavior, but Andy pays no attention to her. Soon enough, he meets an old-time friend, Paulo, who introduces him to Chief Omego, the leader of a gang that traffics in human body parts. To be inducted into Chief Omego's "cult of blood money," he must sacrifice someone dear to him in a ritual ceremony. His wife is the obvious choice, since he has no children, but he is unwilling to do this. Instead, he compels a prostitute to take her place. However, she is rejected during the ceremony when she confesses her belief in "the blood of Jesus." The ritual comes to an abrupt stop, and Andy is given the choice of doing the right thing or being killed in place of his wife. He pleads for his life, and subsequently brings Merit to the ritual site. She is sacrificed in one of the first of a number of disturbing scenes that are now the hallmark of the Nollywood "occult film." Andy becomes rich and then plans a new marriage, against the advice of his parents, who suspect that he had a hand in his wife's unexplained death. At the lavish marriage ceremony, Andy and his new friends spare no expense. But the ghost of Merit appears to him during the traditional wedding ceremony, and he collapses. The marriage is called off, and Ego, his bride-to-be, leaves him, fearing for her life. After a spell in the hospital, he is sent home. Not long after, he falls for another good-time woman, Chichi.

But Andy's problems are far from over. While Chichi enjoys being with a man she considers rich and willing to give her all she wants, strange things keep happening in the home they now share. The ghost of Merit keeps reappearing to Andy, upsetting the couple's life. Disturbed by this turn of events, Andy visits Chief Omego, who tells him, for the third time, that the ghost he refers to is "only in his head." In the meantime, cohabiting with Chichi does not stop his philandering. He soon expresses a desire to take the chieftaincy title to further enhance his social status. Once again, he spares no expense. But during his official investiture, just before he receives the traditional title of Enu-Ani, the ghost of Merit appears yet again. He faints and is carried away. After he recovers, he pays another visit to the cult leader, who demands his eyes and "manhood" to cure him of the constant vision of Merit. He becomes desperate. Feeling the pressure, Chichi leaves him after Merit's ghost appears to her for the first time.

At this point, events begin to move faster. Paulo is killed by an armed gang, and Chichi's friend Caro, Paulo's girlfriend, is devastated. Chichi tells Caro about her difficulties with Andy, and they agree to steal from Andy and use the money to go abroad to make a new start. She steals two huge cash boxes from Andy's home, and then unwisely tells her friend of the sculptured figure "holding a woman's breast"—the repository of Andy's "blood money." They toy with the idea of buying US visas with their loot, but Caro, who has her own plans, kills Chichi by poisoning her drink. On her way to the airport, however, she dies in car accident. Meanwhile, during a contract-signing ceremony Andy is distracted once again by the ghost of Merit. This time he goes mad, and the next time we see him he is eating from a trash bin in a street in Lagos. Eventually he is found by Tina, the prostitute he originally wanted to have killed in place of his wife in the ritual sacrifice. Now a born-again, Tina takes Andy to a church, where he is restored to a degree of sanity, or at least to what he was at the beginning of the story.

NOLLYWOOD, *LIVING IN BONDAGE,* AND THE CRITIQUE OF CULTURE

The success of Nollywood notwithstanding, a flurry of criticism followed after the euphoria of the discovery of this cinema genre died down. University professors, schoolteachers, high-powered public administrators, and a handful of Nigerian celluloid filmmakers wasted no time is telling the public what harm the Nollywood film was doing and would continue to do to the image of the Nigerian people. But Nollywood paid no attention. Frightened by the immense success of Nollywood films across Africa, the critics built up a cultural hysteria and rallied around ideas of cultural nationalism. Ola Balogun and Eddie Ugbomah, two prominent Nigerian filmmakers, publicly denounced the Nollywood film as trash. Like their university counterparts, they also denounced the Africa that was portrayed in the Nollywood film, proposing instead an Africa defined in contrast to the Africa in European-empire films about Africa of the early nineteenth century and the so-called embassy films and literature. Outside Nigeria, the criticism of Nollywood was no less harsh. In referring to the flimsy content of the Nollywood film, Tsitsi Dangarembga, the Zimbabwean filmmaker and author of the highly successful book *Nervous Conditions,* puts it this way: "What you see is what you get." Until 2012, the Nollywood film was not recognized at Africa's most successful film festival, FESPACO, which takes place every other year in Ouagadougou, Burkina Faso. Some Francophone African filmmakers even argued that the success of the Nollywood film outside of Africa was due to its pandering to the idea of the "noble savage."

In Nigeria, *Living in Bondage* was singled out as the Nollywood film Nigerians should not see. It was criticized harshly for blatantly parading "fetish culture"—that is, social acts that involve superstitious beliefs. It was also criticized for valorizing acts of human sacrifice and for contributing to the proliferation of such practices. At the heart of this criticism is the belief that this film, like the others that came after, especially *Ritual* and *Blood Money,* presents Nigeria and the Nigerian people in a bad light to the world. The suggestion is that the content of this film is intended to represent life, not an imitation of life; that the ritual scenes in which Merit is sacrificed reflect reality; and that the sudden acquisition of wealth by the husband afterward is the "cultic" payback for his selling his soul to dark forces. Even today, years after the release of the film, actors and actresses are still recognized on the streets of Lagos and treated as real-life representatives of the roles they played in this film—a reflection of the close relationship in the minds of the audience between the Nollywood story and real life. This is one example of how actors and actresses in Nollywood live—one part of the larger social existence of Africa's most successful popular cinema.

The Africa that is presented in the Nollywood film is spontaneous; it is the everyday Africa unmediated by the power of official legislation or global corporate capital. Nollywood is not even vaguely connected to the debate over the image of Africa in Europe, which the cultural mediators dispute and wish to supplant. In many Nollywood films, the African is a global subject, traveling, or pretending to be traveling, around the world. Andy Okeke in *Living in Bondage* is one such character. The Nollywood film is transnational, its stories told from the perspective of those who truly experience the African street and with it the freedom to play multiple roles in different situations. Andy Okeke lives in both worlds, but, as is true of the characters in many Nollywood films, it is his local affiliations that define how he sees and consumes the global.

ADDITIONAL RESOURCES

Haynes, Jonathan. "Nnebue: The Anatomy of Power." *Critical Intervention* 8 (Spring 2011): 204–17.

Krings, Matthias, and Onookome Okome, eds. *Global Nollywood: The Transnational Dimensions of an African Video Industry.* Bloomington: Indiana University Press, 2014.

Ogunleye, Foluke, ed. *Africa through the Eyes of the Video Camera.* Matsafa, Swaziland: Academic Publishers, 2008.

Okome, Onookome. "Nollywood and Its Critics." In *Viewing African Cinema in the Twenty-First Century: Art Films and the Nollywood Video Revolution,* edited by Mahir Saul and Ralph A. Austen, 26–41. Athens: Ohio University Press, 2010.

———. "Writing the Anxious City: Images of Lagos in Nigerian Home Video Films." In *Under Siege: Four African Cities; Freetown, Johannesburg, Kinshasa,*

Lagos, edited by Okwui Enwezor, Carlos Batualdo, Ute Meta Bauer, Suzanne Ghetz, Sarat Maharaj, Mark Nash, and Octavia Zaya. Berlin: Hatje Cantz, 2002. Okome, Onookome, and Stephanie Newell. "Karin Barber and the Study of Everyday Africa." *Research in African Literatures* 43, no. 4 (2012).

. . .

ONOOKOME OKOME is a faculty member in the Department of English and Film Studies, University of Alberta. He has a special interest in postcolonial literature in general and African literature and literary/cultural productions in particular. His interest in African literature includes popular expressions produced on the continent, especially in Anglophone Africa. Okome's publications include "Nollywood and Its Critics: The Anxiety of the Local," in *Viewing African Cinema: FESPACO Art Films and the Nollywood Video Revolution,* ed. Mahir Saul and Ralph A. Austen (Athens: Ohio University Press, 2010); and "Reading the Popular: Onitsha Market Literature and the Practice of Everyday Life," in *Teaching the African Novel,* ed. Guarav Desai (Chicago: Modern Language Association of America, 2009). He is the coeditor (with Lahouicne Ouzgane) of "Encounters and Engagements with Things Fall Apart," a special issue of *Interventions: International Journal of Postcolonial Studies* (vol. 11, no. 2, 2009) on Chinua Achebe's *Things Fall Apart.*

Globalizing African Islam from Below

WEST AFRICAN SUFI MASTERS IN
THE UNITED STATES

Cheikh Anta Babou

Abstract: In the 1970s and 1980s, two Senegalese Sufi masters, the late Murid and Tijani shaykhs Abdoulaye Dieye and Hassan Cisse, began proselytizing in the United States. Their dual cultural outlooks as global citizens straddling Western and African cultural traditions enabled them to appeal to Europeans, Americans, and Africans in the diaspora. These African Sufi masters were able to develop a vision less bound by the local African context and more meaningful to Western audiences, especially people of African descent. In the process they stretched the appeal of Sufi Islam beyond the confines of the strictly religious and spiritual, where it mostly operates in Senegal.

Keywords: Sufi Islam, Senegal, United States, diaspora, proselytism

INTRODUCTION

In the 1970s and 1980s, two Senegalese Sufi masters, the late Murid and Tijani shaykhs Abdoulaye Dieye and Hassan Cisse, began proselytizing in the United States. Their dual cultural outlooks as global citizens straddling Western and African cultural traditions enabled them to appeal to Europeans, Americans, and Africans in the diaspora. They reinterpreted Sufi teachings to accommodate Western perceptions and contemporary ethical, political, and cultural concerns, including environmental issues, social justice, and women's empowerment. As a result, these African Sufi masters were able to develop a vision less bound by the local African context and more meaningful to Western audiences, especially people of African descent. In the process they stretched the appeal of Sufi Islam beyond the confines of the strictly religious and spiritual, where it mostly operates in Senegal.

Most Muslims in Senegal confess Sufism. Sufism (mystical Islam) emphasizes the building of a personal relationship with God through the purification of one's soul under the guidance of spiritual masters. The Tijaniyya and the Muridiyya form the two largest Sufi orders in Senegal. The Tijaniyya, which is headquartered in Fez, was founded by Shaykh Ahmad al -Tijani, a Muslim cleric of Algerian origin, and has many branches across West and North Africa led by local spiritual guides. The Muridiyya is a home-grown Sufi order established by the Senegalese scholar and cleric Ahmadu Bamba Mbakke.

SHAYKH ABDOULAYE DIEYE AND
SHAYKH HASSAN CISSE

Shaykh Abdoulaye Dieye was born in 1938 in Saint-Louis, in northern Senegal—a city with a unique history not only as the first French colony in Africa but also as a center of Islamic learning and home to prestigious Muslim scholars and educators. Following his forebears' traditions, Shaykh Abdoulaye Dieye received all of his early religious education within his family—principally from his father, who was also a teacher and imam. At a young age he was attracted to Sufism (mystical Islam) and furthered his training in this branch of the Islamic sciences with a Mauritanian disciple of Ahmadu Bamba Mbakke, who later became his spiritual guide. Ahmadu Bamba is the founder of the Muridiyya Sufi order of Senegal.

In contrast to family tradition, Shaykh A. Dieye's education was not limited to religion. He went to a French primary school and attended Lycée Blanchot, a prestigious high school that educated many leaders of colonial and postcolonial Francophone West Africa. Dieye later joined the newly founded National School for Applied Economy, which was designed by Leopold S. Senghor and Mamadou Dia, the leaders of independent Senegal, to train extension agents for the planning and implementation of their policies for rural development. He left Senegal for France in 1977 to pursue training as an engineer at the École Nationale Supérieure de Paysage de Versailles (Institute for Landscaping of Versailles). Shaykh A. Dieye's sojourn in France provided him with a platform for the development and dissemination of his teachings as a Murid shaykh and marked an important turning point in his spiritual growth.

Like Dieye, Shaykh Hassan Cisse also combined Western and classical Islamic education. He was born in 1945 to a family of prestigious Tijani scholars affiliated with Shaykh Ibrahima Niasse, founder of the most influential branch of the Tijaniiya order in sub-Saharan Africa. Hassan Cisse's father was Niasse's closest disciple, husband to his elder daughter, and an imam. Cisse would later replace his father as imam of Medina Baye, the holy city of the Niasse Tijaniyya. Shaykh Hassan was educated in Senegal, Mauritania, Egypt, England, and the United States. He earned a bachelor's degree in Islamic Studies from Ain Shams University in Cairo and a master's degree in English at the School of Oriental and African Studies in London, and started in a PhD program in Islamic studies at Northwestern University, in Evanston, Illinois, before interrupting his studies to assume the position of imam after the death of his father.

Shaykh Hassan traveled to the United States for the first time in the 1970s to visit Ghanaian disciples of his grandfather living in New York City. These disciples introduced him to the African-American Sunni Muslim community of New York. Following in his family's footsteps, he sought to spread the Tijaniyya in the United States, particularly among African Americans. Between the 1970s and his death in 2008, Shaykh Hassan returned to the United States numerous times, traveling on the East Coast but also in California, the Midwest, and the South. In the United States, he controls *zawiyas* (Sufi lodges) and disciples mainly among the African-American community and the West African diaspora. Reflecting on his work at a worldwide Tijani summit convened by King Mohammed VI in Fez in June of 2007, he mentioned that he had expanded or helped reintroduce the Tijaniyya not only in the United States but also in Bermuda, Trinidad, and South Africa.

GLOBALIZING WEST AFRICAN SUFISM

Both Shaykh Abdoulaye Dieye and Shaykh Hassan Cisse are the products of globalization and its modernizing impact. Their calling and that of other Africa-based Sufi orders have benefited from renewed interest in Sufism spawned by the search for an alternative to radical Islam and the disenchantment of black Muslims in Europe and the United States with South Asian and Arab Muslim congregations suspected of racial biases. These two shaykhs belong to a new crop of charismatic and polyglot African Sufi clerics legitimized by their skills as sophisticated global citizens. They may be seen as active agents in an effort to globalize Sufi Islam from below. According to the anthropologist Arjun Appadurai, "globalization from below" refers to "the worldwide effort of nongovernmental organizations and movements to seize and shape the global agenda on such matters as human rights, gender, poverty, environment and disease." Agents of globalization from below are interlopers who harness the technology and resources deployed to promote global capitalism to advance a counterculture of globalization rooted in grassroots agendas. Both Dieye and Cisse were savvy users of the language of Western modernity and new technologies. They were prolific writers and world travelers, their organizations have significant presence on the Internet, and they were frequent visitors to US college campuses.

Dieye's and Cisse's pioneering work in the United States benefited from earlier efforts by Middle Eastern institutions and upper-class white Muslim entrepreneurs to spread Islam and Sufism. But it also surpasses these efforts by focusing its attention on an underprivileged segment of American society (African Americans and the new African diaspora) and by promoting theological traditions often dismissed as peripheral and heterodox. Their initiatives are distinct from an earlier process of globalization of Sufism rooted in Asian and South Asian teachings.

The earlier phase in the expansion of Sufism in the West, especially in the United States, was stimulated by the study of the philosophy of Ibn Arabi, the translation of the poetry of the thirteenth-century Persian Sufi Jalaluddin Rumi (by renowned American poets such as Robert Bly and Coleman Barks), and the popularity of Sufi music and art, especially from South Asia. Print materials produced in the West and on the Internet also contributed to the spread of Sufi thought, which now figures prominently on the "New Age Teachings" shelf. The increasing commodification of Sufi rituals and festivals as tourist products constitutes another reason for the expansion of Sufism in the West. An important characteristic of this early brand of Sufism, sometimes dubbed Euro-American Sufism, is its emphasis on ecumenism, universalism, and secular spirituality; its tendency to de-emphasize Islamic beliefs, religious practices, and sharia; and a willingness to promote the leadership of women. Euro-American Sufism finds most of its followers among highly educated white middle- and upper-class Europeans and Americans.

The movement led by Shaykhs Abdoulaye Dieye and Hassan Cisse, in contrast, is inspired by the thought and teachings of black West African Sufi masters, scarcely known in the Muslim world beyond sub-Saharan Africa, let alone in the Western world. Literacy is important, but intimate contact with the shaykh is highly sought after. The work of proselytizing is done through institutions headquartered in Africa, with chapters abroad led by African and American disciples and supported by the shaykhs, who frequently travel to visit disciples in the United States. These institutions combine characteristics of the Sufi *tariqa* (brotherhood) and those of institutions of civil society such as nongovernmental organizations. They emphasize a personal relationship with the spiritual master, collective *dhikr* (remembrance of God through the chanting of some of his beautiful names), music, religious gatherings, pilgrimages, and pious visits. The shaykhs' discourse emphasizes the Islamic nature of their movements, insisting on the necessity of worship and respect of sharia. In practice, however, there is a certain flexibility, justified in the name of pedagogy, for gradual conversion.

MISSIONARY WORK IN THE UNITED STATES

The global missionary work of Shaykh Abdoulaye Dieye started after he moved to France in 1977 and was pursued through the Khidmatul Khadim International Sufi School he founded in Saint-Louis in the late 1960s. From his base in Paris, Dieye gradually created a network of schools that spanned western Europe, especially France and England; then the Indian Ocean, particularly Mauritius; and the United States. In the process he built a reputation as a global shaykh traveling the world to attend international Sufi meetings and fostering relations with Sufi thinkers worldwide.

The Khidmatul Khadim network became one of the most dynamic chapters of the Muridiyya abroad. It reached the United States in the late 1990s. Dieye was invited to a meeting of the International Association of Sufism held in the San Francisco Bay area in 1997. During his trip, he visited Los Angeles and recruited his first disciples there. He also traveled to a suburb of Philadelphia on the invitation of Jewish disciples of Bawa Muhiddeen, a Sri Lankan Sufi shaykh, who died and was buried there in 1986. One of the leaders of the Bawa movement, Miriam Kabeer, a Jewish woman, joined Abdoulaye Dieye and turned her house into the headquarters of the Khidmatul Khadim. Dieye sent some of his closest disciples from Senegal to Philadelphia to help build a chapter of the organization in the city. The chapter is led today by one of his disciples and includes mostly African-American and white converts to Islam. A chapter was also begun in New Jersey. But California remained the nerve center of Khidmatul Khadim in the United States, with chapters in Los Angeles and Santa Barbara and some disciples in

San Diego and Fresno. Oregon also had a dynamic cell. These chapters are now struggling to maintain their cohesion after the leadership dispute that erupted after Dieye's death in 2002 and the tensions between upper-class white and working-class African-American disciples.

In the United States, Dieye continued to promote some of the ideas he developed in Europe such as the universalism of Ahmadu Bamba's message and nonviolence, but he also championed new ideas such as ecumenism and healing. These last two concepts were central to his ministry in North America and were germane to the country's multiculturalism, religious diversity, and history of racial struggle. Dieye welcomed disciples of all stripes, stressing the Qur'anic notion of People of the Book and Abrahamic tradition, which conceives of Jews, Muslims, and Christians as worshippers of the same God who belong to the same religious tradition. He recruited disciples from the white as well as African-American communities. Many among those who joined him had some experience with Islam or Sufism. Some were former followers of Elijah Muhammad of the Nation of Islam or readers of Ibn Arabi and Rumi, and a small number were following the Sunni tradition of Islam.

In his writings, which were translated into English, Dieye stressed that the calling of his master, Shaykh Ahmadu Bamba of Senegal, was addressed to humanity as a whole. He quoted extensively from Bamba's writings to support his arguments. His favorite quote was a verse in which Bamba called "those of the seas" and "those of the land" to join him because he was an ocean of blessings. He did not ask those who came to him to convert to Islam. Some of his followers were Jewish, Christian, or Hindu. Others were not interested in religion per se but in his persona and in the rituals he performed. Dieye visited synagogues and churches, sang Murid spiritual songs with worshippers, celebrated the Sabbath with rabbis, and built links with a Jewish community in Israel. A rabbi wrote the preface to one of his books, and a second book featured a dialogue he had with a rabbi and Jewish-studies specialist at the University of California Los Angeles. He attended United Nations' meetings advocating recognition of the contribution of Muslim leaders to world peace. Dieye met with Jean-Michel Cousteau, son of Jacques Cousteau, to discuss environmental issues. Son of a fisherman, he denounced the deteriorating economic conditions of the Senegalese fishermen confronted by the unfair competition of international fishing trawlers pillaging the African Atlantic coastline. Dieye conceived of the protection of the environment as the third dimension of *adab,* or proper Muslim ethical behavior, in addition to the two other dimensions that govern the relation of the believer to God and his relation to his fellow human beings.

Healing formed another important aspect of Dieye's writings and activities in the United States. Sufism for him was a prescription for the healing not only of people but also of society. At the occasion of his first visit to the United States, he wrote a pamphlet entitled "Healing of America." In this document, primarily aimed at African-Americans readers, Dieye advises his fellow Muslims in the United States to shun discrimination and competition, to respect each other's faiths, to promote higher education for the youth, to be tolerant, and to be compassionate to their wives and children, and to those among them who had strayed. Dieye made frequent visits to young black inmates in prison and proposed Ahmadu Bamba's spiritual poetry, *dhikr* and meditation, the therapeutic application of the hands, and the use of incense as remedies. He claimed to be a spiritual surgeon. Addressing his American disciples, he wrote, "I will free you by the power of the divine light. You will be reborn as Murids and your songs will soothe your hearts and will transform the injustice and unfairness you have been subjected to. These songs will replace the intoxicants that Satan brought to your houses to pervert your soul." In 2000 Dieye was a delegate to the Millennium World Peace Summit of Religious and Spiritual Leaders convened by the United Nations at its headquarters in New York City. After the events of September 11, 2001, Dieye wrote articles in the press reaffirming the spirit of tolerance and peace in Islam and criticizing Arab extremists, whom he accused of distorting the true meaning of Islam.

Shaykh Hassan Cisse's work parallels that of Abdoulaye Dieye. Like Dieye he was involved with international organizations of Sufi intellectuals, as well as with the Organization of the Islamic Conference and other international Islamic bodies. His actions straddled Islamic education, spiritual enlightening, humanitarian work, and international goodwill diplomacy through the United Nations. While he devoted his life to that of a global shaykh and Sufi teacher, most of his outreach activities were carried out through the African American Islamic Institute, an international NGO based in Medina al-Jadîda, or Medina Baye, in Senegal, which he founded in 1988. This organization is best known for its International Islamic School, which has graduated many young African American and West African students. But its range of activities goes beyond education; it runs the gamut from poverty alleviation, dialogue between the faiths, and women's rights to health-care issues such as the eradication of polio in northern Nigeria (where the Niasse Tijaniyya order counts millions of disciples). The institute has chapters in New York, Detroit, and other major cities in the United States and is run by African-American disciples.

Both Shaykh Abdoulaye Dieye and Shaykh Hassan Cisse were renowned for the prominent role women occupy in their organizations. This is not unusual among Sufis, who tend to embrace less conservative conceptions of gender relations. However, the centrality of the role of women in these two organizations is quite remarkable and could be seen as an effort to reconcile Islam with the aspirations of modernist female disciples. The two largest congregations of Dieye's disciples in the United States, based in Santa Barbara and Philadelphia, were led by women: Farah Michelle Kimbal and Miriam Kabeer, respectively. Kimbal, who now lives in Malaysia with her family, is a graduate of the University of California Berkeley and leader of a nonprofit. She was a major contributor to the funding of the shaykh's trips to the United States and was his host when he visited. She is writing a book on Shaykh Ahmadu Bamba and nonviolence in an effort to disseminate her shaykh's teachings. Shaykha Miriam Kabeer was the first disciple to join Shaykh Abdoulaye Dieye in the United States. As her title suggests, she now enjoys the prestigious position of a Sufi spiritual guide. Kabeer is the founder of the Dieye *zawiya* in Philadelphia and the host of Shaykh Aliu Ndao, a former French high school teacher and Dieye's successor, when he visits disciples in the Philadelphia area. The attraction of women to Dieye's calling is not limited to the United States. In Mauritius, where Dieye has substantial followings, the majority of his disciples are women, including his secretary and translator, who traveled with him around the world. These women of mostly Hindu background were attracted to Dieye partly because of his advocacy for women's rights and freedom and his opposition to strict gender segregation and the seclusion of women.

Shaykh Hassan Cisse pursued a similar path. His first African-American disciple was a woman named Sister Kareemah. Kareemah was already Muslim when she met Shaykh Hassan in the mid-1970s. She was impressed by the depth of the young cleric's religious knowledge and his demeanor. Sister Kareemah convinced Shaykh Hassan to open a Qur'anic school in Medina Baye in Senegal to provide training to young African-American Muslims. She helped take the project off the ground and chaperoned the first African-American pupils sent there. Her own daughter, who was educated in

Senegal, is said to be the first African-American woman to memorize the Qur'an. Hajja Ashaki Taha-Cisse was another prominent member of the Cisse congregation in the United States. She met Shaykh Hassan in the 1980s and was instrumental in the founding of the African American Islamic Institute (a United Nations–affiliated NGO) and remains its executive director. Hajja Ashaki has worked for years as an advocate for women's rights and health care in the United States and was the major inspiration behind Shaykh Hassan's work around the same issues across West Africa. She will go on to become a *muqqadima* of the Tijaniyya—that is, a disciple with the power to initiate new disciples. Both of these women, who were already Muslim before joining Shaykh Hassan's congregation, were cultural nationalists motivated by the fact that Shaykh Hassan was a highly learned black African shaykh just as knowledgeable about the religion of Islam as the Arab clerics that ran the Mosque of New York City that they initially frequented. Shaykh Hassan was also praised for his willingness to accommodate their sensibilities as women and African Americans.

CONCLUSION

The missionary work of Shaykh Abdoulaye Dieye and Shaykh Hassan Cisse in the United States illustrates the flexibility and capacity of adaptation of West African Islam. The encounters between West African Sufi masters and the West resulted in a negotiated process through which Murid and Tijani teachings were reinterpreted to respond to Western cultural and political needs. This led to what could be termed, to borrow from the cultural theorist Stuart Hall and the historian Mamadou Diouf, "vernacular Sufi modernity." This vernacular Sufi modernity is made of the blending and amalgamation of West African teachings and Western concerns. Dieye and Cisse were able to broker this transaction because of their ability to turn Sufi teachings into disembodied and portable universal principles capable of bridging space and temporal boundaries. These teachings, developed in the diaspora, are in turn influencing practices at home, functioning as what scholars term "cultural remittances." The example of these Sufi shaykhs documents the belief, now shared by many scholars, that cultures are not object-like phenomena bound to discrete space but rather consist of mutable and fluid entities that can transcend space and time.

ADDITIONAL SUGGESTIONS

Abdullah, Zain. *Black Mecca: The African Muslims of Harlem.* New York: Oxford University Press, 2010.

Babou, Cheikh Anta. *Fighting the Greater Jihad: Amadu Bamba and the Founding of the Muridiyya of Senegal, 1853–1913.* Athens: Ohio University Press, 2007.

Buggenhagen, Beth A. *Muslim Families in Global Senegal: Money Takes Care of Shame.* Bloomington: Indiana University Press, 2011.

Kane, Ousmane. *The Homeland Is the Arena: Religion, Transnationalism, and the Integration of Senegalese Immigrants in America.* New York: Oxford University Press, 2011.

Wright, Zacharias Valentine. *Living Knowledge in West African Islam: The Sufi Community of Ibrāhīm Niass.* Leiden: Brill, 2015.

. . .

CHEIKH ANTA BABOU is an Associate Professor in the Department of History at the University of Pennsylvania. His research focuses on mystical Islam in West Africa and Senegal as well as the new African diaspora. Publications include *Fighting the Greater Jihad: Amadu Bamba and the Founding of the Muridiyya of Senegal, 1853–1913* (Ohio University Press, 2007) as well as articles in *African Affairs,* the *Journal of African History,* the *International Journal of African Historical Studies,* the *Journal of Religion in Africa, Africa Today,* and other scholarly journals in the United States and in France.

Afropolitanism and Its Discontents

Obadias Ndaba

Abstract: This essay examines what Afropolitanism means through the eyes of its adherents, as well as its potential and limits. Afropolitanism expresses itself through the celebration of African identity and experiences. A way of being and seeing the world through one's own eyes and on one's own terms. But beneath that celebration, there is tension and anger over the representational image of Africa in the imagination of the rest of the world.

Keywords: Afropolitanism, Africa, Western world, African young professionals, identity, diaspora, Pan-Africanism

ON A COOL, CRISP OCTOBER day in 2014, I knocked on Adedeji's apartment door on the eighteenth floor of a luxury apartment building in Manhattan's Midtown West. Wrapped in a reddish towel at his waist, he hurriedly let me in. I had arrived just as he was coming out of his Saturday gym routine in the building's basement, so he needed a shower before our conversation could start. "Something to drink? Wine, beer, juice?" he asked as he opened a fridge.

"Just water," I replied.

So I sat alone in the living room, on a sectional sofa, and waited for him. A flat-screen TV set was there to distract me during that lonely time, plus a bunch of newspapers and a mini bookshelf. When Adedeji finally emerged from his room, in shorts and a tight black T-shirt, we left his apartment and took an elevator to a higher floor—the highest, I suppose—and then out through a garden rooftop with wooden benches. The rooftop had a stunning view of the Hudson River on one side and Times Square and parts of the skyline of Midtown Manhattan on the other. We sat down and talked about Africa.

Adedeji came to America from Nigeria for education and decided to stay. He manages digital marketing for a multinational company. He is young, technologically and culturally savvy, and African. He is part of a small cohort of a globe-trotting, creative class of young Africans. They call themselves

Afropolitans. Afropolitans navigate multiple identities but consider their African identity to be supreme. Adedeji himself carries with him a quadruple awareness of identities.

First, he is African by upbringing and family ties. Second, he's a millennial, the generation born between the early 1980s and 2000s, representing around a third of the American population, who came of age during the Internet era and are wired into technology and the virtual world. Third, he is an African immigrant in America, part of the estimated 1.6 million Africans in the country, according to the 2012 US Census Bureau figures, who constitute one of the most highly educated immigrant groups in America and yet remain underemployed due to cultural and racial barriers. Intent on keeping his African roots as the grounding force of his identity, Adedeji returns every once in a while to reconnect with family and heritage. "Africa is home, man. You feel it when you're there," he told me. Fourth, he is considered an African American, although he doesn't identify himself as such. Adedeji was quick to point out that he is "African, not African American," and that he finds it hard to "connect with African Americans," though noting wittily that he knows how "to nod." He doesn't identify with the experiences of African Americans and the historical racism they suffered over the past four centuries, but he admires their struggle and is aware of sharing the fruit of their hard work without having contributed to it.

On the surface, Afropolitanism is a celebration of African identity and experiences. One way Afropolitans achieve this is by just *being themselves*, doing as they please, and escaping rigid societal norms. At several of the Afropolitan outings and social events I attended, some of which are ostensibly called "African socialites," I heard stories of trips to far-flung places. Of vacation and running routines. Of music, fashion, and other cultural trends. I heard things that, in the old days, might have seemed like an oxymoron in association with Africa or African immigrants. Afropolitans aren't the typical African immigrants in global metropolises; they are a privileged, elite class. Afropolitanism has a racial element, too, though opinions differ on this among Afropolitans. Didier, a self-described New York Afropolitan from Congo, considers "Caribbean and other folks of African descent in the diaspora who are conscious of their heritage" to be Afropolitans. Afropolitanism is a mental space, not a geographical one, where Africans "celebrate their heritage and cultures," as Didier put it.

But there is already a heated debate about Afropolitanism and what it means to be Afropolitan. The term originated with the Ghanaian writer

Taiye Selasi's 2005 essay "Bye-Bye Babar," in which she defined the term as "the newest generation of African emigrants, coming soon or collected already at a law firm/chem lab/jazz lounge near you. You'll know us by our funny blend of London fashion, New York jargon, African ethics, and academic successes. . . . There is at least one place on The African Continent to which we tie our sense of self: be it a nation-state (Ethiopia), a city (Ibadan), or an auntie's kitchen. Then there's the G8 city or two (or three) that we know like the backs of our hands, and the various institutions that know us for our famed focus. We are Afropolitans: not citizens, but Africans of the world."

Cameroonian political scientist and philosopher Achille Mbembe popularized the concept of Afropolitanism in an essay of the same name in which he argued that "Afropolitanism is a way of being in the world, refusing on principle any form of victim identity—which does not mean that it is not aware of the injustice and violence inflicted on the continent and its people by the law of the world."

But critics contend that Afropolitanism is a fad rather than a movement. Something ephemeral like a twitter hashtag, similar to the likes of #BringBackourGirls or #Kony2012, which Afropolitans loathe because of what the Nigerian writer Chimamanda Adichie aptly called the "danger of a single story." Kenyan writer Binyavanga Wainaina's disapproval of Afropolitanism was straightforward: "I am a Pan-Africanist, not an Afropolitan." According to Wainaina, "Afropolitanism has become the marker of crude cultural commodification—a phenomenon increasingly 'product driven,' design focused, and 'potentially funded by the West.'"

The war of words between fellow African writers supporting or objecting to the term continues, and it's unclear who is winning or losing. Despite this wrangling, the term has stuck. A number of websites and blogs about it sprang up in London, New York, Washington, and other global metropolises. And Afropolitanism means different things to different people. For Minna Salami, who runs a popular blog called *Ms. Afropolitan,* Afropolitanism is a philosophical concept and an approach to explaining the world from an Afrocentric viewpoint. But what it means to Selasi, Mbembe, Wainaina, and Salami isn't exactly what it means to the African young professionals I spoke to in New York who identify themselves as Afropolitans.

The common denominator for African young professionals who call themselves Afropolitans but are not necessarily interested in its philosophical or literary meaning is that they are proud Africans who are allergic to poverty-porn, emotion-stricken appeals by NGOs for money and generally skeptical of how outsiders talk about Africa. So they drive hashtags like "The Africa They Never Show You" and congregate on virtual groups such as "The Other Africa" or "L'Autre Afrique," sharing pictures of glittering skyscrapers and new highways from across Africa as a counterattack to prevailing reports about Africa. "A tiger doesn't proclaim its tigerness; it jumps on its prey," the playwright and poet Wole Soyinka once quipped, which aptly sums up the weapon of Afropolitans.

Beneath this celebration of the "other Africa" supposedly unknown to outsiders, there is tension and anger. Afropolitans consider the existing stereotypical tropes associated with Africa (misery, poverty, disease) an affront to their dignity, disingenuous and derogatory. Afropolitans detest the fact that their place in the world has been defined in ways they didn't participate in; neither did their parents or their grandparents. They consider the dichotomous labels imposed upon their world, such as "developed" or "developing" worlds, as passé. It implies that one world is the center—the glue that holds it all together. The other world a mere periphery, doomed to gravitate toward the center or hang in the air. This dichotomy is portrayed in a way that renders it a permanent state of things. One part of the world is "advanced" and the other (Africa in particular) is "behind," the latter being the antithetical image of the status of the former. Afropolitans believe not in static things, but in perpetual change and the fluidity of identities and cultures.

The flux of identities of Afropolitans constitutes a heavy baggage in itself—a crisis similar to what W. E. B. Dubois called the "double consciousness" in which an individual grapples with this "sense of always looking at one's self through the eyes of others, of measuring one's soul by the tape of a world that looks on in amused contempt and pity." Afropolitanism seeks to bend these identities toward some kind of harmony grounded in a new kind of *Africanness*. It is a struggle to define what it means to be African on African terms, to see through African eyes and to judge reality for oneself. It rejects a certain kind of soft power that confers on some people the ability to define who others are in addition to defining who they are. Afropolitans want to make being African cool and interesting. Re-taking pride in their distinctive identity.

At its core, Afropolitanism is not so much an ideology as it is a way of being and seeing the world through one's own eyes and on one's own terms. It is a means to own one's personal existential experience of being an African in a world that has a long history of defining you. It rejects narratives of Africa and its past devoid of history and culture. Afropolitans question things—like the narrative that David Livingstone "discovered" Tokaleya Tonga ("the Smoke That Thunders"), or Victoria Falls, in 1855 after he "was paddled out by the local villagers in a small canoe to approach the thundering smoke." Of the surrounding area he wrote, "No one can imagine the beauty of the view from anything witnessed in England. It had never been seen before by European eyes, but scenes so lovely must have been gazed upon by angels in their flight." How about African eyes?

African eyes have of course seen and touched "the Smoke That Thunders" from time immemorial. Archaeological evidence has shown that the area surrounding the falls has been inhabited since the Middle Stone Age. Weapons and digging tools from the Late Stone Age were in use in the area some ten thousand years ago. And the Khoisan hunter-gatherers, who have lived in this area for millennia, may well have been the ones who paddled Livingston in their canoes to make his "discovery."

But African eyes and ears and vantage points have been ignored or suppressed. Afropolitanism is a conscientious corrective measure, a quest to reclaim the African story, to revisit Africa's narratives, to share African experiences, and to showcase Africa as it is, with its cultures and aesthetics. Afropolitans are good students of Aimé Césaire's and Léopold Sédar Senghor's Négritude, perhaps incognizant of the philosophy itself, and stripped of its Marxist ideals, which trade-loving, aid-hating Afropolitans detest. They also ask not only René Descartes's "Who am I?" but also Césaire's "Who are we?" One is universal and applies to all human beings; the other is unfortunately unique and specific to Africans. In asking the "Who are we?" question, Afropolitanism asserts the acceptance and self-affirmation of being *African,* and finding pride in Africa's heritage, values, culture, and history. It's a "counterattack" celebration, rooted in a troubled history between Africa and the rest of the world.

That troubled history and its remnants still haunt Afropolitans, and inform their worldview. One Sunday I sat in the Bronx Zoo with Paul, another Afropolitan from Kenya, who was then working in consulting, and talked soccer and politics, Africa and America, and everything in between. In the middle of our casual conversation on mundane things, history somehow sneaked in—about that very zoo on whose grounds we were sitting—and it made us shiver. On another Sunday in another period (a mere century ago), in September of 1906, throngs of spectators lined up at this zoo to view Ota Benga, a young Congolese man confined in an iron cage and exhibited in a primate house along with apes. A quarter of a million New Yorkers flocked to the zoo to get a glimpse of him. The *New York Times* headlined the exhibit this way: "Bushman Shares a Cage with Bronx Park Ape," and assured its readers that "the human being happened to be a Bushman, one of a race that scientists do not rate high in the human scale." Mr. Ota Benga, from the Mbuti people of Congo, was brought into the United States by Samuel Verner, a Christ-loving missionary from South Carolina. The oppressor was also the lover. Ota Benga was denied his humanity in a quest to increase the power and privilege of his captors—rendered an object rather than a subject that all humankind shares. Such was the level of barbarity and cruelty with which Africa and its people were treated then, making today seem like a period of sainthood for mankind.

That is the backdrop of what Afropolitans grapple with, perhaps subconsciously: a long history of humiliation, denigration, and dehumanization of all that Africa is and represents. Those days are gone, but their remnants gave birth to Afropolitanism. This entrenched view of Africa, though receding today, took centuries to produce. Colonialism did not spring from a void; it grew and intensified by an active framing of Africa as that big, dangerous, backward, needy, and hostile continent that was close to unknowable. A place that can be anything to everyone. Today such descriptions are never explicit, but touting the "inclusivity mantra" can easily blend in with an implicit belief in one's superiority.

When today's mass media associates Africa with plight and blight, there is nothing new. It is a kind of heritage, for it has been around for close to four centuries. That is why Mr. Adedeji is considered an immigrant, not an expatriate, despite being an executive at a multinational company. But people who move the other way around, even at much junior levels, become expatriates. In the global mental landscape, Adedeji comes from a land rendered motionless and in a state of need. All he and his kin supposedly deserve are care, pity, and compassion. Afropolitans want to shatter such horrendous misconceptions. With their ability to blend in with their new cultures while remaining aware and proud of their African heritage, these young Africans are out to redefine *Africanness*. Africa must be what it truly is, not what the *imagination of the world* says it is.

Afropolitanism celebrates Africa as much as it battles its persistently negative image in the imagination of the rest of world. It questions representations. Afropolitans scowl when they come across things like a Congo-focused NGO named "Jesus Weeps Over Africa" or online adverts of the nameless deformed African child with flies in her eyes on do-gooders' websites seeking funds. A continent of fifty-four countries and over a billion souls is perceived as monolithic—all needy, all powerless, all dependent, all exploitable, all tribal, and other negativities, often in contrast to the goodness of other places. This view of Africa creates a gut-wrenching feeling among Afropolitans that is part of the celebration as counterbalance.

That Africa of *their* mind, not the Africa of Afropolitans, is now the universal Africa. In late 2013, I went to a remote high school in the municipality of Donato Guerra in Mexico, about a three hours' drive west of Mexico City, and gave a talk to some three hundred students. The principal had briefed me before the talk on the school's challenges: students typically walk two hours to get to school from surrounding villages, their families are too poor to afford tuition to complete the high school curriculum, and students are not motivated enough because those who graduate don't go that far from the villages. Opportunities are scarce here; the area is poor and lacks modern amenities. I was the first African most people were meeting face-to-face. I plotted my talk to start with a fun question: What do you know about Africa? In this far-flung poor village, the first student raised a hand and said: poverty; the second: AIDS; the third was more nuanced: economic hardships; the fourth: animals. I was struck with this uniformity of stereotypes reaching a place where TV and modern communication tools are still uncommon. Implicit in their descriptions of Africa was the fact that they, too, are better off than people in Africa. Africa has become a measure of privilege, even for the unprivileged.

Afropolitans want you to know that there is nothing wrong with Africa, but rather something terribly wrong with how Africa is treated. At one time Africa is hopeless; at another time it is rising. One day Africa is an economic laggard; the next day it's the world's fastest-growing continent and hottest investment frontier. It is all things at once. What gets under the skin of Afropolitans isn't that Africa is many things—it is, indeed; it's that Africans seldom drive such narratives. The rage of Afropolitans is less about Africa's own failures and more about the ways in which Africa is treated or what Africa represents in the imagination of the rest of world.

But in expressing this frustration, they might present, perhaps inadvertently, another danger: the danger of the single story the other way around. Africa is the land of milk and honey, and nothing else. What becomes of ineffective, inefficient, and corrupt governments? Extreme poverty in Africa is still stubbornly high, at 48 percent of the population. Slums are all too common for more Africans than those in barbed-wire compounds and gated communities. As much as the Africa of Afropolitans is emerging, it is still a tiny island in a vast, untidy, and messy ocean of slums and shacks and corrugated iron sheets.

Eleanor Khonje, of *OURS Magazine,* another critic of Afropolitanism, argued that the Africa of Afropolitans is "imaginary"—an Africa, she wrote, in which "we get to pick and choose what we like, what we think works with our so called westernized minds and experiences, and we choose what to ignore. It's an Africa which we can market and sell well, one which is acceptable to different persons no matter where they are coming from, and it's an African subculture of palm wine cocktails and ankara pant suits which I very much enjoy, and one which I too partake in."

The paradox of Afropolitanism is that in its attempt to upend the existing narrative, it risks just flipping the coin and revealing an illusory Africa most Africans don't inhabit. An unfair brutal history doesn't make its reverse exactly true.

"One should wash one's dirty linen at home, away from the view of visitors," explained Vincent, another Afropolitan New Yorker. Africa should talk over its issues at home, criticize itself, but not go to outsiders to ask them how it should organize itself.

"Bad things and good things happen in Africa, as they do everywhere. But the negative things are exaggerated while the beauty of Africa is all left out," Vincent told me. He illustrated his point with a recent spat between Kenya and CNN after the latter labeled his country a "hotbed of terror" that posed threats to the visiting US president. Kenyans waged a Twitter war, ridiculed the cable news, and won. (CNN apologized.) Vincent wants more of that kind of spirited reaction and confrontation until the rest of the world, especially Western media, start "putting things in perspective."

In their virtual world, Afropolitans react to and share biased coverage of Africa in the mass media with exasperation. They consider themselves Pan-Africanists, guardians of Africa's online honor, which seems incongruous. Instead of Kwame Nkrumah and Léopold Sédar Senghor, they have blogs and virtual social networks. Pan-Africanism freed us from political imperialism; Afropolitans abhor what they see as cultural and economic imperialism. Call it the Pan-Africanism of the hashtag, Twitter, and Facebook realm.

Afropolitans love freedom and independence, but not in the way of Pan-Africanists who once put their lives on the line to end imperialism during the fight for independence. Afropolitans simply don't want to be told what to do. Like whether to return home or not. They want to explore and live where opportunities take them. For Afropolitans, there are different ways to express love for one's country. Being in a country physically isn't necessarily one of them. They came of age in the digital age, where physical space isn't as important as mental space. Theirs is a view of Africa from afar.

Afropolitans don't, of course, agree with such criticism of superficiality. For them, "Pan-Africanism and Afropolitanism are complementary," as Minna Salami told me, adding that Afropolitanism "grew out of frustration with Pan-Africanism," which did not deliver on its promises. For Salami, Afropolitanism is "boosting new energy and spirit into Pan-Africanism" while "Pan-Africanism is encouraging Afropolitanism to be less superficial."

In America, Afropolitans find their home and belonging in dimly lit barrooms in Manhattan or Brooklyn over tequila and loud music. They are kind of African hipsters, with less coherence of ideas but more idealism and *coolness*. They might enjoy a Bob Marley song like "Exodus," in which he called for the imaginary Jah people to leave Babylon and go to "the Father's Land." But they surely don't heed its message. Nor Marcus Garvey's brilliant Back to Africa movement. For Garvey, social equality was a delusion in America, which meant that only one option was available: return home. For Afropolitans, because of Garvey's work and that of countless others, hard work might get you past the walls of "Garvey's delusion." It is time to wander into the world, not to venture out. Home is where you so desire to call home. And you don't have to have one home; you can enjoy a multiplicity of homes. The world belongs to you, too.

ADDITIONAL RESOURCES

Bwesigye, Brian. "Is Afropolitanism Africa's New Single Story? Reading Helon Habila's Review of 'We Need New Names.'" *Aster(ix)*, November 22, 2013. http://asterixjournal.com/afropolitanism-africas-new-single-story-reading-helon-habilas-review-need-new-names-brian-bwesigye/.
Mbembe, Achille. "Afropolitanism." In *Africa Remix: Contemporary Art of a Continent,* edited by Simone Njami and L. Durán, 26–30. Berlin: Hatje Cantz, 2005.
Salami, Minna. "32 Views of Afropolitanism." *MsAfropolitan* (blog), October 7, 2015. http://www.msafropolitan.com/2015/10/my-views-on-afropolitanism.html.
Selasi, Taiye. "Bye-Bye Babar." *LIP,* March 3, 2005. http://thelip.robertsharp.co.uk/?p=76.
Tveit, Marta. "The Afropolitan Must Go." Africa Is a Country, November 28, 2013. http://africasacountry.com/2013/11/the-afropolitan-must-go/.

. . .

Obadias Ndaba is founder of the Jimbere Fund, a columnist at *Libre Afrique,* and a blogger at the *Huffington Post,* where he writes on economics, development, and African affairs. His articles and views have appeared in the *African Executive, Voice of America,* and the *Africa Review,* among other publications. He has worked in microfinance and commercial banking in Rwanda, and for nonprofits and think tanks in Kenya and the United States.

5.7

Photo Essay

AWRA AMBA: A MODEL "UTOPIAN" COMMUNITY IN ETHIOPIA

Salem Mekuria

Abstract: Salem Mekuria provides a photo essay on her most recent documentary film project—an examination of Awra Amba, a community in Ethiopia that has created a new model for development and built a truly equal society. Its experiences hold lessons for small rural communities as well as for all who are trying to imagine a world in which we can eliminate differences in treatment based on gender, class, and age.

Keywords: utopia, Ethiopia, division of labor, elder care, schooling, development

AN INDEPENDENT PRODUCER, WRITER, AND DIRECTOR, Salem Mekuria was born in Ethiopia but is currently based in the Boston area, where she is a Professor Emerita of Art at Wellesley College. Mekuria worked for many years with the PBS science documentary series *NOVA,* and with numerous international film productions focusing on issues of African women and development. Her prize-winning films include *Ye Wonz Maibel: Deluge* (1996), which tells the story of Ethiopia's tumultuous history following the overthrow of Emperor Haile Selassie in 1974; *Our Place in the Sun* (1988), about the black community on Martha's Vineyard; *Sidet: Forced Exile* (1991), the story of three Ethiopian-Eritrean women refugees in Sudan; *As I Remember It: A Portrait of Dorothy West* (1991); and *Square Stories* (2010) and *Square Stories Too* (2014), the first and second parts of a film trilogy about life on Meskel Square in Addis Ababa.

For Salem Mekuria, "filmmaking is a way of being curious about the world I live in. It is motivated by the need to find effective ways of communicating the stories and themes of exile, difference, and the struggle for justice and equal rights. I am keenly interested in processing these narratives through the stories and experiences of women in Africa and the African Diaspora and am committed to representing these stories as challenges and journeys that are specific but also as universal experiences that can speak to all viewers."

. . .

In a remote area of northern Ethiopia a genuine "utopia" is thriving in a little village called Awra Amba. It is located in the Amhara region of northwestern Ethiopia, about five hundred kilometers or a day's journey from the capital city of Addis Ababa. Forty years ago a small group of people led by a charismatic young man, Zumra Nuru, came together to establish this community—to be based on true equality in all aspects of life, where there would be no difference in treatment based on gender, class, or age, where no organized religion would have a place, and where all people would work to support each other and care for the weak among them.

Division of labor is not based on gender but rather on capability and skill, validating gender equality in a country where women are generally subordinated to men. Everyone works according to her/his ability and contributes to the welfare of the entire community. It is very well organized, unique not only for its advanced outlook toward gender and religion, but also for its commitment to education, its program for the care of the elderly, its work ethic, and its responsiveness to the needs of the entire community.

Through its forty years, Awra Amba has endured hostility and violent confrontations from its neighbors and the government, but has persisted in the pursuit of the dream to sustain a viable "utopian" society. The community manages to survive in one of the most conservative regions in Ethiopia. What is most remarkable about it is that its members are not people who discovered this ideal from books or through exposure to philosophical treatises. Zumra, the leading founder and current cochair, is a man who had no formal education, who doesn't read or write. The members' aspiration to pursue these ideals emanated from direct experience of the consequences of inequality in their own families and communities. Their present community evolved out of the struggle to find meaningful and true equality and self-sufficiency over these forty years. Its members are completely unique in achieving such a revolutionary lifestyle. There is no other community remotely like it, large or small, in the rest of the country, or even in the world.

FIG. 5.7.1. Awra Amba, a tiny community of 180 families. Photo by Salem Mekuria.

FIG. 5.7.2. Zumra Nuru, the founder and charismatic leader of Awra Amba, together with his wife, Enani Kibret; and her mother, Enanu Eshete. Photo by Salem Mekuria.

FIG. 5.7.3. Elderly House, Awra Amba. In a country not known for providing care for senior citizens, Awra Amba leads in its innovation for designing living quarters and full-time care for the elderly. Photo by Salem Mekuria.

FIG. 5.7.4. Enani Kibret with residents in Elderly House. Photo by Salem Mekuria.

FIG. 5.7.5. A classroom in a preschool center. The preschool was locally designed and built with local materials. Through Awra Amba's effort, the government built an elementary school for the surrounding communities. Awra Amba in turn built ninth and tenth grades using its own resources, thus eliminating the need for the children to travel several kilometers to the nearest town. This in turn has encouraged students to continue their education while at the same time fulfilling their obligations at home. The community now looks forward to building for grades eleven and twelve. Several of Awra Amba's children have gone on to college, and many have already graduated. This is no mean achievement for this community. Photo by Salem Mekuria.

FIG. 5.7.6. Library reading room. The library offers resources unlike that of any in the region, let alone in a rural setting such as this one. Photo by Salem Mekuria.

FIG. 5.7.7. The museum documents the community's journey over the last forty years. Photo by Salem Mekuria.

FIG. 5.7.8. Loom in the Weaving Center. Zumra Nura, Awra Amba's founder and co-chair, built the community's looms using parts assembled from discarded metal and ropes. The major sources of livelihood of this unique Ethiopian community are farming, weaving, and spinning. Everyone rotates to do most tasks. In this way they provide for their food and clothing needs. Surplus is sold in nearby markets to buy necessities they can't produce. Photo by Salem Mekuria.

FIG. 5.7.9. The community members are highly creative, innovative, and motivated. One of the most interesting examples of their innovative spirit is this energy-saving stove, designed and developed by the community's cochair, Zumra Nuru. The *mitad* (grill) bakes *injera* (sourdough-risen flatbread), the side stove cooks the *wat* (stew), and the smoke outlet heats a tea or coffee pot—all at the same time. The smoke is channeled outside through a chimney, avoiding the serious smoke-related health hazards to the operators. Its cost effectiveness and flexibility are qualities that have the potential to be duplicated in similar locations through-out the country. Photo by Salem Mekuria.

ADDITIONAL RESOURCES

Awra Amba's (E)Utopia. Short film. https://vimeo.com/145472923.
Zewde, Bahru. *A History of Modern Ethiopia, 1855–1991.* 2nd ed. Athens: Ohio University Press, 2002.
See also the following websites:
Salem Mekuria: www.salemmekuria.com
An interactive website: www.visitawraamba.com

ABOUT THE EDITORS

DOROTHY L. HODGSON is Professor of Anthropology and the Senior Associate Dean for Academic Affairs in the Graduate School-New Brunswick at Rutgers University, where she was a founding member of the Center for African Studies. She has previously served as Chair and Graduate Director of the Department of Anthropology, Director of the Rutgers' Institute for Research on Women, President of the African Studies Association, and President of the Association for Feminist Anthropology. As a historical anthropologist, she has worked in Tanzania, East Africa, for over thirty years on such topics as gender, ethnicity, cultural politics, colonialism, nationalism, modernity, the missionary encounter, transnational organizing, and the indigenous rights movement. She is the author of *Gender, Justice and the Problem of Culture: From Customary Law to Human Rights in Tanzania* (Indiana University Press, 2017), *Being Maasai, Becoming Indigenous: Postcolonial Politics in a Neoliberal World* (Indiana University Press, 2011), *The Church of Women: Gendered Encounters between Maasai and Missionaries* (Indiana University Press, 2005), and *Once Intrepid Warriors: Gender, Ethnicity and the Cultural Politics of Maasai Development* (Indiana University Press, 2001); editor of *The Gender, Culture, and Power Reader* (Oxford University Press, 2016), *Gender and Culture at the Limit of Rights* (University of Pennsylvania Press, 2011), *Gendered Modernities: Ethnographic Perspectives* (Palgrave, 2001), and *Rethinking Pastoralism in Africa: Gender, Culture and the Myth of the Patriarchal Pastoralist* (James Currey, 2000); and coeditor of *Global Africa: Into the Twenty-First Century* (University of California Press, 2017) and *"Wicked" Women and the Reconfiguration of Gender in Africa* (Heinemann, 2001). Her work has been supported by awards and fellowships from the Rockefeller Foundation's Bellagio Center, the National Endowment for the Humanities, the John Simon Guggenheim Memorial Foundation, Fulbright-Hays, the American Council for Learned Societies, the National Science Foundation, the American Philosophical Society, the Wenner-Gren Foundation, the Social Science Research Council, and the Center for Advanced Study in the Behavioral Sciences.

JUDITH A. BYFIELD is an Associate Professor in the History Department at Cornell University. She received her PhD from Columbia University. Her current research focuses on women's social and economic history in colonial Nigeria. She is the author of *The Bluest Hands: A Social and Economic History of Women Indigo Dyers in Western Nigeria, 1890–1940* (Heinemann, 2002) as well as articles in edited volumes and journals such as *Meridians: A Journal on Feminism, Race, and Transnationalism*, the *Journal of African History*, and the *Canadian Journal of African Studies*. She is a coeditor of *Global Africa: Into the Twenty-First Century* (University of California Press, 2017), *Africa and World War II* (Cambridge University Press, 2015) and *Gendering the African Diaspora: Women, Culture and Historical Change in the Caribbean and Nigerian Hinterland* (Indiana University Press, 2010) and the editor of *Cross Currents: Building Bridges across American and Nigerian Studies* (Ibadan, Nigeria: Book Builders, 2009). Byfield serves in a number of organizational capacities: Co-Program Chair, The Seventeenth Berkshire Conference on the History of Women, Genders, and Sexualities (2017); Advisory Board, Cambridge University Press—New Perspectives in African History (2013–present); President of the African Studies Association (2011); and Chair of the Association of African Studies Programs (2002–5). Her research has been supported by numerous fellowships and awards including the Institute for Advanced Study, the National Humanities Center, the National Endowment for the Humanities, Fulbright Senior Scholar, Rockefeller Humanities Fellowship—University of Michigan, and Andrew Mellon Fellowship—Dartmouth College.

INDEX

abductions of women and girls, 330–31, 332
abolitionists, 91–92
Academics Stand Against Poverty, 139
accountability: of elites in justice, 115–18;
  for environmental crisis, 316; in epidemics, 266–67; in HIV responses, 265
Achebe, Chinua, 206, 342
Acquisition of Buildings Act (Tanzania),
  103–4
activists/activism: censorship of in Tunisia,
  308, 315–16; environmental, 154–55,
  315–16; for gender equality, 331–34;
  music in, 237–46, 243; for peace,
  84–89; and soccer, 213; women in,
  84–89
Adeboye, E. A., 183–86, 189–90, 191
Adichie, Chimamanda Ngozi, 208, 368
aesthetics: in fabric, 4, 171, 173, 176–77; in
  literature, 208–9
"Africa for Africans," 102–3
African American Islamic Institute,
  362–63
African Americans: and Afropolitanism,
  367; in the Harlem Renaissance, 165–
  66; literary networks of, 207; and
  Pan-Africanism, 59–69, 93–95, 97–98;
  in Pentacostalism, 189; and Sufism, 358,
  360–64
African Association, 92
African Blood Brotherhood, 166
African Diaspora in Asia (TADIA), 72–73
African languages in African literature,
  202, 204–6

African Methodist Episcopal (AME)
  Church, 59–60, 65–66
African Union (AU), 90, 98–99, 111, 139
African Writers Series, 203–4
Africa Progress Panel, 135
Afro-Asian economic engagement, 141–51
Afrocentrism, 98
Afro-Iberians in the Spanish Empire,
  39–47
Afro-Peruvians, 47
Afro-pessimism, 109–10, 371–72
Afropolitans/Afropolitanism, 366–74
Agbogbloshie Makerspace Platform, 278
agriculture, Chinese-owned, 146
Aje Ni Iya Mi movie, 349
al-Bakrî, Abû Abayd Abd Allâh, 17–18
Algeria, 238
All-African Peoples Conference, 97
Álvares, Domingo, 53–54
Amata, Jeta, 348
Amazing Grace movie, 348
American colonies, 40
American Pentecostalism, 189–90
Americo-Liberians, 85
Amin, Idi, 104
"Angola" ethnonym, 55–57
Annan, Kofi, 135, 139
ANPE (Tunisia's environmental protection
  agency), 315
Anti-Caste Journal, 63
anti-colonialism, 73–75, 213, 239–40
anti-lynching movement, 62–63
antiracism, 73, 215

Dakar-Casablanca network, 33–34

Damas, Léon, 95

Declaration of the Rights of the Negro Peoples of the World, 94

decolonization: and Chinese migration, 144–45; in literature, 204–8; in the Sahara, 32–34, 73; in South-South cooperation, 73

Delany, Martin, 91–92

democracy/democratization: beneficiaries of, 126; in entrepreneurship, 327–28; soccer in, 214–15; in the Tunisian environmental crisis, 308

Democratic Republic of Congo (DRC), 289–97

devaluation of currency, 340–41

development: and bioprospecting, 306; gender equality in, 335–36; global, in epidemic responses, 267–68; mobile money in, 287; in pollution in Tunisia, 313–15; in South-South cooperation, 73

diabetes, 262–63

Diagne, Raoul, 216

diaspora: in the African Union, 99; Afro-Iberian, 40–41; Afropolitanism in, 366–74; cultural links in, 207; in Harlem, U. S. A., 166; hip-hop music in, 241; identities in, 49–58; in India, 71–77; Nollywood films in, 349, 350–51; in Pan-Africanism, 90–99; soccer in, 216–17; Sufism in, 356–64

dictators, accountability of, 115–16

Dieye, Abdoulaye, 356–62, 363

diggers. see mining/miners

digital age: Afropolitanism in, 374; artisanal mining in, 289–97; materiality of, 296–97

disease, 259–68, 312–13

DIY (do it yourself) movement, 275–78

"double consciousness" in Afropolitanism, 369–70

Douglass, Frederick, 61–63

Draft Room (Gaba), 339–41

drug trafficking, 76, 130, 135–36

Du Bois, W. E. B., 92, 93–94, 166

Dutch East Indies Company, 172–73

dynastic decline, theory of, 13–15

Early Warning and Response Network (ECOWARN), 111

ebola, 263–64

"Economic Challenge—Dialogue or Confrontation" (Nyerere), 105

Economic Community of West African States (ECOWAS), 111

economic crime, 138

economic crisis, 104–6

economic growth, 118–19, 131, 186–87, 323

economics/economies: in dynastic decline, 10; inequality in, 20–21, 122; of Lesotho, 329; in Pan-Africanism, 97; in public health spending, 264–65; reforms in, 144; of soccer, 215–16; women's empowerment in, 334–35

Economic South, 107

Economist magazine, 110, 119

education: at Awra Amba, 377; in entrepreneurship, 325; in gender equity, 331–32; health, 261–63; in Pan-Africanism, 91–92; and soccer, 210–11; in South-South cooperation, 73–75, 78; in ujamaa, 106–7; for women, 86

elites: accountability of, 115–18; Afropolitanism of, 367; and gold, 18–19; in the golden age, 20–21; and hip-hop music, 243–44

emancipation: of Moroccan women, 232–33; and Pan-Africanism, 61–62, 91

embezzlement in illicit financial flows, 130

empowerment of women, 334–35

energy services in environmental justice, 160

English language, 202, 204

enjawulo (reciprocity), 150

entrepreneurship, 321–28

environmental crisis in Tunisia, 308–17

environmental justice: activism in, 154–55, 315–16; defined, 154; radicalization of in South Africa, 153–62; and waste management, 311–13

Environmental Justice Networking Forum (EJNF), 156–57

environmental protection in Sufism, 361–62

environmental racism, 156, 158–60

epidemics, 259–68

government of India (GoI) scholarships, 74–75
governments: coalition, 113–15; and economic growth, 118–19; in entrepreneurship, 323–27; and illicit financial flows, 132
grassroots organizations, 86–87, 88, 156–57
grave goods in the Middle Ages, 18–19
Great Depression, 96
Group of 77, 105
Guangdone Province, China, 143
Guangzhou, China, 183–88, 193–200
Gugulethu Seven, 121, 123–25, 129

Haiti, 90, 351
Harem (Essaydi), 233–34
harems, North African, 233–34
Harlem Renaissance, 165–66, 207
Havelange, João, 215
Healing of Memories Workships, 125
health education, 261–63
health science, 250–57
health services, 77–78, 260–63
henna, 231
Hernandez, Barbola, 39–40, 41–42, 45–46
Hersman, Erik, 276
Hill, Allan, 203
hip-hop music, 240–46
historiography, 12–15
HIV/AIDS pandemic, 259–68, 372
hoodia, 298–301
Horton, James Africanus, 91
Hughes, Nick, 282–83
Humanist Space (Gaba), 344–45
human rights: in environmental justice, 159–60; and epidemics, 262, 265–66; in HIV/AIDS responses, 262, 265–66; and soccer, 213; violations of in South Africa, 123, 125; for women, 329–36
hypertension, 262–63

Ibero-Atlantic world, 41–44
Ibn Battûta, Muhammad ibn Abdullah, 22–23, 24
Ibn Khaldun, 'Abd al-Raḥmān, 10–16
Ibrahim, Mo, 321–28
iconography in textile arts, 176–79
identity: and Afropolitanism, 366–74; in

art, 221–22, 231–33, 235; and bioprospecting, 302–5; Catholic, 43–44, 45–46; Christian, 42, 46–47; in India, 75–77; linguistic, 54–57; music in, 245; Pentecostal, 188–89; in rap music, 242; Saharan, 36–37; Siddi, 72–73; of slaves in colonial Mexico, 49–58; soccer in, 214
Illicit Financial Flows and the Problem of Net Resource Transfers from Africa: 1980–2009, 130–31
Illicit Financial Flows: Track It! Stop It! Get It!, 132, 134, 135, 136
iMfolozi Community and Wilderness Alliance, 159
immigrants/immigration: entrepreneurship by, 326–27; in India, 71–77; in the Spanish Empire, 43. *see also* migrants, African
imperialism, 3, 63–64, 210–11
Impey, Catherine, 63
inclusion: mobile money in, 284; in national parks, 157; soccer in, 214–15; in *ujamaa*, 103
independence, national: and Asafo flags, 179; in Ghana, 97; in the Saharan region, 29, 32–34, 37; in soccer, 213–14; transitional governments in, 114, 115–16
India, 71–78
India-Africa Forum Summits (IAFS), 74
Indian Ocean, 71–72
Indian Technical and Economic Cooperation Grants, 78
indigenous peoples and bioprospecting, 298–306
industrial waste dumping, 313–15
inequality: and bioprospecting, 306; and disease, 266–67; economic, 20–21, 122; environmental, 311–13; in soccer, 217–18; social, 331–32, 334–35; in South Africa, 82, 122, 123, 125–27; and *ujamaa*, 101, 104–5
infrastructure, 151, 261, 322–23, 325–26
Intergovernmental Authority on Development (IGAD), 111
International Criminal Court (ICC), 116–18
International Monetary Fund (IMF), 106–7

Mauritania, 33
Mbeki, Thabo, 107, 131–32
Mbelo, Thapelo Johannes, 124, 125
Mbembe, Achille, 368
media: censorship of in Tunisia, 308;
    imagery of Africa in, 371–73; and soccer,
    218–19
mediation of conflicts, 112–13, 114
medical services, 77–78
Mekuria, Salem, 376–82
memory: in art, 222, 232–33; and the TRC,
    125, 128
merchants, 19, 37
Merhari, Mohamed, 241–42
Mexico City, 49–58
microfinance, 283–84
Middle Ages, 17–25
Middle Passage, 51–52
Mighty Be Our Powers (Gbowee), 85
migrants, African: in China, 183, 184–85,
    193–200, *196–200f3.4.1–10*; to India, 76;
    and music, 245; and soccer, 216–17. *see
    also* diaspora; immigrants/immigration
militias, political, 111
millennials and Afropolitanism, 367–68
Mining Affected Communities United in
    Action (MACUA), 159–60
mining/miners: for cell phone minerals,
    289–97; and environmental justice,
    158–59
mint Ali ould Ali Wali, Sophie, 27–37
missionaries, 60, 65–68, 183–91
Mittal, Lakshmi, 154
mobile money, 277, 280–87
Mobile Systems International (MSI), 321,
    324
modernization: in Afro-Asian working
    relationships, 144; in Nollywood films,
    351; and soccer, 212; of Sufism, 358–59,
    364
Mofolo, Thomas, 206–7
Mo Ibrahim Foundation, 321
Mokoena, Samson, 154, 155
money laundering, 138
Morocco: in the art of Lalla Essaydi, 230–
    35; colonial, 32–34, 35, 37; music in, 238;
    war on terror in, 244
Morris, Charles, 59–69

M-PESA, 277, 280–87
M-Shwari, 286
mulattos, 45–46
multiculturalism, 73, 157–58, 336, 361
multinational firms: in illicit financial
    flows, 130, 131–32, 133–35; in land dispos-
    session, 160; in pollution in Tunisia,
    308, 313–15, 316
Mulungushi textile factory (Zambia), 145
Mumbai, India, 75–77
Muqaddimah (Ibn Khaldun), 11–15
Muridiyya Sufism, 357
Mûsâ, king of Mâli, 18–19, 20
museum at Awra Amba, 381
Museum of Contemporary African Art
    (Gaba), 5, 338–45
Museum Restaurant Room (Gaba), 344
music: hip-hop, 240–46; North African,
    237–46; and Pan-Africanism, 98; ragga
    style, 242; raï, 237, 239–40, 245; rap,
    240–46; Siddi, 72–73
Muslims: in China, 185; Chinese, 23–25; in
    Senegal, 356–57; in the Spanish Empire,
    45–46. *see also* Sufi Islam
Muslim world: contemporary studies of, 15;
    travelers in, 21–25

Nagoya Protocol, 299–300, 306
Nama people, 303–4
Nardal, Jane and Paulette, 95–96
Nas El Ghiwane, 242–43
National Baptist Convention (NBC),
    59–60, 65–66
national conflict early warning systems,
    111–12
National Environmental Management Act
    (South Africa), 157
nationalism: in *Living in Bondage,* 353–54;
    and soccer, 214
National Khoisan Council, 302–5
National Liberation Front (Algeria), 213
national parks, 157
National Union of Metal workers of South
    Africa (NUMSA), 160
natural resources: colonial exploitation of,
    131; coltan, 289–97; in environmental
    justice, 161–62. *see also* resource
    extraction

Négritude, 95–96, 207, 370
Negro newspaper, 92
Nehru, Jawaharlal, 73–75
neocolonialism, 97, 218, 255–56
neoliberalism, 145–46, 150–51, 156, 159, 306
"New Christian" status, 46
New Delhi, 76
Newton Theological Seminary, 63–64
"New World Economic Order" (Nyerere), 104
Ngũgĩ wa Thiong'o, 202–9
Niasse, Ibrahima, 358
Nigeria: cell phone adaptations in, 277; Chinese-owned firms in, 146, 149–50; Nollywood, 5, 319–20, 347–54; and pelete bite, 176; repatriation of stolen wealth to, 136–37; soccer in, 211, 216–17
Nigerians: in China, 183–91; in India, 75–77
Njoya, Ibrahim, King of Cameroon, 179–80
Nkrumah, Kwame, 95, 96–98
Nnebue, Kenneth, 348, 349
Nneka the Pretty Serpents movie, 348
Nobel Peace Prize, 88
Nollywood, 347–54
nomads, 35–36
Non-Alignment International Program of Cooperation, 104–5
noncommunicable diseases (NCDs), 260–61, 262–63, 264–65
nongovernmental organizations (NGOs): in the DRC, 290; environmental, in Tunisia, 310–11; in environmental justice, 156–57, 159; and resource extraction, 295–96
North Africa, 13–15, 237–46
Nuru, Zumra, 377
Nyerere, Julius, 100–108

occult beliefs, 212
Oguibe, Olu, 234–35
"Old Christian" status, 46–47
ONAS (Tunisia's wastewater agency), 312–13
open-source software, 274–75

Organization for Economic Cooperation and Development (OECD), 137
Organization of African Unity, 74, 97–98, 111
Organization of Afro-American Unity, 97
organized crime syndicates, 82, 132
Osakwe, Amaka, 181
Our Mother (Marasela), 223–29
outreach in HIV/AIDS prevention, 262

Pacific nations, 105
Padmore, George, 95, 96
Pan-African Association, 92
Pan-African Congress, 93–94, 96–97
Pan-Africanism: in Africa, 97–99; and Afropolitanism, 373–74; defined, 90–91; forerunners of, 91–92; in literary tradition, 203–4; Morris's campaign for, 59–69; and Nollywood films, 350–51; and rap music, 241; and soccer, 215
Pan-African magazine, 92
Pan African Parliament, 99
Pan-Arabism, 242–43
Panel of the Wise, 113
Pan-Negroism, 93
Pawlowska, Aneta, 276
peace-builders, 84–89, 121–29
peace monitors, 112
pelete bite, 175–76
Pentecostalism, 185–91, 351
Peru, 43–44
PesaPoint, 284–85
photography, 180, 223–35
police in South Africa, 124–25
political philosophy, 10, 11–15
political will: in gender equality, 335–36; in public health, 262–63, 264–65
politics: epidemics in, 259–61; music in, 238, 242–43; soccer in, 219; violence in, 110–11
pollution: DIY solutions to, 278; in environmental discourse, 156–57; and environmental justice, 153–55; and extractive industries, 162; from mining, 158–59; in Tunisia, 308–17
Portugal, 40
Portuguese America, 53–54
Portuguese language, 204

poverty: and bioprospecting, 302–3; and conservation, 157–58; and disease, 266–67; and environmental justice, 160–61; illicit financial flows in, 130–31; in images of Africa, 372–73; and reparations, 127; and waste management, 311–13

power: and accountability, 115–18; in conflict and justice, 109–19; in the golden age, 20–21; of grassroots organizations, 86–87; language in, 205–6; of women in Morocco, 231

Pray the Devil Back to Hell documentary, 88

preschool at Awra Amba, 380

prison labor, 141–42

prosperity gospel, 188–89, 191

protests, 155, 243, 276

public health, 253–54, 260–61, 264–65

Puigaudeau, Odette du, 27–37

race and religion, 41–44

racialization: of Afro-Asian working relationships, 142, 143; of North African harems, 233; of sub-Saharan Africa, 2

racial profiling, 75–77

racism: in the HIV/AIDs pandemic, 265–66; in India, 75–76, 77, 78; and Pan-Africanism, 91, 93–94

radicalization of environmental justice, 153–62

ragga style music, 242

raï music, 237, 239–40, 245

Rally for Congolese Democracy, 293–94

rap music, 240–46

razzia (traditional attacks on trade), 35–36, 37

rebel groups, conventional, 111

Reborn heavy metal band, 243

reciprocity *(enjawulo)*, 150

record keeping, 19, 20, 174–75

Redeemed Christian Church of God (RCCG), 183–86

Red Rooster Restaurant (New York City), 165–67

regional organizations, 111, 113

regulation: of bioprospecting, 299–306; of mining, 295–96

religion: African missions in, 183–91; and art, 342–43; and race, 41–44; and

soccer, 212; Sufi Islam, 356–64; and travel rights, 39, 41–44, 45–47

Remitti, Cheikha, 239–40

reparations: and bioprospecting, 298–306; and the TRC, 127

repatriation: in Pan-Africanism, 91; of stolen money, 136–37

resource extraction: in the DRC, 289–97; in environmental justice, 161–62; and environmental policy in Tunisia, 148–49, 309; in illicit financial flows, 133. *see also* natural resources

Rhodes, Cecil, 65–66

rights: of citizens, 118; socioeconomic, 122; in *ujamaa*, 102. *see also* human rights

Rihla ("Journey") (ibn Battûta), 22–23

risks in mobile money, 285–87

Ritual and Blood Money movie, 353–54

Rodney, Walter, 98

rooibos, 302, 304–5

Rooibos Tea Control Board, 304–5

Rubusana, Walter, Rev., 66–67

rule of law in entrepreneurship, 323–24, 326

Rwanda, 114, 117

Safaricom, 281–87

Sahara, 27–37

sailors, 42–43, 72

Salami, Minna, 368, 374

Salon (Gaba), 344

salt industry, 37

salt route, 35

Samuelsson, Marcus, 165–67, 169

San Buenaventura Brotherhood, 42, 43

San peoples (Southern Africa), 298–306

Save Mapungubwe Coalition, 159

Save the Environment (SOS BIAA), 310–11

sceletium tortuosum, 301–2, 303–4

Schomburg Center for Research in Black Culture, 166

security, personal, 88, 285–86, 287

Selasi, Taiye, 367–68

Senegal, 356–57

Senegalese restaurants, 168

Senghor, Léopold, 95

Senones, Marion, 31

sexuality, 265–66, 267

Shonibare, Yinka, 174